11-18-74

WOMEN
IN POLITICS

CONTRIBUTORS

JoAnn Aviel	*California State University, San Francisco*
Louise M. Bachtold	*University of California, Davis*
Kay Boals	*Princeton University*
Elsa M. Chaney	*Fordham University*
Warren T. Farrell	*New York University*
Cornelia B. Flora	*Kansas State University*
Jo Freeman	*State University of New York, Old Westbury*
Lynne B. Iglitzin	*University of Washington*
Barbara Jancar	*International Science Exchange*
Jane S. Jaquette	*Occidental College*
Temma Kaplan	*University of California, Los Angeles*
Marjorie Lansing	*Eastern Michigan University*
Gail Warshofsky Lapidus	*University of California, Berkeley*
Mary M. Lepper	*Health, Education and Welfare Office of Civil Rights*
Naomi B. Lynn	*Kansas State University*
Nancy McWilliams	*Rutgers University*
Ann B. Matasar	*Mundelein College*
Mary Cornelia Porter	*Barat College*
Susan Kaufman Purcell	*University of California, Los Angeles*
Eleanor Cutri Smeal	*University of Pittsburgh*
Judith Van Allen	*University of California, Berkeley*
Audrey Siess Wells	*Syntex Laboratories, San Jose*
Emmy E. Werner	*University of California, Davis*

WOMEN
IN POLITICS

Edited by

Jane S. Jaquette

Department of Political Science
Occidental College
Los Angeles

A Wiley-Interscience Publication

JOHN WILEY & SONS

New York   London   Sydney   Toronto

Library of Congress Cataloging in Publication Data:

Jaquette, Jane S.   1942–   comp.
    Women in politics.

    "A Wiley-Interscience publication."
    Bibliography: p.
    1. Women in politics—United States—Addresses,
essays, lectures.   I. Title.

HQ1236.J38   329   74-1037
ISBN 0-471-44022-1

Printed in the United States of America

10 9 8 7 6 5 4 3 2 1

Preface

Politics has traditionally viewed itself as a male field, and, with the possible exception of economics, it is the social science discipline which has responded with the least enthusiasm to the impact of the modern feminist movement. While a number of books have appeared which explore feminist approaches to psychology and sociology, there are very few studies of female participation in politics, and still fewer which challenge the predominant male interpretation of what that participation means or how it reflects the female character. Why should this be so?

One possibility is that fewer women have been attracted to careers in political science as compared to sociology, psychology, or anthropology. This is true despite the large number of women undergraduates attracted to the field and despite the fact that sociology and psychology require more quantitative skills and thus might discourage women who are, as both tradition and data show, "less mathematically inclined."

There is also the question of subject matter. Sociology and psychology differ markedly from political science in that they are practically and theoretically concerned with female behavior. In sociology, the emphasis on the family as a key social institution and the use of sex as a basic variable insure that women will be studied and that female perspectives will be sought to enhance the quality of research design and analysis. Psychology, so closely tied historically to the concept of sexuality and concerned with early childhood experiences, must of necessity include the study of women, however biased that study may have been. Today, as a result, sociologists and psychologists who are building feminist critiques of their respective disciplines have visible targets to attack: psychology "constructs" the female, Weisstein charges, and sociology creates a "nonconscious ideology" of proper female role behavior, according to the Bems. (Naomi Weisstein, "Psychology Constructs the Female . . . ," and Sandra L. and Daryl J. Bem, "Training Woman to Know Her Place: The Power of a Nonconscious Ideology," in M. H. Garskof, ed., *Roles Women Play: Readings Toward Women's Liberation.* Belmont, Ca.: Brooks/Cole, 1971, pp. 68-83, 84-96.)

v

In political science, this is not the case. The issues which have traditionally absorbed the discipline—questions of individual freedom and political obligation, international conflict, nationalism, laws and constitutions, and public administration—appear on the surface, at least, to transcend sex. Classical attempts to inject female values into politics—*Lysistrata*, for example—make the intrusion of sex into political theory seem misguided or inappropriate. On further reflection it will be seen that the basic questions of political science almost invariably arise out of male social behaviors. Thus Lionel Tiger sees politics as a form of "male bonding," and argues that "it is clear that there is a close relationship between maleness, politics and territory . . . Male dominance coupled with sexual dimorphism occurs cross-culturally; it may be a phenomenon rooted in the nature of *Homo sapiens* (Lionel Tiger, "Sex and Politics," in C. S. Stoll, ed., *Sexism: Scientific Debates*. Reading, Mass.: Addison-Wesley, 1973, pp. 44, 56). Thus it might be legitimately asked whether politics *transcends* sex, or merely ignores women.

Whether male dominance of what is conventionally seen as political activity is a result of our primate inheritance, natural predispositions, cultural norms, or enforced social sanctions, it is a fact. As a result, there has been little to say about women in politics and there are few women who have acquired prestige as political scientists or political theorists. The articles in this book have been collected at a time when women (and men) in the field have begun to examine this problem and to do research on the motivations, self-perceptions, role conflicts and institutional parameters of female political participation. This book begins with the individual American woman—her position as a voter, her response to socialization, the conflict between motherhood and participation, her response to women in elective office. The second section views political institutions from the urban machine to the Federal bureaucracy and the Supreme Court as arenas of female participation and as sources of societal norms for female political behavior. Finally, the issue of how the modern feminist movement is affecting our definition of politics and our understanding of power is raised and debated.

Part II provides a perspective on women in American politics by looking at case studies of female political participation in developing countries, some of which, like the Soviet Union, have experimented with radical attempts to change the traditional female role. These chapters raise questions which have not been central to the study of American politics. How effective is ideology in changing customs, particularly well-ingrained traditions regarding the treatment and status of women? What are the theoretical issues of communism versus capitalism in the context of female emancipation? What effect does the application of technology to production—the industrial revolution or modernization—have on the range of options available to women? What effect has education? Given the analogies between imperialism, racism and sexism, how does consciousness arise and to what degree does it alter the relationship between the dominant and the dependent?

Most of the articles which appear here were originally presented at annual meetings of the American Political Science Association or at regional meetings within the past few years, and some were written especially for this volume. Few have been published elsewhere. I wish to give special thanks to my contributors who have in every case been responsive to requests and supportive of this effort. In addition, I am grateful to Susan Kaufman Purcell who worked with me on the original idea for this collection, and to Anne Howells, Sara Latz, Ann Manning and others at Occidental College who have given me many kinds of invaluable aid and advice.

Los Angeles, California   *Jane S. Jaquette*

Contents

Part
II
COMPARATIVE PERSPECTIVES   215

Introduction:
Women in American Politics

Jane S. Jaquette

Any review of the literature on the role of women in politics in the U.S. must begin with the observation that there have been very few studies which compare male and female patterns of political participation, despite the interest in this topic engendered by the political activity of the suffrage movement and the potential threat of a female bloc vote. The absence of studies may in part be explained by the fact that, with regard to voting at least, there are few variations that can be attributed to sex. Women tend to vote somewhat less than men and to be interested in different kinds of issues, but a significant determinant of voting, party affiliation, does not vary by sex [1]. However, studies of female political elites—women's pressure groups [2], women as party workers [3], as legislators [4], and as bureaucrats [5]—show marked sex differences in levels of participation. Women account for less than 5% of legislators and top-level bureaucrats.

Thus it would seem that women's suffrage, though hard-fought and hard-won, did not bring about the massive changes in the nature of politics that some of its supporters had predicted. Almond and Verba summarize the gap between expectations and results as follows:

> Some of the advocates of feminine suffrage a few decades ago made exaggerated claims about the consequences of extending equal rights to women. A polity that included women as active participants would, they said, abolish poverty, protect family life, and raise educational and cultural standards; an international society made up of nations in which woman had the suffrage would not tolerate war. Certainly these expectations have not been realized. Wherever the consequences of women's suffrage have been studied, it would appear that women differ from men in their political behavior only in being somewhat more frequently

A version of this paper was presented at the American Political Science Association Annual Meeting, New Orleans, 1973.

apathetic, parochial, conservative, and sensitive to the personality, emotional and esthetic aspects of political life and electoral campaigns [6].

Or, as Carl Degler put it, women's suffrage "ushered in no millenium [7]." Despite the vote, women remain on the periphery of politics and continue to have their interests defined, debated and often ignored by their "husbands and fathers," as in the 19th century. Why is this so?

Degler's argument is that women's rights were extended not as a result of political activity but as a consequence of economic changes. The women who knew "the discipline of the clock, the managing of their own money, the excitement of life outside the home, and the exhilaration of financial independence . . . could not be treated then nor later in marriage, as the hopeless dependents Victorian ideals prescribed." For this reason American feminism is nonideological, that is, incapable of creating a rationale for political participation, or the political leverage of a female bloc vote. "When American women obtained the vote, they simply did not use it ideologically; they voted not as women but as individuals [8]." As a further explanation for the same phenomenon, it has been pointed out that women are more divided by class and interest than they are united by sex [9]. Lower levels of voting participation are universally attributed to patterns of female dependence on the male [10], and data showing that husbands and wives vote alike is also taken as evidence of male dominance.

All in all, the pattern of female participation in American politics seems to provide the occasion for a mild tut-tut or a studied ho-hum, to be seen as less than it should be but never very different from male participation at similar class, education, and age levels. The failure of women to be elected to public office or to participate more effectively in political party organizations is seen as a result of *role conflicts* which must be resolved by women themselves. We might conclude that we should have paid less attention to the reformers and more to such diverse souls as Elizabeth Cady Stanton and Chicago's Bathhouse John [12] who both predicted (presumably without benefit of mutual consultation) that the women's vote "wouldn't make any difference anyway."

It has been argued that the failure of women to become a political force as a group is only a reflection of broader sociological trends. Riesman has observed that, while homogenization and differentiation seem to be occurring at the same time in this country, differences between city and country, social and occupational strata, and *sex differences* are disappearing, while differences are increasing "among the age-grades, . . . between North and South, and between the college educated and those of lesser academic exposure [13]." If Riesman and Degler are correct, the now revived goal of a feminist politics will be very difficult to achieve.

Voting and Female Political Culture

In the United States (and in most countries) "at every social level women vote less than men [14]." This occurs despite the fact that women had to fight to win the right to vote, in spite of the fact that they show more concern than men for certain kinds of issues [15], and in spite of the fact that in some cases (in elections studied in Finland, Czechoslovakia, and Ann Arbor, Michigan, for example) the percentage of women voting has been higher than that of men [16].

In probing the causes of lower voting turnout among women, Campbell and his associates note that female involvement in politics is lower than that of males. However, lower voting rates are not associated with weaker party identification or with lack of sense of civic obligation, but with a weak sense of political efficacy. "Men are more likely than women to feel that they can cope with the complexities of politics and to believe that their participation carries some weight in the political process [17]."

To explain this weaker sense of efficacy, *The American Voter* turns to the larger issue of dependency in male/female relations: "The man is expected to be dominant in action directed toward the world outside the family; the woman is to accept his leadership passively. She is not expected, therefore, to see herself as an effective agent in politics [18]." Data to support his view is taken from many sources, among them a pioneer study of female voting by Merriam and Gosnell [19] which was later reinforced by a major study in 1940 [20]. Individual female responses to the question of why they did not vote included: "Women have no business voting," "Voting is for the men," and "I have never voted. I never will . . . a woman's place is in the home [21]."

Levitt finds that "Men are expected to be dominant in action directed toward the world outside the family; women are to accept that leadership passively [22]," and then quotes Riesman to explain, with that "women 'feel pressured to play any role they are accepted in by the men [23].' " The reverse is apparently not the case. Here the tendency to opt for the dependent role is not seen entirely an artifact of past stereotypes still too close at hand, as Lane [24] put it; it is a product of ongoing role relationships. Married women vote more than single women, but in married couples "husband and wife have a tendency to behave in the same manner—either they vote together or not at all. The husband may vote and the wife abstain frequently, but the wife rarely votes without the husband's doing likewise [25]."

The suffragists believed that women were less politically aware due to the influence of the home itself which limits female exposure to political experience and information [26]: "the isolated household is responsible for a large share of woman's ignorance and degradation. A mind always in contact

Table 1   Relation of Sex, Education and Region to Sense of Political Efficacy, 1956

	Men			Women		
	Grade school	High school	College	Grade school	High school	College
Non-South						
High efficacy	32%	47%	83%	13%	40%	68%
Medium efficacy	31	29	12	20	34	25
Low efficacy	37	24	5	67	26	7
	100%	100%	100%	100%	100%	100%
Number of cases	150	267	116	198	382	110
South						
High efficacy	16%	37%	78%	3%	31%	56%
Medium efficacy	12	28	15	20	36	22
Low efficacy	72	35	7	77	33	22
	100%	100%	100%	100%	100%	100%
Number of cases	89	82	55	90	147	27

SOURCE: Angus Campbell, et al., *The American Voter.* New York: Wiley, 1960, p. 491.

with children and servants, whose aspirations and ambitions rise no higher than the roof which shelters it, is necessarily dwarfed in its proportions [27]." In support of this view we find that education levels are correlated with levels of political information, political involvement, and voting itself. Education "frees the mind from bondages of authority and oppression" and provides an adequate "frame of reference" to give "meaning to political events [28]." Education increases civic obligation.

Yet which is more important, education or work? Duverger, in his well-known study for UNESCO, concluded that, while there are some differences between working women and non-working women, education is a more important cause of discrepancies in participation: "economic independence has no more succeeded in banishing a general mentality born of a tradition dating back thousands of years than has the conquest of political rights [29]." This position is reinforced by research on party elites, which shows that working women are not more leadership-oriented than housewives [30]. Campbell et al. focus on education as a major causal factor in participation. Education is a powerful stimulus to voting for women at all ages and particularly in the South. (See Table 1.) The one study which directly compares employment and education to voting turnout and feelings of efficacy is based on data from the University of Michigan's Survey Research Center for the Presidential elections of 1956, 1960, and 1964. It concluded that working was a more important factor than education: "When working women and (housewives) were compared at each education level, it was found that women

Table 2 Relation of Age, Education, Sex, and Region to Presidential Vote Turnout[a]

	34 or less			Age 35–54			55 or over		
	Grade school	High school	College	Grade school	High school	College	Grade school	High school	College
Non-South									
Male	60% (52)	78% (175)	88% (81)	80% (156)	87% (222)	96% (103)	87% (179)	93% (96)	100% (31)
Female	44% (55)	73% (285)	90% (70)	71% (170)	85% (312)	91% (85)	71% (173)	91% (126)	93% (30)
South									
Male	19% (32)	55% (69)	81% (32)	55% (87)	80% (54)	88% (33)	63% (72)	71% (21)	82% (11)
Female	13% (47)	41% (111)	74% (23)	22% (97)	56% (86)	82% (38)	31% (75)	58% (33)	86% (22)

SOURCE: Angus Campbell, et al, *The American Vote*. New York: Wiley, 1960, p. 495.

[a]The primary entry in each cell indicates the proportion voting for president within the category. The number of cases involved in each proportion is indicated in parentheses. Figures in this table are based on a combination of data from the 1952 and 1956 election samples.

who engaged in work were more politically involved and participated more in the political process than those who stayed at home; and further, that they had a higher sense of political efficacy and a higher sense of citizen obligation [31]." Nonetheless a Census Bureau study found that "the voting percentage of college educated women was (marginally) higher than that of college educated men [32]." Jennings and Niemi's study of politicization of husbands and wives concluded that education and employment status had a cumulative or additive effect, particularly among working class couples [33].

An additional factor is age. Although both men and women tend to vote less below thirty and when they are past their midsixties [34], age has a more radical effect on female voting patterns (see Table 2). Age raises the issue of participation as a function of *stake*, that is the degree of economic or other direct interest which might produce voting and deeper involvement in political issues. Lane makes this argument as follows:

> In maturity certain things occur in the normal lifetime which tend to increase the motivation and the pressure to take part in the political life of the community. A person acquires property, hence one of the most important forces politicizing the local citizen comes to bear on him—the question of assessment and tax on his house. Then too, the family includes children who need playgrounds and schools and therefore the mother finds new stakes in politics [35].

Or, as one of the female nonvoters in Merriam and Gosnell's 1924 study commented, she would vote "if she were a widow" or "had property in her own name [36]."

> As for the elderly, apparently several things happen at these later stages in life. Persons over fifty-five lose their sense of political effectiveness to some extent, and perhaps, with retirement, lose their feeling of vital economic stake in political decisions of many kinds [37].

The concept of stake may thus explain why younger and older women vote less than middle-aged women (who are more likely to be married and have young children), and why women are generally more interested in local issues than in national ones. More importantly, it provides an alternative to the standard explanation given for lower levels of female participation, an argument which might be labeled *insufficient masculinization*. If only women were more like men (were more informed, had greater feelings of efficacy, were more involved in the real world), so the argument runs, the problem of female deviance from male norms of participation would be solved. The implication here is that women should take on male political characteristics. To the degree that they do not, they are seen as weak, unable to overcome outworn stereotypes and lacking participatory elan.

By contrast, to raise the question of female stake in politics brings different issues to the fore: what reasons do women have (other than a sense of civic duty which they feel more strongly than men) to participate in politics? What results may they reasonably expect from any political efforts they make? The kinds of reasons brought forth to explain lower levels of male participation should be applied to women as well. Are women more alienated from the political system? Does pluralism remove from the political arena issues of first importance to women? The fact that the modern feminist movement has politicized issues formerly reserved for the private sphere (childcare, housework, sex itself) indicates that earlier definitions of practical politics may have been too restrictive to give women a real stake in the political process.

In addition to the issue of what gains women actually achieve from participation in politics, the concept of stake has broader implications related to feelings of psychological well-being and personal efficacy. Gosnell has observed that among voters in general, "a lack of tension and anxiety, generalized into a basic satisfaction with oneself and one's life (euphoria), tends to increase a person's interest and participation in the nondeviant areas of American politics [38]." It is interesting then that there is some data to indicate that female politicians experience more tension and anxiety than male politicians, and that for women in general, contemporary studies suggest a high degree of tension and anxiety arising out of the conflict between female role behaviors and those behaviors (usually reserved to men) which society values most highly. Gosnell does not conclude that the dissatisfied should resolve their problems by becoming more satisfied and thus conform more closely to the American norm. Rather, he argues that the system is biased in favor of expressing "the needs and wishes of the more contented and satisfied citizens at every level of society, rather than the discontent and alienation of the dissatisfied [40]." This statement can be construed as another version of the rich get richer. The poor, including women, go unrepresented.

Not only does politics tend to discourage the expression of alienation, it further denies women a stake by labeling their complaints and needs as exclusively private and thus inappropriate to the public sphere [41]. Duverger makes this point a very telling part of his General Conclusions:

Faced with the same basic set of circumstances—an inferior social and economic position, leading to a sense of deprivation and frustration and a feeling of belonging to a 'proletariat,' young men tend to turn towards the revolutionary parties or the trade unions, young women towards the expectation of a rich and handsome 'prince charming' who will deliver them from the poverty and ugliness of their everyday world . . . (S)entimental magazines simply supply this basic need, by giving their readers their weekly dose of hope and illusion. To denounce the very real damage they do is, to some extent, hypocritical, for they meet a need, resulting from the general attitudes of present-day Western society and the upbringing it gives to women [42].

While there are good reasons for avoiding the politicization of such personal decisions as choosing a husband, these reservations should not prevent us from considering such basic questions as why marriage is the most promising, perhaps the only step a woman can take to improve her status and upgrade her material existence, or why marriage is an inadequate psychological substitute for a career. These issues must become political if we are to change present-day attitudes and the heritage of Western tradition; without such politicization the female stake in politics is necessarily, and quite realistically, limited.

We have dealt at some length with voting levels, efficacy, and political involvement; now we will turn to the issue of female attitudes toward political issues. A number of students of politics have been interested in the question of whether female suffrage has affected the outcome of presidential elections. Gosnell cites evidence that women supported Wilson, were "consistently in favor of Harding" and were less inclined to vote for the Socialist candidate, Eugene V. Debs, based on separate records for male and female votes kept in Illinois between 1913 and 1920 [43]. In the 1950s and 1960s, women were said to favor the paternal figure of Eisenhower against the divorced Adlai Stevenson and to have given an edge to Nixon in the 1960 race with Kennedy [44].

Candidate Orientation and Political Sophistication

A number of studies have shown that women are more interested in candidates than issues. This presumably contributes to the sporadic character of the female vote [45], a quality which Duverger, on the basis of European data, interprets as independence: women are "less rooted in party traditions and habits, less hidebound, more 'open-minded'. . . and thus more unstable and 'floating.'" He sees this as a result of the relative newness of female participation [46]. American analysts have viewed greater candidate orientation as linked to greater female moralism [47]" and lack of sophistication about politics. In Lane's words, "it is relatively easy to compare political acts and statements with moral symbols to assay moral worth, while it is difficult, indeed, to ascertain causes and estimate results [48]." This description implies that male voters make decisions in a more sophisticated way. Whyte argues that women find it easier to view politicians, compared with issues, as either good or bad [49]. *The American Voter* finds that women,

Table 3   Relation of Sex and Education to Level of Conceptualization, 1956

Level of concept formation	Grade school		High school		College	
	Male	Female	Male	Female	Male	Female
A. Ideology	8%	1%	17%	5%	34%	27%
B. Group benefit	43	33	52	44	35	34
C. Nature of times	30	26	19	26	19	21
D. No issue content	19	40	12	25	11	18

SOURCE: Angus Campbell, et al., *The American Voter.* New York: Wiley, 1960, p. 491.

even college-educated women, have "a more impoverished level of (political) concept formation." (See Table 3.)

Campbell notes that of those in Category D (no issue content), women fall less into the candidate-oriented type, as might be hypothesized . . ." Instead they fall into the least sophisticated category, those who were "unable to venture any political content at all [50]." The role of education in increasing ideological conceptualization is clearly seen in this data, although it might be possible to question the degree to which *level of conceptualization,* as an abstract quality, was being measured.

Conservatism

Studies in the U.S. and in Western Europe provide considerable data that women tend to vote more conservatively than men. Duverger reports that women in France support the center and Catholic-oriented parties but do not vote for the Communist and Socialist parties in spite of the fact that these parties have done the most "to increase the number of women entering Parliament or holding office [51]." Tingsten found that women in the Weimar Republic supported center parties against the extremes until 1933 when they supported the Nazi party, and noted that "the precarious position of the democratic regime in Germany, particularly after the successes of the National Socialists and the Communists in the election of 1930, to a certain extent was camouflaged by women suffrage [52]." In Spain, after the leftist Republican-Socialist coalition won in 1931, women were granted the vote. In the 1933 election the parties of the Right and Right-Center won important gains, and the "leaders of the revolution discovered that more Spanish women were against them than for them [53]." Devaud states flatly that women's votes "prevented the establishment of communist regimes" in France, Germany and Italy [54].

In the U.S., an early study of referendum voting in Portland, Oregon showed women "more opposed to the 8-hour day for women; to a single tax; to extending certain forms of government; and that they were more in favor of prohibition . . . [55]." Gosnell argues that, in contrast to European political parties, parties in the United States "are tinged innocuously enough so that probably fewer women are determined in their voting behavior by convictions for or against radicalism," although a study of voting in Illinois found low support for the Socialist party (58.3% that of men) and high support for the Prohibition party (246.7% that of men) [56]. A conclusion drawn from female participation in and support of the Soviet political system is that women tend to be system-maintaining rather than doctrinally conservative, although it is clear that intensive socialization of females played a part in the Soviet Union. It could be argued, of course, that females are just as intensively socialized to system-maintenance in the U.S. and Europe.

Campbell and associates found that women tended to be 3-5% more Republican, although they argue that this difference should be attributed to income, education and regional factors determining levels of voting. That is, more women vote who are wealthier, more highly educated, and live in the North, and these types of individuals tend to be more Republican [57]. Yet some analysts have credited women with extending the concept of the *service state* in the U.S.—a *liberal* ideological position [58]. This may be due in part to female interest in protective legislation, child labor laws, and food and drug regulation, all of which require some limitation of free enterprise. Gruberg has pointed out that most women's groups are "on the liberal portion of the political spectrum [59]." While groups like the League of Women Voters clearly have not represented a majority of American women, they have provided a public image of women as liberal reformers. In the 1930s, the League was the only major interest group to support the establishment of the TVA [60].

A recent study of college students found that females tended to have more liberal views than males, when liberalism was defined as a preference for the Democratic party. 56% of freshmen women as compared with 43% of freshman men considered themselves Democratic. Further, 43% of the students' mothers were perceived as Democrats as compared with only 35% of the fathers. Women showed more tendency to deviate from parents' allegiances when the parents both belonged to the same party (although the total number of deviants in this situation was quite small—6.3%). 62% of the women supported McGovern over Nixon for President (as compared with 58% of the men) which reflected stronger support on the part of mothers for McGovern (48% to 32% for fathers) [61]. Thus it is not clear that women in the U.S. are as conservative as their European counterparts.

Moralism

Not all evaluations of the female bias toward reform are positive. Lane writes, "Consider the image of the female vote as a reform vote, that is, impersonal and detached from personal gain, qualitatively different from the male vote which is imbued with matters of self interest . . . (it is) a kind of bloodless love of the good." Idealistic approaches to politics could be one cause of sporadic female participation as the reform vote is a cyclical phenomenon "kicked off periodically in municipal elections by revelations of newer and greater corruption." The roots of this approach in women, Lane believes, are the female focus on childrearing with its concern for a "suitable morality," and the "more limited orbits" of women which reinforce the view that "the values they are familiar with are the only values—a lack of cultural relativism [62]." He quotes Lipset to the effect that those who are excluded from "activities which have the highest value in society" often become moral custodians [63].

Women are considered politically naive because of their strong support of prohibition and for their opposition to prostitution, legalized gambling and horse racing—for votes against sin [64]. Women tend to favor peace and to vote for candidates committed to peace, even in times of international crisis. Female support for President Wilson during World War I and for President Johnson in 1964 is attributed to the salience of the peace issue, and 1964 marks the first time when females are thought to have voted more Democratic than Republican [65]. Gosnell reports a striking difference between male and female attitudes toward Chamberlain's appeasement policy in Britain in 1938. 67% of the men were indignant at the betrayal of the Czechs, as compared with 22% of the women [66].

Polls have found women less in favor of universal military training, more disturbed by the Korean War, and more in favor of the 1963 Test Ban Treaty [67]. Gruberg, who finds women more security-oriented, quotes Rear Admiral Fiske on the female peace vote: "Women have an insatiable desire to interfere in matters they do not understand. War they understand least, and from it they instinctively recoil . . . There must be some action by the men which will bring women to realize that it is for their comfort and protection that all wars are fought . . . In spite of themselves, we must protect the ladies [68]!"

Finally, there is the issue of clean government. Women have traditionally been concerned with local rather than national issues. March found a division of labor in families with men most involved and informed on issues involving labor and foreign affairs and women taking local issues as their proper sphere [69]. Women have decided most school board elections [70]. They have been associated with efforts to eliminate corruption along the lines suggested by the Progressives, particularly the depoliticization of urban administration. Women were instrumental in having the city-manager form of government adopted in some cities, and have favored bipartisan approaches and direct primaries at the state level.

In the latter case, Key argued that support of direct democracy was undermining the party system at the state level. Participation in primaries he judged both unrepresentative and ineffectual. Nominations "by minorities . . . seriously handicap the party in carrying the battle to the opposition" in general elections and at times lead to the election of the "most improbable sorts of characters [71]." Key was very concerned with the damage women could do to the party system; he did not ask however what the party system had done for women [72].

The oft quoted phrase to the effect that female political idealism has resulted in female concentration on the trivial and irrelevant in politics has been impossible to track down. It is often used to support the widely held view that the organization and style of American politics, involving machines, parties, interest groups and some degree of corruption, is necessary and appropriate to the true function of politics: that of brokerage among competing interests. Conversely, any interference with the process in the name of *do-goodism* is not only naive but harmful. A glance at the current critiques of pluralism with their emphasis on the unrepresentative nature of group conflict [73], the failure of pluralist politics to deal with important issues [74], and its encouragement of citizen apathy [75] might put female political idealism into a very different perspective. That women have always been sensitive to the gap between the norms and reality of democratic politics in the United States seems clear; however, such sensitivity has until very recently been very unfashionable. Instead the male realist school, represented by Key, Dahl, Lipset, Lane, and others, has been dominant.

Intolerant But Permissive

In a famous if now somewhat dated study, Stouffer found that women were less tolerant (that is, less likely to allow civil liberties to Socialists, atheists, and Communists) than men at all levels of education, almost all age levels, and in every major region of the country [76]. Stouffer further discovered no significant differences between workingwomen and housewives when housewives were classified by their husbands' occupational levels; that is, both operatives and semiskilled workers and the wives of men in these categories were equally intolerant.

Of greater interest, perhaps, than Stouffer's analysis of this phenomenon [77], which rests almost entirely on the fact that more women than men are churchgoers and that churchgoers as a whole tend to be less tolerant, is Riesman's discussion of the Stouffer data. Riesman points out that education plays a decisive role in creating tolerance "because for many it constitutes acculturation to the ideology of the assured and the successful, and that this leads . . . to a 'cosmopolitan' leadership . . ." which encourages tolerance [78]. Yet education may not produce assurance or success for women in the way that it does for men. That men and women 60 and over show higher levels of intolerance may suggest an analysis of this variable in a

Table 4 Scores on Scale of Tolerance, by Sex, Level of Education and Age

	Less		In-between		More	
	Female	Male	Female	Male	Female	Male
Education						
College graduates	6	4	33	21	61	75
Some college	11	7	42	32	47	61
High school graduates	14	9	50	43	36	48
Some high school	19	14	55	53	26	33
Grade school	23	21	62	62	15	17
Age						
21–29	10	9	49	36	41	55
30–39	14	8	47	45	39	47
40–49	19	12	48	48	33	40
50–59	15	21	54	49	31	30
60 and over	23	20	62	59	15	21

SOURCE: Samuel Stouffer, *Communism, Conformity and Civil Liberties.* New York: Doubleday, 1955, p. 134.

manner parallel to the lack of stake argument developed earlier. Older people in general are less successful, therefore have less stake, vote less and are more intolerant.

Riesman argues persuasively that values like tolerance are the result of complex and often conflicting factors. For example, women may be less tolerant of allowing subversives the exercise of their civil liberties—such as the right to speak in schools—yet may be more tolerant than men of nonconformity in other dimensions: "The men are . . . rugged individualists, while their wives believe in cooperation and groupism; yet, when it comes to dealing at home or at school with their own children, it is the wives who defend them against patriarchal legalism and who insist on their right to be idiosyncratic." He concludes, "It would seem that fathers want children prepared 'realistically' to cope with the tough world; the fathers, that is, move in orbits that lead to political aeration and domestic severity." On the other hand, "the greater political intolerance of women can in part . . . be linked with their cultural role in protecting the young: it is, the Stouffer study makes clear, 'insidious' teachers they fear, and ideas and books—not sabotage or direct political threats [79]."

The reason for heightened fear, Riesman suggests, is lack of experience. "Though women do not bind their feet, as Chinese women did, it remains true that at every class level save the very top (and perhaps among the Bohemians) they get around less than men do [80]." Interestingly, he concludes that efforts to "get out the vote" have often brought the "uninformed and the ill-informed" to the polls who should have been "counted as 'don't knows' until they widen their grasp of political communications [81]."

A different sort of intolerance is exemplified by the attitudes women voters

Table 5   Percent of Men and Women
Who Would Vote for a Qualified Woman
for President

Year	Men	Women	Difference
1937	27%	40%	+ 13
1947	29	37	+ 8
1949	45	51	+ 6
1955	47	57	+ 10
1963	58	51	− 7
1967	61	53	− 8
1969	58	49	− 9

SOURCE: Hazel Erskine, "The Polls: Women's
Role" *Pub. Opinions Quart.*, **35.** 275 (Summer
1972).

have toward female candidates running for public office. The Gallup Poll
has regularly asked whether individual respondents would support a qualified
woman for President. The results show that women have a decreasing tendency to vote for a woman candidate relative to men (see Table 5). In
view of the publicity surrounding women's liberation in 1968 and 1969, the
drop in female acceptance of female candidates in 1969 can hardly be taken
as an encouraging sign by the National Woman's Political Caucus.

As a final note on attitude and voting research, Duverger comments on
the issue of whether women's votes should be counted separately from men's
in national and local elections:

(The) opposition to a separate count of votes appears to be as strong among
men as it is in feminist circles. It may well be asked whether this does not
point to the existence of a more or less unconscious masculine mentality of
domination which would be the exact corollary of the feminine minority mentality; the aim would be to maintain the fiction of women 'voting like men,'. . .
by preventing any definite test of the originality and the possible independence
of the political behavior of women [82].

Women as Legislators and Party Elites

The act of voting is a limited act of political participation, particularly
when compared to party work or running for office. Thus women who vote
may experience some role conflict because voting is perceived as a male
behavior, but this conflict is heightened considerably for women who are
more involved in politics and may be assumed to be particularly acute for
female legislators.

Studies made of female party workers and delegates to national party conventions [83] and studies of women legislators [84] have produced some findings which may be compared to the characteristics ascribed to the general population of female voters. Thus interviews of female state legislators carried out by the Eagleton Institute's Center for the Study of Women in Politics find evidence of what has been described as the moralistic image of female participation. In comparison with their male colleagues, women state legislators "tend to perceive themselves as more honest, less corruptible, less willing to compromise, more concerned with the public interest, nicer to the legislative staff, less interested in personal gain, more accessible to constituents, more oriented to issues and less to fulfilling their own egos, and more independent of party demands [85]."

Women appear to be more honest than men, this study reports, "partly because there is less opportunity for women to be involved in conflicts of interest because few have outside employment, partly because they have not been co-opted by the power structure, and may therefore be subject to fewer temptations [86]." The report adds that women are less susceptible to lobbyists as they are less vulnerable to the informal pressures of male-to-male friendships, or flattery [87]. This is not only consistent with the idealistic view that politics should follow universalistic and affectively neutral norms. It is further mirrored in the behavior of the most important female pressure organization, the League of Women Voters, which relies on letter writing campaigns, informal coffee hours with legislators, and on "wooing legislators in a dignified and League-like" manner—an attitude which Gruberg has described as "political virginity" [88].

On the other hand, "because women in general are expected to be more emotional, more talkative, less familiar with the facts, women legislators are determined to be none of these things [89]." Women legislators, in contrast to women voters, have limited options because they must constantly avoid typically female behavior which their male colleagues would consider inappropriate. Thus women must talk less and avoid emotional displays.

Yet typical male behavior is not acceptable either. Women must accept the double standard of morality and avoid openly promoting their own interest, namely women's issues. While some female legislators felt their power had been enhanced by the activities of the women's movement, others found support of women's rights an expensive strategy:

> In your first term, your colleagues are delighted to have you sponsor education, health, conservation, consumer legislation. Bills on such subjects do not threaten men or hurt your image as a legislator. Also, in the first term you can move into areas other than these where it is known that you have previous experience or expert knowledge . . . But I waited until my second term to introduce anything to do with women's rights because then the red flag goes up [90].

Many women who were not strong supporters of the movement were associated with it by voters and other legislators simply because they were women [91].

Both Werner and Gehlen note that women in Congress have tended to be older than their male counterparts, a difference which has been attributed to the female responsibility for childrearing. Women come from the field of teaching rather than law or business as do male legislators. The linkage between occupation and political resources is an important one, for as Gruberg has noted, "merely to have women among the employed . . . will not guarantee that women will emerge as leaders." Leaders are largely businessmen and professionals. "Unless women can attain importance in these feeder hierarchies, they will never amount to much in government [92]."

A study by Jennings and Thomas of Michigan delegates to the 1964 national party conventions shows that even among women self-selected to political participation of this type, there are important differences in occupational background. Men are younger, have more education, and are more experienced than women in their study. This, they argue, is a result of their own role expectations and those of society. Men were "much more likely to have performed key campaign activities, to have held either appointive or elective public office, to have sought public office, and to have succeeded in their quest [93]." Women delegates were more timid and content with rewards and ambitions other than elective office, many of which were symbolic. Both men and women delegates saw the political system as Pluralist rather than Popular Democratic or Elitist, and both substantially disagreed with the notion that the party role should be one of brokerage. Yet only 45% of the women as compared with 79% of the men felt that a delegate should make decisions using his best individual judgment [94]. Women, especially Democratic working women, preferred the other alternatives of following party leaders or public opinion.

The study concludes from these responses that: "Men are more accustomed to making their own decisions in non-political as well as political matters. Women tend to be less self-sufficient and to seek certainty in people, institutions, and concepts outside themselves." Further, "employed women are even more likely than housewives to use external rather than internal reference points in making their decisions. The fact that a woman works does not necessarily mean that she is likely to be an independent, self-reliant individual [95]." If lack of a personal sense of independence were the only rationale for choosing to make decisions in accordance with party leaders and public opinion the thesis that women are by nature more dependent might be substantiated and employment would not appear to equalize the differences between the sexes. The possibility that women might legitimately view their function as party delegates as representative rather than Burkean seems not to have occurred to the authors.

Two separate studies have found similar sex-related differences in class and educational backgrounds between male and female convention delegates. Both the Jennings and Thomas study in Michigan and a study by Costantini and Craik [96] in California found that female delegates came from lower class backgrounds and had lower levels of educational achievement than the male delegates. Jennings and Thomas suggest that women who are less privileged have "fewer opportunities to become involved in the community through high-status civic and social organizations. Consequently (they) turn to politics where the major requirements for successful feminine involvement are energy, talent, and commitment [97]." Costantini and Craik argue that the composition of party elites reflects the "differential socioeconomic opportunities and attainments of men and women in contemporary society," and they note that upper class women who participate in public affairs are more likely than men at the same socioeconomic levels to prefer nonpartisan activities and organizations [98]. Marvick and Nixon found that Republican women are more likely to use party work to *reflect* their status in the community while Democratic women tend to *create* status by party work, although that status was generated within the party and not generalized to the community as a whole [99].

The examination of personality characteristics in the Costantini and Craik study found that women delegates "are forceful, effective, ambitious and socially ascendant individuals" as compared with other women. "However, their dominant and self-confident approach to life and their strong, purposeful style appear to be complicated by doubt and concern about their place in society and their push toward achievement seems constrained by a sense of caution and propriety . . . (F)emale party workers try harder and worry more [100]." This description fits that of the women state legislators in the Eagleton Institute study and reinforces the point made at the beginning of this section: that women often feel conflict between their political role and their role as women. However, it is not clear that women experience anxiety and try to act feminine solely because of abstract societal norms. Rather, women may find it impossible to be effective in individual interactions with men who reject aggressive behavior on the part of the women they are with while at the same time chiding women for being typically female.

It is not clear, as Costantini and Craik would argue, that the problem would be solved if women themselves would change their attitudes and motivations. There is no question that female legislators and politicians simply do not have the range of behavior options that are available to men. Under these circumstances no amount of masculine motivation is going to make it possible for a woman to be perceived as a man and thus be granted the latitude of acceptable (and self-enhancing) behavior that men possess. It is more likely that women will be punished for assuming male prerogatives as the Eagleton Institute study shows.

It is quite possible to imagine, however, that as more women enter politics and run for office there will be less of a tendency for their constituencies or colleagues to perceive them as female first, and there will be increased tolerance for individual styles. Today, women still find it very difficult to be elected to public office (though this is less true at the local level) and must often rely on their husbands to finance their campaigns because of attitudes beyond their control. The inaccessibility of public office means that women often enter the party for rewards obtainable within the party structure while men tend to use the party as a vehicle for personal enhancement and career advancement. It is not clear that women choose to be relegated to "a supportive role of more or selfless service," a role which Costantini and Craik compare to the female role in the family (what choice even there?), while "the male partner or co-partyist pursues a career in the outside world [101]." Such behavior may instead be based on a rational calculation of their alternatives. Half a loaf (and indirect power) is better than none at all.

Women state legislators and party elites report that they are outside the informal communications network, not included in strategy sessions, and in some cases even in formal meetings where they should be present ex officio. State and some county party committees have adopted the national party rule of 50–50 representation of men and women adopted by the Democrats in 1920 and the Republicans in 1924. Yet formal representation does not guarantee real representation. As a female national committee member commented:

> I have seen many women develop to a point where they could defeat men at their own tactics . . . But the result has not been that intended by the proponents of the (50–50) measure. For in many cases, as soon as women use their knowledge to their own advantage against some men on the committees, they found themselves replaced by women who did not have such knowledge [102].

Perhaps it would be useful to view the above information in a comparative perspective. Duverger finds the participation of women in federal parliaments to average about 5% in Western Europe in the mid-1950s [103]. Since then, participation has increased notably in the Scandinavian countries, to the 10–15% level by 1966 [104]. Female participation in the Soviet Union and East European countries has been higher: 20% in the Yugoslavian federal parliament and 28% in the Supreme Soviet in 1966 [105]. The figures for

Britain and the U.S. are depressingly low: women were 4% of the House of Commons membership during this period. In the U.S. there were 65 women elected to Congress and 10 female Senators by 1968 [106]. In mid-1972 women were 4.5% of the membership of state legislatures [107]. As Almond and Verba have argued that the quality of female participation in general is higher in Britain and the U.S. than in Italy, Germany, or Mexico, we see a surprising gap between the political culture of women and their direct representation in legislative bodies. This gap is even more significant when it is recognized that both England and the U.S. have long histories of feminist movements and are seen as egalitarian in their approach to male/female relations.

In concluding this discussion of studies of women and politics I would like to comment on the issue of male bias in political science. Certain patterns of analysis seem to recur in the literature which could be taken as evidence of a male perspective, regardless of whether the authors are male or female. These are usually more subtle than Lane's ambivalence toward the prospect of politicizing the female role, which he felt might have negative consequences:

> It is too seldom remembered in the American society that working girls and career women, and women who insistently serve the community in volunteer capacities, and women with extracurricular interests of an absorbing kind are often borrowing their time and attention and capacity for relaxed play and love from their children to whom it rightfully belongs. As Kardiner points out, the rise in juvenile delinquency (and, he says, homosexuality) is partly to be attributed to the feminist movement and what it did to the American mother [108].

As a woman (and thus by nature more concerned with insidious threats) I am less bothered by Lane's obvious prejudices than by the helpful paternal approach. As was noted above in the discussion of party elites and legislators, the male perspective views women as needing to come up to male standards of participation, independence, or political realism to achieve equality. This approach does not acknowledge the fact that women may be prevented from assuming male roles by the application of sanctions nor does it question the legitimacy or the necessity of doing things the way male politicians have always done them. What starts out as an objective study of male/female differences all too often ends up as a diatribe against female weaknesses and a paean to male virtues. In addition to Jennings and Thomas' study of leadership behavior discussed above, I would cite the extreme example found in Greenstein's well-known article on "Sex Related Differences in Childhood." In supporting his argument that boys exceed girls in "interest in and information about matters of relevance to politics," Greenstein uses

Preston's study of children's reactions to World War II. To establish the relationship between interest and level of information, Greenstein employs Preston as follows:

> Neither sex exceeded in the meager factual awareness of war at this age, but when asked which of a series of pictures they preferred, nine of the boys and *none* of the girls were described by the authors as "enthusiastic" or "excited" about the war [109].

If excitement about the war at the first grade level is what it will take to have women informed about the political system, then perhaps there is more wrong with the system (or with our current definition of it) than with women.

To turn to another aspect of the male perspective, it is interesting to note that when weaker nations call upon law and world public opinion in their behalf, it is considered a legitimate restraint on power or even a clever bargaining tactic utilized by small states [110]. When women similarly inject ethical considerations into politics (or object to corruption, perhaps because they do not have the resources to make it work for them), they are considered hopelessly moralistic, unsophisticated, or at worst, a threat to the proper functioning of the system, as Key argued. Women are not to tamper with politics-as-it-is.

Finally, as Lynne Iglitzin has argued in a study of political information and sex stereotyping [111], important methodological questions must be raised about the way in which political socialization research has been done in the past. Questionnaires implicitly reinforce the idea that it is males who perform political activities, and research that proves that women are, after all, apolitical, itself becomes a socialization agent in the direction of reduced participation. The lack of interest in micropolitics—the politics of the family, the school and the peer group—imposes rigid limits on what is considered political behavior. It is interesting in this regard that studies by Jennings and Niemi [112] and Langton and Jennings [113] show that women play a much stronger role in political discussion and have more influence on political attitudes within the family than the conventional view of the man as the political mediator would hypothesize. This is not to suggest a return to the narrow women have power in the home view, but rather to argue that women do have political resources available to them and that politics cannot be defined as something that, for traditional, biological or functional reasons, men do. This should become more evident as women become more involved in political struggles to achieve ends they have defined as important—day care and equal rights, for example—and as more women run for public office.

As the definition of politics expands to include issues which were formerly relegated to the private sphere, issues involving sexual relations, new forms of marriage, changes in the family structure, and areas of corporate decision-making such as hiring and promotion, the examination of the role of women in politics and a conscious awareness of male bias may revitalize our thinking on some of the fundamental questions of equity, obligation, and representation on which the study of politics has traditionally been based.

NOTES

1. Maurice Duverger, *The Political Role of Women* (UNESCO, 1955), Chap. 1 and Appendices; Harold F. Gosnell, *Democracy, The Threshold of Freedom.* New York: Ronald Press, 1948, Chap. 4.; Angus Campbell, et al., *The American Voter.* New York: Wiley, 1960, pp. 489–493. Robert E. Lane, *Political Life.* Glencoe, Ill.: The Free Press, 1959; Gabriel A. Almond and Sidney Verba, *The Civic Culture.* Boston: Little Brown, 1965; Fred I. Greenstein, "Sex-Related Political Differences in Childhood," *Jour. of Politics,* **23,** pp. 353–371 (1961); Kenneth P. Langton and M. Kent Jennings, "Mothers versus Fathers in the Formation of Political Attitudes," in Kenneth P. Langton, ed., *Political Socialization.* New York: Oxford Press, 1969, p. 52ff.; Rosamonde Ramsay Boyd, "Women and Politics in the United States and Canada," *Annals of the American Academy of Political and Social Science,* **375,** pp. 53–57 (1968); Bernard Berelson and Paul S. Lazarsfeld, "Women, A Major Problem for the PAC," *Public Opinion Quarterly,* **9,** pp. 79–82 (1945); Earl R. Kruschke, "Level of Optimism as Related to Female Political Behavior," *Social Science,* **41,** pp. 67–75 (1966); Morris Levitt, "The Political Role of American Women," *Jour. of Human Relations,* **15,** pp. 23–35 (1967); William F. Ogburn and Inez Goltra, "How Women Vote, A Study of an Election in Portland, Oregon," *Political Science Quarterly,* **34,** pp. 413–433 (1919); Martin Gruberg, *Women in American Politics.* Oshkosh, Wis.: Academia Press, 1968, Chap. 1; Samuel A. Stouffer, *Communism, Conformity and Civil Liberties.* Garden City, N.Y.: Doubleday, 1955, Chap. 6; M. Willey and S. Rice, "A Sex Cleavage in the Presidential Election of 1920," *Jour. of the American Statistical Association,* pp. 519ff 1924; Herbert Tingsten, *Political Behavior Studies in Election Statistics.* London: P.S. King and Sons, 1937; Angus Campbell, Phillip E. Converse, Warren E. Miller, and Donald Stokes, *The American Voter.* New York: Wiley, 1960.

2. Sophinisba P. Breckinridge, *Women in the 20th Century: A Study of Their Political, Social and Economic Activities.* New York: McGraw Hill, 1933; Duverger, *op cit.,* Chap. 2; Mary Helen Robertson, "Constitutional Revision in Illinois: The League of Women Voters' Role," *National Civic Review,* pp. 438ff (September 1971); Judith Axler Turner, "League of Women Voters Backs Study With Lobbying to Influence Policy," *National Jour.,* **4,** pp. 860–870 (May 20, 1972); Gruberg, *op. cit.,* Chap. 4.

3. Marguerite J. Fisher, "Women in Political Parties," *Annals of the American Academy of Political and Social Science,* **251,** pp. 87–93 (1947); M. Kent Jennings and Norman Thomas, "Men and Women in Party Elites: Social Roles and Political Resources," *Midwest Jour. of Political Science,* **12,** pp. 469–492 (1968); Edmond Costantini and Kenneth A. Craik, "Women as Politicians: The Social Background, Personality and Political Careers of Female Party Leaders," *Jour. of Social Issues,* **28,** pp. 217–236 (1972); Dwaine Marvick and Charles R. Nixon, "Recruitment Contrasts in Rival Campaign Groups, in Dwaine Marvick, ed., *Political Decision-Makers.* Glencoe, Ill.: The Free Press, 1965.

4. Peggy Lamson, *Few Are Chosen.* Boston: Houghton Mifflin, 1968; Emmy E. Werner, "Women in Congress: 1917–1964," *The Western Political Quarterly,* **19,** pp. 16–30 (1966); Frieda Gehlen,

xxxiv INTRODUCTION

"Women in Congress: Their Power and Influence in A Man's World," *Transaction*, **6**, pp. 36–40 (1969); Eagleton Institute Center for the Study of Women in Politics, *Women State Legislators, Report From a Conference*. New Brunswick: May, 1973; Frank Colon, "The Elected Woman," *The Social Studies*, **58**, pp. 256–261 (1967); Dorothy A. Moncure, "Women in Political Life," *Current History*, **29** (1929); Lakshimi N. Menon, "From Constitutional Recognition to Public Office," *Annals of the American Academy of Political and Social Science*, **375**, pp. 34–43 (1968). (See also Breckenridge, *op. cit.*; Duverger, *op. cit.*; Gruberg, *op. cit.*)

5. Helene S. Markoff, "The Federal Woman's Program," *Public Administration Review*, pp. 144–151 (1972); Margaret Mead and Frances B. Kaplan, eds., *American Women: The Report of the President's Commission on the Status of Women*. New York: Scribners, 1965, pp. 65–95.

6. *Op. cit.*, p. 325.

7. Carl N. Degler, "Revolution Without Ideology: The Changing Place of Women in America," in Robert Jay Lipton, ed., *The Woman in America*. Boston: Houghton Mifflin, 1965, p. 204.

8. *Op. cit.*, p. 204.

9. Arnold W. Green and Eleanor Melnick, "What Has Happened to the Feminist Movement?" in Alvin W. Gouldner, ed., *Studies in Leadership*. New York: Harper and Brothers, 1945, p. 285; and H. Gosnell, *op. cit.*, p. 60.

10. See, for example, discussions by Duverger, *op. cit.*, Lane, *op. cit.*, and Campbell, et al., *op. cit.* Duverger's view is considered a classic expression of the case: "Under a democratic system, political activity is essentially adult . . . But, while women have, legally, ceased to be minors, they still have the mentality of minors in many fields and, particularly in politics, they usually accept paternalism on the part of men. The man—husband, fiancé, lover or myth—is the mediator between them and the political world." *The Political Role of Women*, p. 129.

11. See Costantini and Craik, *op. cit.*; and Jennings and Thomas, *op. cit.*

12. John D. Buenker, "The Urban Political Machine and Woman Suffrage: A Study in Political Adaptability," *The Historian*, **33**, p. 279 (1971).

13. Riesman, "Orbits of Tolerance . . . ," p. 50.

14. See Lane, *op. cit.*; Campbell, et al., *op. cit.*; and Almond and Verba, *op. cit.*

15. See M. Kent Jennings and Richard G. Niemi, "The Division of Political Labor Between Mothers and Fathers," *The American Political Science Review*, **65**, pp. 69–82 (1971). Gosnell, *op. cit.*; and James C. March, "Husband-Wife Interaction Over Political Issues," *Public Opinion Quarterly*, **17**, pp. 461–470 (1953–1954).

16. Gosnell, *op. cit.*, p. 59; Lane, p. 209, ft. 22.

17. A. Campbell, *The American Voter*, pp. 489–490.

18. *Ibid.*, p. 490.

19. Charles E. Merriam and Harold F. Gosnell, *Non-Voting*. Chicago: University of Chicago Press, 1924.

20. Paul Lazarsfeld, et. al., *The People's Choice*. New York: Columbia University Press, 1948.

21. Quoted in Lane, *Political Life*, p. 211.

22. Morris Levitt, *op. cit.*, p. 25.

23. *Ibid.*, p. 25. The Riesman quote is from *The Lonely Crowd*. New Haven: Yale University Press, 1962, p. 81.

24. R. Lane, *op. cit.*, p. 212.

25. H. Gosnell, *op. cit.*, p. 60.

26. Women get their political information from magazines, radio and television, men from newspapers. See Lane, *op. cit.*, p. 209 and Jennings and Niemi, *op. cit.* Ashley Montagu has

argued that women are better equipped to adapt to new political communication patterns in an increasingly technological age.

27. Quoted in M. Levitt, *op. cit.*, pp. 29–30.

28. *Ibid.*, p. 31.

29. M. Duverger, op. cit., p. 152.

30. Jennings and Thomas, *op. cit.*, p. 488.

31. M. Levitt, op. cit., p. 32. See also Frank Kent, *Political Behavior.* New York: 1928, p. 288.

32. M. Gruberg, *op. cit.*, p. 11.

33. Jennings and Niemi, *op. cit.*, pp. 80–81.

34. A. Campbell, et al., *op. cit.*, p. 494.

35. R. Lane, *op. cit.*, p. 218.

36. *Ibid.*, p. 212.

37. *Ibid.*, p. 218.

38. H. Gosnell, op. cit., p. 157. See also an analysis of the relationship between income level, optimism and female political behavior in E. Kruschke, *op. cit.*

39. Costantini and Craik, *op. cit.*

40. H. Gosnell, *op. cit.*, p. 157

41. See Alice Rossi, "Sex Equality: The Beginnings of Ideology," *The Humanist,* **29** (1969).

42. M. Duverger, *op. cit.*, p. 129.

43. H. Gosnell, *op. cit.*, p. 64.

44. Harris poll data, reported in D. Riesman, *op. cit.*, p. 58.

45. Rosamonde Boyd, *op. cit.*, p. 56.

46. M. Duverger, *op. cit.*, p. 143.

47. A. Campbell, et al., op. cit., pp. 152–156.

48. R. Lane, *op. cit.*, p. 213.

49. Of course, the opposite case can be made just as logically—that it is easier to judge discrete issues and policies as "good" or "bad" in comparison with complex personalities. But the case I would like to make is that, for presidential elections at least, in a system where the Chief Executive is very powerful, where party discipline and no confidence votes are weak or unavailable, and where the parties themselves are almost indistinguishable ideologically, "intuition" about a candidate (candidate-orientation?) may be the only rational basis for a voting decision. In U.S. presidential elections, in short, "sensitivity to emotional and esthetic characteristics" of campaigns and candidates may be not just "functional," but a practical necessity.

50. A. Campbell, et al., *op. cit.*, p. 492n.

51. M. Duverger, *op. cit.*, pp. 143–45, 147.

52. H. Tingsten, *op. cit.*, p. 47.

53. H. Gosnell, *op. cit.*, p. 68.

54. Marcelle Stanislas Devaud, "Political Participation of Western European Women," *Annals of the American Academy of Political and Social Science,* **372,** p. 61 (1968). Based on research by Mattei Dogan and Jacques Narbonne in Duverger, *op. cit.*

55. Ogburn and Goltra, *op. cit.*, *passim.*

56. H. Gosnell, *op. cit.*, p. 71.

57. A. Campbell, et al., *op. cit.*, p. 493.

58. Although specific data is hard to find.

59. M. Gruberg, *op. cit.*, p. 95.

60. *Ibid.*, p. 89.

61. Richard Hallin, "The New Voter: An Analysis of Political Views of Occidental College Freshmen," Los Angeles: mimeo., 1973. See also Costantini and Craik's study of California party elites, *op. cit.*, in which Democratic women are "more liberal," p. 234.

62. R. Lane, *op. cit.*, pp. 212–213.

63. *Ibid.*, p. 212f.

64. M. Gruberg, *op. cit.*, p. 13.

65. From Gallup and Harris polls. Women also favored Johnson's stand on civil rights in 1964 more than men did, although they voted against Kennedy in 1960 to a greater extent than men did because they "feared a Catholic in the White House." *Ibid.*, p. 15.

66. H. Gosnell, *op. cit.*, Chap. 4.

67. M. Gruberg, *op. cit.*, p. 15.

68. *Ibid.*, p. 13.

69. Melnick and Green, *op. cit.*

70. J. March, *op. cit.*

71. V.O. Key, Jr., *American State Politics: An Introduction.* New York: Knopf, 1956.

72. The "party system" itself has been one of the causes of low female representation in Congress. The lack of proportional representation has favored two consensus-seeking parties against the formation of a spectrum of ideological parties. In Europe, it has been the leftist and Catholic parties which have supported and elected women. A similar argument can be made for Britain. See M. Duverger, *op. cit.*, and H. Gosnell, *op. cit.*

73. Robert Paul Wolff, "Beyond Tolerance," in Wolff, et al., *A Critique of Pure Tolerance.* Boston: Beacon Press, 1965.

74. See essays by Theodore Lowi and others in William Connolly, ed., *The Bias of Pluralism.* New York: Atherton, 1967.

75. Peter Bachrach, *The Theory of Democratic Elitism.* Boston: Little Brown, 1967.

76. S. Stouffer, *op. cit.*, pp. 132–135.

77. He finds some evidence of greater female anxiety as a possible causal factor in creating greater levels of "intolerance" in females. For a general discussion of "psychological distress" in women, see Jessie Bernard, *The Future of Marriage.* New York: World Publishing, 1972, Tables 23 and 27.

78. D. Riesman, *op. cit.*, p. 51

79. *Ibid.*, p. 57.

80. *Ibid.*, p. 58.

81. *Ibid.*, pp. 58–59.

82. M. Duverger, *op. cit.*, p. 155.

83. See Note 3.

84. See Note 4.

85. Eagleton Institute Center for the Study of Women in Politics, *op. cit.*, p. 5.

86. *Ibid.*, p. 9.

87. *Ibid.*, pp. 9–10.

88. M. Gruberg, *op. cit.*, pp. 90–91.

89. Eagleton Institute Center for the Study of Women in Politics, *op. cit.*, p. 8.

90. *Ibid.*, p. 18.

91. *Ibid.*, pp. 16–17.

92. M. Gruberg, *op. cit.*, p. 42.

93. Jennings and Thomas, *op. cit.*, p. 490.

94. *Ibid.*, p. 487.

95. Ibid., p. 488.

96. "Women as Politicians: The Social Background, Personality and Political Careers of Female Party Leaders," *op. cit.*

97. Jennings and Thomas, *op. cit.*, p. 478.

98. Costantini and Craik, *op. cit.*, p. 220.

99. Marvick and Nixon, *op. cit.*, p. 207.

100. Costantini and Craik, op. cit., p. 226.

101. *Ibid.*, p. 235. On female "unelectability" see Peggy Lamson's introduction to *Few Are Chosen, op. cit.;* contrast Jennings and Thomas' view, p. 483.

102. Quoted in H. Gosnell, *op. cit.*, p. 62.

103. M. Duverger, *op. cit.*, p. 145.

104. M. Devaud, *op. cit.*, pp. 62–64.

105. Kamila Chylinska, "Political Activity of Women in Eastern Europe," *Annals of the American Academy of Political and Social Science,* **375,** pp. 68–71 (1968).

106. M. Gruberg, p. 118, 123.

107. Computed from figures in the Eagleton Institute Study on Women State Legislators.

108. R. Lane, op. cit., p. 523. Contrast Duverger's discussion of the purpose of counting male and female votes separately, quoted above. (Duverger, p. 155.)

109. F. Greenstein, *op. cit.*, p. 359.

110. Hans Morgenthau, *Politics Among Nations.* New York: Knopf, 1973, Chap. 15.

112. *Op. cit.*

113. M. Kent Jennings and Kenneth P. Langton, "Mothers vs. Fathers: The Formation of Political Orientations Among Young Americans," *Jour. of Politics,* **31** (1969).

Part
I
THE AMERICAN SYSTEM

Section

1

CHANGING PATTERNS OF PARTICIPATION:
VOTING AND
POLITICAL ATTITUDES

Chapter

1

The American Woman:
Voter and Activist

Marjorie Lansing

In the massive research on voting behavior which began in 1940, women have generally been portrayed as uninterested and uninvolved in the great game of politics. Recent empirical research, however, suggests a very different picture. In the last three general elections, more women than men voted for President. (Table 1.1). Demographically, it is clear that women will continue to be a majority of the voting age population for some time. Therefore, any tendency for them to vote as a cohesive bloc has implications for political parties and candidates. The electoral balance between the American political parties is quite delicate; in 1948 or 1960, for example, a minuscule shift would have changed the outcome of the election.

The movement for equality by women in the 1960s challenges the model of the politically apathetic woman. There is a fairly general perception that women, at least some women, are becoming more politicized. In this study we shall seek to investigate this process, to determine in which ways changes in the status and role of women have affected their voting and activism patterns.

The analysis will concentrate on two aspects of political behavior: voting and activism. In the first section, female voting patterns in the most recent seven presidential elections are analyzed with the aid of survey data from the Center for Political Studies at The University of Michigan [1]. Voting behavior will be measured against key demographic variables: education, age, labor force participation, region, and race. The background for this analysis is the combined role theory/theory of the voter of Campbell, et al. [2]. The role concept provides our central hypothesis: that changes in the structure of society, beginning with women's suffrage in 1920, have led to a redefinition of political roles for American women. It is our contention

An earlier version of this paper was presented at the Annual Meeting of the American Political Science Association, Chicago, 1971.

that in the 50-year interval since 1920 the major shift concerning American women in political behavior has resulted from the general acceptance of the legitimacy of the female vote, that is, of a participant role as appropriate for women.

The role changes can be dramatized by a comment from Flexner that few women or men under 70 years of age realize there was a time when women could not vote, or earn their livelihood, or go to college, or choose a profession [3]. McLuhan updates her observation: "The pill makes woman a bomb. Watch for traditions to fall." He believes that contraception is the most important discovery in the history of women and more important than the vote in freeing women from their ancient bondage [4]. The Director of the Census, George Hay Brown, analyzed the 1970 census, noting the 1960's as a decade of striking change. In his analysis women are now considerably more likely to attend college, work, live alone, marry late, and outlive their husbands than they were at the beginning of the 1960's [5]. In our study some of these changes in life-style can be correlated with political behavior.

Survey analysis provides us with a means of lending empirical support to these propositions [6]. But, status changes cannot be related directly to the political variables. Status change is a gradual process, and the survey data apply only from 1948 through 1972. While longitudinal strength is supplied by comparisons over the span of 25 years, some tables will provide data for only one presidential election in order to simplify the data array. (And for some tables the 1972 data are not yet available). In this study the most useful variable as a general indicator of change in women's place is education. Education can be related systematically to political variables, and is undoubtedly the most well documented variable in all of voting

Table 1.1.   Women Are Out–Voting Men

	Potential vote		Total vote cast	Women out-voted men by	Women's percentage of total vote
1964	Men	51,991,000	37,419,000		51
	Women	53,318,000	39,130,000	1,711,000	
1968	Men	54,464,000	38,014,000		52
	Women	62,071,000	40,951,000	2,937,000	
1970	Men	56,431,000	32,048,000		51
	Women	64,270,000	33,840,000	1,792,000	
1972	Men	63,834,000	40,906,000		52
	Women	72,369,000	44,858,000	3,952,000	

SOURCE: U.S. Bureau of the Census, *Current Population Reports: Population Characteristics,* **P-20,** No. 143 (October 1965); No. 192 (1968); No. 244 (December 1972).

research. In this study, three levels of education are considered: Low (elementary); Medium (high school); High (attended some college).

The theory of the voter is derived from the model of the voter developed over 20 years of joint research by Campbell, et al. Their explanatory theory sees the individual voter as influenced by a field of forces made up of long and short-term components connecting her to her environment. We consider only the consequences of the changes in sex roles. We cannot measure changes in sex roles directly, but we can trace their effects.

Part Two considers the dimensions of female activism, that is the extent to which women have become involved in grass-roots political party activity and candidate support. A Scale of Political Activities standardized by the Campbell et al. team measures the degree of activity. Here we will consider three crucial questions:

1. Are the women who have attended some college as active in formal and informal politics as similarly educated men?
2. Is the proportion of college women engaging in activist politics remaining constant as the membership in that group rises?
3. Are sex differences in a activism within education groups being narrowed?

We begin with Part I.

Part I. Voting Turnout in Presidential Elections

The crucial test of political participation in America is the casting of votes for the election of President and other elite officials. For our purposes, previous research and data permit an enquiry to test our central hypothesis that a change in status and role of American women since they received the right to vote in 1920 shows a direct relationship to their voting and activism. We predict that among women who have shown less change in status, generally defined as related to *traditional environments* which approximate conditions for women at the time of the adoption of equal suffrage, there has been less change in political role. These women will vote at lower rates than women who have experienced a new definition of political role. The conditions which we specify for consideration begin with our key variable, education, followed by age, region, race and labor force status.

We can examine the recent vote from survey data, beginning with the 1948 through the 1964 election, relying for these years on data from the Center for Political Studies, University of Michigan. Additional data on age, from the Bureau of the Census, extend the investigation to the 1972 election.

Table 1.2 summarizes the comparison between the sexes. All women increased their rate of voting by approximately 11% from 1948 to 1964, and by 14% from 1948 to 1968. The increase for men was between 1948 and 1960—an increase of 11 points. The difference between men and women was about 10% in 1948 and 1960, but dropped to 3% in 1964 and 1968. The difference was 6% in 1972. The postelection survey by the Bureau of the Census found only a 2% difference between men and women in 1972 [7]. (See also note 8.) This gradual increase in voting by women and decline in the differential between the sexes reflects the gradual politicizing of women.

We turn now to a consideration of several variables affecting voting behavior, as they pertain to women.

Education

If we stratify the presidential vote by education, we may test our questions in Table 1.3.

1. Are women who have attended some college voting at the same rates as men of similar education? We find in Table 1.3 that these women voted 7 percentage points less than men in 1948, and 4 percentage points less than men in 1956. In three elections these women voted at the same rates as men of similar education.

2. Does the rate of voting observed at the start of the period under investigation remain constant (or rise still higher) for the college women as the number of women with a high level of education rises? The percentage of college women who voted increased from 70% in 1948 to 84% in 1956 and 1960. Table 1.3 makes clear that the discrepancy between men and women at this educational level in presidential vote was erased in three of five elections, and was reduced over the period.

3. Are sex differences within education groups in level of education being narrowed? Men of elementary and high school education continued to vote at higher rates than women, but the differential was lower in 1964 and 1968

Table 1.2.   Sex Differences in Voting for President

	1948	1952	1956	1960	1964	1968	1972
Men (%)	69	72	80	80	73	76	76
Number	(303)	(821)	(784)	(883)	(703)	(684)	(975)
Women (%)	56	62	69	69	70	73	70
Number	(356)	(978)	(970)	(1071)	(668)	(873)	(1308)
Difference between the sexes (M-W) (%)	13	10	11	11	3	3	6

SOURCE: Center for Political Studies, University of Michigan.

than in 1948. Women of low education increased their vote from 48% in 1952 to 59% in 1964. Women of medium education increased from 58% to 70% over the same period. This decline is consistent with our thesis of an increasing politicizing of women over time within the same level of education.

The significant finding in this table is that education makes more difference for women than for men as to whether or not they vote. This tendency is especially obvious for women who have received elementary school education.

Since 1900 women have been graduating from high school at about the same rate or a slightly higher rate than men [9]. For both sexes graduation from high school has become more common. By 1965 the average citizen in America had become a high school graduate. Thus a category especially applicable to women, that of poor education, is disappearing.

It should be noted that if a woman has attended college, in the past four elections she has usually been found in the voting column. It is relevant to point out that this is where some of the gains in women's voting are found, and will increase, since more and more women are going on to college. For example, between 1900 and 1967, the proportion of B.A. degrees earned by women increased from 19% to 40%. M.A. degrees increased from 19% to 34%, and Ph.D.'s from 6 to 12% [10].

Age

Age serves as a useful variable to locate longitudinal evidence of change in the total electorate and to pinpoint sex differences where they exist. Table 1.4 reports voting by sex and age in the presidential elections of 1964, 1968, and 1972, utilizing census data which are available in this form. These data

Table 1.3. Relation of Education by Sex Differences in Voting for President[a]

| Year of Election | Education | | | | | | | | |
| | Low | | | Medium | | | High | | |
	Men	Women	M-W	Men	Women	M-W	Men	Women	M-W
1948	57%	48%	+9%	72%	58%	+14%	77%	70%	+7%
1952	66	47	+21	74	69	+5	80	80	0
1956	70	52	+18	80	68	+12	88	84	+4
1960	74	52	+22	80	66	+14	84	84	0
1964	64	59	+5	73	70	+3	80	80	0

SOURCE: Center for Political Studies, University of Michigan.

[a]Figures in this table are based on a combination of data from the national election samples. The primary percent entries in each cell represent a simple subtraction of the proportion of women within the category voting for president from the same proportion among men. Positive percentages indicate that men turned out to vote at a higher rate than women. Negative percentages indicate higher female vote proportion.

Table 1.4. Relation of Age to Sex Differences in Voting for President

Sex	Age (years)	Voting (%) 1964	1968	1972
Men	18–24			48
Women				49
Men	21–24	53	53	50
Women		52	53	52
Men	25–34	66	63	
Women		65	63	
Men	25–29			58
Women				58
Men	30–34			66
Women				67
Men	35–44	75	74	66
Women		72	72	67
Men	45–54	79	78	72
Women		75	76	70
Men	55–64	80	79	72
Women		74	74	69
Men	65–74	78	79	73
Women		67	69	64
Men	75 and over	67	68	67
Women		50	51	49

SOURCE: U.S. Bureau of the Census, *Current Population Reports, Population Characteristics,* **P-20,** No. 244 (Dec. 1972); No. 143 (Oct. 1965); No. 192 (Dec. 1969).

make clear that women in the younger years vote in almost the same proportions as men of similar age.

If we look at the 1972 election, we find that until the age of 45 women voted in the same proportions as men, or cutting across all other variables, a percentage point or two higher than men. It is not until we examine the age category beginning at 55–64 that we find men out-voting women. This difference rises steeply at age 65 and over. It is obvious that a high proportion of the nonvoting by women is found in the older age categories. This is significant because women outlive men.

Since younger female cohorts up to age 55 voted in the same proportions as men across the three most recent presidential elections, it is evident that their voting is not an artifact, but a stable phenomenon.

Region

It is well documented that voting turnout is influenced by the effects of variables other than age, sex, and education. By examining age in relation to region we can explore the areas where changes in sex differences are taking place in relation to presidential vote.

Campbell et al., found sex differences in voting turnout generally sharper in the South than in other regions. Their findings from the 1952 and 1956 presidential elections can be used as a rough comparison against the 1964 data which we report from the Bureau of the Census. Campbell et al., found in 1952 and 1956 that the average differences between white men and women were as shown in Table 1.5 [11]. They concluded that sex differences were greater in the South than elsewhere.

We examined census data to check for the persistence of this regional pattern in the 1964 and 1968 elections. In Table 1.6 (1964) as before, the difference between the sexes is much larger in the South than in other regions.

For our purposes it is also important to note that the percentages indicating the differences between men and women progress up the age scale. For the national electorate the youngest group, ages 21–24, showed the least variance between the sexes. The age group 25–44 also showed a small difference between the sexes, only 5% even in the South. The group aged 45–64 showed more difference than the younger voters. The age group 64 years and over reflected a wide difference, 16% in the Northeast, 11% in the North Central, 18% in the South, and 4% in the West. We examined a similar set of statistics for the 1968 presidential election and found the same pattern.

It is to be noted that the sex differences were least in the West. States in the West, and in particular less populated states, tend to produce smaller

Table 1.5. Average Differences in Presidential Vote

Whites only, men minus women

Age	South	Non-South
Under 35	+7	+6
35–54	+20	+5
55 or over	+21	+8

Table 1.6. Participation by Region in 1964 National Election in Relation to Sex and Age for White Voters

	North East	North Central	South	West
Men				
Age: 21–24	56%	61%	39%	53%
25–44	74	77	60	69
45–64	84	83	68	80
65 and older	78	78	64	77
Women				
Age: 21–24	57%	62%	36%	54%
25–44	74	76	55	70
45–64	79	81	59	79
65 and older	62	67	46	73
Difference between the sexes (M-W)				
Age: 21–24	+1	−1	+3	+1
25–44	0	+1	+5	−1
45–64	+5	+2	+9	+1
65 and older	+16	+11	+18	+4

SOURCE: U.S. Bureau of the Census, "Voter Participation in the National Elections, November 1964," *Current Population Reports: Population Characteristics,* **P-20,** No. 143 (Oct. 25, 1965).

differences in political participation for the sexes. This development appears to be related to the ratio of the number of women to the number of men. We have been interested in the findings of Werner [12] that women have gone to Congress or state legislatures more often from the West or New England. We note also that when women are perceived as a minority which is not in direct competition with men, there seems to be a tendency for women to be more involved in politics at the grass-roots level.

The significant development in the regional picture in relation to voting, however, is found in the increasing vote in the South. If we turn the data around in Table 1.7 to examine nonvoting, we find that about half of the nonvoters in America live in the South. More than two-thirds of these are women. About 8% of nonvoters are found outside the South. This figure has remained constant over the past decade or so. But nonvoting in the South has declined from 38% in 1952 to 15% in 1968.

From our data on regional differences we have tried to locate areas where change is taking place in relation to the voting patterns of women. The lag in voting by women in the South supports our hypothesis that women who live in traditional environments where sex roles are slow to change are less inclined to vote. The decline in nonvoting, however, parallels the

Table 1.7. Men and Women by Race and Region Who Have Never Voted (Percentage)

	1952		1956		1960		1964		1968	
	White	Black	White	Black	White	Black	White	Black	White	Black
South[b]										
Men	12	65	14	60	8	33	5	26	9	25
Women	33	87	27	70	17	63	14	39	26	31
Non-South										
Men	6	17	6	17	6	11	7	10	9	0[a]
Women	7	11	10	32	7	28	7	18	7	17

SOURCE: Center for Political Studies, University of Michigan.

[a]Sampling problem.

[b]Includes Alabama, Arkansas, Florida, Georgia, Kentucky, Louisiana, Maryland, Mississippi, North Carolina, Oklahoma, South Carolina, Tennessee, Texas, Virginia, West Virginia.

movement for the equality of women, and is especially dramatic for black women. Next we shall consider black voters. In 1964, 1968, and 1972 the increase in black voting appears to exceed that of any other group.

Race

Black women have entered the electorate during the postwar era in America when their status in many ways has undergone significant change. In a regional study of the South, Matthews and Prothro commented in 1966:

> We might expect sex differences in political participation among southern Negroes to be even greater than among Americans in general. Negroes tend to be disproportionately clustered at the lowest status levels where the general deficit in female participation is greatest [13].

Since the enactment of women's suffrage black people represent the newest bloc of potential voters. The estimated number of black voters in the South was 250,000 in 1940, doubling in 1955, and by 1964 it had climbed to 2,164,000 [14]. The comparison between black men and women as a new bloc of voters therefore takes on added interest. Moreover, recent research in sociology has provoked controversy over family relations and politics, especially in light of Moynihan's statement that black women have played the dominant role in marriage and family relations [15]. The question has political implications which suggest further study.

Table 1.8, which presents figures that compare black and white voters for the entire United States, reports that black women in the 21 to 24 age category voted at a rate of 10% more than black men in 1964 and 6% more

Table 1.8.   Comparison by Sex, Age, and Race of Persons of Voting Age Voting for President in 1964 and 1968

| | | | | 1964 | | | |
| Age (years) | White | | | Black | | |
	Men	Women	M-W	Men	Women	M-W
21–24	53%	52%	+1%	39%	49%	–10%
25–34	66	65	+1	58	62	–4
35–44	76	73	+3	64	62	+2
45–54	80	75	+5	65	66	–1
55–64	80	74	+6	65	60	+5
65–74	79	51	+28	57	48	+9

| | | | | 1968 | | | |
| Age (years) | White | | | Black | | |
	Men	Women	M-W	Men	Women	M-W
21–24	53%	53%	0%	36%	42%	–6%
25–34	64	63	+1	56	57	–1
35–44	73	71	+2	65	65	0
45–54	77	75	+2	66	66	0
55–64	79	69	+10	65	60	+5
65–74	68	51	+17	51	32	+19

SOURCE: U.S. Bureau of the Census, *Current Population Reports, Population Characteristics,* **P-20,** No. 143 (October 25, 1965); and No. 192 (December 2, 1969).

in 1968. In the next age category, 25 to 34, black women voted 4% more than black men in 1964 and at about the same rate in 1968. Black women at the ages 25 to 34 voted at 4% lower rates than white women in 1964 and 5% in 1968. Only at older ages (over 55) is there a clear tendency for women, white or black, to vote at lower rates than men. On the basis of these election statistics, it appears quite probable that black women will be voting in significantly greater numbers in future elections.

Labor Force Status

Whether women work as a member of the labor force or not can be related to their voting behavior. Table 1.9 makes clear that 71% of the women who were in the labor force voted for president in 1968. Of those women who were not in the labor force 63% voted. It should be noted that whether a woman works in agriculture appears to make a difference. Some 64% of the women in agricultural employment voted as compared to 71% who were engaged in nonagricultural employment. There is variation by age among women who are not employed. Women who were under 25 years

Table 1.9. Voting for President by Sex and Employment Status in 1968

	Men	Women	Difference (M-W)
Civilian labor force	70%	66%	+4%
Employed	71	71	0
Agriculture	70	64	+6
Nonagricultural	72	71	+1
Unemployed	51	53	-2
Not in the labor force	64	63	+1
Under 25 years	54	63	-9
25 to 64 years	55	46	+9
65 years and over	70	59	+11

SOURCE: U.S. Bureau of the Census, "Voter Participation in the National Election, November 1968." *Current Population Reports, Population Characteristics,* **P-20,** No. 192 (December 2, 1969).

of age voted at a rate of 63%. For those women 25 to 64 years of age, some 46% voted, and for those 65 and over 59% voted for President.

It should be noted that only about 20% of the women in the labor force have attended college from one to four years or more. Since education appears to be highly related to political participation, as is well documented in all voting research, it is interesting to observe that employment status apparently

Table 1.10. Voting for President by Sex (Percentage)

	1956		1960	
	Stevenson	Eisenhower	Kennedy	Nixon
Men	45	55	52	48
Women	39	61	49	51

	1964		1968		
	Johnson	Goldwater	Humphrey	Nixon	Wallace
Men	60	40	41	43	16
Women	63	38	45	43	12

	1972	
	McGovern	Nixon
Men	30	65
Women	37	59

SOURCE: *1956, 1960,* George Gallup, *The Political Almanac* (1956, 1960); U.S. Bureau of the Census, *Current Population Reports,* **P-20,** No. 143 (Oct. 1965); No. 192 (Dec. 1969); No. 244 (Dec. 1972).

also has its effects. This finding is offered as evidence for our central hypothesis that when women move from the traditional homemaker role, as to go out of the house to take jobs, their voting rates increase.

Female Choice for President

It is generally reported in voting research that women vote for candidates very similarly to men. To a considerable extent this observation is correct, but it is worthwhile to note any differences in view of the close balance between the political parties in some national elections. Table 1.10 reports the vote for President by sex over the past five elections. The sharpest difference between men and women occurred in the vote for McGovern, a difference of 7%. It is necessary to go back to the 1956 election to find that degree of difference when 39% of the women voted for Stevenson (45% of men), and women voted 5 percentage points more for Eisenhower than did men. Women voted at a rate of 4 percentage points less than men for Wallace. The significance in reporting these data is to suggest that women occasionally perceive political candidates differently from men.

Part II. Activism

Key has written that the empirical evidence on the political activist is weak, that this area is a missing piece of the puzzle. This is due to the fact that the individuals who are actually involved in political party work or working for candidates do not turn up in survey data in sufficient numbers to explain the personality or attitudes of the activist. The fact is that no more than 4 to 8% of the population, even in the most recent elections, participate actively in party or candidate work. Dahl has described this characteristic of the mass electorate: "One of the central facts of political life is that politics, local, state, national, and international—lies for most people at the outer periphery of attention, interest, concern, and activity [16]." In 1952 Campbell, Gurin, and Miller developed a Scale of Political Activities which has made it possible to make a systematic comparison over time, and to document characteristics of activists on some measurements, which can be quantified. However, it is the opinion of this researcher, derived from historical evidence, a few local studies in political science, and life experience, that women participated in political party work in greater numbers by 1952 than they had in any previous years. If this impression is correct, then the scale is time-bound in catching the full flavor of women's entry into activism. For a more systematic report on the question we turn now to the survey data. The following questions appear on the Scale of Political Activities as developed by Campbell, Gurin, Miller (1954) [17]:

1. Did you go to any political meetings, rallies, dinners, or things like that?
2. Did you do any other work for one of the parties or candidates?
3. Do you belong to any political club or organizations?
4. Did you give any money or buy tickets or do anything to help the campaign for one of the parties or candidates?
5. Did you wear a campaign button or put a campaign sticker on a car?
6. Did you talk to any people and try to show them why they should vote for one of the parties or candidates?

For any individual the score on the scale is the number of *yes* answers to the six questions. We find only 4% of the men and 4% of the women in the country participating in four or more activities on this scale in 1964.

If we examine the Scale of Political Activities in terms of our key questions, we may ask:

1. Are the women who have attended some college as active in formal and informal politics as similarly educated men?

Table 1.11 reports respondents divided by sex and three levels of education who reported that they had engaged in one or more activities on the Scale of Political Activities. It is clear that in 1952 and 1956 men of college experience were more active than women. The differences were 13 percentage points in these election years. However, in 1960 college women exceeded

Table 1.11. Sex Differences by Education of Activists Participating in One or More Political Activities Across Four Presidential Elections[a]

Education	1952	1956	1960	1964
Low				
Men (%)	24	39	39	29
Women (%)	14	19	19	18
Men minus women (%)	+10	+20	+20	+11
Medium				
Men (%)	32	44	46	44
Women (%)	27	33	34	34
Men minus women (%)	+5	+11	+12	+10
High				
Men (%)	50	60	54	54
Women (%)	37	47	60	52
Men minus women (%)	+13	+13	−6	+2

SOURCE: Center for Political Studies, University of Michigan.

[a]This table reports respondents scoring one or more on the 6-point Scale of Political Activities.

Table 1.12.   Sex Differences of Activists Participating in Four
or More Political Activities Across Four Presidential Elections[a]

Education	1952	1956	1960	1964
Low				
Men (%)	0.3	1.6	4.9	2.6
Women (%)	0	1.0	0.8	0
Men minus women (%)	0.3	0.6	4.1	2.6
Medium				
Men (%)	1.6	1.7	4.5	2.8
Women (%)	0.8	1.1	1.7	2.1
Men minus women (%)	0.8	0.6	2.8	0.7
High				
Men (%)	2.5	8.0	4.8	6.9
Women (%)	2.6	5.3	7.6	9.3
Men minus women (%)	−0.1	2.7	−2.8	−2.4

SOURCE: Center for Political Studies, University of Michigan.

[a]These data report respondents scoring four or more on the 6-point Scale
of Political Activities.

college men by 6 percentage points, and in 1964 the difference virtually
disappeared (2%).

2.   Is the proportion of college women engaging in activist politics remaining
constant as more women enter that group?

Table 1.12 provides evidence that the better educated women are increasing
in political activism. On the same Scale of Political Activities which reports
the number of respondents divided by sex and education who engaged in
four or more activities, college women tripled their rates from 1952 through
1964. The proportion of college women participating in four or more political
activities rose regularly in each election from 1952 through 1964. Over this
period college men doubled their rates, but the percentages for them have
fluctuated from one election to the next.

3.   Are sex differences in activism within educational groups being narrowed?

As already remarked, at the college level sex differences have been reduced.
If anything, more women than men are now highly active. At the levels
of elementary and high school education there is fluctuation for men and
women. Men showed consistently higher participation in one or more activities appearing on the Scale of Political Activities. It is remarkable, however,
that neither men nor women at these educational levels increased very much
in participation over the four elections.

Table 1.13. Sex Differences in Percent Participating in One or More Activities by Education and Age

Age:[b]	20–29			30–39			40–49			50–59		
	Men	Women	M-W	Men	Women	M-W	Men	Women	M-W	Men	Women	M-W
High education												
1952	57%	40%	+17%	30%	35%	−5%	58%	38%	+20%	64%	39%	+25%
1956	a	a	a	63	45	+18	61	46	+15	62	47	+15
1960	49	59	−10	58	71	−13	51	61	−10	49	51	−2
1964	60	61	−1	49	58	−9	64	50	+14	49	40	+9
Medium education												
1952	22%	26%	−4%	32%	19%	+13%	38%	25%	+13%	48%	35%	+13%
1956	29	34	−5	45	31	+14	46	33	+13	42	33	+9
1960	42	45	−3	53	37	+16	47	25	+22	33	30	+3
1964	32	33	−1	43	47	−4	47	37	+10	56	35	+21
Low education												
1952	16%	21%	−5%	18%	10%	+8%	32%	13%	+19%	27%	18%	+9%
1956	a	a	a	39	11	+28	41	19	+22	44	22	+22
1960	a	a	a	38	0	+38	39	23	+16	37	21	+16
1964	a	a	a	38	24	a	37	17	+20	28	23	+5

SOURCE: Center for Political Studies, University of Michigan.

[a] Less than 20 cases.

[b] In 1956 the age brackets shown are, respectively, 21–24, 25–34, 35–44, 45–54.

We extend the data to examine the effects of age in Table 1.13 which presents the proportion of politically active individuals among respondents in the high education groups divided by sex and age. The most interesting figures in Table 1.13 are those which show the significant increases by young women of some college education in the 1960 and 1964 election campaigns. This is the age group which has been found previously among both sexes to have the poorest participation. Of women aged 20–29 in 1952, 40% participated in one or more activities: in 1960, 59%; and in 1964, 61%. For women aged 30–39 the results are similar in trend. In 1960 and 1964 the women aged 20–39 were more active than older women, and in 1960 the women of some college experience were more active than the men of the same age and education.

In Table 1.14 we consider the percentage of women engaged in one or more activities for three educational levels. As before, the younger and better educated women are more active than men, especially in the more recent elections. Women of medium education aged 20–29 are slightly more likely to be active than comparable men, but the men are usually more active at age 30–39 and above. Women of high education may be more active than men of similar education even after age 30.

Table 1.14. Age + Sex Differences Among Higher Educated Participating in One or More Political Activities During Four Presidential Campaigns[a]

High education	20–29	30–39	40–49	50–59
1952				
Men (%)	57	30	58	64
Women (%)	40	35	38	39
Men minus women (%)	+17	–5	+20	+25
1956				
Men (%)	b	63	61	62
Women (%)	b	45	46	47
Men minus women (%)	–	+18	+15	+15
1960				
Men (%)	49	58	51	49
Women (%)	59	71	61	51
Men minus women (%)	–10	–13	–10	–2
1964				
Men (%)	60	49	64	49
Women (%)	61	58	50	40
Men minus women (%)	–1	–9	+14	+9

SOURCE: Center for Political Studies, University of Michigan.

[a]This table combines the number of yes answers to one or more questions on the Scale of Political Activities for respondents of high education only.

[b]Less than 20 cases.

Table 1.15. Sex Differences of College Educated *Strong Democrats* versus *Strong Republicans* Who Participated in One or More Political Activity[a]

High education	Strong Democrats			Strong Republicans		
Year	Men	Women	M-W	Men	Women	M-W
1952	59%	35%	24%	61%	44%	17%
1956	62	33	29	78	63	15
1960	71	60	11	74	72	2
1964	56	51	5	69	79	-10

SOURCE: Center for Political Studies, University of Michigan.

[a]These data report the percentage of respondents identifying as *Strong Democrats* or *Strong Republicans* on the measurement of party identification correlated with respondents reporting one or more political activities on the Scale of Political Activities in the same sample surveys.

Table 1.15 shows that respondents of high education identifying with *Strong Republicans* reported political activities in higher proportions than similar Democrats. With the exception of 1964, college-educated women identifying as Strong Republicans were more likely to be as active as similar men than were Democratic women. In both parties the difference, men minus women, decreased steadily from 1952 to 1964, with Republican women moving ahead of comparable men in 1964. This finding correlates with the evidence that voters of some college experience tend to identify in greater strength with the Republican party than with the Democratic. In terms of activist politics these statistics suggest also why the Republican party women's division historically has attracted women in greater numbers than the Democratic party, and why its organization has been more widespread. More generally political activism increases among people of higher education if they identify strongly with a political party.

In summary, the simple facts are that women over the past 25 years have become more involved in activist politics. The data reported from the Scale of Political Activities shows a definite increase for some categories of women. The topic generally, however, awaits future research.

Conclusions

Education, age, race, and employment appear to be the key variables in relation to changes in role and status of women as they affect female voting behavior. Relying on the theory of the voter developed by Campbell, et al., we have presented data to support the following propositions:

Voting

1. There was an increased politicization of women within the same level of education over the presidential elections, 1948–1968. During this period women increased their rate of voting 11%, while men increased only 4%. Further, the rate of voting by women who had received some college experience increased relative to similarly educated men.

2. Younger women, 21 to 28, voted more often than older women, 55 and over.

3. Younger black women since 1964 voted more often than older black women, and proportionately with black men.

4. Women who are members of the labor force vote at somewhat higher rates than do women who are not employed outside the home.

Activism

1. Women who have had some college experience definitely increased their rates of involvement in political party and candidate support.

2. In the 1964, 1968, and 1972 presidential elections younger, better educated women appear to be more active in politics than men of the same characteristics. There is some evidence that college-educated women may be more active than men even after the age of 30.

3. In both political parties female activism (as compared with male activism) increased steadily from 1952 to 1968, and Republican women moved ahead of comparable men in 1964.

Overall, there is abundant evidence that the level of participation of women in politics has increased steadily over the past two decades and is now accelerating.

Demographic projections to the year 2000 identify an increasingly younger population. Our data found a gradual but significant dying-off of older women lacking in education. Our data located the two youngest female cohorts with some college participating in voting and activism in 1960 and 1964 at higher rates than similar men.

Economists forecast a more automated technology less and less based on differences in physical strength. Career lines are subject to change as suggested by recent studies at Vassar and Stanford. In the midfifties most Vassar graduates wanted marriage with or without career. The same study repeated in the 1960's found that most of the women were insisting on a career with or without marriage. Women at Stanford University made the same choice in a study in 1972. The Women's Bureau predicts increasing labor force participation by women.

Projections for education suggest increasing numbers of women will be graduating from high school and attending college. Women are also entering professional schools as never before. Entry into law schools leads to opportunities for elite careers in politics. (Half of the members of Congress have law degrees.) Education has been found in our study to politicize women more than men. Thus predictions of a younger, better educated, and more highly employed population suggest increasing political participation by women.

A major determinant, however, undoubtedly relates to the general status of women in the social structure, and predictions in this area are less clear. One point of view has been stated by Mead:

> The recognition of the population crisis . . . may result in a reconsideration of the present family style . . . There would be a growing disregard for sex as a basic mode of differentiation. Boys and girls would be given a similar education, and like demands would be made on them for citizenship, economic contribution, and creativity [18].

Other social scientists such as Tiger, from a study of men in groups, predict a general economic, and biological, revolt by women [19].

The combined power of the demographic variables reported in this study suggests that more and more women will vote and get involved in grass-roots politics. These variables, education, age, race, employment, are predictive of trends which are not easily reversed in the short run. This means that the new political woman is here to stay.

NOTES

1. The data utilized in this study were made available by the Inter-University Consortium for Political Research. The data (1948–1968) were originally collected by the Survey Research Center Political Behavior Program, Institute for Social Research, University of Michigan. Neither the original collectors of the data nor the Consortium bear any responsibility for the analyses or interpretations presented here.

2. Angus Campbell, Philip Converse, Warren Miller, and Donald Stokes, *The American Voter.* New York: Wiley, 1960.

3. Eleanor Flexner, *Century of Struggle.* New York: Atheneum, 1968.

4. Isabel Ross, *Sons of Adam, Daughters of Eve.* New York: Harper and Row, 1969, p. 277.

5. Jack Rosenthal, *The New York Times*, p. 1, (April 10, 1974).

6. For a good general discussion of the problems of statistical inference, see W. S. Robinson, "Ecological Correlations and the Behavior of Individuals," *Amer. Sociological Rev.,* **15** (1950), and Austin Ranney, "The Utility and Limitations of Aggregate Data in the Study of Electoral Behavior," in Ranney, ed., *Essays on Behavioral Study of Politics.* Urbana: University of Illinois Press, 1962.

7. U.S. Bureau of the Census, "Voter Participation in the National Election, November 1964," *Current Population Reports: Population,* **P-20,** No. 244, p. 21 (Dec. 1972).

8. This measurement of turnout is from survey data which are dependent on postelection self-report, and vary somewhat from actual statistics. For comparative purposes the overreport or underreport is internally consistent since the data for 1948–1964 are from an identical research design. The proportion of women in these samples tends to be slightly higher than the proportion of men since the excluded population elements are disproportionately male. For a more rigorous explanation see an analysis by Aage R. Clausen, "Response Validity, Vote Report," *Pub. Opinion Quart.,* **XXXII,** No. 4, pp. 588–606 (Winter 1968–1969).

9. U.S. Department of Health, Education, and Welfare, Office of Education, *Digest of Educational Statistics.* Washington, D.C.: GPO, 1965 and 1966.

10. U.S. Department of Labor, *1969 Handbook on Women Workers* (Women's Bureau Bulletin 294). Washington, D.C.: GPO, 1969, p. 191.

11. Campbell, et al., *The American Voter, op. cit.,* p. 486.

12. Emmy E. Werner, "Women in Congress, 1917–1964," *Western Poli. Quart.,* **19,** pp. 16–30 (Mar. 1966); "Women in State Legislatures," *Western Poli. Quart.,* **19** (Mar. 1968).

13. Donald R. Matthews and James W. Prothro, *Negroes and the New Southern Politics.* New York: Harcourt, Brace, and World, 1966. Chap. 1.

14. These estimates are rough approximations because of the decentralization organization of records, *Report of the U.S. Commission on Civil Rights.* Washington, D.C.: GPO, 1959; "Commission on Civil Rights Report: Voting, Book One, 1961," *The New York Times* (November 22, 1964).

15. Lee Rainwater and William L. Yancey, eds., *The Moynihan Report and The Politics of Controversy.* Cambridge, Mass.: MIT Press, 1967.

16. Robert A. Dahl, *Who Governs: Democracy and Power in an American City.* New Haven, Conn.: Yale University Press, 1961, p. 279.

17. These questions were identical across the 1952–1964 presidential elections in the questionnaire of the Center for Political Studies. Angus Campbell, Gerald Gurin, Warren Miller, *The Voter Decides.* Evanston, Ill.: Row, Peterson 1954.

18. Margaret Mead, *Daedalus,* pp. 872–873 (Summer 1967), at a conference on predictions for American social structure.

19. Lionel Tiger, *Men in Groups.* New York: Random House, 1969.

Chapter

2

The Making of the Apolitical Woman:
Femininity and Sex-Stereotyping in Girls

Lynne B. Iglitzin

Many feminists charge that society has institutionalized a sharp demarcation of social roles according to sex, in which one-half of its members voluntarily accept a role subordinate to the other half. The fact that such a division of labor, extending into both economic and political spheres, has existed throughout history and in most areas of the world, does not lessen the deleterious impact of such a secondary role on women. Rather it is important to learn how far such a division of labor is the product of socialization. This chapter argues that agents of socialization, particularly family and school, combine to channel young women into lowered occupational expectations and a willingness to play a marginal role in the economic, political and social aspects of society.

As Mead and others have long said, the roles assigned to women (childbearing and childrearing) are low in prestige and social status in every known society. Men virtually monopolize the high status positions of decision-making and formulation of goals in the major economic, political and cultural institutions of society [1]. The standard rationale for this unequal division of labor is that women want it that way—studies which show that women are apolitical when compared with men [2] imply that the women prefer the domestic sphere of home and family and thus choose to leave political and civic affairs to men.

Although physical force has certainly been used throughout history to keep women in *their place,* as in the use of the harem, the suttee, the veil, and

An earlier version of this paper was presented at the Annual Meeting of the American Political Science Association, Washington, D.C., 1972.

purdah, contemporary society is more sophisticated in inculcating women's willing support of the status quo. John Stuart Mill recognized this, and explained that institutions of society combine to teach the woman submission to her role: "men do not want solely the obedience of women, they want their sentiments . . . not a forced slave but a willing one . . .[3]."

A huge body of research attests to the influence of childhood experiences and learning on adult attitudes and behavior. Indeed, it seems hardly controversial to argue that childhood is the major formative period for later adult behavior [4]. Accordingly, the opinions and attitudes of children should provide insight as to why most women willingly support the existing division of labor, and play their appointed roles even when, by so doing, they are assuring themselves of lowered rewards, status and prestige. The socialization of a sexual division of labor based upon conventional norms of masculine and feminine social roles ought to be well-entrenched even in the very young.

A growing body of literature indicates that as the socialization process proceeds girls are taught to accept *femininity*, a role equated with dependency, submissiveness, conformity, and passivity [5]. This chapter explores some of the consequences of the holding of traditional female values for young girls.

Research studies focusing on girls and women have been sparse until the last few years. Recently, a number of studies indicate that the holding of traditional values tends to lessen the self-esteem and career expectations of young women [6]. This raised the question of whether it is traditional feminine values and sex-stereotyping which cause girls to lower their own aspirations, not only with respect to social roles, but within the full spectrum of political attitudes and participation. If an interrelatedness between traditional feminine values, sex-stereotyping, and political awareness could be demonstrated, it might serve to explain the well-known findings from major political socialization research [7] that girls are apolitical compared to boys.

This chapter reviews some beginning attempts to explore the effects of sex-stereotyping and traditional feminine attitudes upon young girls. The research reported on raises more questions than it answers, as is to be expected in such a new and provocative research area. Accordingly, the last part of the chapter focuses on some of the unanswered questions and speculates on possible future research avenues which need to be explored.

In 1971 and 1972, a two-part research project dealing with sex-stereotyping was conducted on schoolchildren in three suburbs of Seattle. A total of 437 fifth graders took part (221 boys and 216 girls) [8].

The study involved a series of questions designed to show sex-stereotyping based on views of career and employment patterns, social roles in home and family and the child's view of his/her future life as an adult. Both boys and girls demonstrated sex-stereotyping (as measured by the response *men* or *women* rather than *either* or *both* to the questions). However, significantly higher proportions of girls had nonstereotyped responses in all categories.

Career and Employment Patterns

We gave the children a list of jobs and asked them to indicate whether *men, women,* or *both men and women* should perform these tasks. A majority of both sexes thought that bosses, taxi drivers, mayors, factory workers, and lawyers should be men and that nurses and house cleaners should be women.

Stereotyping was common for both boys and girls. In fact, in some cases, girls were even less inclined than boys to see traditionally masculine jobs become feminine jobs. For example, 3.6% of the boys said mayors should be women, but only 2% of the girls said this. Although girls were as little inclined as boys to reverse sex roles in traditionally sex-tied jobs, girls were much more willing to see jobs open to either sex.

Home and Family

Fifth graders have been thoroughly inculcated with a sex-typed view of home and household. Women wash dishes, cook, dust, scrub floors, and get up at night with a sick child. Men pay bills, fix things, and weed the yard. The men's list was shorter than the women's—even taking out the garbage was bestowed by our children on women! Girls' views were as traditional as boys', though the girls showed a slightly greater tendency to see both parents performing household tasks.

Sex-Typing in Girls' View of Their Future

The pattern of traditional sex-typing which emerged in girls' views of social roles carried over into their career aspirations and descriptions of their lives as adults. While the boys wanted to be craftsmen, engineers or scientists, professionals (doctors, lawyers, dentists), sportsmen, and pilots, the girls wanted to be teachers, artists, stewardesses, nurses, and veterinarians.

Overall, the girls had varied job and career aspirations, albeit heavily weighted toward traditional female occupations. They seemed in little doubt that they would have careers. Only 6% said they would be simply a mother or a housewife.

Yet when we correlated the career-choice question with an open-ended essay—"Imagine you are grown up. Describe how you would spend a typical day"—a different picture emerged. The girls showed a marked discrepancy between their stated career goals and their descriptions of an actual day.

Girls in the sample emphasized marriage and family much more than boys. Despite the small number (6%) who said they would be housewives and mothers, well over 25% of the girls made marriage and family the predominant focus of their projected day, and an even larger group emphasized details of family life in their description. In contrast, boys overwhelmingly ignored domestic life—well over 83% gave no details of family activities and fewer than one-fourth even mentioned marriage or family.

Typically, many of the girls commented extensively and in detail on housewifely routine. Even girls who had chosen a variety of careers in the earlier question saw themselves doing traditional "women's work" around the house. In fact, for many, the description of the household chores seemed far more salient than the job. A girl who had said she wanted to be "an artist, maybe a beautician" described her typical day as follows:

> I would start the morning after getting out of bed by eating breakfast. Then I would clean house. If I was done before lunch I would probably visit a friend. Then eat lunch. After lunch I would go shopping. Then I would come home and rest for a while. When my husband came home (if I was married) he would probably tell me how his day went and I would tell him how mine went. If he was in a real good mood he would take me out to dinner. When we were done with dinner we would go to a movie. Then we would go home and go to bed.

Boys tended much more to focus exclusively on details of job and career. The following statement by a boy who wants to be a lawyer and who never discusses marriage, family, or home was quite typical:

> I would talk to my clients on what their problems were. If I thought his thoughts were right I would explain the right procedures to take depending on his problems, and I would fight for his thoughts.

The comments of girls who said they wanted to be housewives could be described as typical of persons leading what has been called the *contingent life*—seeing one's actions as derived from and dependent on the wishes of others. Thus such statements as "I would try to please my husband" or "If my children wanted to" were common in their essays.

This study indicated that the degree of traditional sex-stereotyping of the major social roles in society is very strong by the fifth grade level. The fact that so many of the girls clearly opted for career choices they appear to be unwilling or unable to translate into consequences in their own lives is particularly interesting.

What is the explanation for this dichotomy between career choice and visualization of future life that our data showed applied unequally to the boys and girls in our sample? It appears that social stereotypes restrict girls in expressing a free choice of future roles. If this is true, it may be that the first question, suggesting that such decisions are possible, permitted the girls freedom to state their wildest wishes. The later question, however, brought them down to earth by asking them to imagine a typical day. The realities of societal pressure took over, they saw themselves doing things women always do, and thus fell back into the traditional activities society sanctions for women.

One significant finding was that the girls were consistently less stereotyped than the boys. This was a puzzling finding that we were at a loss to explain, particularly in view of the literature that attests to women as tradition bearers and upholders of conservative values.

One variable that seemed to be relevant in determining which children had less traditional sex-stereotyped attitudes was whether or not their mothers worked. As other studies have shown [9], our data indicated that children with working mothers—especially girls—had more liberal views on roles of men and women in society.

A year later, a further study was undertaken in the same schools and with the same age children to determine what effect, if any, the strongly stereotyped views children hold have on their political attitudes and beliefs. More particularly, the interest was with girls who had always emerged as less politically interested and aware than boys in previous socialization studies. Was there a relationship between strong adherence to traditional feminine values and weak political interest among girls?

As before, the new questionnaire dealt with children's own view of their future roles in job and family; the degree of openness/stereotyping in their view of social roles for men and women; and, new in this study, a series of questions designed to explore their political information and awareness.

Sex Differences and Political Responses

A number of questions dealt with the degree of stereotyping in children's views of both public and private roles. Was the sexual division of labor that extended into family and social roles also true for the civil and political areas?

The democratic norm of equal opportunity implies that anyone can be President, a goal theoretically open to both sexes. Which was more salient for the girls, the rhetoric of equal access or the reality of male dominance in virtually all positions of political power? For boys, the log-cabin-to-Presidency myth or an impenetrable power elite? Do 11-year-olds find the prospect of someday becoming powerful political leaders attractive? What degree of realism do they have about their actual chances of attaining such posts?

To get answers to some of these queries, a number of questions were asked dealing with national and local politics. Children were asked to assume that they were adults and could choose any political job, such as President, governor, judge, head of the school board, and mayor. Although well over half of the children picked none of these posts, strong sex differences were apparent in the answers of those who did pick political jobs. While about the same small proportion of boys and girls chose President, and a sizable number of boys wanted to be mayor, not a single girl chose this. For girls, the popular choices were head of the school board and judge.

Other sex differences emerged that were in line with previous socialization studies [10]. When asked to decide why they might vote for a candidate, girls were more likely to choose candidates who were peace-oriented, honest and sincere. Over twice as many boys as girls chose the candidate whose ideas would contribute to the country's economic wealth.

A composite index was drawn to include the determinants of political information and awareness. The information score consisted of correct answers to the various political identification questions; the awareness score was composed of any response other than "don't know" to the various questions dealing with voting and elections. On each of these scores, the girls did more poorly than the boys.

In areas beside the political, sex-stereotyping was as strong in the attitudes of these children as it had been in their counterparts the year before. Girls saw themselves eventually marrying and having children; boys saw themselves as adults with jobs. Over half the children thought only men should do certain jobs and only women, certain others. Only 10.6% of the girls and 14.7% of the boys said a woman should work "anytime she wants to."

Stereotyping and Politicization

After establishing the existence of sex differences, we were still concerned to see if stereotyping, in and of itself, could be isolated as a determinant of low politicization. Stereotyping was measured by how strongly children saw social roles (housework, medical care, and so on) in the traditional sexually dichotomous terms. The stereotyping index and the political information and awareness indices were matched against each other for all the children. For girls, in particular, the femininity index (adherence to traditional female careers and values) was matched against their political scores.

Results were inconclusive. Stereotyping clearly exists, but the data did not show any strong relationship with levels of political information and awareness, except in a few cases.

Summary

The degree of traditional sex-stereotyping of the major social roles in society is very strong, according to the data reported on here. There is a clear demarcation of roles both at home and in the outside world. Moreover, the girls in the study were more strongly affected by the factors of stereotyping and feminization than were the boys. Not only did they see their own futures in strictly female occupations, but they could not translate their career choices into realistic conceptions of how they would be spending their daily lives when grown. Such discrepancies did not appear for boys.

The effect of stereotyping and feminizing influences upon the political interests and attitudes of girls produced puzzling results. Girls who had the least narrowly feminine aspirations appeared to score higher on political information and awareness, but the relationship was weak. Similarly, while the occupation of the mother (housewife or occupation outside the home) clearly affected the girls' aspirations and degree of stereotyping, it was less apparent in influencing their politicization scores. The hoped-for correlation between stereotyping and feminization in girls as an explanation for their low politicization had not materialized.

Some Remaining Questions

The substantive findings reported on here raised a number of questions which challenge the discipline of political science as sexist in its fundamental paradigms and methodology.

This study demonstrated the wide extent of sex role stereotyping in the attitudes of one group of 11-year-old youngsters, and the particularly damaging effect of such stereotyping on girls. Views were ascertained at only one particular point in time. Other research needs to be done on such questions as the following: Where does stereotyping come from? What are the primary socializing agents inculcating sex role stereotyping? What is the comparative socialization influence on young children of parents, schools, and the media? How does stereotyping change over time? How can it be modified, changed, eliminated? Questions such as these need to be dealt with in longitudinal studies, and in other research efforts with children of different ages and different social and economic strata.

Other more basic questions, not so easily operationalized into empirical studies, are needed if sex-stereotyping is ever to be modified or eliminated. Is it possible to make such modifications without basic changes in the economy, the family and the school? How will future research cope with basic societal role expectations and normative values prescribed for males and females? Such expectations have long been accepted as *givens* by many previous researchers to explain the differential attitudes and behavior of men and women, and have influenced the paradigmatic framework of the social sciences. For example, the work of Parsons has affected much subsequent research. Parsons suggests that society prescribes a dichotomy of instrumental and expressive standards and expectations for men and women [11]. In the Parsonian framework, male roles revolve around task-orientation and include economic achievement, self-reliance, competition, managerial skills, power and physical aggression. Female, expressive expectations center around personal sensitivity to others, and include nurturance, affiliation, solidarity, tension-management, kindliness and a desire to please others. The man's role revolves around his occupation; the woman's around her family role. Children model their behavior after same sex parents, and boys and girls perceive their sex role identity in conformity with these general expectations. In the Seattle study, occupational aspirations of girls were linked to traditional femininity values such as marriage and family, while boys were more oriented to economic and occupational pursuits. But these results do not prove the existence of *inborn* roles and further research needs to be done to ascertain how far *expressive* and *instrumental* behavior and attitudes are already the fruit of prior socialization.

The constraints on career aspirations and self-images of the girls in the Seattle study raise other questions for future research. What direct experiences does the young girl have which serve to strengthen or weaken such sex role images? Since existing research in at least one study showed that sex role expectations were clearer for older children [12], one wonders what happens to women as they grow older in our society. In what ways do they get the message that they are supposed to play certain feminine roles and that politics is a man's business? What are the various sources of these messages and how can they be modified? In order to bring about change in something as basic as societal expectations regarding male and female roles, we need empirical data to probe the degree to which sex and gender are, in fact, linked to masculinity and femininity.

Reflections on these and other sex role differences indicate some serious shortcomings in political socialization research. A neutral definition of socialization research is inadequate in dealing with the views of women. Our interest should not be simply how girls learn existing adult orientations and political roles *because these roles are unsatisfactory for women* at the present time. In terms of civic involvement, full self-development and participation in the decision-making and public process, women are in secondary and second-rate positions. Research into socialization must deal with this. It must raise questions as to how change and diversity can be built into women's view of politics and of themselves within the political system. We need to ask what the possible consequences are for the individual woman as result of being brought up to expect to play a lesser role in the political system. How far does she fall short of being a complete human being, able to exercise power over her own self and to take moral responsibility for decisions which concern her?

Attempts in this project to connect training in femininity and low politicalization in young girls did not succeed. Girls in this study, as in most earlier research, continued to test more apolitical than boys. Is it possible that the previous explanations (biological unsuitability; psychological predispositions to domesticity; emotional instability in coping with the rough-and-ready world of politics) are indeed valid? Another explanation seems plausible: perhaps the existing tools and techniques of political socialization research are themselves sexist, biasing results to favor boys over girls. If this is the case, it will serve to perpetuate a status quo which finds these girls, as adult women, accepting the fact that politics is a man's business. When grown, they can be expected to continue playing a less active role in politics than men, acquiescing in the virtual male domination of the political scene throughout the world.

Political socialization research may have failed to uncover the entire picture with respect to the politicalization of girls because its methodology reflects an unconscious ideology of sexism. This ideology is reflected in two dimensions: the sexist language in which questionnaires eliciting opinions are written; the sexist subject matter with which they deal.

Questionnaires used in three major political socialization studies were scrutinized [13]. Politics is portrayed as a male-only world by the unvarying use of the male gender, the pictures chosen, and the limited and stereotyped choices of answers provided. Adult models are presented only in traditionally sex-typed social and political roles (Example: "Here are some people. Which ones work for the government?" pictures of male milkman, policeman, soldier, judge, postman; "Does the teacher work for the government?" picture of female). Males are the only ones listed as choices for national political leader, party leaders, government workers. The belief is fostered that only the father in the family deals with politics and authority questions, since equivalent questions relating to the mother are never included. Women are either completely invisible ("If the President came to your school, to give a prize to two boys who were the best citizens . . . which two boys would he pick?"—*no equivalent question for girls*) or they are expected to get vicarious satisfaction through their husband's status ("Check all the jobs you would like when you are older. Girls can also check jobs they would want their husband to have.") The supposedly neutral questionnaire has indeed sent through some distinctly nonneutral *messages!*

The present study was premised on the theory that language is important because it symbolizes an underlying ideological position, and so a conscious attempt was made to avoid the sexist pitfalls described above. *He/she* was used instead of the ubiquitous *he*, women were included as examples of political leaders, and men and women were suggested as role models in every type of social and political roles. In spite of this, the girls still made a poor showing on the political information and awareness scales. Obviously, something more than language must be at work reinforcing and perpetuating a sexist view of the political world [14].

It is immediately apparent that the typical questions which test for political information and awareness are male-designed and male-oriented: who runs the country, political party labels, names of mayors and governors—male-oriented, because these posts historically have been held by men. How many girls given the task of memorizing the names of the Presidents of the United States will visualize themselves in that role? As young girls and women sense the exclusiveness of the male club which has dominated the political scene, their resulting disinterest and low involvement in politics is easy to understand. Even more important, when politics is conceptualized solely in terms of aggressive, exploitative and manipulative power it is not surprising that women, trained in submissiveness, dependence and passivity, should find little in it with which to relate.

Sexism underlies our conception of politics and the consequent research techniques designed to illuminate political questions. It has taken the feminist challenge to redefine many questions, previously considered strictly private, as political issues. Through the efforts of the women's movement, such topics as birth control, abortion, and childrearing have become politicized as women learn to define their difficulties in political, rather than individual and psychological, terms. Yet while this has been happening, political science has remained imbedded in its narrow, traditional view of politics, concentrating on the exercise of power by Presidents, governors and mayors, and dealing almost exclusively with houses of parliament, congresses and legislatures. The notion that politics also includes shared values and civic concerns in which power is only one aspect has been ignored. It is not surprising then that our research techniques as well as our basic paradigms, have distorted the political by emphasizing only its narrow, institutional side.

Further socialization studies need to reflect the feminist challenge to a narrowly masculine conception of politics. Politics is more than a one-sided focus on what government officials do and it is also more than aggressive, exploitative power. To the degree that politics is seen as involving individuals, and not merely as residing in the remote, inaccessible realms of *the government,* all of us, men and women alike, will find it easier to break out of the apolitical role. Feelings of impotence and futility with respect to politics may be supplanted by feelings of individual strength and self-reliance in the politics of personal relationships, and apolitical acquiescence may shift imperceptibly into civic awareness and involvement.

Future socialization questionnaires need to broaden the conception of politics so that children will be asked questions dealing with the political aspects of their own lives in home and school. In reflecting about unequal

1831849

power distributions, immovable hierarchies and the authority structure of parents, teachers, and peers, children will come to sense the very real ways in which politics touch their lives at all times. Apolitical may well become a thing of the past, for men as well as women, and the entire political system may benefit from the interest and concern of previously alienated citizens.

NOTES

1. Kirsten Amundsen, *The Silenced Majority*. Englewood Cliffs, N.J.: Prentice-Hall, 1971. Chaps. 4 and 5.

2. Maurice Duverger, *The Political Role of Women* (Paris: UNESCO, 1955); A. Campbell et al., *The Voter Decides*. Evanston, Ill.: Row, Peterson, 1954; H. Cantril and M. Strunk, *Public Opinion: 1935–1946*. Princeton, N.J.: Princeton University Press, 1951; Campbell et al., *The American Voter*. New York: Wiley, 1960; G. Almond and S. Verba, *The Civic Culture: Political Attitudes and Democracy in Five Nations*. Boston: Little Brown, 1969. Lionel Tiger, *Men in Groups*. New York: Random House, 1968.

3. John Stuart Mill, *The Subjection of Women*. Cambridge, Mass.: MIT Press, 1970, pp. 84–85.

4. Robert D. Hess and Judith V. Torney, *The Development of Political Attitudes in Children*. Garden City, N.Y.: Doubleday Anchor, 1968, p. 7.

5. Nancy Chodorow, "Being and Doing: A Cross-Cultural Examination of the Socialization of Males and Females: in Gornick and Moran, *Women in Sexist Society*. New York: Basic Books, 1971; Judith Bardwick and Elizabeth Douvan, "Ambivalence: The Socialization of Women" in Gornick and Moran, *Women in Sexist Society, op. cit.*, S. Bem and D. Bem, "Case Study of a Nonconscious Ideology: Training the Woman to Know Her Place," D. Bem, ed., *Beliefs, Attitudes and Human Affairs*. Belmont, Ca.: Brooks/Cole, 1970; J. Lipman-Blumen, "How Ideology Shapes Women's Lives," *Sci. Amer.*, **226**, 34–42 (1972).

6. M. S. Horner, "Femininity and Successful Achievement: A Basic Inconsistency," in Garskof, ed., *Roles Women Play: Readings Towards Womens Liberation*. Belmont, Ca.: Brooks/Cole, 1971; I. Frieze, J. Parsons, D. Ruble, "Some Determinants of Career Aspirations in College Women," paper presented at the UCLA Symposium on Sex Roles and Sex Differences, Los Angeles, May 1972.

7. Fred Greenstein, *Children and Politics*. New Haven: Yale University Press, 1965; R. D. Hess and J. V. Torney, *Development of Political Attitudes, op. cit.;* D. Easton and J. Dennis, *Children in the Political System*. New York: McGraw-Hill, 1969; Charles F. Andrain, *Children and Civic Awareness*. Columbus, O.: Merrill, 1971.

8. The research was carried out as part of a political science course entitled "Women and Patriarchal Politics" conducted by the author at the University of Washington. During the first part of the study (1971), sociologist Judith Fiedler supervised all phases of the research and collaborated on the report of the data.

9. See, for example, E. T. Peterson, "The Impact of Maternal Employment on the Mother-Daughter Relationship and on the Daughter's Role-Orientation," unpublished Ph.D. dissertation, University of Michigan, 1950; also, S. R. Vogel et al., "Sex-Role Stereotypes: A Current Appraisal," *Jour. of Soc. Issues*, **28** (Summer 1972).

10. Girls scored lower in information and awareness (Greenstein, *Children and Politics, op. cit.*);

girls personalized authority (Hess and Torney, *Development of Political Attitudes, op. cit.;* Easton and Dennis, *Children in the Political System, op. cit.);* girls saw their identity linked with marriage not occupation (Andrain, *Children and Civic Awareness, op. cit.);* girls were less wealth-oriented than boys (Andrain, *Children and Civic Awareness, op. cit.).*

11. Talcott Parsons and Robert F. Bales, *Family, Socialization, and Interaction Process.* Glencoe, Ill.: Free Press, 1955, pp. 45–46.

12. Andrain, *Children and Civic Awareness, op. cit.,* pp. 135, 139.

13. Hess and Torney, *Development of Political Attitudes, op. cit.;* Greenstein, *Children and Politics, op. cit.;* Andrain, *Children and Civic Awareness, op. cit.*

14. Political science textbooks do a lot to contribute to the sexist view of the world the discipline presents. Research done by students under the direction of the author attests to the virtual invisibility of women in standard introductory and American politics texts. In many books, the only women who appear are the little old ladies beloved of political cartoonists—they are either uninformed, silly and irrational, or totally disinterested in politics. "Henry," asks one of her husband of many years, "I've always meant to ask you, what are you, a Republican or a Democrat?" (Cartoon in James Prothro and Marian Irish, *The Politics of American Democracy,* Englewood Cliffs: Prentice Hall, 1965).

Chapter

3

Women and Political Socialization:
Considerations of the Impact of Motherhood

Cornelia B. Flora and Naomi B. Lynn

Politics traditionally has been viewed as a male activity. Men are elected and appointed to the vast majority of policy-making positions at all levels of government. Scholars, perceptive of this tendency, have focused on men in their studies of politics and how people become politicians. When women are treated, it is generally in light of how they influence the male, who is the politician, or how they compare with men in terms of the political process. Here we compare women with women, showing the impact of a single vital event on a woman's self-perception and her political activity.

Sociologists have long stressed the primacy of the role of mother in the identification of the adult female. Lopata describes and analyzes the changes in a woman that take place during the life cycle, stressing the importance of becoming and being a mother [1]. LeMasters, Dyer, and others have pointed to the crisis accompanying initiation to motherhood [2]. For young women, in particular, absorbtion in the care of young children is the norm [3]. As the *self* of an individual can be seen as emerging through the internalization by the individual of social processes of experience and behavior, the new set of interactions and experiences proscribed by the role of mother can be seen to give a woman new criteria for self-evaluation and to remove many of her previous interactions which reinforced her old identity [4].

For women themselves, becoming a mother is viewed as radically changing a woman. Often, in popular mythology, simply being pregnant endows a woman with special attributes and causes monumental alterations in her

A version of this paper was presented at the Annual Meeting of the American Political Science Association, Washington, D.C., 1972.

character. Women who are not mothers, or who haven't experienced pregnancy, are often seen as somehow incomplete individuals.

Motherhood and Self-Image

Many sociologists see the role of mother as the crucial one in limiting female behavior, and, by extension, her resulting self-image. Ginzberg points out that although a husband may broaden or narrow a woman's margin of choice, children almost always narrow it [5]. While the nuclear family dyad is expanded into a triad, tripling the types of potential sets of interactions, the emphasis on the mother as the sole or primary guardian of the child's everyday needs limits to a large degree any other kind of interaction she may experience. Lopata points to two types of self-modification that occur with motherhood: an *identity crisis*, the feeling that the whole personality is affected by constant physical work and contact mainly with infants in a small confined space, and an increase in maturity, in capacities, and abilities [6].

Past research has seemed to agree that motherhood is the major role of women, particularly young women, and that motherhood is a confining role. But the results of the saliency of motherhood among young women has not been systematically analyzed for its political implications.

Motherhood and Political Socialization

Political socialization does not end with adulthood; it is a continuing process which may be affected by any major change in the life of the individual [7]. Dawson and Prewitt point out that acquiring a political self is a natural corollary to general social maturation [8]. Almond and Verba have concerned themselves with the relationship between nonpolitical roles and the political role and suggest that there is a tendency to generalize from one social sphere to the other [9]. If motherhood does indeed have such a tremendous impact on women and their self-image, political socialization should be radically affected as well. New forces play upon a woman's life, a new political self emerges.

Radical members of the women's liberation movement have linked woman's lack of political activity to her role of wife and mother. As pointed out by Gordon, one of the institutions of this society that the women's liberation movement has been particularly vocal in condemning is the nuclear family. The method of child care of the nuclear family is seen as destructive to both adults and children, turning the mother's "adult mind into mush"—a prosaic way of describing the changing self resulting from a new set of interactional processes [10]. In organizations where the responsibility of child care is communalized, mothers maintain a high degree of political participation, as in the organization Rising Up Angry, which is a leftist collective in Chicago engaged in a variety of political organizing endeavors.

The nuclear family, with stress on the childrearing function of the adult female, is claimed by members of the movement to separate people into small, isolated units which distrust outsiders. This distrust, according to Gordon, is one of the forces making it difficult for people to join together to act politically. But it is the family as an institution, rather than the mother-child relationship, which is identified as the antipolitical force.

Children, because of low monetary value placed upon caring for them, serve as one of the many factors that assign a low degree of worth to women, contributing to women's low self-esteem that hinders them in attempting to participate in politics [11]. The myths surrounding motherhood also entrap women into false consciousness, allowing women to define the status quo as the most desirable and secure state. Political socialization is almost completely negative for women in a nuclear family childrearing experience. The sphere of politics is defined as male, because males are the only ones able to cope with it.

Are women totally removed from political activity and political thinking, as suggested by Gordon? Or does a different kind of political thinking emerge, one that is oriented less to personalities and more to policies?

The traditional male view of politics can be seen as personified by Metternich in the nineteenth century and Kissinger in the twentieth. Men make history, therefore real politics is that which involves the struggle between men for power. In American political science, this means an emphasis on electoral politics. The larger the arena, the more important it is. Thus someone who is not concerned with international, or at least national issues, and the personalities—primarily male—involved, is not political.

Women, because of their close contact with the exigencies of life, which men, particularly men who are political actors, are shielded from by wives, secretaries, and other service workers, do have a different view of reality. The most important thing is that which is closest, which affects one most directly. Thus getting a stop light put in by the school is more important than who is on the Public Works Commission, or even who is President of the United States, because that stop light helps insure the survival of that woman's children. And it is with the onset of children that women in our society leave the public arena, at least in terms of labor force participation, and enter a childbound world.

To determine the differences in political participation between mothers and nonmothers, we utilized the 1968 National Election Study conducted by the Survey Research Center at the University of Michigan. We analyzed only women between 20 and 40 to determine their feelings of political efficacy (see Lynn and Flora, 1973, for a more complete discussion of our results). Mothers definitely felt less efficacious politically than nonmothers, even when a number of controls for socioeconomic status were introduced. Differences between mothers and nonmothers was greatest at the higher socioeconomic levels, where motherhood constitutes a greater change in life-style than in the working class [12]. The removal from the public sphere is more dramatic for upper status women, as more of them are in the male political world to begin with.

The question we used to determine political efficacy was one shown to be most reliable in these circumstances [13]. It was: "Would you say that voting is the only way people like you can have a say about the way government runs things, or that there are lots of ways that you can have a say?" The term *government* can be construed as a male province, and although the level of government was not specified, it is likely the women responding interpreted it to mean on the national or at least the state level. The differences between mothers and nonmothers tend to be consistent on these global measures of political efficacy and participation, but disappear on questions related to participation and interest in local policy.

Depth interviews of new mothers were undertaken to try to determine the process of political socialization when a woman becomes a mother. Part of this investigation included examining their definition of the political process and in what ways they were acting or were willing to act on the outside forces touching their lives.

Our sample was drawn randomly from hospital listings of all women 21 to 29 in 1970 who had had their first birth in 1970. As we conducted our interviews in May and June of 1972, these children were between 1½ to 2½ at the time of study. This time span allowed the mothers to completely recover from the traumas of birth, but still to maintain a perspective of their prematernal state.

There were many women in our original sample who had moved from the area since the birth of their first child. We could only make initial contact with 50 women who appeared to be currently living in the Manhattan, Kansas, area. Contact with our sample was initiated by a letter and followed up by a telephone call. Of our original 50 women, nine had left the area, one had experienced the death of her first-born, three were out of town, and two refused completely to respond to our questionnaire.

The analysis below is based on interviews with the remaining 32 women. Our aim in this portion of the study is to try to get a perspective on the process and interaction between the conditions imposed by motherhood and political participation. Thus we claim no representativeness for the sample. The biases present in the sample are discussed below. Basically, the group is of above average socioeconomic status.

For whites in the United States in 1965, the median age of mothers at the birth of their first child was 22.2 years [14]. Presser reports the same median age at first births for whites in 1967 [15]. The median age for our sample was 23.5, and the mean age was 24. Pohlman, citing Ryder, mentions as results of delaying the age of mother at the time of first birth: (*a*) increased education, (*b*) increased employment of women, (*c*) increased capital formation, (*d*) increased geographical and social mobility, (*e*) individualism instead of familism, and (*f*) loosening of ties to traditional patterns, by delaying the time when young people are tied down [16]. All of these results also have consequences for political participation. Presser suggests that the timing of the first birth is an important determinant of subsequent role behavior among women [17]. She suggests that if a woman has her first birth early, the nature of her options in nonfamilial roles may be limited. Conversely, by postponing the first birth, nonfamilial role options may be multiplied.

Our sample, by the definition of the universe, seems to be biased toward potentially political participants, to women who might actually develop a political self, given the right conditions of what Burstein calls formal roles and network interaction. However, their potential as political participants is somewhat restrained by the fact that political participation generally reaches its peak at a later age.

Socioeconomic Characteristics of the Sample

As predicted by choosing women over 20 at age of first birth, the sample had an above average median education of 15.2 years. All had at least high school education, with only four with no training past high school. One respondent had a Ph.D. and several are currently working toward advanced degrees.

The age at marriage of our sample varied between 16 to 27. The mean age at marriage was 21.32. The mean length of marriage was 5.1 years, varying between 3 and 9 years. All the women were currently mated, although one woman in our sample had a husband absent due to overseas military service. None had been previously mated or had any conceptions previous to their first birth. The period of time between marriage and first birth varied between slightly under one and 7 years. The mean was three years. None of our sample was pregnant before marriage. This data suggests that these women were efficacious in their personal lives. All the births were wanted and the majority were planned.

Thirty-one of the women had had only one birth, although five were currently pregnant. Only one had had a second child, two months old at the time of the interview. Most stated family size preferences—only three were unsure of their total desired family size. One woman wants one child, 10 women want two, six want two or three, 12 want three (with one couple planning to adopt the third child). Twenty-eight plan the spacing of their children.

In terms of seeing herself as an effective person, and thus capable of making an impact on the larger world, an effective family planner can gain the self-confidence to act politically.

Manhattan, Kansas, is a community of 27,600, located in the northeastern part of the state, about two hours west of Kansas City along Interstate 70. Kansas State University and Fort Riley, a large Army base, account for a major part of the economic structure of the town, although Manhattan does house a few small factories and a major pattern factory. It is the marketing center for an agricultural hinterland. Of the persons employed in Manhattan in 1970, 4% were in manufacturing industries and 41% were government workers. It is basically a middle class community, with 64% of the labor force in white collar occupations.

The economic structure of the community is reflected by our sample. Currently 10 of their husbands are students, although most of them hold other jobs on the side. Three are in the Armed Forces, six are teachers, elementary to college level, while the other men are in lower level white collar or skilled blue collar jobs. One is currently unemployed.

Median income in Manhattan in 1970 was a little more than $9,000. The poverty level included 9% and 19% made more than $15,000. Manhattan had a somewhat higher level of income than did the state as a whole. For our 32 woman interviewees, family income varied between $2,500 and $35,000. The mean income was approximately $10,000. The generally high income of our sample is usually associated with high political participation. It should be noted that those with the lowest incomes were students, who are subjectively, at least, members of the middle class.

Due to the university and the fort, the population is highly migratory. In 1970, 46% of the population of Manhattan over five was classified by the Bureau of the Census as migrants (living in a different county in 1965), over twice the rate of the state as a whole. The 1970 Manhattan population was 58% native—residing in their state of birth. This is about the same percentage native as was found in Kansas City. For Kansas as a whole, 64% of the population was native in 1970. The majority—65%—of our sample was born in Kansas. None of the women interviewed had lived in Manhattan, Kansas, her entire life. Length of time lived in Manhattan varied from 3 to 20 years. The mean number of years in Manhattan is 5.3. This gives our sample a potential for higher community identification—and thus political participation—than a large portion of the local population.

In Manhattan as a whole, 44% of the married women with husbands present were in the labor force, while 27.4% of the married women with husbands present and children under six were in the labor force. Female labor force participation in Manhattan in 1970 for both mothers of young children and nonmothers, was considerably lower than for the Kansas City SMSA and for the state as a whole. This might in part be due to the sharp competition for jobs among the wives of students and military personnel. All but one of the 31 mothers had some labor force participation. Thirty wives were employed before marriage. Eight were students, with odd jobs to help support themselves. Ten had secretarial or clerical jobs before marriage. Two were nurses and three were nurses aides. Six had other jobs requiring specialized training, including teaching. Interestingly, one in our sample had been a nun. One of the women had worked primarily as a waitress. Thus almost all our women had been part of the public sphere, where participation is generally higher.

Labor force participation continued for the women after marriage but before the baby was born. Fifteen were in secretarial or clerical jobs. Six were technicians of various sorts. Three were graduate assistants or instructors at the university. Four were registered nurses and one was a nurse's aide. One was a beauty operator. The wages varied between $100 and $800 a month, with a mean of $360. The relatively high level of their occupations (for women) can be related to the postponement of childbearing among our sample.

Six of the women worked right up to the birth of their first child. Eleven quit their jobs between 6 weeks to a month before the baby was born. Three quit two months before, and the rest quit working from 3 to 12 months in anticipation of childbearing. Childbearing was therefore the catalyst of separation from the public sphere for many women we interviewed.

At the present time, with the child between 1½ and 2½, 14 of our respondents are no longer in the labor force. Eight are working part time and nine are working full time. Those that continue full-time employment are in professional or technical fields, and relatively well remunerated. Thus we are able to assess the process of becoming a mother and its interaction with political socialization for workers and nonworkers as distinct female types.

The women in our sample did not view themselves as highly political, although 25 out of the 32 replied that there were more ways than voting for them to influence the government, a proportion well above that of our national sample of college-educated mothers with children under five. They were able to cite concrete ways they could influence the government other than voting, although only a minority had attempted to do so.

Ten respondents identified as Republicans (Kansas is a strongly Republican state—64% of the presidential vote went to Nixon in 1970; although currently a Democrat, Dr. William Roy, is the Congressional Representative from the district which includes Manhattan), eight are Democrats, 12 classify themselves as Independents, and two frankly stated they did not know what their political leanings were. Few were deeply involved in the preconvention political turmoil, although we had one avid supporter of Governor Wallace and two women working for McGovern.

Sixty % of our respondents voted in the 1968 presidential election, 43% voted in the 1970 congressional election, and 39% of those eligible voted in the 1971 city-wide election. (Five of our respondents were living in university housing, which is not part of the city, or in mobile home parks outside the city limits at the time of the city election.) From this, it would appear that national personalities were viewed as more salient than local ones.

In our interviews of these 32 women, we discovered three major types of intermediate variables which seem to influence how motherhood will influence a woman's political socialization and thus her political participation. These are: anticipatory socialization, interaction networks, and husband helpfulness.

Anticipatory Socialization

The life cycle of a woman can be conceptualized as a series of roles and concomitant statuses. Becoming a mother is a major status change for many women. All the women we interviewed reported at least some changes in themselves resulting from motherhood. Role theory allows us to focus on role transitions as the point where crucial changes in the self occur [18]. Ease of role transition is defined as the degree to which there is freedom from difficulty and availability of resources either to stop or begin a role [19]. Anticipatory socialization, according to Merton, includes taking on the values and orientations of the nonmembership group to which a person aspires [20]. While for many formal roles, explicit training and education is involved in anticipatory socialization, for many roles—particularly the traditionally feminine ones—it is ". . . *implicit, unwitting,* and *informal* . . . [21]."

Deutscher has used the concept of anticipatory socialization to explain ease of role transition for couples whose children have left home [22]. Dyer's examination of the crisis occurring at the onset of parenthood relates the severity of the crisis to degree of education for the role of parent [23]. Burr suggests a general proposition relevant to new mothers: the amount of anticipatory socialization positively influences the ease of transition into roles [24].

In analyzing a national sample of 343, we found that among women with a high school education or less, political efficacy was generally low. Motherhood did not seem to influence it. Among women with education past high school, presence of children made a difference, with mothers having a significantly lower sense of political efficacy than nonmothers (chi-square probability .05). We attribute this differential impact of children on political participation to differential anticipatory socialization for the role of mother

[25]. The lives of women of lower educational attainment have been aimed primarily at gaining the status of mother. This greater degree of anticipatory socialization means that actual achievement of the role does not create great psychic and physical disruption in the life of a working-class woman [26]. Less anticipatory socialization occurs among middle-class women, according to Lopata [27]. The unexpected trauma of motherhood, with the accompanying increased repetition of tasks and the social isolation which is so common in the life of a young mother, may lead to a change in the sense of self resulting in low political efficacy among the better-educated women.

A high degree of anticipatory socialization for the role of mother tends to account for a low degree of political participation. Active political socialization does not occur, as no disjuncture in the female sphere occurs which allows entry of the elements of the public sphere.

The least amount of anticipatory socialization for the role of mother was exhibited by an ex-nun in our sample. Motherhood, although not unwanted, was much more limiting than she had ever imagined. The constant demands of a two-year-old left her no time to "just sit and think," as in meditation in the nunnery. While she identified problems in individualistic terms, she was much more prone to act to change things which bothered her than were the women who had spent a lifetime anticipating being mothers. Our ex-nun had circulated petitions on building a local bridge and boycotted certain businesses whose policies (mainly prices) she disapproved of.

Husband Helpfulness

An individual has to have more than minimal free time if she is going to engage in writing letters to influence policy, circulate petitions, or join or organize political groups. For the young mother who is feeling the constant pressure of taking care of her child, the time just doesn't seem to be there. Lane mentions lack of leisure time in explaining why lower-class women are not politically active [28]. This same reason can apply as well to middle-class young mothers. The tasks of child rearing are never-ending, as one of our respondents pointed out. "Once you get everything all done up (laugh) and you sit down and you think 'Ah! It's all finished' and you turn around and here they've got a pile here and a pile here and you about pull your hair out." In a nuclear family situation, only the husband can provide the mother with the extra free time necessary for political activity to take place. For communities such as Manhattan, Kansas, alternatives such as daycare centers and domestic help are available only to a few—and thought of as immoral by many others.

Resource theory of family power, as stated by Blood and Wolfe [29], assumes that spouses' familial behavior is influenced and regulated by relative personal resources: education, income, occupation, and social participation. Social participation, which includes politics, can be viewed as caused by equality of family power, as well as causing such equality to emerge. A number of researchers have shown that education is a power resource [30].

A large number of studies show that working wives have more power within the family than nonworking wives, validating the use of occupation as a power resource [31]. There are few studies of couples where income is separated from occupation as a measure of relative resources of husband and wife, and fewer studies of differential social participation and family power. However, these are still potential sources of differential power, and thus, differential facilitators for husband helpfulness and female political participation.

We had expected the working mothers, who would have more family power and thus might be seen as more likely to equitable division of labor within the family, to be the ones with high political participation. However, our analysis of the SRC data showed that motherhood was more important than labor force participation in explaining women's political efficacy.

Even with the nonworking mothers, those that could count on their husbands to help with the child were the ones more likely to engage in politics at any level. For other working mothers, the job just meant that their household tasks dominated a major portion of their nonworking time. They too were dependent on a willing husband to free their scarcest resource— time—for political activity.

Analysis of Cuba and other cultures where there is ideological commitment to changing the role and status of women show the difficulty of changing only the female sex role [32]. If a change in the traditional female role of nonparticipation in politics is to change, some male roles must also change to facilitate female involvement.

Interaction Networks

The network interactions of mothers, the voluntary behavior conditioned by their formal roles, are crucial when explaining the political socialization occurring with motherhood. These networks provide the *significant other* through which the self is defined and the importance of the other in the formation of self conceptions has been established by sociologists [33]. We look at four types of interaction networks: child-centered, job-centered, voluntary organizations, and the media.

The active individual is most likely to be found near the center of relevant communications networks with high rates of interaction [34]. It is the individual's location in this network of social-political relationships that determines whether or not he is exposed to political stimuli [35].

Child-Centered Networks

The typical nonworking housewife we interviewed interacts primarily with her family and others in her neighborhood. She is preoccupied with carrying out the duties and responsibilities of motherhood which have been specified for her by society. She has no personal and direct ties to the intermediary groups which intervene between citizens and the larger polity. The political isolation of the child-centered neighborhood places her in the peripheral dimension of the relevant communications network [36].

Women we interviewed tended to think it very important to live in neighborhoods where there were lots of peers for their children to play with. Many of them were successful in geographically locating in such areas. Although there was much visiting back and forth, this social interaction still meant political isolation. The women mentioned that most of their conversations with their neighbors were about children and the problems of child-rearing with a minimum of political discussion. One mother discussed her personal contacts in these words, "I also found that I made new friends and most of our neighbors had children which gave me something in common with them." Another stated: "Now that I have a child, there's more to talk about with my friends since they also have children."

The personal interactions of these young mothers still left them politically isolated. Their interpersonal channels of information were restricted and they were exposed to few politically knowledgeable people. Heiskanen has observed that "through differential accessibility and participation in different opportunity structures, females are given less opportunities for exposure to phenomena that are here suggested to be indispensable components of effective political participation [37]."

The depoliticalizing influence of friendships with neighboring mothers is best illustrated by a negative example, a woman outside the child-centered networks and highly politically active.

Mary Ann has no close friends with small children. Lacking social interaction with young mothers which tends to satisfy the social needs of most of the nonworking mothers we interviewed, she feels especially tied down with the birth of her daughter.

". . . once you get to feel tied down that's when you want to get out and do something else." Previously concerned about social issues but now active toward them, she joined the League of Women Voters and worked to elect McGovern people at the county-level delegate caucus.

Job-Related Networks

Both working and nonworking mothers were politically active and inactive. Only when they found a reflection of an active self outside the work sphere or the neighborhood sphere did such activity occur. Most of our respondents were in female occupations—nurse, secretary, etc.—and politics was seldom discussed at work. The job-related political socialization which did occur seemed to result in cynicism rather than participation, as this comment by one of our working mothers illustrates: "Unless you have a lot of the money and the pull behind you and then as a single person you're going to have a lot of clout. Sure, you're going to have a lot to say and people are going to sit up and listen. But me as a small person, I'm—if I said something, people are going to say, you know, 'Look at that dummy sitting down there.' You know, I feel like this, I really do."

Media Networks

Various forms of mass media were mentioned by all the women we interviewed as sources of information. Some spoke with pride about reading at least one newspaper daily and listening to the 5:30 news each evening. Although the news was on television, they were involved in meal preparation and thus could not concentrate fully. One would normally expect that exposure to the mass media would lead to increased political activity, but since they felt they did not have the time to get involved, this preoccupation with the media served as a means for fulfilling their civic duty. Although lack of time may make this displacement necessary, it may also serve as a *narcotizing dysfunction* with respect to activating political activity. Some respondents were substituting the passive intake of information for the more demanding and active political activities which they denied themselves either through choice or necessity.

Although radio, television, magazines and newspapers were utilized by the women we interviewed, they were generally selective and preferred the nonpolitical items. Although most of the women listened to the radio, as an accompaniment to housework, many did not listen to radio news. They enjoyed instead a musical background to their domestic activities. The social page, Heloise and Ann Landers were popular among the newspaper readers, although only one person said she deliberately skipped the news.

One respondent with low political participation mentioned that she had written a letter to a senator. When asked what motivated this letter, she answered that Ann Landers had suggested that a letter be written encouraging the passage of a health bill. This was the only time she had taken any political action other than voting. Another respondent, in expanding the political efficacy question, mentioned petitions as a way an individual could influence the government. She had read about a woman who had effectively used this tool in an article in *Good Housekeeping* magazine. This suggests that women are being politically socialized and activated by newspaper and magazine reading not normally associated with high political participation. For these mothers, their political *generalized other* were media figures rather than their immediate neighbors.

The majority of women, even those with minimal political participation, at least skimmed the front page, which, in the local paper, emphasizes local news. Many of the more politically conscious read local and national news quite thoroughly. Those who did not read a newspaper at all or who read only the nonpolitical sections were also those who felt voting was the only way someone like them could influence the government and did not intend to get more involved in the community when their children were older.

Television viewing habits were similar to radio and newspaper consumption. The totally uninvolved never saw the television news or only watched it occasionally. Those in the high participation group watched regularly, although one of these mothers mentioned that since the baby came, she watched the news just as regularly, but "now with more interruptions."

Although differences in education and social class may account for this lack of interest in political activity, more attention needs to be paid to the effects which daytime television viewing may be having on the housewife. Politics by definition is a group activity. If changes are going to be made in the polity they will have to come as a result of group effort. Life as it is portrayed by the television actor is a series of personal mishaps. If there are problems, they are caused by individual weaknesses; if solutions are to be discovered the individual hero will have to do it (see Mattelart and Flora for discussions of individualism in women's magazine fiction and its relation to social change) [38]. Personal tragedy resulting from social forces beyond the individual's control are largely ignored. The value of organizing and working with others to tackle the societal ills is virtually nonexistent. Women for whom life on television may have become as real as their own will find little motivation for political participation. The advantages of political solutions to life's problems may be more unreal to them than the complicated maze of plots on which they focus their attention every day. That the women who were the most devoted soap opera fans were also the most apolitical, and did not in the future plan to become more active in community affairs, supports this, as does an analysis by Katzman of soap opera audiences and content [39].

Voluntary Organization Networks

We found that the women we interviewed who were members of voluntary organizations were more likely to engage in some sort of political behavior. This type of voluntary organization a woman belonged to influenced the type of issue which she would get involved in. The members of fundamentalist religions tended to get involved only in moral issues, such as whether or not Kansas should have liquor by the drink. Although this is a traditionally feminine sphere of interest, they still acted through petitions, letter writing, and the grass-roots organizing necessary. Other churches urged concern with issues such as war and racism, but the reactions elicited among our respondents varied from anger to apathy at the exhortations.

The League of Women Voters was mentioned by several of our mothers as a way other than voting by which they could influence the government. Some of the women, currently moderately politically active but who proposed more community activity in the future, mentioned the League as the vehicle they would use to increase their participation. For these women, a reinforcement for a more politically active self was already latently present. However, these women who looked forward to League activity when their children were older were college graduates and not members of the labor force.

The type of voluntary organization, as well as participation per se, seemed to greatly influence a woman's political socialization and sense of self. New mothers are unlikely to participate in any organization outside their church, where their activity is at a lower level than at other stages of their life cycles.

In general, our respondents tended to have an individualistic view of the need for themselves to get involved in the political process. One respondent who had acted politically viewed her activity this way: "Guess it all depends on the magnitude—how much it would affect me personally. That's probably a selfish point of view . . ." Because they act on personal, individual level issues, they are basically content with the system. They have found that their personal difficulties, from being cheated on promised discounts to being denied Blue Cross-Blue Shield by the Air Force, can be solved through individual pressure. They are personally efficacious people, and their private lives they see as well-organized.

"We don't like to get out on our high horse and yell and scream around because we don't feel that's the way to do these things and we've found that—you know—it takes a little time, but by working through the system—however long it takes—why, we usually get something done."

These women define their area of interest by what they can feel and what they can anticipate affecting their family. Local issues interest them most, and, as one woman stated, the time to get involved is while there is still time for action to be taken for their children. "You're voting for a school tax bond because by the time your children are in school, that school will be built, or you're voting a new swimming pool or you're voting for the commissioners that will be in office during the period of time your children will be growing up—this type of thing."

Although most of our sample ranked the role of wife as more important to them than the role of mother (contrary to findings of Lopata [40]), their political interest had a child-centerness, particularly among the nonworking wives. The working wives also saw their children as a basis for political activity, but were to a lesser extent mobilized as well on issues that directly influenced their profession, such as licensing of x-ray technicians.

Becoming a mother had a definite influence on the political socialization of our sample. New mothers are socialized in politics by different mechanisms than are men and women at other stages of their life cycle. Their very definition of politics, as it interests them, is a personalistic, practical one. The urgencies of motherhood, when one suddenly finds oneself totally responsible for a young life, have repercussions for the issues a woman is interested in. What action, if any, she might take is mediated by her degree of anticipatory socialization for the role of mother, the degree to which her husband is willing to share female tasks, and the kind of interaction networks in which she is involved.

NOTES

1. Helena Z. Lopata, *Occupation: Housewife*. New York: Oxford University Press, 1971.

2. Daniel F. Hobbs, Jr., "Parenthood as Crisis: A Third Study," *Jour. of Marriage and the Family*, **XXVII.** pp. 367–372 (1965).

3. Talcott Parsons, "Age and Sex in Social Structure," *Amer. Sociological Rev.*, **VII.** pp. 604–616 (Oct. 1942).

4. George H. Mead, *Mind, Self and Society*. Chicago: University of Chicago Press, 1934.

5. Eli Ginzberg with Ivan E. Berg, *et al.*, *Life Styles of Educated Women*. New York: Columbia University Press, 1966, p. 55.

6. Lopata, *op. cit.*, pp. 192–193.

7. By political socialization, we mean the interaction between a social system and an individual whereby both predisposition for and skills related to participation in the political sphere are internalized.

8. Richard E. Dawson and Kenneth Prewitt, *Political Socialization*. Boston: Little, Brown. 1969, p. 19.

9. Gabriel A. Almond and Sidney Verba, *The Civic Culture: Political Attitudes and Democracy in Five Nations*. Boston: Little, Brown. 1965, p. 272.

10. Linda Gordon, *Families*. Boston: New England Free Press, 1970, p. 3.

11. *Ibid.*, p. 16.

12. Lopata, *Occupation: Housewife, op. cit.*, Chapter 3; Richard Rainwater, Richard P. Coleman, and George Handel, *Workingman's Wife: Her Personality, World, and Life Style*. New York: Oceana. pp. 88–89.

13. Shanto Iyengar, *The Problem of Response Stability: Some Comparisons Between Items and Scales*. Paper Delivered at the Midwest Political Science Association, Chicago, 1972.

14. Donald J. Bogue, *Principles of Demography*. New York: Wiley. 1969, p. 687.

15. Harriet B. Presser, "The Timing of the First Birth, Female Roles, and Black Fertility," *Milbank Memorial Fund Quart.*, **XLIX.** p. 333 (1971).

16. Edward Pohlman, "The Timing of First Births: A Review of Effects," *Eugenics Quart.*, **XV.** pp. 252–263 (Dec. 1968).

17. Presser, "Timing of First Birth," *op. cit.*

18. Leonard Cottrell, "The Adjustment of the Individual to His Age and Sex Roles," *Amer. Sociological Rev.*, **VII.** pp. 617–620 (Oct. 1942).

19. Wesley R. Burr, "Role Transitions: A Reformulation of Theory," *Jour. of Marriage and the Family*, **XXXIV.** p. 407 (Aug. 1972).

20. Robert K. Merton, *Social Theory and Social Structure*. Glencoe, Ill.: Free Press, 1957, pp. 265, 384.

21. *Ibid.*, p. 384.

22. Irwin Deutscher, "Socialization for Post-Parental Life," in Arnold M. Rose, ed., *Human Behavior and Social Processes*. Boston: Houghton Mifflin, 1962.

23. Everett D. Dyer, "Parenthood as Crisis: A Restudy," *Marriage and Family Living*, **XXV.** pp. 196–201 (1963).

24. Burr, *op. cit.*, p. 408.

25. Naomi B. Lynn and Cornelia Butler Flora, "Motherhood and Political Participation: A Changing Sense of Self," *Jour. of Mil. and Poli. Soc.*, I (March 1973).

26. Rainwater, *op. cit.*

27. Lopata, *op. cit.*

28. Robert Lane, *Political Life*, Glencoe, Ill.: Free Press, 1959, p. 235.

29. Robert O. Blood, Jr. and Donald M. Wolfe, *Husbands and Wives*. New York: Free Press, 1960.

30. Robert O. Blood, Jr., *Love Match and Arranged Marriage*. New York: Free Press, 1967; Oliveria Buric and Andjelka Zecevic, "Family Authority," *Jour. of Marriage and the Family*, **XXIX.** pp. 325–336 (May 1967); Andree Michel, "Comparative Data Concerning the Interaction in French and American Families," *Jour. of Marriage and the Family*, **XXIX.** pp. 337–344 (May 1967); Eugene Lupri, "Contemporary Authority Patterns in the West German Family: A Study in Cross-National Validation," *Jour. of Marriage and the Family*, **XXXI.** pp. 134–144 (Feb. 1969).

31. Sheldon Glueck and Eleanor Glueck, "Working Mothers and Delinquency," *Mental Hygiene*, **XLI.** pp. 327–352 (July 1957); David M. Heer, "Dominance and the Working Wife," *Soc. Forces*, **XXXVI.** pp. 341–347 (May 1958); Robert O. Blood, Jr. and Robert M. Hamblin, "The Effect of the Wife's Employment on Her Family Power Structure," *Soc. Forces*, **XXXVI.** pp. 347–352 (May 1958); Lois Weadis Hoffman, "Parental Power Relations and the Division of Household Tasks," *Marriage and Family Living*, **XXII.** pp. 27–35 (Feb. 1960); Francena L. Nolan, "Rural Employment and Husbands and Wives," in F. Ivan Nye and Lois W. Hoffman, *The Employed Mother in America*. Chicago: Rand McNally. 1963; Robert O. Blood, Jr., *op. cit.*; Buric and Zecevic, *op. cit.*; Constantina Safilios-Rothschild, "A Comparison of Power Structure and Marital Satisfaction in Urban Greek and French Families," *Jour. of Marriage and the Family*, **XXIX.** pp. 345–352 (May 1967); Robert H. Weller, "The Employment of Wives, Dominance, and Fertility," *Jour. of Marriage and the Family*, **XXX.** pp. 437–442 (Aug. 1968); Lynda Lytle Holmstrom, *The Two-Career Family*. Cambridge: Schenkam. 1972.

32. Susan Kaufman Purcell, "Modernizing Women for a Modern Society: The Cuban Case,"

in Ann Pescatello, ed., *Female and Male in Latin America*. Pittsburgh: University of Pittsburgh Press, 1973, pp. 257–271.

33. Mead, *op. cit.*: Charles Cooley, *Human Nature and the Social Order*. New York: Schoken. 1964; Elihu Katz and Paul F. Lazarsfeld, *Personal Influence*. Glencoe, Ill.: Free Press, 1955; Joseph Woefel and Archibald O. Haller, "Significant Others, The Self-Reflective Act, and the Attitude Formation Process," *Amer. Sociological Rev.* **XXXVI.** pp. 74–87 (Feb. 1971).

34. Lester W. Milbraith, *Political Participation*. Chicago: Rand McNally. 1965, pp. 110–113.

35. Kenneth Prewitt, *The Recruitment of Political Leaders: A Study of Citizen Politicians*. Indianapolis: Bobbs-Merrill. 1970, p. 10.

36. Lynn and Flora, *op. cit.*

37. Veronica Stolte Heiskanan, "Sex Roles, Social Class and Political Consciousness," *Acta Sociologica*, **XIV.** p. 86 (1971).

38. Michele Mattelart, "El nivel mitico en la prensa seudo-amorosa," *Cuadernos de la Realidad National*, **III.** pp. 221–284 (Marzo 1970); Cornelia Butler Flora, "The Passive Female and Social Change: A Cross-Cultural Comparison by Class of Women's Magazine Fiction in the United States and Colombia and Mexico," in Ann Pescatello, ed., *Female and Male in Latin America*. Pittsburgh: University of Pittsburgh Press, 1973, pp. 59–85.

39. Nathan Katzman, "Television Soap Operas: What's Been Going On Anyway?" *Pub. Opinion Quart.* **XXVI.** pp. 200–212 (1972).

40. Lopata, *Occupation: Housewife, op. cit.*, p. 48.

Chapter

4

Women's Attitudes Toward Women in Politics:
A Survey of Urban Registered Voters and Party Committeewomen

Audrey Siess Wells and Eleanor Cutri Smeal

Political scientists have been generally surprised by the recent surfacing of a viable political movement stemming from the women's rights movement. The profession as a whole has found itself hard pressed to deal with the movement, either in analyzing the factors that provoked its emergence, or in explaining its implications for policy-making and the operation of political institutions in general. Such unpreparedness can be partially explained by the focus of political research, which has almost excluded women from its concern. This has been accomplished by either defining political to exclude women or studying institutions which are predominantly male in orientation, occupancy, or style. We have seen little research on women that would explain the current phenomena or events [1]. Only recently has research been directed at women and politics with an interest in women as the focus. The research of those few who worked in this area earlier is only now receiving adequate attention as the subject becomes legitimatized as a research concern.

It has been assumed in the past that women would not organize as a group for political purposes in the way ethnic and racial groups have done. The assumption was that women would never form a voting bloc because

An earlier version of this paper was presented at the Annual Meeting of the American Political Science Association, Washington, D.C., 1972.

their other diverse characteristics prevented such alliances. It was believed that differences in social class, race, or religion were more likely to divide women politically than sharing the same sex characteristic was likely to unite them. The fact that they lived with the enemy—males—was another rationale supporting this belief. An underlying assumption was that women as a group did not receive differential treatment at the hands of the political system—in other words they did not suffer in the allocation of resources by that system because of their sex classification. For example, no one asked if women's interests were being represented by men who predominated in the decision-making positions. The political science profession has done little until recently to question the widely held belief that politics is strictly a masculine affair and that woman's place is in the home. On the contrary, the profession has ignored the question by relying on cultural sex role definitions as the unifactor explanation for the status of women in politics rather than actually investigating that status. The lower status of women in politics was perpetuated and accepted because the culture supported the myth that politics is a man's world. If that status was not acceptable to some women, the rationale was that they had only themselves to blame because women are their own worse enemies in politics.

Women's attitudes toward women in politics is an area of information which is crucial to understanding the current political phase of the women's rights movement and its future. The overall significance and impact of the movement will be determined by its support among women. Explanations of why women are supportive of women in politics or not, as well as knowledge of characteristics that distinguish supporters from nonsupporters, are necessary to understand the viability of the movement. Such information is also essential to potential women candidates planning their campaigns. For example, a female candidate wants to know which women are likely to support her and whether women's issues are potentially useful in attracting additional support from women.

Despite the importance of mapping women's attitudes toward women in politics, which would thereby provide information to understand better the increasing involvement of women in politics, little research has been done to obtain such information [2]. The Gallup Poll with its question regarding the likelihood of a woman voting for a woman for President, and more recently Congress, has received the most widespread coverage [3], and that is probably because its results are used to support the idea that women are less supportive than men of other women in politics. From 1963 through 1969 the Gallup Poll has reported that more men than women have said they would vote for a woman for President. This question however provided insufficient information regarding the support for women candidates among women because it questioned support only for the highest office, for which women had had no role model. The fact that the wording of the question varied over the years and that the unidimensional character of the question was suspect were additional factors which convinced us of the need for new research. We felt support for women in different public offices of varying status levels would provide more worthwhile information than questions only about the highest status positions. Knowing that women held a greater percentage of positions at the state and local levels than at the national level, we suspected support would decrease with the increased status of the office. Not only is the whole question of support for women far more complex than allowed for in the interpretation of one question in the Gallup Poll, but also the conclusions based on that one question are dubious.

The study of women's attitudes toward women in politics has been left at this superficial level, and, as a consequence, we know very little in depth about the support for women in politics. As noted, the wording in the Gallup question has varied over the years. The original 1936 version "Would you vote for a woman for President if she was qualified in every other respect?" is certainly biased. As worded from 1945 through 1971 the question suggests the existence of another dimension. The 1945 version "If the party whose candidate you most often support nominated a woman for President of the United States, would you vote for her if she seemed best qualified for the job?" suggests a second question of loyalty to your party in the event they nominate a woman. The wording in 1949 excluded "best." In 1958 and 1963 the wording became "If your party nominated a generally well-qualified woman for President, would you vote for her?" and in 1967, 1969, and 1971, "If your party nominated a woman for President, would you vote for her if she were qualified for the job [4]?" In the "best" version one is being asked whether he or she would support the best candidate even if she were female.

It is in 1963 that the trend of women being more supportive changed, but it should be noted that the wording of the question changed also. The female candidate became only generally well-qualified rather than best qualified. These findings bring to mind the commonly held belief that women have to be twice as good as men to get a position. Perhaps the female respondents were being realistic in recognizing an equally qualified woman could not get elected in the 1960's. In the 1967 and 1969 polls in which the female candidate was "qualified for the job," male support still surpassed that of women. Then two years later in July, 1971, the poll results showed a dramatic increase of 18 percentage points in female support compared to a seven point gain in male support. This increase placed female support ahead of male support by two points. Among the females, 67% said yes to the question, still in its 1967–1969 form, compared to 65% of the men [5]. This large change in two years time further suggests the inadequacy of this single indicator for a complex cluster of attitudes.

Description of Research

The major goals for our research were: (a) to ascertain the characteristics of women who are supportive, as well as nonsupportive, of women in politics, (b) to investigate reasons for their support or nonsupport, and (c) to establish the differential in support levels between politically active women and female voters. Such information is essential for an assessment of the potential support for women candidates as well as broadbased support of the political phase of the women's rights movement.

Assumptions

Prior to the study, several assumptions concerning the attitudes of women toward women in politics were present in the thinking of the researchers. It seemed logical to assume that party committeewomen would be more supportive of women in politics than female voters in general. One, they could better witness the status of women in politics from their positions, and, two, the improvement of the status of women in the political arena would enhance their own power within the party. It seemed reasonable to assume that support for female candidates and leadership in the promotion of women would come from those already active in electoral politics. But we also had strong suspicions that committeewomen might, in fact, be less supportive than women voters. In that case, the committeewomen would identify more with male issues and male candidates than would registered women voters. This factor was believed to be related to the party-entrance route or the methods by which women were recruited to party positions. The males who controlled the party would more likely select go-along types for committee positions and contain the personal ambitions of any highly motivated female activists.

It was also believed that those women who were conscious of the status of women in American society would be more supportive of women in politics than those lacking such knowledge. The consciousness raising of the American female by the women's rights movement was having an impact on the American culture in 1971. It was felt that such a variable indicating the recognition of the outgroup status of women in politics would be more related to support levels than educational, income, or occupational status, or even interest in politics.

Hypotheses

The hypotheses that served as the focus for the research reported here are as follows:

There is no difference in propensity to support women in politics between registered women voters and local party committeewomen.

Propensity to support women in politics is not related to awareness of the outgroup status of women in politics.

Methodology

The research hypotheses were operationalized via a field survey during the first three weeks of August, 1971, in Pittsburgh, Pennsylvania. We planned parallel studies directed at local party committeewomen and rank and file women voters. Two separate questionnaires which shared some identical questions, the field materials, and the training of interviewers were planned to be compatible even though each study was actually conducted separately.

The respondents in the two groups were selected by a slightly different random method from two different sources. The names of the voters were selected from the most recent lists of registered voters and the committeewomen's names were chosen from current lists of both Democratic and Republican committee people. There were 192 (69.7%) usable interviews from the female voters' group and 172 (69.4%) from the committeewomen's group. Some reasons for nonparticipation varied between the two groups, but having moved, being ill or hospitalized, having died, being on vacation, or outright refusal were common to both populations. Having moved accounted for the largest loss of interviews.

The survey groups closely matched the age and racial characteristics of the city's female population of voting age taken from the census data for 1970 [6]. Age and racial characteristics were not available for the actual universe of registered female voters and committeewomen from which the samples were drawn.

Propensity to support women in politics was operationalized with an index based on five checklist-type items. The question read:

Would you be just as likely to vote for a qualified woman as a qualified man for the following political offices? Please answer yes or no.

_____ Judge
_____ President
_____ U.S. Senator
_____ Governor
_____ City Council

The index ranged from a score of zero to five. The index was split into two levels of support, low and high, at the combined median for the two groups. Those scores under four were defined as low support and those of four or above, high.

Research Findings

Propensity to Support

There is little difference in the levels of support for women in politics between committeewomen and registered voters. In spite of their participation in party activities, committeewomen evidenced only 57% of their members in the high support group, while 60.4% of voters were found there.

The breakdown of potential votes for individual offices shows an interesting difference in the two groups. A higher percentage of committeewomen than registered voters would vote for women for lesser offices—city council, judge, and U.S. senator, but registered voters demonstrate potentially higher support for women in the executive positions of governor and President. (See Table 4.1.) This difference is not statistically significant. There is a fall off in support as the office becomes higher in status and an apparent cleavage in support between nonexecutive and executive offices. Both group means fall below a score of four. One possible explanation for this break between executive and nonexecutive positions is the presence of female role models for the lower level positions and their absence for higher levels. Women in this survey were familiar with women in the offices of city council, judge, and congresswoman, but unfamiliar with women governors. And, of course, they have been denied exposure to a woman President.

In another question suggesting support for more women in public office in general, there again was no significant difference in the responses of the two groups. This question introduces a different dimension than the previous

Table 4.1. Propensity to Support Women for Individual Offices by Registered Female Voters and Local Committeewomen

Office	Registered female voters (N = 192)	Party committeewomen (N = 172)
City council	88.9%	94.4%
Judge	88.0	91.1
U.S. senator	76.8	85.4
Governor	62.6	60.5
President	46.2	42.7
Spread, from lowest to highest office	−42.7	−51.7
Not significant		

Table 4.2. Expression of Support for More Women in Public Office
by Registered Female Voters and Local Committeewomen[a]

Favor more women in public office	Registered female voters (N = 178)	Party committeewomen (N = 157)
Yes	77.0%	80.9%
No	23.0	19.1
Not significant		

[a]"Some people feel that more women should hold public office. Others disagree. How about you? Do you think there should be more women holding public office?"

index in that it questions support for more women running for public office
in general, while the earlier checklist question solicits voting support for
a female candidate for a specific office. A respondent might be in favor
of more women holding public office but not specifically in any of the
positions named in the checklist question.

Only 77% of the female voters and 80.9% of the committeewomen were
in favor of more women running for public office. (See Table 4.2.) In fact,
fewer registered voters and committeewomen answered yes to the general
support question than would vote for a woman candidate for city council,
judge, or U.S. senator. As it turns out, women who might not be in favor
of more women going into public office will not deny their vote to a woman
for these lower level positions. That is much like the restaurant owner who
claims he would not seat an Oriental in his place of business, but who serves
such an individual when he is actually on the premises.

The respondents were asked why they wanted or did not want more women
in public office. There was a qualitative difference in the answers depending
on whether the respondent supported women or not. Those answering yes
offered the following reasons: (a) more women in public office would advance
the status of women in politics, (b) their participation would benefit society,
(c) women have superior qualifications, or (d) women are just as qualified
as men. The interesting differences among those who answered no was the
large number who could give no reason other than the cultural myth that
politics is a man's role and women belong at home. Over 60% who answered
negatively gave this reason. The balance of those who answered negatively
believed men to be better qualified.

When asked to choose between equally qualified candidates, distinguished
only by sex, for an unspecified office, a statistically significant difference
occurred in the response patterns of the two groups. Of the three responses
(male, female, no choice), a higher percentage of committeewomen than
voters chose the female, while a much lower percentage of committeewomen

Table 4.3.   Preference of Male or Female for Unnamed Office by Registered Voters and Committeewomen[a]

Choice for office	Registered female voters $(N = 191)$	Party committeewomen $(N = 164)$
Female	26.2%	30.5%
Could not answer	36.6	45.7
Male	37.2	23.8
$P = 0.0239$		

[a]"If there were two equally qualified candidates for political office, one female and one male, which one would you vote for?"

than voters chose the male. (See Table 4.3.) It is difficult to analyze this question because of the large "Could not answer" category. Committeewomen chose this category at a much higher rate than voters. The two choices were meant to force the respondents into stating a definite sex preference for public office holders if they had one. Many could not make the choice either because they were unwilling to discriminate on the basis of sex or they believed that there would be some other characteristic which would influence their choice.

The results above indicate there is little difference in the attitudes of local party committeewomen and registered female voters regarding support of women in politics. This was true in spite of the fact that committeewomen gave a significantly higher proportion of better ratings when asked to evaluate the potential performance of women in office compared to men. While 31.6% of the committeewomen gave better ratings; only 18.2% of the voters did. Voters were more egalitarian with 72.9% giving a same rating compared to 58.2% for committeewomen. (See Table 4.4.)

Table 4.4.   Evaluation of Capability of Women in Office by Registered Voters and Committeewomen[a]

Evaluation of capability	Registered female voters $(N = 181)$	Party committeewomen $(N = 158)$
Worse	8.8%	10.1%
Same	72.9	58.2
Better	18.2	31.6
$P = 0.0105$		

[a]"How do you feel about the job qualified women would do in political office as compared to the job qualified men would do? Would you say women would: do a better job? . . . do about the same? . . . or do a worse job?"

Possible Explanations

It may be surprising to find that women who are personally involved in active politics and, therefore, likely to benefit from the enhancement of the status of women in politics, do not have a greater propensity to support females than women voters in general. The mode of entrance into a committeewoman's position must be considered. It has been pointed out that even national committeewomen have little influence on the party [7] and suggested that women are selected by the men for party positions [8]. In fact, over 25% of the committeewomen in this study indicated they had been selected by the party to run for the position. (Only 28.2% of the committeewomen had opposition from one or more candidates for the position.) Another 9.5% gave job-related reasons; either they themselves or a member of their family had a government job. Another 15.4% ran because of a commitment to a family member or friend. A total of 51% were recruited for other than their own personal interest in politics. When mode of entrance was checked against support propensity, 60.5% of the self-motivated committeewomen were high supporters while only 52.6% of the nonself-motivated were. Although the difference between the self-motivated and nonself-motivated committeewomen was not statistically significant, the trend of the data supports the suggested explanation that nonself-motivated participants are less likely to be supportive of women because they are recruited to maintain the status quo and therefore the control by men. These findings suggest that the current recruitment of women into party positions is much like that of Uncle Tom blacks in the past. They are window dressing and not expected to promote themselves or other women into higher positions of power. If this is an accurate interpretation, then women already holding office in the party are not likely to provide leadership in the drive for raising the status of women in politics. The difference in support levels between women in the voting group who have participated in party campaigns versus those who have not further corroborates the finding above. The women voters who had party experience in electoral campaigns in Pittsburgh were not significantly more supportive of women than those who had only participated to the extent of voting on election day. Among participators, 65.6% were in the high-support category, but 59.4% of the nonparticipators were also.

Several conclusions about the status of women in party politics are suggested by these findings, but there is a need for similar research in other locations to determine if these patterns hold elsewhere. Perhaps women who might advance the cause of women in politics are being shut out of party power by recruitment practices. Also, even if they attain the position of committeewomen, females may leave because of frustration with their impotence as women in the party. Such information would help clarify why women have been less politically involved, as measured by party participation. The question is whether involvement is based on cultural sex role preferences or on a perception of overt discrimination against women in attaining decision-making positions. Perhaps both are operating.

In further attempts to interpret the findings we checked differences as indicated by a question to determine the respondents' perception of the influence politics has in their lives. Quite unexpectedly we found very little difference in the percentages of committeewomen and voters who felt politics had no effect on their lives; the percentages were 25.5% and 21% respectively. These results seem to undermine the studies that assume politics is more central to officeholders than nonofficeholders. We again suspect these figures support the idea that women are recruited into politics by men with the intention that they will maintain the status quo. We discovered involvement in party politics should not be necessarily equated with an interest in politics when dealing with women.

We were curious to know the reasons for nonparticipation among the voters. Over 20% of the voters group who had never worked in a campaign stated that they were never asked as their reason for nonparticipation. Such an answer indicates these respondents viewed party politics as a closed club to the uninvited. Other reasons given with a similar frequency were *not interested* and *don't have enough time.* Lack of child care was the reason given by roughly 15% of the nonparticipators, and less than 5% thought "such things were for men."

We next examined the socioeconomic characteristics of the two groups for differences which might provide further explanation for the failure of committeewomen to achieve higher support levels. Race, childhood religion, marital status, number of children, and income characteristics did not exhibit any statistically significant differences between committeewomen and registered women voters, but age, education, party affiliation, and employment status characteristics were found to be significantly different. While the median and mean ages of the two groups were not so dissimilar, the distribution of the age variable was. Committeewomen underrepresented the youngest and oldest women voters, i.e., 20–29 and 70–89 years of age. Of the voters group, 14.3% were in the youngest category, while only 4.2% of the committeewomen were. Committeewomen had roughly 7% fewer of its members in the oldest cohort group than did the voters group. Such a variance in age distributions is not surprising in our political system, but the difference is important in the context of our study. Since we would expect feminist ideas to be associated with younger women in our culture, such differences in age between the groups would affect the representation of such interests by committeewomen. The underrepresentation of the youngest category

Table 4.5. Characteristics of Registered Female Voters and Local
Committeewomen

Characteristics		Registered female voters	Party committee-women
Party[a]			
Democrat		73.8%	39.0%
Republican		26.2	61.0
		100.0%	100.0%
	Number	(191)	(172)
Education[a]			
8 years or less		19.3%	14.0%
9 to 12 years		56.8	71.3
1 to 4 years of college		19.3	9.4
Post college		4.7	5.3
		100.1[b]	100.0%
	Number	(192)	(171)
Employment[a]			
Yes		33.3%	46.5%
No		66.7	53.5
		100.0%	100.0%
	Number	(192)	(172)
Occupation[a]			
Professional and managerial		7.3%	6.2%
Clerical and sales		15.8	29.0
Blue collar and service		11.3	13.6
Student		1.7	0.6
Housewife		63.8	50.6
		99.9%[b]	100.0%
	Number	(177)	(162)
Age[a]			
20–29 years		14.3%	4.2%
30–39		11.1	13.2
40–49		25.4	31.1
50–59		17.5	25.7
60–69		17.5	19.2
70–89		14.3	6.6
		100.1%[b]	100.0%
	Number	(189)	(167)

[a]Percentages significant at less than 0.05 level in the chi-square test.

[b]Some percentages do not total 100 due to rounding.

among committeewomen partially explains the lower support for women
in politics than might be expected.

The educational characteristic also appeared as an important variable in
distinguishing supporters from nonsupporters. Committeewomen as a group

had substantially less education than voters. Only 14.7% of the committeewomen had any college or professional education beyond high school, while 24% of the voters group did. The differences in educational attainment and age explain the variance in employment status. More committeewomen were currently employed even though, on the basis of some work experience versus none, there was no difference between the two groups. Only 50.6% of the committeewomen were housewives compared to 63.8% of the voter group. The proportionately younger voter group was staying home in larger numbers than the committeewomen because of family responsibilities. Also, there was an expected variance in the distribution of occupational choices which educational differences help explain. Of the employed committeewomen, 58.8% were in the clerical and sales occupations, while only 43.8% of the voters were found there. The voters group had more of its members in professional and managerial jobs than the committeewomen group; while 20.3% of the voters had these higher status occupations, only 12.5% of the committeewomen did. We shall see later that these differences in educational and occupational status relate to differences in support levels.

The distribution of party affiliations for the committeewomen group did not match that of the voter group, but we did not expect that variance to be important in relation to support levels. While 73.8% of the voters were Democratic, only 39% of the committeewomen were [9]. There had been no evidence that party relates to support for women in politics. (See Table 4.5.)

The suspected importance of differences in age and educational distributions in explaining the unexpected conservative stature of committeewomen regarding support for women in politics was supported by our analysis of the relationship between socioeconomic characteristics and support levels for the combined sample of respondents. Both age and education are linked to support propensity; the latter varies directly with education but inversely with age. Income, party registration, childhood religion, marital status, race, and employment status (employed or not) were not strongly related to support propensity but the trends of the data indicated liberal Jews and those with an income over $15,000 tended to be more supportive than members of other religious or income level groups. Higher occupational status also tended to be related to higher support levels. A much higher percentage of respondents with professional and managerial occupations were found in the high support level when compared to other occupations, but the difference was not statistically significant. (See Table 4.6.)

Outgroup Consciousness

We were looking for variables that distinguish supporters from nonsupporters of women in politics. An important indicator, learned through per-

Table 4.6. The Relationship Between Standard Socioeconomic Variables and Level of Support Propensity for Women in Politics for the Combined Sample of Voters and Committeewomen

| Characteristics | Level of support propensity | | |
	Low	High	Total
Age[a]			
20–29 years	17.6%	82.4%	
30–39	34.9	65.1	
40–49	41.0	59.0	
50–59	43.4	56.6	
60–69	53.8	46.2	
70–89	36.8	63.2	
	40.4%	59.6%	100.0%
Number	(144)	(212)	(356)
Education[a]			
8 years or less	45.9%	54.1%	
9 to 12 years	44.2	55.8	
1 to 4 years of college	34.0	66.0	
Post college	11.1	88.9	
	41.3%	58.7%	100.0%
Number	(150)	(213)	(363)
Income			
Under $7,000	44.2%	55.8%	
$7,000–$15,000	40.6	59.4	
Over $15,000	21.9	78.1	
	40.6%	59.4%	100.0%
Number	(136)	(199)	(335)
Party			
Democrat	39.4%	60.6%	
Republican	43.9	56.1	
	41.3%	58.7%	100.0%
Number	(150)	(213)	(363)
Childhood religion			
Protestant	39.8%	60.2%	
Roman Catholic and Orthodox	45.3	54.7	
Liberal Jewish faiths	10.0	90.0	
Orthodox and Conservative Jewish	33.3	66.7	
	41.7%	58.3%	100.0%
Number	(149)	(208)	(357)

(Continued)

Table 4.6 (Continued)

Characteristics	Level of support propensity		
	Low	High	Total
Marital[b]			
Single, separated, or divorced	42.3%	57.7%	
Married (husband present)	37.3	62.7	
	38.6%	61.4%	100.0%
Number	(78)	(181)	(295)
Race			
White	41.7%	58.3%	
Black	38.0	62.0	
	41.2%	58.8%	100.0%
Number	(150)	(214)	(364)
Employment status			
Unemployed	40.9%	59.1%	
Employed	41.7	58.3	
	41.2%	58.8%	100.0%
Number	(150)	(214)	(364)
Occupation			
Professional and managerial	21.7%	78.3%	
Clerical and sales	42.7	57.3	
Blue collar and service	52.4	47.6	
Student	25.0	75.0	
Housewife	41.5	58.5	
	41.6%	58.4%	100.0%
Number	(141)	(198)	(339)

[a] Percentages are significant at less than 0.05 level in the chi-square test.
[b] Widows not included.

sonal experience talking to women of all ages and backgrounds over the years as a social worker, teacher, and housewife, was the awareness of discrimination against women based on their sex either in employment, education, or in general social encounters. Such an awareness or consciousness seems to trigger responsiveness to additional information regarding the often property-like treatment of women in the American culture. With such awareness women begin to reevaluate their own previously accepted views regarding women's capability and the role of women in society. This awareness comes to different women in different ways. A personal experience with discrimination, exposure to such information from friends, reading books such as *Born Female* or *The Feminine Mystique*, and introduction of evidence through an educational mode, are some sources of original information which further develop awareness of the treatment of women [10].

For the purposes of research this awareness has been called outgroup consciousness. An index of this outgroup consciousness was developed using items in the survey instrument. The items were chosen because they indicated the respondent's positions on acknowledged feminist issues. The eight point index was divided into low and high levels using the median score as the dividing point. Scores of zero to three were considered low and four through eight high.

The items that were used to form the outgroup consciousness index included open-ended and structured questions. A point was tallied for respondents on this index when they identified a feminist issue as one of the most important problems facing American women in the open-ended format and one to three when they identified one, two, or three feminist issues in a group of structured items as local problems in Pittsburgh. The other structured responses worth one possible point each were believing that women's interests and problems are not represented in local politics, that a group of men would have more influence on city council than a group of women in deciding an issue, that a man would be more influential in taking a problem or complaint to city council than a woman, and personal experience with sex discrimination.

In the cross-tabulation between outgroup consciousness and support propensity, 66.9% of the combined sample fell in the high support category while only 52.5% of the low-group consciousness level respondents fell in the high support category. The breakdown in percentages was similar for the two sample groups separately, although the relationship was not statistically significant for committeewomen. This relationship was probably not significant because of the age and educational background of committeewomen; these characteristics were also found to be significantly related to outgroup consciousness (see Table 4.7.). Subsequent analysis to determine if the relationship between outgroup consciousness and level of support propensity was spurious, substantiated the existence of the relationship between the two variables [11].

The strength of the relationship between outgroup consciousness and support propensity was compared to the relationships of other characteristics with support propensity in subsequent analysis of the voter group study alone. The outgroup consciousness variable had the strongest correlation with voting support, while interest in politics, as measured by interest in political issues, education, and age, varied in the strength of their relationship with support propensity in that order. Other variables which were found to be statistically significant in their relationship with voting support in the analysis of the voter group separately include nationality, leadership experience, past organizational membership, age of youngest child, self-role, and frequency of ticket-splitting [12].

Table 4.7. The Relationship Between Levels of Outgroup
Consciousness and Support Propensity for Female Voters and
Party Committeewomen Combined

	Level of outgroup consciousness ($N = 364$)	
Level of support	Low	High
Low	47.5%	33.1%
High	52.5	66.9
	100.0%	100.0%

$P = 0.0076$

Discussion of Findings

The survey on the whole failed to locate significant differences in the
attitudes of registered women voters and local party committeewomen toward
support for women in politics. The two groups did differ significantly in
their evaluation of the capability of women in office; committeewomen gave
a similar proportion of "worse" ratings, less "same" ratings, and more "better"
ratings than the voters. Yet this difference in evaluation did not produce
significant differences in support propensity for either specific offices mentioned or for public offices in general.

There was a substantial gap in support by the combined groups between
the city council and presidential positions, where the percentage difference
between the highest and lowest positions was 47.1 points. Although 94.4%
of the sample would be ʲᵘˢt as likely to choose a woman for city council
as a man, only 43.4% of the group would be just as likely to choose a woman
for President.

The existence of the cleavage in support levels between nonexecutive and
executive levels, as well as the gradation of support according to position
level, suggests the Gallup Poll question regarding propensity to vote for
a woman for President is the most extreme measure of support for women
in politics and, therefore, an imperfect indicator of support among women
for women. Such a measure overlooks the broad support for lesser offices.

Three meaningful and distinct categories of potential supporters arise from
the data. There are the hard core nonsupporters or myth holders who
represent 10–30% of the combined sample depending on the level of commitment to women in politics. These women have not brought any information
to their stance of nonsupport other than the cultural myth that woman's
place is in the home and, its inverse, politics is a man's role. Less than
10% of the combined group would evaluate women as being less capable
than men, a little over 20% do not desire more women in office, and around
30% would choose a male in a race between equally qualified candidates
distinguished only by sex.

The second and largest group are the egalitarians who feel women and men are equally capable of holding public office and believe women should be given an equal opportunity to secure a political position. They recognize individual differences as being more important than those of gender in regard to the realm of politics. This group varies in size again depending on how extreme the question probing their attitudes of support for women is.

The last group we have called the female boosters. This group prefers women over men for office for one or more of the following reasons: (a) they view females as being more qualified to hold public office, (b) they have a high evaluation of female capability, or (c) they want to compensate for past discrimination against women in politics. Over 20% of the combined sample have a higher evaluation of female political capability than of male and 28% would choose a woman in the match between a male and female.

The standard variables of social status and role such as religious affiliation, age, income level, educational level, occupational status, marital status, political participation level, and party affiliation appear less valuable in locating support among women than the level of consciousness of the outgroup status of women in society. The variable outgroup consciousness has a stronger correlation than the other variables mentioned with support propensity. Such a finding suggests that a change in the dependent variable can be brought about by exposure to information on the status of women in society. If that is an accurate assumption, increased support for women in politics might be fairly easily gained. In order to better assess such a possibility, research needs to be done to learn how well the nonsupportive attitudes are integrated into the total personality system. If nonsupportive attitudes toward women in politics are a part of the core identity and self-definition, then such attitudes would be more difficult to change.

Overall, the results of this survey help explain why political scientists are generally surprised at the sudden prominence of the status of women in politics as an issue. Previous political perspectives, having lacked information of any depth regarding the potential for a female voting bloc and female interest in the status of women in politics, were not prepared for the political ramifications of a resurfacing feminist movement.

Implications for Further Research

A national sample of female voters and local party committeewomen would be most useful in further exploring the indications found in this survey based on one urban center. A larger sample size would be extremely valuable in validating the findings reported here. Regional and patronage versus nonpatronage environments might also prove important influences on propensity to support women in politics.

A larger study would enable researchers to look more carefully at the interesting behavior of data for the variable of age. Although increasing age is inversely related to support propensity, there are some curious findings for the age group over 70. This group within our data shows higher than expected support for women. The attitudes of the respondents over 70 may be interpreted by either a life cycle or generational explanation. Perhaps women past the childbearing stage are less involved in the culturally defined female role and therefore more objective toward women in society; or perhaps the influence of the feminist movement in the twenties produced greater support than expected among the group over 70 years of age.

The need for a careful study of female party leaders at all levels, directed at their support propensity and their representativeness of the female voting population, is indicated by these research results. A comparison with male party leaders would provide further information useful in evaluating the status of women within the party. A study of recruitment patterns, task allocation, and grooming for candidacy might explain why so few women run for office. Finally, we need data on the success rate of women candidates, their proportion of the candidate pool, and their comparative campaign resources to understand the full range of factors, including voter and party worker attitudes, that have limited female participation in elective politics.

NOTES

1. Notable exceptions are the research of Kirsten Amundsen, *The Silenced Majority.* Englewood Cliffs, N.J.: Prentice-Hall, 1971 and Martin Gruberg, *Women in American Politics.* Oshkosh, Wis.: Academia, 1968. Emmy Werner has given us some long overdue information about women in Congress and state legislatures, and Marjorie Lansing has informed us of new trends in the political participation rates of women.

2. The more recent Harris Poll done for Virginia Slims in 1972 entitled "Women in Politics and the Economy," treated the topic in more depth but exhibits some of the same shortcomings as the Gallup Poll in regard to question design. The latter poll, which was conducted after the research reported here, has been interpreted to suggest that women's attitudes toward women in politics are more favorable than previously believed. Their findings regarding characteristics associated with supportive attitudes toward women in politics have corroborated the present study's results.

3. Pollsters asked the most questions regarding women and politics in the 1930s and 1940s. See Hadley Cantril and Mildred Strunk, *Public Opinion 1935–1946.* Princeton, N.J.: Princeton University Press, 1951. pp. 1052–1054.

4. Hazel Erskine, "The Polls: Women's Role," *Pub. Opinion Quart.,* **XXV.** pp. 277–79 (Summer 1971).

5. *Gallup Opinion Index,* No. 74, pp. 25–26 (August, 1971).

6. U.S. Bureau of the Census, *Census of Population: 1970 General Population Characteristics, Final Report PC (1)–B40 PA.* Washington, D.C.: GPO, 1971, pp. 115, 129.

7. Cornelius Cotter and Bernard Hennessy, *Politics Without Power.* New York: Atherton, 1964, p. 59.

8. Harold R. Gosnell, *Democracy: The Threshold of Freedom.* New York: Ronald, 1948, p. 62.

9. The reason there are more Republican committeewomen in the sample is that Republicans in Pittsburgh choose two committeewomen per district while Democrats choose only one.

10. Caroline Bird, *Born Female: The High Cost of Keeping Women Down.* New York: Pocket Books, 1969; and Betty Friedan, *The Feminine Mystique.* New York: Dell, 1963.

11. Partial correlation analysis was used with the voter sample to ascertain whether or not the relationship between outgroup consciousness and the support variable might be spurious. Kendall's tau rank-order correlations were first computed for the relationship between the variables of interest and support propensity in the form of the 8-point scale. (Kendall's tau was selected because of the few categories and large number of ties.) These correlations also formed the basis for a comparison of the strength of the relationship between outgroup consciousness and support propensity as compared to the other variables of interest and support propensity. The correlational matrix was fed into the Statistical Package for the Social Sciences' partial correlation program. The rank-order correlational analysis indicated significant relationships between education and interest in politics and the support propensity variable based on a sample size of 150 with listwise deletion for missing values. With age removed from the relationship the partial correlation between outgroup consciousness and the voting support variable became 0.2175 at .004. (The original correlation was 0.2328 at .001 level of significance.) When education was removed, the partial correlation was 0.1964 at .008 level of significance. The removal of interest in politics produced the biggest effect on the original correlations. The partial was 0.1895 at .010. Taking all three variables of age, education, and interest in politics together, their removal produced a partial of 0.1642 at .023 level of significance for the relationship between the voting support and outgroup consciousness variables. The relationship between the consciousness and support was diminished, indicating that education and interest in politics was influencing the relationship, but the relationship was not wiped out by the control for age, education, and interest in politics.

12. Audrey Siess Wells, *Female Attitudes Toward Women in Politics: The Propensity to Support Women.* University of Florida, 1972, unpublished dissertation.

Section

2
WOMEN AS POLITICAL ELITES

Chapter

5

Personality Characteristics of Women in American Politics

Emmy E. Werner and Louise M. Bachtold

"Remember the ladies," wrote Abigail Adams, wife and mother of a president, to her friend and husband John in a letter to the Continental Congress, nearly two hundred years ago [1]. Her gentle plea went largely unheard in American political life until women won the right to vote five decades ago.

Today it is heard—more forcefully and perhaps more shrilly—in the voices of the women's liberation movement and the newly founded National Women's Political Caucus whose aim is equal political representation for women in every political office, on the local, state and national levels.

There is a startling gap between the rhetoric about sexual politics [2], and research on women in American politics, and between the goals of the National Women's Political Caucus and the present reality of American women's participation in the process of political decision-making.

A recently published assessment and sourcebook on women in American politics [3] lists only a few studies that deal directly with this subject. A search of the *Psychological Abstracts* from Volume I (1928 to the present) showed more index entries under "gold—fish" than under "government—women." There have been no studies so far which deal exclusively with the personality characteristics of women who achieve political leadership positions. The senior author has published two studies on women in Congress and in the state legislatures [4] which examined the political experience of women politicians, their motivation for seeking office, and their evaluation of their assets and liabilities in political life.

This paper was originally presented at the Annual Meeting of the American Political Science Association, Washington, D.C., 1972.

In addition, there have been several books which presented short biographical sketches of individual women politicians [5]—among the most recent Lamson's *Few Are Chosen: American Women in Political Life Today* which highlights contributions of a few outstanding women politicians on the national, state and local levels [6].

In 1955, Young surveyed three decades of women's political activities in *Understanding Politics*. She noted that, at that time, the trend for women in the state legislatures, though slow, was upward and grew at a faster rate than women's representation in Congress (4% versus 1%). She recognized, however, that the political arena is highly competitive, and that women encounter the same forces at work as in the economic arena. The number of women in the legislatures resembled the employment curve. When times were good and public confidence was high, women stood a better chance in the political arena. In times of public unrest or anxiety, social pressures operated to keep them outside the political arena [7].

Her assessment appears prophetic today, when one notes the declining numbers of women in the state legislatures and in Congress. After a climb from 31 women in the state legislatures in 1921, to 144 in 1941, to a peak of 351 in 1961, there has been a gradual, but steady, decline among women in the state legislatures in the last decade, at the very time when women's rights have become a fashionable issue again. There were 323 women in the 1967 state legislatures, 305 in the 1969 state legislatures, and 293 in the 1970–1971 state legislatures [8]. The trend is similar in Congress, where after a peak of 19 women in 1961, women's representation dropped to 13 in 1963 and has remained so until the present.

The decline in women's representation in the legislatures has been mostly among the larger industrialized Eastern, Midwestern and Southern border states, while there has been an increase in the number of women in the legislatures of the West and South, possibly reflecting a national trend in the shift of political power centers.

What kind of women, in the face of these odds, have become successful political officeholders, and what are the antecedents of their political behavior? Smith has recently provided a map for the analysis of personality and politics. He reminds us that political behavior results from the interaction of psychological variables with three classes of social variables: (a) the immediate situation in which the behavior occurs; (b) the immediate social environment extending from birth through adult life within which the politician's personality develops (including sex roles learned); and (a) the distal social environment which includes the features of the contemporary social and political system and the historical antecedents of these features. Within the central portion of his map, Smith includes personality processes and dispositions, among them "self-other relationships," "ego defenses" and cognitive and temperamental traits [9].

Greenstein has stressed the need to explore those personality determinants in political situations that encourage the expression of personal differences in behavior. Ambiguous situations tend to leave room for personal variability to have an impact. Ambiguity is to be found in new, complex and contradictory situations—situations that women active in politics face constantly, since their political roles deviate from sex-role expectations, and they often combine the multiple and seemingly contradictory roles of wife, mother, professional, and politician.

The present study is concerned with salient personality characteristics which set women in political office apart from adult women in the general population and elected male leaders. The study is not concerned with ego-defensive behavior or psychopathology, but with cognitive and temperamental traits which differentiate women politicians from apolitical women and from men in leadership positions [10].

Methodology

The subjects of this report are 103 women who served in the 1970–1971 state legislatures. They represent one of every three women in the current state legislatures and come from 37 states of the Union: Alabama, Alaska, Arizona, Arkansas, Colorado, Connecticut, Delaware, Florida, Hawaii, Idaho, Illinois, Indiana, Iowa, Kentucky, Louisiana, Maine, Maryland, Minnesota, Missouri, Nebraska, Nevada, New Hampshire, New Jersey, New Mexico, New York, North Carolina, North Dakota, Ohio, South Dakota, Texas, Utah, Vermont, Virginia, Washington, West Virginia, Wisconsin, and Wyoming.

The sample represents states with wide ranges in population rank and proportion of women in their legislatures. It includes women from the most and least populated states, as well as from state houses which contain the highest and the lowest percentage of women legislators.

All major geographical regions are represented. There is an equal proportion of Democrats and Republicans in the sample.

Most of the women in this sample are middle-aged (the majority were first elected to the state legislatures in their late forties), are or have been married and have reared children. The majority of the women worked in one or several occupations: business and public relations (insurance, banking, real estate), education, work with the mass media, law, and social service were the most frequently mentioned professions.

The women were selected from the *Book of States: Supplement 1: State elected officials and the legislatures* [11] and from *Women in Public Service* [12]. They were invited to complete the Sixteen Personality Factor Questionnaire (16 PF), a self-report inventory which had been used in two other studies of leadership, one of elected male leaders [13] and one of male and female leaders of campus political action groups [14]. The same inventory had also been used in several studies of the personality characteristics of outstanding women in the social and natural sciences [15].

The handbook for the 16 PF Questionnaire [16] provides norms and descriptive information on the standardization, validity and reliability of this objective personality test. Each personality factor, relatively independent from the others, is presented as a bipolar measure, and is summarized with a high score corresponding to the description on the right, and a low score to the behavior on the left, as shown below:

	Low Score Description	High Score Description
A.	Reserved, detached, aloof	Outgoing, easygoing, participating
B.	Less intelligent, concrete-thinking	More intelligent, abstract-thinking
C.	Affected by feelings, easily upset	Emotionally stable, faces reality, mature
E.	Mild, accommodating, conforming	Assertive, stubborn, competitive
F.	Sober, prudent, serious	Lively, gay, enthusiastic
G.	Expedient, disregards rules, feels few obligations	Conscientious, persevering, staid
H.	Shy, restrained, timid	Venturesome, socially bold, spontaneous
I.	Tough-minded, self-reliant, realistic	Tender-minded, overprotected, sensitive
L.	Trusting, adaptable, easy to get along with	Suspicious, self-opinionated, hard to fool
M.	Practical, careful, conventional	Imaginative, bohemian
N.	Forthright, natural, unpretentious	Shrewd, calculating, worldly
O.	Self-assured, confident, serene	Apprehensive, worrying, troubled
Q_1.	Conservative, respecting established ideas	Experimenting, liberal, free-thinking
Q_2.	Group-dependent, a "joiner" and follower	Self-sufficient, resourceful
Q_3.	Follows own urges, careless of protocol	Controlled
Q_4.	Relaxed, tranquil	Tense, frustrated, driven

Responses of the women politicians are reported in sten scores for each of the 16 personality factors. Stens are standard scores with a mean of 5.5

Table 5.1. Mean Sten Scores and Standard Deviations for Women Legislators ($N = 103$) and Mean Sten Scores for Elected Male Leaders ($N = 92$) on the 16 PF

	Factor	Women legislators Mean	Women legislators S.D.	Elected male leaders Mean
A	Sociability	5.5	2.0	6.0
B	Intelligence	8.1	1.5	7.3
C	Egostrength	5.4	1.5	5.7
E	Dominance	6.9	1.9	5.8
F	Enthusiasm	5.9	1.8	7.1
G	Conscientiousness	5.9	1.8	6.3
H	Adventuresomeness	7.3	1.7	6.7
I	Sensitivity	6.1	2.2	5.2
L	Trust	5.6	2.0	5.2
M	Unconventionality	6.5	2.0	4.8
N	Sophistication	6.0	2.2	5.7
O	Guilt-proneness	4.9	1.9	3.9
Q_1	Radicalism	6.5	2.2	4.9
Q_2	Self-sufficiency	6.0	1.8	4.9
Q_3	Willpower	6.1	2.0	6.4
Q_4	Drive, excitability	5.3	1.4	4.9

and a standard deviation of 2. Computation of mean stens and standard deviations for the women politicians provides a basis for comparison of their personality characteristics with women in the general population [17] and with elected male leaders who had earlier responded to the same instrument [18].

Results and Discussion

As can be seen in Table 5.1, the women legislators in this sample differed from women in the general population on the following personality factors: $B+$, $E+$, $H+$, $M+$, and Q_1+. The women politicians were generally more intelligent, more assertive, more venturesome, more imaginative and unconventional, and more liberal in their attitudes than women in general. There was no evidence of defensiveness or egopathology in the responses of the women legislators to this self-report inventory.

Figure 5.1 compares each sample, the women legislators and elected male leaders, with their respective reference groups, i.e., adult men and adult women in the general population. Both male and female elected leaders resemble the norms for their sex on measures of sociability (A), egostrength

Standard ten score (sten) → Average

Low score description	1	2	3	4	5	6	7	8	9	10	High score description
Reserved, detached, critical, aloof (sizothymia)											**Outgoing**, warmhearted, easy–going, participating (affectothymia, formerly cyclothymia)
Less intelligent, concrete thinking (lower scholastic mental capacity)											**More intelligent**, abstract–thinking, bright (higher scholastic mental capacity)
Affected by feelings, emotionally less stable, easily upset (lower ego strength)											**Emotionally stable**, faces reality, calm, mature (higher ego strength)
Humble, mild, accommodating, conforming (submissiveness)											**Assertive**, aggressive, stubborn competitive (dominance)
Sober, prudent, serious, taciturn (desurgency)											**Happy–go–lucky**, impulsively lively, gay, enthusiastic (surgency)
Expedient, disregards rules, feels few obligations (weaker superego strength)											**Conscientious**, persevering, staid moralistic (stronger–superego strength)
Shy, restrained, timid, threat–sensitive (threctia)											**Venturesome**, socially bold, uninhibited, spontaneous (parmia)
Tough–minded, self–reliant, realistic, no–nonsense (harria)											**Tender–minded**, clinging, over–protected, sensitive (premsia)

A B C E F G H I

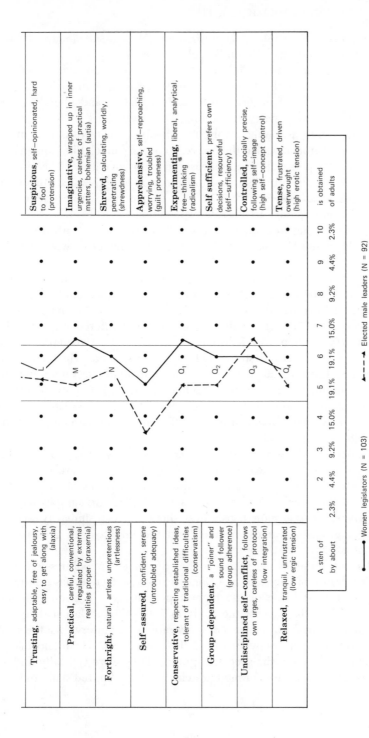

Figure 5.1. Personality profiles of women legislators and elected male leaders.

Trusting, adaptable, free of jealousy, easy to get along with (alaxia)

Practical, careful, conventional, regulated by external realities proper (praxernia)

Forthright, natural, artless, unpretentious (artlessness)

Self–assured, confident, serene (untroubled adequacy)

Conservative, respecting established ideas, tolerant of traditional difficulties (conservatism)

Group–dependent, a "joiner" and sound follower (group adherence)

Undisciplined self–conflict, follows own urges, careless of protocol (low integration)

Relaxed, tranquil, unfrustrated (low ergic tension)

Suspicious, self–opinionated, hard to fool (protension)

Imaginative, wrapped up in inner urgencies, careless of practical matters, bohemian (autia)

Shrewd, calculating, worldly, penetrating (shrewdness)

Apprehensive, self–reproaching, worrying, troubled (guilt proneness)

Experimenting, liberal, analytical, free–thinking (radicalism)

Self sufficient, prefers own decisions, resourceful (self–sufficiency)

Controlled, socially precise, following self–image (high self–concept control)

Tense, frustrated, driven overwrought (high erotic tension)

| A sten of by about | 1 2.3% | 2 4.4% | 3 9.2% | 4 15.0% | 5 19.1% | 6 19.1% | 7 15.0% | 8 9.2% | 9 4.4% | 10 2.3% | is obtained of adults |

●——● Women legislators (N = 103)   ▲– – –▲ Elected male leaders (N = 92)

(C), sensitivity (I), trust (L), sophistication (N), self-sufficiency (Q_2) and drive (Q_4). But irrespective of their sex, elected leaders appeared more intelligent, bold and venturesome. While elected male leaders appeared more enthusiastic (F), self-assured (O) and self-controlled (Q_3), women holding political office appeared to be more assertive, imaginative and liberal in their attitudes—regardless of party affiliation.

Thus, despite assuming a role historically conceived as masculine, these women legislators revealed themselves to be very much like women in general on most of the personality traits measured in this inventory. Their intelligence, assertiveness, adventuresomeness, imagination and liberal attitudes appeared to be the major assets in their success in a political role that is powerful, but also contradictory to sex-role expectations.

It is interesting to compare the results of this study with the few reports in the literature that have dealt with characteristics of women in political life.

Kruschke, in a comparison of female politicals and apoliticals, attempted to trace a relationship between political personality and political participation. He compared 46 women active in politics (a movement for the construction of a civic center, a school bond referendum, and the 1960 presidential election) with 58 women who were not active in politics, matched on the basis of marital status and higher education. He found significant differences favoring the political women on the following dimensions: sociability, optimism, willingness to risk, liberalism, and a sense of political efficacy—characteristics that resemble our findings of greater assertiveness, adventuresomeness, imagination, and liberal attitudes among the women in the state legislatures [19].

Winborn and Jansen, in a study of the personality characteristics of campus social-political action leaders, used the 16 PF to compare political leaders with other types of leaders on campus. Comparisons of the 16 PF group means of the female social-political action leaders on campus with those of the women in the state legislatures show a great similarity between the younger group of campus women and the middle-aged group of women legislators [20].

The only other study which included women in politics is a report on the legislature of the state of Connecticut—a state that has a large number of legislators and one of the highest percentages of women among them (about 15% at the time of the study in 1963–1964). Barber delineates four legislative "types" on the basis of observations and interviews: the spectators, the advertisers, the reluctants, and the lawmakers. He found many of his women legislators in the spectator group. They were typically middle-aged, lower-status housewives of modest achievements, limited skills and restricted ambitions, who had little sense of individuality, were other-directed, and were especially sensitive to approval and disapproval [21].

The findings of our study resemble more closely the description of Barber's *effective lawmaker* who enters politics from a position of personal strength, not as a compensation for weakness. Barber rates the effective lawmaker high in activity, and describes him as having a strong and realistic sense of personal identity and personal and moral standards, coupled with self-confidence, high achievement motivation, and a fundamental respect for and empathy with people unlike himself.

It may be noted that we sampled a wider universe of state legislatures (37 states instead of one), representing all geographical regions in the country. Among them are many large industrialized, urban states, where it is much harder to compete for the legislature than in Connecticut, because the number of available seats and the proportion of women elected are much smaller (less than 5%). However, within this wider range of state legislatures we sampled only one of every three women serving in 1970–1971, and we may well have obtained the personality profiles of the most cooperative, effective and least-threatened among them.

However, the consistency of our findings with those reported for elected male leaders, for women active on the local level and for campus social-political leaders lends credence to our belief that our results describe a generalizable personality profile of the effective woman in politics.

Conclusions

This study was concerned with the salient personality characteristics that set women legislators, atypical incumbents of a role normally defined as masculine, apart from adult women in the general population, and from elected male leaders.

It was anticipated that the role stress of contradictory expectations of what it is like to be a woman and a legislator might be reflected in certain cognitive and temperamental dispositions, which in turn might influence political behavior. It appears that the women legislators in our sample were able to combine and maintain their multiple roles of women and politicians successfully because they shared certain key personality characteristics with both reference groups.

In this particular sample of cooperative women legislators there was little evidence of ego-defensiveness or anxiety. However, their high scores on intelligence, dominance, adventuresomeness, unconventionality, and radicalism (regardless of party affiliation) seem a testimony to the effort it takes to create a new role for oneself rather than to adopt a ready-made self.

NOTES

1. F. C. Adams, ed., *Family Letters of John Adams and His Wife Abigail Adams During the Revolution.* Freeport, N.Y.: Books for Libraries, 1970.

2. K. Millett, *Sexual Politics.* Garden City, N.Y.: Doubleday, 1970.

3. M. Gruberg, *Women in American Politics: An Assessment and Sourcebook.* Oshkosh, Wis.: Academia, 1968.

4. E. Werner, "Women in Congress: 1917–1964," *Western Poli. Quart.,* **19,** pp. 16–30 (1966); E. Werner, "Women in the State Legislatures," *Western Poli. Quart.,* **21,** pp. 40–50 (1968).

5. S. Breckenridge, *Women in the 20th Century: A Study of Their Political, Social and Economic Activities.* New York: McGraw-Hill, 1933; E. T. Douglass, *Remember the Ladies.* New York: Putnam, 1966; A. Paxton, *Women in Congress.* Richmond, Va.: Dietz, 1945; E. Roosevelt and L. Hickock, *Ladies of Courage:* Van Rees, 1954.

6. P. Lamson, *Few Are Chosen: American Women in Political Life Today.* Boston: Houghton Mifflin, 1968.

7. L. M. Young, *Understanding Politics.* New York: Pellegrini and Cudahy, 1955.

8. *Women in Public Service.* Washington, D.C.: Republican National Committee, 1971.

9. M. B. Smith, "A Map for the Analysis of Personality and Politics," *Jour. of Soc. Issues,* **24,** pp. 15–28 (1968).

10. F. Greenstein, "Personality and Politics: Problems of Evidence, Inference, and Conceptualization," *Amer. Behavioral Sci.,* **11,** pp. 38–53 (1967); F. Greenstein, "The Need for Systematic Inquiry into Personality and Politics: Introduction and Overview," *Jour. of Soc. Issues,* **24,** pp. 1–14 (1968).

11. *Book of States: Supplement I: State Elective Officials and the Legislatures.* Lexington, Ky.: Council of State Governments, 1970.

12. *Women in Public Service, op. cit.*

13. R. B. Cattell and G. F. Stice, "Four Formulae for the Selection of Leaders on the Basis of Personality," *Human Relations,* **7,** pp. 493–507 (1954).

14. R. B. Winborn and D. G. Jansen, "Personality Characteristics of Campus Social-Political Action Leaders," *Jour. of Counseling Psych.,* **14,** pp. 509–513 (1967).

15. L. Bachtold and E. Werner, "Personality Profiles of Gifted Women: Psychologists," *Amer. Psychologist,* **25,** pp. 234–243 (1970); L. Bachtold and E. Werner, "Personality Profiles of Women Psychologists: Three Generations," *Developmental Psychology,* **5,** pp. 273–278 (1971); L. Bachtold and E. Werner, "Personality Profiles of Women Scientists," *Psychological Reports,* in press.

16. R. B. Cattell, H. W. Eber, and M. Tatsuoka, *Handbook for the Sixteen Personality Factor Questionnaire (16 PF).* Champaign, Ill.: Institute for Personality and Ability Testing, 1970.

17. Cattell, Eber, and Tatsuoka, *Handbook, op. cit.*

18. Cattell and Stice, "Four Formulae," *op. cit.*

19. E. R. Kruschke, "Female Politicals and Apoliticals," *Dissertation Abstracts,* **24,** pp. 2546–2547 (1963); E. R. Kruschke, "Level of Optimism as Related to Female Political Behavior," *Soc. Sci.,* **41,** pp. 67–75 (1966).

20. Winborn and Jansen, "Personality Characteristics," *op. cit.*

21. J. D. Barber, *The Lawmakers.* New Haven: Yale University Press, 1965.

Chapter

6

The Role and Status of Women in the Daley Organization

Mary Cornelia Porter and Ann B. Matasar

Hypothesis

American women, with few exceptions, do not participate in public life or in meaningful party activity [1]. In this respect there is nothing remarkable about the Daley organization. What we have examined, however, is the relationship between the style of the last of the old-fashioned urban political machines on the one hand, and on the other, its treatment of women and its responses to their recently articulated political aspirations.

We approached the study initially from a Banfieldian perspective and hypothesized that while the Daley organization has heretofore excluded women, it will now respond, after its own fashion, to the new demands. This would be managed either by making concessions, as the organization does, occasionally and minimally, to civic groups and reformers [2], or by co-opting women as it has blacks and other challengers [3].

We soon abandoned this hypothesis. We discovered that the Chicago Democratic machine has always utilized a few women, and that just as the characteristics of the machine have remained essentially unchanged for the past forty years, so the characteristics of the handful of women whom it sponsors have varied but little. Either their backgrounds, interests, assigned tasks and attitudes toward political power present a composite picture of a *womanly* woman who restricts herself to woman's work, and/or these

Presented as a paper at the American Political Science Association Annual Meeting, Washington, D.C., September 1972.

Table 6.1   Women Slated by the Central Committee of the Cook County Democratic Party, 1955–1972

Office	Name	Term or electoral outcome	Ethnic identity	Marital status
Ward Committee-man	Lillian Piotrowski	1970–Present	Polish/Catholic	S
Alderman	Marilou Hedlund	1971–Present	Irish/Catholic	M
State	Lillian Piotrowski	1950–1964	Polish/Catholic	S
Representative	Esther Saperstein	1956–1966	Jewish	W
	Floy Clements	1958–1959	Black	?
	Joanne Saunders[d]	1972–Lost	Jewish	D
	Odas Nicholson[d]	1972–Lost	Black	S
State Senator	Esther Saperstein	1966–Present	Jewish	W
Cook County	Elizabeth Conkey[c]	1933–1963	Irish/Catholic	M/W
Board	Ruby Ryan[ab]	1961–Present	Irish/Catholic	W
of Commissioners	Josephine Sneed[a]	1961–1964	Black	W
	Lillian Piotrowski	1964–Present	Polish/Catholic	S
Associate Judges of the Circuit Court	Kathleen Nohelty[c]	1956–1962	Irish/Catholic	?
Cook County Judicial	Helen McGillicuddy	1962–Present	Irish/Catholic	?
Circuit	Edith Sampson	1962–Present	Black	?
City of Chicago Trustee of the Municipal Sanitary District	Joanne Alter	1972–Won	Jewish	M
U.S.	Helen Kelleher	1964–Lost	Irish/Catholic	?
Representative	Cardiss Collins[a]	1973–Won	Black	W

[a]Denotes widow appointed to replace dead husband or slated to run for his seat.

[b]Denotes widow who subsequently ran on her own.

[c]Denotes deceased.

[d]Indicates primary election.

women are useful to the organization because they are women. (See Table 6.1.) The attitude of the present leadership toward women indicates that the Daley organization will continue to support such women, and only such women. While more women have been permitted to run for office in recent years, women are not and will not, because they are women, be taken seriously as politicians. Thus, no concessions need be made to claims which cannot exist in the nature of things.

le 6.1.   (Continued)

Political family, sponsor or ability to pay	"Women's" civic work	Party service	Does "women's" work in office, or useful as a female candidate	Occupation and/or training
Yes	No	Yes	No	?
Yes	Yes	No	Yes	Housewife
Yes	No	Yes	No	?
Yes	Yes	No/Yes	Yes	Teacher
?	Yes	Yes	?	?
Yes	Yes	No	Yes	Attorney
?	Yes	Yes	Yes	Attorney
Yes	Yes	Yes	Yes	Teacher
Yes	Yes	Yes	Yes	?
Yes	Yes	?	Yes	Housewife
Yes	Yes	Yes	Yes	Housewife
Yes	No	Yes	No/Yes	Teacher
?	?	?	?	Attorney
?	?	Yes	Yes	Attorney
?	?	Yes	Yes	Attorney
Yes	Yes	Yes	?/Yes	Political/ Activist
?	?	Yes	Yes, as	Attorney
Yes	?	?	appointed magistrate	Civil Service Auditor, Illinois Department of Revenue

Our original proposition, then, gives way to one more modest: While women have a role in the Daley organization, they have no status, never have had status and will not attain status. The more things change as far as women are concerned, the more they remain the same for women and the Daley organization.

Methodology

Our research methods were dictated, in large part, by the difficulty of getting any specific information from anyone connected with the Daley organization. Two examples will suffice: A visit was paid to party headquarters in order to find out the names and numbers of Chicago women who have asked for party endorsement. All we could learn was that there "hadn't been many," and that no records were kept of the slate-making meetings. A questionnaire was sent to the 50 Chicago ward and the 30 suburban township committeemen. The return from the former, directly beholden to Daley, was 26%, and from the latter, who are autonomous, was 53%.

We relied, then, largely upon official election returns, the *Illinois Blue Books* [4], the scholarly and journalistic literature on Chicago government and politics [5], newspapers, such interviews as we could obtain with the leadership and subleadership of the Daley organization, interviews with the women studied, our numerous contacts with independent Democrats in Chicago and the Cook County suburbs, and, finally, on the questionnaire.

From these sources we determined the following: (*a*) historical patterns of female political participation; (*b*) the characteristics of women supported by the organization; (*c*) leadership attitudes toward female political participation; and (*d*) the activities of Chicago Democratic women who have run for office as independents, that is, without support of the organization.

The Daley Organization

The Chicago machine [6] has been competently described and analyzed elsewhere. Only a brief summary is necessary here.

The base of the machine's power has not changed since the 1930s—a ward-based system of political organization with its nucleus of virtually unchallengeable ward committeemen, a vast patronage army; control over the election machinery; the hegemony of the Irish, and a constituency which, in the words of former Alderman "Paddy" Bauler, "ain't ready for reform."

It maintains itself by the informal centralization of formally decentralized power—this due to Daley's dual role as mayor and chairman of the central committee of the Cook County Democratic party (CCDP)—the close working relationship between the mayor and the president of the Cook County board of commissioners (when he is a Democrat) and the close relationship between Chairman Daley and the chairman of the state central committee of the Democratic party; by alliances with labor and the business community, and performing the service of mediating conflicts between and among them. It coexists peacefully with the Republicans who usually control the governorship and the upper house of the general assembly.

The Daley organization's existence is further assured by demographic patterns which keep independents in a minority. Only a few wards and districts on the north and west sides of the city, one in the University of Chicago area and two black wards, send mavericks to the city council, Springfield or Congress. Furthermore, the movement to the suburbs further dilutes the strength of the independent Democrats. While Chicago has lost population to the suburbs, the base of power in the Cook County Democratic party remains with the Chicago ward committeeman. The Democratic township committeemen, islands in Republican seas, do not come to the slate-making sessions with enough votes to be taken seriously [7].

Finally, the machine has survived by its determination to survive. While it has supported blue-ribbon candidates for some state offices and for Congress, it does not permit itself to be distracted by issues and/or ideology. It concentrates on maintaining control over the electoral process and over the jobs which control jobs. Between 1937 and 1973 only three of its major slated candidates failed to win nomination and only once has such a candidate lost a general election. While there are some who claim that the machine is dying [8], we agree with Gosnell that its most outstanding characteristic is its durability [9]. It is from this point, and eschewing all judgments, that we present our findings.

Historical Patterns of Participation

Elected Offices

Since our study centers about the locus of the Daley organization's power, Chicago, we have concentrated on the offices and activities which relate directly to the organization's interests. We are not here concerned with women who have received endorsement from the central committee of the CCDP, but who represent areas outside the organization's sphere of influence, or with women who have been willing to run hopeless races in Republican districts. The Daley organization's record on its Chicago women is as follows: It has sent one woman to the U.S. House of Representatives. Of the three whom it has sent to the state general assembly, one has served as both representative and senator [10]. These have been the only women whom the machine has sent to Washington since 1945 and to Springfield since 1933. It has carried on in the tradition of its predecessor, the Kelly-Nash machine, by successfully slating at least one woman for the 15 member board of Cook County commissioners. It has made one woman a ward committeeman, another serves on the 50-member city council, and another as trustee of the nine-member sanitary district. Two have been elected to serve among the 48 circuit and associate Chicago area judges on the Cook County circuit court. Two slated women have lost primary elections and one has lost a general election. (See Table 6.1.)

Organization

The Daley organization does not look kindly upon organizations-within-the-organization unless, of course, it sponsors them [11]. About

10 years ago an effort was made to organize an ongoing group of Democratic women in Chicago. Word of Daley's disapproval was quickly transmitted and the project was abandoned [12]. There is now something in existence called the Cook County Democratic Women's Club. The membership is composed entirely of precinct workers, and the club's sole function is to help swell the crowds at election rallies.

A very different kind of organization, the Illinois Democratic Women's Caucus (IDWC) assembled itself in 1971. It was the direct outgrowth of the Women's Leadership Conference called by the Women's Activities Division of the Democratic National Committee, which, in turn, was held in order to promote interest in the McGovern-Fraser Committee [13] recommendations concerning an increase in women delegates to the 1972 nominating convention. The IDWC has attracted, for the most part, upper middle-class, college-educated, issue-oriented women.

As far as the Daley organization is concerned, the IDWC has two objectives: to persuade the slate-makers to endorse more women, and to pressure the central committee of the CCDP into promulgating party rules, as required by the McGovern-Fraser guidelines, for delegate selection. Thus far the only tangible results of the IDWC's efforts have been a hearing before the slate-makers and the slating of three women, one of whom (running unopposed) survived the 1972 primary.

The Daley organization has, clearly, kept women on a short lead—just how short will be apparent after the description of the "Daley woman" which follows.

The Daley Woman

General Characteristics

Mayor Daley, it has been reported, wishes that more women would become active in politics [14]. If they would but step forward . . . This may indeed be the case, but she who would present herself for the organization's blessings would do well to determine if she meets most, if not all, of the following requirements. (See Table 6.1.) Some are the same as for a man. Her loyalty must be unquestioned. She should have an ethnic identity—if she is white she cannot be a WASP, if black she need not be Catholic [15]. She should come from a long-trusted political family or have a reliable political sponsor. If neither, her willingness to finance her campaign is evidence of her sincerity.

Since she will never have influence, she need not prove herself, as must a male hopeful, by delivering the vote or by serving the organization's interests in Springfield [16]. Her apprenticeship is of a different order. She should be involved in community and/or church affairs, and active in voluntary service organizations. When elected it is her responsibility to bring a woman's touch to the problems of the young, the old, the needy and the troubled—matters which concerned her in private life. She should "care about people [17]."

Close analysis of the careers of women who, at first glance, do not appear to fit this mold, discloses that the differences are of degree and levels of sophistication. "Caring about people" does not preclude having a law practice, or a specialized knowledge of housing, or an interest in the rights of minorities—and women. Intelligence, competence, professionalism and expertise are valued as long as these attributes remain properly channeled. Traditional or nontraditional in her outlook, the Daley organization is only interested in her candidacy if her sex fulfills a political function.

What follows are descriptions of the handful of "Daley women" and an analysis of their particular utility to the machine.

Cook County Commissioner Elizabeth Conkey

When Richard Daley was elected mayor in 1955, Mrs. Conkey, the quintessential machine woman, had already been around for some 30 years. Her natural and earned credentials were impeccable. She was Irish, Catholic, sister of a state senator, and active in her parish. In the 1920s she organized and remained active in local and state Democratic party auxiliary groups, did odd jobs by serving as jury commissioner and commissioner of public welfare, and as delegate to the national nominating conventions [18].

When the Republicans slated a woman, Mrs. Ruth Hanna McCormick, for the U.S. Senate in 1933, the Kelly-Nash machine responded by running Mrs. Conkey as commissioner of the Cook County board [19]. She held that job for 30 years, successfully fighting off efforts to dump her in favor of younger party stalwarts. While on the board, she turned her attention to public welfare, the Cook County Hospital, and the Audy Home for delinquent and runaway children which she helped to found. She was, in her own words, "dedicated (to) service to the sick, the poor, the blind, the aged . . . (and) children." In 1943, President Roosevelt appointed her a member of the U.S. delegation for the organization of the United Nations Relief and Rehabilitation Agency.

The eulogies delivered after her death sum up, as well as anything, the organization's appreciation of its complete woman. "She belonged to the old school," said Mayor Daley, "in which there was a deep sense of responsibility and loyalty," and she was, added the president of the county board, a "gracious lady."

Since Mrs. Conkey's election, women have served regularly on the Cook County board and, in fact, the leadership wants women on the board because the commissioners are responsible for the "kinds of things" which interest women and which need the "compassionate" and "patient" attention which "only a woman can give [20]."

Two of these women were appointed to fill out their late husbands' unexpired terms. One, Ruby Ryan, Irish and Catholic and whose husband had been president of the board, was later slated to run for the job. She is currently serving as a commissioner. When the other, Josephine Sneed, a black, was not slated to run, she retreated quietly, bearing perhaps her son's patronage job in mind. Both women, as commissioners, continued their interests in the sick, the poor and the young [21].

State Senator Esther Saperstein

Of the three Daley women who have gone to Springfield, little is known of one who served only a single term [22]. Another, Lillian Piotrowski, "did time," as do many Daley men, in Springfield. Esther Saperstein is the only Daley woman who can be said to have had a purely legislative career.

Mrs. Saperstein is Jewish, and her association with Jewish causes and organizations has reinforced this identity with her constituency [23]. Unlike Mrs. Conkey, she got her start outside of the regular organization and with the support of the Independent Voters of Illinois (IVI)—a group strongly opposed to the Daley organization. However, her interest in politics was not sparked by an urge to challenge the organization, but by proper womanly concerns— she was the founder and first president of the Chicago PTA. While she ran as an independent for the city council in 1955, she also backed Daley, a personal friend, for mayor in his first election for that office. The next year, with organization backing, she won a seat in the state legislature, and in 1962 was elected state senator, and has subsequently been reelected.

Her legislative efforts reflect her major interests. Like Mrs. Conkey, she has concentrated on the problems of the young, the sick, the poor, and the deprived. She is more modern to the extent that she has added mental health and women's rights to the list [24]. She believes that it is in such areas, where women have greater insights than men, that she can be most effective [25].

While Mrs. Saperstein's irregular political beginnings have not been entirely forgiven, her loyalty has been rewarded and assured by a patronage job—suitably enough with the Chicago Board of Health, and useful for a widow who must support herself [26]. She has no interest, she says, in having a voice in party affairs, satisfied to leave matters of *realpolitik* to the men [27].

Alderwoman Marilou McCarthy Hedlund

Mrs. Hedlund, Irish, Catholic, Catholic-educated, and the daughter of a businessman with close ties to the Daley organization [28], is one of two women ever to be elected to the city council and the only one to receive organization support [29]. In one respect she is quite different from Mrs. Conkey and Mrs. Saperstein. She does not believe that there are particular matters upon which she, as a woman, should concentrate her attention and energies. And while we never met Mrs. Conkey and can make no comparisons, there is no doubt that Mrs. Hedlund is more self-assured vis-à-vis her male colleagues than is Mrs. Saperstein. By her admission not an ardent feminist, she nonetheless is determined that she can be accepted on her own merits, and be neither tolerated nor cherished as a woman in a man's world.

The fact remains that Mrs. Hedlund fills a female role. With her husband she took an active part in neighborhood groups formed to combat deteriorating conditions in her ward. Her "anger" and "despair" drove her (after her husband said he could not run) to seek the Democratic ward committeeman's endorsement for the 1971 aldermanic race. Thus, our updated scenario finds Mrs. Hedlund, citizen housewife (not to mention mother of two) [30], asking for organization support to attain objectives with which no one could quarrel—decent housing, improved schools, more parks and quiet neighborhoods [31].

Mrs. Hedlund gives three reasons for the approval of her candidacy:

1. She could finance her own campaign.

2. Through her volunteer activities, she was well-known in the ward.

3. Her committeeman's hope that if she lost to the incumbent Republican, her defeat could be blamed on her sex and less on his failure to deliver the vote. This was especially important because the committeeman, recently appointed to fill out an unexpired term, was anxious to make his reputation on his own.

Another reason, and one which she of course did not mention, is that she is young, elegant, bright and articulate—in short, an attractive candidate.

Her campaign was directed to her opponent's failure to address himself to the problems of the ward. She received major newspaper endorsement, and carried, by four hundred votes, a ward which the organization cannot count on [32]. She thinks that while her sex may have handicapped her with older women voters, it was an asset, perhaps the decisive one, with young, single and married, working women.

As a member of the council, she feels she has earned the respect of her pro-administration colleagues by being hard-working, well-prepared on legislative matters, and by developing her own field of expertise—housing [33].

While she does not consider herself a regular, and cannot be so considered, she does go along with the leadership in order to get what she wants for her ward. She sees herself as an essentially apolitical, imaginative, and effective ombudswoman for the 48th Ward and, as of now, her ambitions go no further.

Ward Committeeman Lillian Piotrowski

Miss Piotrowski is the only woman to have been a ward committeeman and thus is the only Daley woman in any position of authority in the organization. Our many efforts to interview her were of no avail, and since, unlike other women in politics, she has never been the subject of a news story (the kind which usually appear in the women's pages), we assume that she deliberately keeps a low profile [34].

She is Polish, Catholic, and Catholic-educated. We were told that her political sponsor was Otto Janousek, alderman and Democratic committeeman of the 22nd ward. He, in turn, got his start in politics by serving as Mayor Anton Cermak's chauffeur [35]. Miss Piotrowski has served the organization in a number of capacities—precinct worker, deputy sheriff for the juvenile courts, juvenile and adult probation officer (the latter two are also patronage jobs), and state representative for seven terms [36]. In 1964 she was elected Cook County commissioner, and she succeeded Janousek as committeeman following his death in 1970. She holds a patronage job with the Cook County board and as a ward committeeman, commands patronage. She has been described as "very tough" and "not really a woman [37]," and insists, according to her secretary, on being called committee*man* [38].

From all outward appearances, it seems as though Miss Piotrowski weakens our hypothesis about the "Daley woman." However, despite the fact that she is the only one who has taken a male route to advancement (Springfield), and has the attributes of power (patronage [39], a voice in the slate-making process, and holds more than one job [40]), she does fulfill a function because she is a woman. As cochairwoman, with the very feminine Ruby Ryan of the Democratic Women's Club of Cook County she keeps a close watch on the city's estimated 3,500 women precinct workers. She is the general of the female troops.

Women and the 1971 Slate

In December 1971, what was probably an unprecedented number of women appeared before the slate-making body of the CCDP. Some requested slating, others, representing the IDWC, pled the cause of women. While some of the slate-makers expressed hostility, it is reported, Chairman Daley treated the women with genial courtesy [41]. When Joanne Alter, a spokeswoman for the IDWC, suggested that the slate-makers give consideration to women seeking endorsement as trustee of the metropolitan sanitary district [42], she was asked to run for the office. After she recovered from her surprise, she accepted.

While Mrs. Alter's liberalism, independence, and insistence that women have a greater voice in party affairs might not sit too well with the slatemakers [43], she was a good choice from other standpoints. She is Jewish, and apparently it was felt that more ticket balancing in that direction was in order. She can finance her campaign. She has proven herself in 20 years of organizational Democratic Party work [44], and represents an important component of electoral politics—the woman volunteer. Intelligent, attractive, capable, and politically experienced, she is considered a good match for the well-qualified woman whom the Republicans had earlier endorsed for the same post. Furthermore, slating Mrs. Alter might have been viewed as a convenient way of silencing the demands of the women activists [45]—a factor which Mrs. Alter herself takes into account [46]. Be that as it may, Mrs. Alter performed a particularized function for the organization because she was a woman.

Two other slated women were given women's jobs to do. Odas Nicholson, black, and Joanne Saunders, Jewish, were endorsed to run against male Democratic state representatives who were vocal critics of the Daley organization. Neither Miss Nicholson nor Mrs. Saunders received the support of liberal or feminist organizations [47]. Their opponents, as was predicted, won handily.

Miss Nicholson and Mrs. Saunders are both attorneys and active in civil rights and women's causes. Mrs. Saunders did not appear before the slatemakers. Miss Nicholson did and requested slating as state's attorney general, a request which was, to her distress, turned down. She is considered to be a party regular, a designation which she emphatically rejects [48]. She won election as a delegate to the 1970 state constitutional convention against an IVI backed opponent. She is liked and respected by both organization and independent Democrats, and her cosponsorship of the first meeting of the IDWC was considered essential [49]. Her future appears uncertain now that she has failed the machine as a woman.

Some Miscellaneous Women: Judges, Constitutional Convention Delegates, City Employees

At present, eight Chicago women are serving on the circuit court of Cook County. Seven are Democrats, five of whom, formerly magistrates, were appointed and will be up for election in 1973 [50]. Three of the Democratic judges have Irish names [51]. All attended one or the other of the two Catholic law schools in the city [52]. They have earned their laurels. As one candidly explained: "Only a few spots are open, so naturally service and loyalty to the party count when judges are selected [53]." The five magistrates, like all magistrates, were patronage workers. The Chicago Council of Lawyers found them, as it found all but a few of the magistrates, "unqualified" to serve as associate judges [54].

Whatever their competence, the magistrates were given assignments in which they could exercise their womanly, if not legal talents. They dealt with human problems such as alcoholism and family difficulties. One of the elected judges, who deals only with forcible detainer actions, finds much of her time spent in advising women who cannot pay the rent because their husbands have deserted them [55].

Of the 42 Chicago delegates to the 1970 state constitutional convention, four were women—two regulars and two independents. Odas Nicholson, one of the regulars, served as secretary of the convention. The other, Gloria Pughsley, is also black, and according to her biography, should be considered a good Daley woman. Widow of an army officer, she has a civic job (coordinator for the mayor's committee for a cleaner Chicago), has been active in the U.S.O., the Red Cross, and a variety of community and church groups, many of which are youth, health, and civil rights oriented [56].

While not strictly within the purview of our study, the status of women in the city government provides further evidence concerning the status of women in the Daley organization. An independent alderman, Leon Despres, has undertaken a study of ranks and pay-scales of municipally employed women in Chicago. His preliminary findings indicate that of those serving in high appointive position, none are in major decision-making posts [57]. Further investigation discloses that, with one exception, these women deal with women's matters"—consumerism, health, welfare and youth [58].

Attitudes Toward Female Political Participation

Interviews [59]

Independents and regulars alike stressed the importance of Daley's traditional, puritanical Irish Catholicism. His mother may have been a suffragist, but he still believes women belong at home. He also has strong convictions about marital fidelity, and will no more forgive a man's "playing around" (as the phrase kept cropping up) than he will forgive disloyalty to himself or the organization. These sins are, in his eyes, cardinal and equally heinous. Women also should remain on their pedestals. As long as the organization is dominated by this Irish Catholic ethos, we were told, women will be excluded from any meaningful participation.

All of the regulars with whom we spoke agreed on at least one point: Women are good precinct workers. Different explanations, though, were offered. One mentioned that young and pretty women, once apartment doors were opened to them, were more persuasive than older, and thus presumably less appealing, women. Widows with families to support and holding patronage jobs, on the other hand, while lacking in sex appeal could be counted on as loyal and hard workers. Another said that women are more effective than men with other women, especially if the woman precinct workers had day by day contacts with their neighbors. Women do the job well because they appreciate the opportunity to "get out of the house." (All said that women precinct workers could not go out at night unless escorted by a male.)

When we asked about elected offices the replies were mixed. One alderman admitted to his uneasiness over women in the council. Because they might "cry" he could not be as "honest" or as "tough" with them as he is with male colleagues. What is more, he feels that women are handicapped because so much of the council's business is discussed in bars, often at night. Unable (naturally) to participate in these informal work sessions, women must miss out of an essential part of the legislative process. (When this observation was reported to Mrs. Hedlund, she replied, "I just follow them on in.") In contrast to this view, a representative, also a ward committeeman, shrugged off the suggestion that a female legislator could never be one of the boys. But too many mentioned this as a factor for us to dismiss it.

All interviewed reported "liking" Mrs. Hedlund. Reactions from the regulars to mention of Anna Langford, the black independent alderwoman [60], were swift and vehement. She is described as a "hater" who cannot "even get along with the other independents." She is "all talk" and so ineffective that she would be unable to "get a constituent's dog out of the pound." Whether this has to do with Mrs. Langford's abilities, her sex, or her strong anti-organization position, is a matter of speculation.

Two of those interviewed, one an alderman, the other a township committeeman who, unlike most township committeemen, holds a patronage job, commented upon the correlation between class and female political participation. Suburban women active in community affairs, and college-educated and professional women have, as lower middle-class women do not, the training and leisure necessary to stimulate an interest in politics. Therefore, they predicted that few Chicago women would ever become politically active. One ward committeeman commented on this score that many downstate Democratic women are as competent and politically astute as their suburban sisters.

With one exception, all regulars expressed a wish that more women would participate in the party and indicate a willingness to run for office. The mayor himself, for example, is "always" telling the ward committeemen to activate the ladies. In fact, Daley has singled out for praise one committeeman, who in order to stimulate female interest in politics, holds card parties and fashion shows at ward headquarters—at the same time and on different floors. All, in various ways, tried to tell us that they held no biases against professional women. And although we never posed the question, we were repeatedly told that they did not object to "taking orders" from women—as indeed they do all the time from their wives and daughters [61].

The Questionnaire

The return rates on the two questionnaires, 13 of the 50 ward committeemen and 16 of the 30 township committeemen, were disappointing but not surprising. While this may reflect the latter's autonomy, it also undoubtedly reflects their overall attitudes. For instance, on the question, "Do you think women participate sufficiently in Democratic party politics?", 69% of the ward and 19% of the township committeemen responding, replied in the affirmative.

We had hoped to make more specific comparisons of the attitudes of the ward and township committeemen toward women serving in different elective offices, and to determine if ward committeemen would be more likely to support women for office in jobs which command no patronage than in jobs which do command patronage. However, the meager returns from the ward committeemen precluded making meaningful comparisons and drawing any conclusions other than that, for whatever reasons, almost three-fourths of the ward committeemen did not answer a brief anonymous questionnaire about women and politics [62]. Furthermore, since we have no way of knowing which ward committeemen responded (i.e. were Mayor Daley, County Board President Dunne, State Central Committee Chairman Ronan, Aldermen Holman, Keane and Marzullo among them?), there is no way to attach any significance to the responses we did receive.

Independent Democratic Women

While not many Chicago women have run as independents, they are now doing so and in increasing numbers. This does raise questions about the Daley leadership's assertions that they are willing to endorse more women if only women were more willing to participate. Of course the women who have run may not have sought endorsement, not because they were anti-organization, but because they thought their chances of receiving endorsement were slim [63]. On the other hand, some do hold very strong views about the organization in general and Daley in particular [64].

Turning first to the aldermanic races (see Table 6.2), the rise in the numbers of women who have filed (some of whom withdrew or were eliminated) and run has increased steadily. Three ran or filed in 1955; six in 1959; nine in 1963 (four ran in special aldermanic elections of 1964 and 1965); seven ran in 1967; and, including Mrs. Hedlund, not listed because she is not an independent, 11 ran in 1971. What is also significant is that as the numbers who have filed have increased the proportion of those withdrawing or being eliminated has *decreased*. In 1959 and 1963 six women filed, but did not run. In 1971 only one withdrew, and that because she was persuaded that her elimination from the race would enhance the chances of a male independent who, as a matter of fact, did win [65].

Since the aldermanic races are nonpartisan, we do not know the party preferences of all the candidates. However, we have identified nine candidacies as Democratic (we have counted each of Mrs. Scala's and Mrs. Langford's candidacies). What the list does indicate, whatever party preferences, is that in a city tightly controlled by a Democratic machine, women have kept on trying to be elected to the council despite the odds against their candidacies.

As can be seen from Table 6.3, women have also been running in Democratic primaries for national and state offices. Two have even tried to storm the impregnable fortress of ward committeeman. Before 1972, two independent women have run every two years with the exception of 1958. In 1972, six women sought four offices and two, Peggy Smith Martin for state representative and Dawn Clark Netsch for state senator, won.

While the successes of these two groups of women have been modest, some tentative and *very* general conclusions can be drawn about their efforts and the results:

1. The greater the numbers of women who run, the greater their chances of success.

2. There seems to be a payoff in "try, try again." Both Mrs. Langford, who barely lost her first race for the council, and Mrs. Martin, who filed for an aldermanic race and lost four primaries for state representative, were subsequently victorious. (Mrs. Martin's defeated opponent, in the 1972 primary, was the Democratic committeeman of Mrs. Langford's ward.)

3. Black and Spanish-speaking women are showing an interest in electoral politics. Only three of the 37 women who have filed and/or run for alderman have been black, but five of the 13 who have run for other offices have represented minority groups. In 1970 and 1972, four of the eight women independents were either black or Spanish-speaking.

Table 6.2.   Independent Aldermanic Women Candidates, 1955–1972

Year	Name	Result	Occupation
1955	Dorothy Morgenstern	Lost	?
	Dorsey Crowe	Lost	?
	Esther Saperstein[a]	Lost	Teacher
1959	Ruth Porter[ab]	Lost	?
	Margaret N. White	Lost	?
	Frances Vestuto	Lost	?
	Ursula Rihs	Lost	?
	Peggy Smith[ab]	Withdrew	Welfare lobbyist
	Marian Cleveland	Withdrew	?
1963	Florence Scala[a]	Lost	Housewife
	Marian Smith	Lost	Political activist
	Henrietta Stashwick	Lost	?
	Catherine Anagnost	Lost	Attorney
	Marian Cleveland	Lost	?
	Margaret Schimon	Withdrew/ Eliminated	?
	Hilde Deemar	Eliminated	?
	Clory Lee Bryant[ab]	Eliminated	Machine tool operator
	Ann Ackerman	Eliminated	?
1964	Florence Scala[a]	Lost	Housewife/Political activist
1965	Lucy Jean Jones	Lost	?
	Maria Anagnost	Lost	?
	Ruth Tracy	Lost	?
1967	Anna Langford[ab]	Lost	?
	Gertrude Jones	Lost	?
	Delores Peck	Lost	?
	Lillian Karamaczyn	Lost	?
	Stephanie Pietruszka	Lost	?
	Mardean Cole	Lost	?
	Jane Ward	Lost	?
1971	Cynthia Burk	Lost	?
	Marylee Leahy[a]	Lost	Attorney
	Mary Sweeny	Lost	?
	Anna Langford[ab]	Won	Attorney
	Marcella Dempsey	Lost	?
	Delores Chadwick	Lost	?
	Naomi Allen	Lost	?
	Priscilla Dombek	Lost	?
	Mary Anne Dory	Lost	?
	Laura Keith[a]	Withdrew	Legal secretary

Although Chicago aldermanic elections are nonpartisan, the majority of the council members are supported, with the mayor's approval, by the Democratic ward organizations.

[a]Denotes women who are Democrats.

[b]Denotes women who are black.

4. Independent women, as opposed to their regular counterparts, are more apt to be employed and/or have professional training [66]. (See Table 6.3.)

5. There appears to be a correlation between the women's liberation movement, however defined, and the increase in the numbers of women running, without organizational backing, for office.

Elections: 1972 and 1973

Mrs. Netsch won easily. Mrs. Martin's otherwise sure chances were jeopardized by the candidacy of her defeated primary opponent, an incumbent state representative and patronage worker, who ran as an independent for one of the district's three legislative seats. He gathered enough votes to assure his election, but not enough to prevent hers.

Mrs. Alter, backed by the Independent Voters of Illinois and the Independent Precinct Organization as well as by the regular organization, led six contenders for the three available trusteeships. The other woman on the ticket, Republican Joan Anderson, also supported by the same independent groups, followed close behind. This marks the first time, in a contest in which votes are cast along party lines, that a Republican has placed between the two leading Democrats [67].

With more in common with Mrs. Anderson than with her fellow Democrats, Mrs. Alter rose above partisanship and campaigned against the "sludge" which travels through the some three hundred and fifty miles of sewers under the sanitary district's supervision and into Lake Michigan and other waters. Her ongoing concern about pollution was intensified, she said, when one of her children required medical attention after falling into one of Cook County's filthier lagoons. Her campaign literature carried a picture of a magnified drop of water, in the center of which appeared her very photogenic face. However else the Daley organization may view the independent-minded Mrs. Alter, there could have been nothing but approval for an attractive mother taking a public stand in favor of healthy children and pure water.

In December, 1972, a black congressman, George Collins, was killed in a plane crash. His widow, Cardiss, slated for his seat, was not seriously challenged in either the special primary or general elections. She is the first black woman from Illinois to serve in the house.

Summary and Conclusions

Women have been and continue to be useful to the Daley organization in a number of ways, but not as politicians capable of wielding and holding

Table 6.3. Independent Chicago Democratic Women Who Have Sought Office, 1955–1972

Year	Name	Office	Result	Occupation	Marital status
1956	Beulah Wheeler[a]	State Representative	Lost	?	?
	Mary Trais[a]	State Representative	Lost	?	?
1960	Helen Boyle[a]	U.S. Representative	Lost	?	?
	Peggy Smith Martin[ac]	State Representative	Lost	Welfare lobbyist	D
1962	Clory Lee Bryant[ac]	State Representative	Lost	Machine tool Operator	D
1964	Brenetta Howell[ac]	U.S. Representative	Lost	Social worker	M
	Clory Lee Bryant[ac]	U.S. Representative	Lost	Machine tool Operator	D
1966	Peggy Smith Martin[ac]	State Representative	Lost	Welfare lobbyist	D
1968	June Sochen	U.S. Representative	Lost	Professor of history	S
1970	Peggy Smith Martin[ac]	State Representative	Lost	Welfare lobbyist	D
	Brenetta Howell[ac]	U.S. Representative	Lost	Social worker	M
	Peggy Smith Martin[ac]	State Representative	Lost	Welfare lobbyist	D
	Rhea Hammer[ad]	U.S. Representative	Lost	Producer TV show	D
	Peggy Smith Martin[bc]	State Representative	Won	Welfare lobbyist	D
	Judith Lonnquist[a]	State Representative	Lost	Attorney	S
1972	Jaren Parker[a]	State Representative	Lost	?	?
	Dawn Clark Netsch[ab]	State Senator	Won	Professor of law	M
	Anna Langford[ac]	Ward Committeeman	Withdrew	Attorney	D
	Carmen Chico[d]	Ward Committeeman	Lost	Spanish-speaking Political activist	M

[a]Indicates primary election.

[b]Indicates women who also won general election.

[c]Denotes women who are black.

[d]Indicates women who are Spanish-speaking.

power in the CCDP. An examination of the historical data, the characteristics of women supported by the organization, and leadership attitudes toward women and elective office indicates that while the Daley organization has endorsed more Chicago women for office than its predecessors the services and contributions of these women to the party have hardly changed at all. What we might call the *Conkey syndrome,* although in modern dress, still prevails. The Daley women are like children as far as influence in the CCDP goes—they are to be seen and not heard.

This does not mean that the organization will continue to support only a few women. If Mrs. Alter performs as well in office as on the campaign trail, if Mrs. Netsch is not troublesomely independent in the state senate, or if Mrs. Hedlund's horizons should extend beyond the 48th ward, there is no reason why these women could not go on to Congress or to high state office with the organization's blessing. A female Paul Douglas or Adlai Stevenson is not out of the question. This much has been accomplished.

What is out of the question is the possibility that women will, in the foreseeable future, have power within the CCDP. For one thing, since there is not, as far as we know, a "woman's vote" in Chicago, and no signs of one developing, women who aspire to power have no constituency to deliver. They may have supporters who need silencing, but that is quite a different matter. Therefore, there is no need for the organization to co-opt women as it has blacks. Also, most women who aspire to office, and some who have been slated, such as Mrs. Alter and Mrs. Hedlund, are good-government types who neither need nor want patronage jobs, and who would not be comfortable dispensing patronage. In other words, the kinds of women who in the past few years have been politically active do not fit into, although they may go along with, the organization.

The only way this picture can change, is, we think, if ethnic Catholics, particularly the Irish, lose control of the organization to blacks and/or the Spanish-speaking [68]. Women from these groups, as has been noted, are becoming aggressive politically while other ethnic women remain passive. Furthermore, it is the black and Spanish-speaking women who represent the groups most in need of patronage jobs. Mrs. Langford and Mrs. Martin, Mrs. Hammer and Mrs. Chico [69] may represent the vanguard of women who might, in the distant future, hold power in a black/Latin machine. And the Mrs. Sapersteins and Miss Piotrowskis, the Mrs. Hedlunds and the Mrs. Alters, will either serve the party as representatives of their respective ethnic and interest groups, or as ornaments in Springfield or Washington.

NOTES

1. Kirsten Amundson, *The Silenced Majority*. Englewood Cliffs, N.J.: Prentice-Hall, 1971; Martin Gruberg, *Women in American Politics*. Oshkosh, Wis.: Academia, 1969.

2. Edward C. Banfield, *Political Influence*. Glencoe, Ill.: The Free Press, 1961.

3. For a discussion of the Daley organization's co-optation of the NAACP, see James Q. Wilson, *Negro Politics*. New York: The Free Press, 1960, pp. 63–65. For the "surrender" of the issue-oriented, liberal Democrats to Daley, see James Q. Wilson, *The Amateur Democrat*. Chicago: University of Chicago Press, 1960, Chap. 3.

4. Published annually and issued from the office of the Secretary of State, Springfield, Ill.

5. Edward C. Banfield, *Political Influence*. Glencoe, Ill.: The Free Press, 1961; Harold F. Gosnell, *Machine Politics*. Chicago: University of Chicago Press, 1937 and 1968; James Q. Wilson, *Negro Politics, op. cit.;* Edward C. Banfield and Martin Meyerson, *Politics, Planning and the Public Interest*. Glencoe, Ill.: The Free Press, 1955, pp. 64–75; Harvey M. Karlen, *The Governments of Chicago*. Chicago: Courier, 1958; *The Key to Our Local Government*. Chicago: The League of Women Voters, 1971; Edward M. Levine, *The Irish and Irish Politicians*. South Bend, Ind.: University of Notre Dame, 1966, Chap. 6; Mike Royko, *Boss*, New York: New American Library, 1971.

6. We have referred to the *machine* as a phenomenon which has persisted over a period of some 40 years. The "Daley organization," or "the organization" refers to the present regime.

7. The slate-making committee of the CCDP is drawn from the membership of that body—the 50 ward and 30 township committeemen. Of the 80 eligible to serve as slate-makers in 1972, Daley selected 35 ward and 14 township committeemen. Daley is Democratic committeeman of the 11th ward.

8. *Election Trends in Cook County: An Analytical Symposium*. Chicago: Center for Research in Urban Government, Loyola University, 1967; Perry L. Weed, "Will Polarization Kill Daley Machine?", *Chicago Sun-Times* (May 7, 1972).

9. Harold F. Gosnell, *Machine Politics, op. cit.*, "Postscript to the Second Edition: Chicago Politics 1937–1967."

10. Between 1933–1970, 1.2% of all state senators and 2.5% of all state representatives were women. The Daley organization has supplied one of the three women senators and three of the 18 women representatives. *Illinois Blue Book, 1969–1970.*

11. Black pro-administration aldermen have recently formed a black caucus. They have not been joined by the independent black alderman and alderwoman.

12. Interview document.

13. *Mandate for Reform*. Washington, D.C.: Democratic National Committee, 1970.

14. Interview documents.

15. Chicago politics are ethnic politics. Anton Cermak, elected in 1933, was the first ethnic mayor. The three who succeeded him were Irish. The Irish, an ethnic minority, have performed a broker function among other ethnic groups. Anglo-Saxon names seldom show up in positions of trust and/or power.

16. Daley served as state representative and state senator. Other powerful leaders who have been members of the general assembly are: Vito Marzullo, George Dunne, John D'Arco, Charles Weber, Thomas Keane.

17. The phrase came up in an interview.

18. The information about Mrs. Conkey came from her obituaries in the *Chicago Tribune* and the *Chicago Sun-Times* (Jan. 1, 1964).

19. Martin Gruberg, *Women in American Politics, op. cit.,* p. 154.

20. Interview document with a male member of the board.

21. Sources of information about Mrs. Ryan and Mrs. Sneed: *Chicago Tribune* (April 19, 1961); *Chicago-American* (July 14, 1964); *Chicago Daily News* (Aug. 15, 1964). Mrs. Ryan, in her first campaign for election to the board, pledged to continue her interest in the Audy home and hospitals under the board's jurisdiction. Mrs. Sneed's volunteer activities included raising money for medical research and for Half-Way House, a rehabilitation center for released prisoners. She was a member of the executive committee of the Illinois Federation of Democratic Women. An acquaintance described the refusal of the slate-makers to endorse Mrs. Sneed as a candidate for the board as a "shaft." Interview document.

22. Floy Clements, a black woman, was for 20 years a precinct captain in the 4th ward and a ward committeewoman. (This is an appointed auxiliary position, and up to the discretion of the ward committeeman to fill). *Illinois Blue Book, 1961–1962.*

23. North Shore B'Nai B'rith, Hadassah, National Council of Jewish Women, Board of Directors of Jewish Community Center of Rogers Park, Zionest Organization of Chicago. *Illinois Blue Book, 1959–1960.*

24. She is a member of the Senate standing committee on education and of the commissions on mental health and the status of women.

25. Interview with Mrs. Saperstein.

26. Interview document.

27. Interview with Mrs. Saperstein.

28. Unless otherwise designated, the information about Mrs. Hedlund was obtained from the interview with her, and from interviews with those who know her.

29. Elections to the city council are nonpartisan. However, those receiving support of the Democratic ward committeemen may be presumed to also be Democratic. Mrs. Hedlund received the endorsement of the 48th ward Democratic committeeman.

30. Mrs. Hedlund noted, with some distaste, that one newspaper, citing reasons for endorsing her candidacy, contrasted her family life with her opponent's bachelorhood.

31. High-rise apartments edge the east (lake) side of the ward. The west side contains a large number of "half-way" houses for mental patients, discharged from state hospitals, but still in need of care. In the last decade the character of the ward has changed with the arrival of large numbers of Appalachians, Spanish-speaking and Orientals. Mrs. Hedlund's interest in the stability of the ward could only meet with the mayor's approval. The mushrooming of high-rises reflects his interest in keeping the middle classes in and attracting suburbanites back, to the city. Mrs. Hedlund has summed up what she considers her accomplishments: "We have stopped the federal government from burdening us unjustly with more subsidized apartment buildings. We have slowed the flood of discharged state mental patients into the community. Slum landlords expect to see me in court, and two of our worst have sold their property here, probably to plunder elsewhere. The park district has pledged us a full new park playground and three playlots. The board of education is committed to the immediate development of a new middle school. We are forming a neighborhood development corporation to both rehabilitate and build family-type housing. . . . The department of streets and sanitation is reviewing traffic patterns and creating new plans for our streets to serve the people who live on them rather than the cars that commute through them. . . . We are recycling the 48th ward for the people who live in it." *Chicago Tribune* (March 4, 1972).

32. While the Democrats carried the ward in the mayoral elections of 1963 and 1967, they lost the aldermanic elections.

33. As a means of solving difficulties resulting from a court-ordered freeze on Model Cities

Funds (a long and complex affair which will not be discussed here), Mrs. Hedlund suggested that the Department of Housing and Urban Development issue rent stamps which the poor could use toward paying rent in housing of their choice.

34. It was suggested to us that Miss Piotrowski, something of a diamond in the rough, is self-conscious about her appearance and manner of speech, and would shy away from an interview with college professors.

35. Interview document.

36. While Mrs. Saperstein's committee assignments reflect her womanly interests, Miss Piotrowski's reflected matters of interest to the Daley organization, such as the committees on industrial affairs, pensions, insurance, and public utilities.

37. Interview document.

38. The Illinois election code provides for the election of ward committeemen, with no mention made of committeewomen. While occasionally ward committeewomen have been elected, we have not found any in Chicago other than Miss Piotrowski. Ward and township committeemen do sometimes appoint committeewomen as auxiliaries. One of the present 30 Cook County suburban committeemen is a woman.

39. Miss Piotrowski holds one of the patronage jobs at the disposal of the county board.

40. The practice, a common one, is known as "double-dipping." One's unsalaried position as ward committeeman might be balanced by one's salaried position as a county commissioner and another job on the public payroll. Precinct workers have been known to be employed by private firms as well as being on the public payroll.

41. Information about this particular slate-making session came from a number of women who were present.

42. The metropolitan sanitary district is one of the many special government districts of Chicago and its outlying areas. While it used to be a patronage haven, it is now professionalized. Four women asked to be slated for the job, only one of whom was sponsored by her committeeman.

43. It should be born in mind that the organization has always been willing to endorse a few good-government types—but only for offices which do not carry any weight in the organization. Such candidates help the ticket in the suburbs and the *newspaper wards*. If they prove to be big winners, as did Senator Adlai Stevenson in 1970, their support of candidates who challenge the organization is tolerated.

44. She has worked in numerous campaigns, and organized the state-wide, home headquarters for Adlai Stevenson's senatorial campaign.

45. *New York Times* (February 11, 1972).

46. Interview document.

47. The IVI and the Illinois Women's Political Caucus, both bi-partisan groups, supported their opponents.

48. Miss Nicholson was interviewed the day after she was refused slating as attorney general. She was angry and upset, vowing that she was through with politics.

49. Miss Nicholson was described as "a doll" by a Daley alderman, and as an intelligent, highly professional woman by a suburban Democratic state representative.

50. Magistrates were appointed by and served at the pleasure, according to law, of the circuit court judges. Under the new state constitution magistrates were promoted, by the state supreme court, to the position of associate judge.

51. Judge Helen McGillicuddy, Judge Kathleen Nohelty (deceased); former magistrates, now judges, Margaret O'Malley and Helen Kelleher. Judge Edith Sampson is black.

52. Loyola and De Paul.

53. *Chicago Daily News* (Oct. 11, 1965).

54. The appointments were not challenged by the Chicago Bar Association. The CCL is composed of young nonestablishment lawyers with a lively interest in politics and public affairs. They found only three of the 107 magistrates to be qualified. The report on one of the women magistrates was especially critical: "Magistrate Stryker is hopelessly unqualified. Some of the comments by lawyers who have appeared before her are: 'Horrible'. . . 'Doesn't know the law'. . . 'Lazy'. . . 'While she may respect the rule of law, she does not have the cerebral equipment to determine what the law might be'. . . 'Unwarranted outbursts . . . screams'. . ." *A Report by the Chicago Council of Lawyers: the 107 Cook County Magistrates Who Are Scheduled To Become Associate Judges of the Circuit Court on July 1, 1971,* undated.

55. *Chicago Tribune* (Feb. 8, 1970, Dec. 17, 1970); *Chicago Daily News* (Oct. 11, 1965).

56. *Illinois Blue Book, 1969–1970.*

57. *Hyde-Park Herald* (Apr. 4, 1970).

58. Executive director of the antipoverty program; director of consumer weights and measures; director of relocation services; chief epidemiologist; director of public health nursing; director of institutional and medical care inspections; director of correctional services for the human resources department; director of the alcoholic rehabilitation center. The municipal reference librarian is a woman. The one exception is assistant commissioner of public works. For an assessment of the performance of the director of consumer weights and measures, see: Camille S. Jilke, "Jane Byrne: Our Lady of Open Coding," *The Chicago Guide,* **22,** No. 3, pp. 95–101 (Mar. 1973). In 1973, Mayor Daley appointed Professor Pastora San Juan Cafferty of the University of Chicago to fill her late husband's post on the urban transit board.

59. All whom we interviewed and all recipients of the questionnaire were assured anonymity.

60. When we queried members of the administrative staff of the CCDP about Mrs. Langford, they told us that she was not a Democrat, adding that there was no such thing as an independent Democrat. One ward committeeman attributed Mrs. Langford's election to the council to the incompetence of her ward committeeman who failed to make himself available to the residents of the ward.

61. Alderman Thomas Keane, the mayor's floor leader in the council, was opposed by a Republican woman in the 1963 aldermanic election. Keane correctly predicted that no woman would be elected to the council that year, but added, "I like women. I have three daughters and a wife." *Chicago Daily News* (Jan. 1, 1963). Keane did not give us an interview, but spoke with one of us briefly on the telephone. When asked about his views on the future for women in the party, he replied, "Ever since Eve, the future for women has looked good." He said we could quote him.

62. We cannot compare 26% of the ward with 53% of the township committeemen without producing gross distortions of the data which are impossible to correct. The variance in our sample is too great for significant comparisons to be made.

63. Peggy Smith Martin started out as a party regular and served as a precinct captain. She was informed by, then County Clerk, Richard J. Daley in 1955 that failure to support him over the incumbent Mayor Kennelley would result in the loss of her job. Her break with the organization came with Daley's election as mayor, *Chicago Sun-Times* (Feb. 2, 1970). Clory Lee Bryant, also black, said that while she admired the one-man leadership of William Dawson (Congressman Dawson was boss of Chicago's black wards—see James Q. Wilson, *Negro Politics,* Chap. 3), she objected to his "putting party over his people," *Chicago Sun-Times* (Apr. 16, 1964).

64. Alderwoman Anna Langford's criticisms of the organization are always pungent. At city

council judiciary hearings on the mayor's proposed equal rights legislation (attended by one of the writers), pro-administration aldermen successfully tabled a motion to strengthen the proposal until their cohorts could be rounded up to vote it down. "Bring them in," Mrs. Langford shouted, "bring the male chauvinist pigs in." Turning to the witnesses and observers, she added, "that's democracy—Chicago style." Later she announced that she was going to run for ward committeeman so that she could be right in the center of things, meeting the "male chauvinist pigs on their own territory." She did file. Her petitions were challenged and refusing to challenge the challenge, she withdrew.

65. Laura Keith left the independent field open to Richard Simpson, a professor of political science at the University of Illinois, Chicago Circle Campus, *Chicago Sun-Times* (Feb. 4, 1971).

66. We note that women attorneys have become politically active in the past 2 years. In 1971, two of the 11 women aldermanic candidates, Mrs. Langford and Mrs. Leahy, were attorneys. In 1972, three of the seven women independent candidates for other offices were attorneys. In 1972, the two slated women who lost were attorneys.

67. *Chicago Sun-Times* (Nov. 19, 1972).

68. Chicago's population has dropped 5% during the past decade—due, mostly, to the white exodus to the suburbs. During the same period the black population grew from 23% of the total population to 33%. The Spanish-speaking comprise 10% of the population.

69. Between 1937 and 1967, the machine was challenged three times in contests for ward committeemen and lost one election. That Mrs. Chico managed to get on to the ballot is something of an achievement. Candidates for national and state office and for the city council need to have signatures on their petitions amounting to ½ of 1% of the party's vote in their district in the last election, and candidates for ward committeemen need signatures amounting to between 10% and 16% of the ward's electorate.

Chapter

7

A Study of Career Structures of Federal Executives:
A Focus on Women

Mary M. Lepper

This Government owes it to the women of the country . . . that they shall no longer be held in a subordinate position and treated as inferiors; that it shall say to them there shall be hereinafter no position under this Government for which they are fitted which shall not be open to them equall(sic) with men.

CONGRESSIONAL GLOBE [1]

The Nation's many highly qualified women represent an important reservoir of ability and talent that we must draw on to a greater degree. In this Administration we have firmly espoused the rights of women, and we must now clearly demonstrate our recognition of the equality of women by making greater use of their skills in high level positions.

RICHARD M. NIXON [2]

The last ten years have seen a tremendous growth in the feminist movement. Much of this growth has come about as a result of the increasing awareness that women were being systematically discriminated against in

This study (originally presented at the American Political Science Association Annual Meeting, Chicago, 1971) was made possible by the cooperation of several bureaus of the U.S. Civil Service Commission. However, all interpretations are the author's and do not represent official Commission positions. Support for the project was provided by the Bureau of Training. The career structure pattern was based on the Executive Inventory Record developed by the Bureau of Executive Manpower. Glenn Sutton from BEM provided the needed programming assistance. Ms. Helene Markoff, Director of the Federal Women's Program, and her staff were helpful at all stages of the research. S. Lee Seaton, University of California, Berkeley greatly aided me in the interpretation of the factor analyses.

109

areas of employment and education. In order to remedy this situation, women have begun to insist they be allowed to participate in the determination of policy which affects the total society, especially that directly related to women as a group.

Increasingly large numbers of women are seeking higher education to equip themselves with the skills requisite for a professional career.

At the same time, there has been unparalleled growth in the number and scope of government programs at the national level necessitating a growth in the number of employees. Indications are this growth in the public service will be reflected at other levels of government in the near future. Given these trends, concern is growing over the role women play in making public policy. Will women share in determining how the future will be shaped? They can only do this if they occupy policy-making positions. Will government service offer a career alternative for women with higher education? It will only if women have access to and are placed in administrative positions.

A recent article in *U.S. News & World Report* states that "Quietly and rapidly, 'woman' power is making unparalleled headway in the upper ranks of the federal government, which by tradition has been dominated by a male hierarchy [3]." A cause for rejoicing among women's groups if this is indeed fact and not rhetoric. The present study will examine the relative status of women and men in the federal service at the executive levels. This study will seek to determine not only what the status of women is at present, but also what trends appear to be developing.

The time frame selected for the study is 1967 to the present. The reasons for the choice of 1967 were twofold, one substantive and the other pragmatic. In 1967, President Lyndon B. Johnson issued Executive Order 11375 which prohibited sex discrimination in federal employment and gave the Federal Women's Program the same emphasis throughout the government as all other elements of the Equal Employment Opportunity Program. In addition, that same year the Civil Service Commission developed the Executive Inventory which makes it possible to research the career structure of the entire federal service at the executive level [4].

The grade parameters of the study are General Schedule Grades 15 through 18. Technically an executive in the government service is defined as any full-time employee of the executive branch whose base salary equals or exceeds the beginning salary ($29,678) of a GS 16 regardless of the personnel or pay system involved. By including the "feeder" group, GS 15, it was possible to broaden the base of the executive inventory since there are about three GS 15's for every "supergrade" (GS 16–18) [5]. Substantively this seemed to be desirable since numerous studies have tended to indicate that in many cases, especially in the field duty-stations as opposed to headquarters, the

GS 15's are performing comparable work to the GS 16's. This study of the career structure of the federal service will include, then, GS 15–18.

In addition, a numerical breakdown on women at the mid-level managerial ranks (GS 13–14) is included. (See Table 7.1.) With the increased emphasis on executive development within the federal service, these ranks provide access to the policy-making strata. With a starting salary for GS 13 of $18,737, these ranks appear to offer, at least financially, a reasonable career alternative to teaching for women with higher education. The demographic and background data on the GS 13–14 population are not readily available to allow for the study of the career structure as has been done for the higher grades; however, it is expected that it will be possible to do so within the next year.

The number of cases used for various parts of the study will vary somewhat. This is due to the variety of reporting dates for different types of data and it was desirable to use the most recent to reflect the changing conditions. In addition, the Executive Inventory is always being updated. The inventory is based on an 11-page questionnaire which each person appointed or promoted to a position at GS 15 or above is asked to complete. Completion of the questionnaire is voluntary and some of those eligible fail to complete it for a variety of reasons.

Evolution of Federal Employment Practices Toward Women [6]

Women were employed as postmistresses before the adoption of the Constitution. The first known woman federal employee was a postmistress in Baltimore, Maryland in 1773. Beginning in 1853, women were appointed as lighthouse keepers, and by 1871 there were 56 of them. The Treasury Department employed women as clerks between 1863 and 1868. This probably was a result of a shortage of men during the Civil War period as the number of women declined after 1868. Appointments of women were sporadic events and were seldom to a position of any significance. In 1870 a law was passed which allowed agency heads at their "discretion" to hire females at higher clerkships with the same salary as males. Despite the fine sentiments expressed by Congress in passing this law as illustrated by the first quote in this paper, it resulted in the development of the practice of agencies requesting men only or women only when filling positions. As a consequence, openings at higher levels always specified *men only.*

The passage of the Civil Service Act of 1883 marked a major breakthrough in the status of women as employees of the federal government. Under the newly created merit system, women could compete in civil service examinations on the same basis as men. The Classification Act of 1923 established

Table 7.1. Full-time White Collar Employment by General Schedule and Equivalent Grades[a] (All Agencies Worldwide)

	Employment as of October 31, 1967				Employment as of October 31, 1972[b]		
		Women				Women	
Grade[c]	Total[d]	Number	%	Grade[c]	Total[d]	Number	%
13	85,308	3,632	4.2	13	102,968	4,797	4.7
14	42,938	1,583	3.7	14	50,257	1,924	3.8
15	22,901	577	2.5	15	27,373	883	3.2
16	6,321	124	2.0	16	5,356	98	1.8
17	2,349	35	1.5	17	1,869	30	1.6
18	756	5	.7	18	1,334	14	1.0
18 (above)[e]	609	15	2.5	18 (above)[e]	299	6	2.0
Total	161,182	5,962	3.7	Total	189,456	7,752	4.0

[a]Bureau of Management Services, U.S. Civil Service Commission. *Study of Employment of Women in the Federal Government, 1967.* Washington, D.C.: GPO, 1968.

[b]This is data based on a U.S. Civil Service Commission news release of May 16, 1973.

[c]The grades or levels of the various pay systems have been considered equivalent to specific general schedule grades solely on the comparison of salary rates, specifically, in most instances by comparing the 4th step GS rates with comparable rates in other pay systems.

[d]Excludes employees of Central Intelligence Agency, National Security Agency, Board of Governors of Federal Reserve System and Foreign Nationals Overseas. Also excludes Post Office in 1971 data.

[e]This category includes individuals who are not part of the career service. The salaries in this category are not part of the General Schedule.

the concept of equal pay for equal work. From 1940 on, women increasingly filled positions at the lower levels of the federal service, but as recently as 1959 only eighteen of the 1500 supergrade positions were filled by women. A breakthrough came in 1962 when Attorney General Robert F. Kennedy ruled against the interpretation of the 1870 law as allowing agencies to specify a single sex for openings. Finally, in 1965 Congress declared the 1870 law invalid. When President John F. Kennedy created the Commission on the Status of Women in 1961, there were 24 women and 2026 men in the supergrade positions, a very slight decline from 1959 [7]. Among the committees created by the first Commission on the Status of Women was one on Federal Employment Policies and Practices.

Late in 1961, John W. Macy, Chairman of the Civil Service Commission, began to question practices of agencies which appeared to be discriminating against women. Stating that personnel actions should be taken on the sole basis of merit and fitness, Macy directed federal appointing officials to include reasons when asking for a referral of men only or women only from examination lists. At that time the commission could not overrule these requests but did make an analysis and evaluation of the legitimacy of such requests. A study based on a 6 month period showed that 29% of the requests were for men only and 34% were for women only, but that 94% of the requests for positions at GS 13, 14, and 15 were restricted to men only. After the agencies had to justify their specification of sex, 99.8% of the requests did not specify sex [8].

Despite these actions, women were still not being promoted to higher ranks, and as recently as 1964, a number of major agencies had no women other than personal secretaries, historians or librarians, including The White House Staff, Internal Revenue Service, Bureau of Customs, Bureau of Budget, Federal Aviation Agency, Federal Mediation and Conciliation Service, and the Federal Power Commission [9]. During the Kennedy administration 18 women were appointed to major decision-making positions and during the Johnson administration 27 women were appointed to high-level positions. The Nixon administration has made considerably more progress with 125 by July 1, 1972.

With the issuance of Executive Order 11375 by President Lyndon B. Johnson, a series of actions were taken to alter the status of women in federal employment. The executive order prohibited sex discrimination in federal employment and gave the Federal Women's Program the same emphasis as all other elements of the Equal Employment Opportunity Programs. The Civil Service Commission was given the task of implementing the order. Several directives were issued designed to achieve three main objectives: (*a*) to create the regulatory and administrative framework for achieving equality of opportunity without regard to sex, (b) to bring practice in closer accord with merit principles through the elimination of attitudes, customs and habits which have previously denied women entry into certain occupations as well as into high-level positions throughout the career service, and (c) to encourage qualified women to compete in examinations for federal employment and participate in training programs leading to advancement. In addition the commission issued a directive that it would only agree to selective certification based on sex if the following conditions prevail: (a) when sharing of common sleeping quarters is required, (b) when institutional or custodial services can properly be performed only by a member of the same sex as the recipients of the Services [10].

In August of 1969, President Richard M. Nixon issued Executive Order 11478 which was the strongest and most comprehensive executive order on equal employment opportunity to be issued by any President. This order directed each department and agency of the federal government to "establish and maintain an affirmative action program of equal employment opportunity for all civilian employees and applicants . . ." To implement the executive order the Civil Service Commission made the Federal Women's Program part of the Equal Employment Opportunity Programs. All agencies were directed to appoint a Federal Women's Program coordinator or an advisory committee to serve on the staff of the agency's Director of Equal Employment Opportunity who is usually a person at the assistant secretary level.

Finding that this still had not substantially increased the number of women executives in federal employment, President Nixon issued a memorandum for the heads of executive departments and agencies on April 21, 1971 in which he called for more use of women at executive levels. He directed agencies to take the following actions: Develop and put into action a plan for attracting more qualified women to top appointive positions (GS 16 through Presidential appointees) in each department or agency; develop and put into action a plan for significantly increasing the number of women, career and appointive, in mid-level positions (GS 13 to 15); to ensure that substantial numbers of the vacancies on advisory boards and committees are filled with well-qualified women. Finally, the President requested that each agency designate an overall coordinator responsible for these actions and that he be provided with the name. He indicated that his special assistant, Fred Malek, would be monitoring the project. Subsequently, President Nixon appointed Barbara Hackman Franklin as special assistant in the White House staff specifically to recruit more women to high-level positions.

The most recent piece of legislation designed to change the status of women in federal employment is the Equal Opportunity Act of 1972 which includes federal employees and agencies under the equal employment opportunity provisions of the Civil Rights Act of 1964 for the first time. The Civil Service Commission is given direct authority to see that all personnel actions in federal government are free from discrimination. This responsibility for state and local jurisdictions is assigned to the Equal Employment Opportunity Commission. Among the key provisions is the requirement that federal agencies submit Equal Employment Opportunity Affirmative Action plans to the commission annually. Each action plan must provide for programs of training and education which will afford employees an opportunity to acquire skills and abilities needed to compete for advancement to positions of greater responsibility. In order to implement the provisions of the act, the Civil Service Commission has issued Federal Personnel Manual directives which lay out the provisions for reviewing the plans and for on-site inspections as well as the procedures for handling complaints and appeals. In addition, the coverage has been expanded to include the regions as well as the central offices of executive agencies [11].

A Composite Picture of Federal Executives

The legislative and administrative actions taken since 1967 point to women receiving greater equity in employment in the federal service in the future than they have in the past. In studying the current status of women in the federal service, it is possible to examine a number of characteristics of federal executives and make some comparisons of male and female executives. In examining the distribution of women executives by grade and agency several hypotheses can be tested.

1. Gender makes no difference in predicting success as measured by high grade.
2. Women are not clustered in a specific occupational group at the executive levels.
3. The number of women in managerial/executive positions (GS 13 and above) has not increased proportionally to men in these grades.

The study is based on the population of the Federal Executive Inventory as of July 1, 1972. The universe is composed: total population 35,538; male, 34,700; female, 838; female percentage of total, 2.3.

Table 7.2. The Comparative Distribution of Males and Females by Grade

Grade	Male	Female
GS 15 and equivalent	75.8%	87.6%
GS 16 and equivalent	13.3	8.1
GS 17 and equivalent	5.2	3.1
GS 18 and equivalent	2.9	0.7
Special Authorization	2.8	0.5

Table 7.2 demonstrates the dramatic difference between the males and females. Sheer numbers (34,700 to 838) indicate that presently a male has a much greater chance of success in the Federal Executive Service than a female. The comparative distribution percentage in the top four grades adds emphasis to this disparity.

Hypothesis one must be rejected. Indeed, there is so little variance in the distribution of gender that the variable identifying gender was not at all related to the common space defined by the other career structure vari-

Table 7.3. Federal Executive Service Identif/Variables Used in Career Structure[a]

Variable	Mean	Standard deviation	Cases
Gender	1.0236	0.1517	35540
Year of birth	21.1322	9.3924	35605
Grade	15.3741	0.7477	35607
Veterans preference	1.7846	0.6679	35535
Number of professional societies (member)	2.9318	2.0037	19767
Number of professional societies (officer)	0.7900	1.9806	29686
Number of agencies employed in at GS-13 and above	1.3988	0.8797	30314
Number of agencies employed in throughout federal career	1.7976	1.2514	30246
Number of awards received from agency in which employed	1.6542	2.2516	29857
Number of awards received from other organizations	0.6073	1.7037	29601
Number of employees supervised	4.3709	1.5902	29922
Year entered federal service	50.7581	9.7974	29402
Grade at entry in federal service	8.4365	4.4019	28561
Education level at entry in federal service	6.9701	2.2747	29906
Years of federal civilian service	16.2428	8.9356	29864
Years in present agency	12.4438	8.8559	29863
Years of military service	2.9300	4.0213	29630
Number of times left government service	0.1942	0.7583	29610
Years in grade 11	2.1805	1.4385	16890
Years in grade 12	2.5269	1.6716	19317
Years in grade 13	3.0890	1.9206	22306
Years in grade 14	3.7241	2.2012	24551
Number of times changed jobs in last five years	0.9035	0.9712	27938
Highest level of education	7.5807	1.9931	30619
Number of honor society memberships	0.6476	1.2351	30367

[a]Executive Inventory Data, July 26, 1972.

ables. The communality of the gender variable was .049. That is, less than 5% of the variance in gender is associated with the overall career structure of federal executives. The decision to reject the hypothesis is further strengthened by evidence from Table 7.1. Not only do women occupy less than 5% of any grade from GS 13 through 18, but, also, women tend to cluster in the lower GS grades.

The distribution of women at the senior levels by agency is shown in Table 7.3. The latest official distribution is October 31, 1970. According to the report the Departments of Health, Education, and Welfare, Labor, and the Library of Congress show the largest percentages of women at the executive level. In terms of numbers, HEW and Veterans Administration have the most women. This would seem to follow an expected pattern that these agencies have the most programs related to the educational backgrounds traditionally associated with women.

Comparing highest level of education, it is found that 25.4% (7588) of the men have a Ph.D. or equivalent (e.g., M.D.) while 49.3% (340) of the women do. This is probably directly related to the clustering of women in the medical occupation in government service. In occupations, 23.9% of the male federal executives are in general administration, followed by 17.1% in engineering and 13.5% in medical. Three occupational groups thus account for 54.5% of male executives. For women executives the largest single occupational group is medical 37.9%, followed by administration 19.9%, and social science with 13.2%. Thus, three occupational groups account for 71.0% of female executives. Hypothesis 2 must be rejected since women are clustered in a specific group.

Hypothesis 3 is tentatively rejected. There are 1601 more women in managerial/executive levels (GS 13–18) as of October 31, 1971, than in 1967 (see Table 7.1). However, the percentage of increase for the top six grades is only 0.2. Preliminary data suggests that there have been further gains in these grades between October 1971, and June 30, 1972, which marked the close of fiscal 1972.

A related comparison of years of federal service shows a marked difference for women and men. The modal group for males is 20–24 years of service (20.3%), closely followed by 15–19 years (19%); for females the modal is 5–9 years (22%), followed by 10–14 years (18.4%). A shorter service period for women is indicative of the move into full-time employment by women in the society as a whole, in the last ten years, as well as the pressures which have been exerted for employment of women by government. This is also reflected in the mode of entry figures. Entry for 55% of males was by competitive examination while for 49.1% of females entry was by some other means. However, since the actual numbers involved are small, the difference may be significant in terms of determining career patterns. The entry grade pattern was somewhat surprising. For males the modal entry grade was 1–2

(27.2%) and a second clustering at grades 5-6 (18%). For women the modal grade was also 1-2 (37.2%), but the secondary clustering took place at grades 13-14 (18.5%). This is probably related to entry being by means other than examination. Together these figures on years of service and entry mode suggest a dynamic component to the male/female balance in the executive service.

In addition to testing the three hypotheses, cross-tabulations were made with grade-controlling for sex on the following items: age, duty station, and birth state. These demographic variables provide some environmental information on career structures.

In examining the cross-tabulations of grade with age, it was found that there was no significant relation between age and grade for males. There was a very weak one for females. (Raw chi square 58.49 with 56 degrees of freedom, significance 13839.) The modal age category for males and females is 51-55 years but the next largest clustering for males is in the 46-50 bracket while for females it is 56-60, an indication that the female executive is currently somewhat older than the male.

The two final categories, duty station and birth state, did not show any significant differences by gender. Well over half of the executives, male and female, are stationed in the Washington, D.C. area. The states of birth reflect population distributions of 10 to 20 years ago. It is worthy of note that 6.2% of the males and 15.8% of females in these higher grades were born outside the United States.

Using modal groups and median characteristics tends to present a limited and static picture. It would be a mistake to assume that there is a typical federal executive. However, there are some clusterings around certain characteristics which suggests a pattern.

Career Structure of the Federal Executive Service

In order to pursue questions of the relative position of men and women at the executive level as well as to suggest whether government service does offer a career alternative for professional women, it becomes necessary to ask the question "What is the pattern of career variation in the Federal Executive Service?" Subsidiary questions include "What is the structure of success (grade)?", "Is it predictable?", and "What is the importance of gender?" Two specific hypotheses follow from these questions:

1. Career patterns of women are no different from the overall career pattern.
2. There is no significant relation between educational level, length of service, grade at entry, and grade achieved.

The analytic model used for the study includes the use of factor analysis for developing the structure [12]. One factor analysis was used for the entire universe (35,540 cases) and a subsequent one was done for the subset of females (838 cases) [13].

The variables were all developed from data contained in the Executive Inventory Record [14]. The inventory is a questionnaire developed by the Bureau of Executive Manpower of the U.S. Civil Service Commission which has been used since 1967 to develop a manpower management system for staffing executive positions within the federal government. The record contains demographic information, work experience, education, publications, awards, promotions, and career interests.

The 25 variables used in the factor analysis are gender, year of birth, grade, veteran preference score, number of memberships in professional societies, number of professional societies an officer of, number of agencies employed in at GS 13 and above, number of agencies employed in throughout federal career, number of awards received from agency in which employed, number of awards received from other organizations, number of employees supervised, year entered federal service, grade at entry in federal service, education level at entry in federal service, years of federal civilian service, years in present agency, years of military service, numbers of times left government service, years spent in grade 11, years spent in grade 12, years spent in grade 13, years spent in grade 14, number of times changed jobs in last 5 years, highest level of education, number of honor society memberships. Statistical descriptors for these variables for the entire universe are given. (See Table 7.3.)

The matrix factored is the correlation matrix with the largest off-diagonal element used as the estimate of communality. Seven factors having eigenvalues greater than one were rotated and account for 57.4% of the total variance [15]. The varimax rotation to simple structure is displayed in Table 7.4.

Interpretation of the Factors

Factor 1—Service

There are positive loadings for "years of federal service," "years in present agency," "years in grades 11, 12, and 13" with a lower contribution from "years in grade 14"; negative loadings for "year of birth" and "year entering federal service" with low negative contribution from "number of times changed jobs in the last five years." It is clear that "Time" is an important

Table 7.4. Varimax Rotated Factor Matrix

Variable	Factor 1, Service	Factor 2, Education	Factor 3, Agency mobility	Factor 4, Grade	Factor 5, Veteran	Factor 6, Entry	Factor 7, Honors	Communality
GENDER	0.01952	0.05444	0.00020	-0.04222	-0.20503	0.04762	0.00503	0.04946
YRBIRTH	-0.65296	0.02515	-0.09621	-0.11696	-0.11504	-0.00861	-0.04331	0.47288
GRADE	-0.09089	0.07938	0.05746	0.91545	0.01075	-0.04010	0.06832	0.86230
VETPREF	-0.06806	-0.03444	0.00921	-0.05743	0.59475	-0.04201	-0.00352	0.36470
PROFSOC	0.08343	0.37684	-0.01596	-0.00111	-0.07672	0.14212	0.37996	0.31968
PROFOFF	0.04153	0.15849	0.03422	0.01152	-0.06114	0.01406	0.45008	0.23466
NOAGY13	-0.05465	-0.05172	0.74820	0.02326	0.01379	0.09103	0.07010	0.57940
NOAGYTOT	0.01226	-0.12015	0.88667	-0.00928	0.03301	-0.14795	-0.00471	0.82386
AGYAWRD	-0.03048	-0.19009	0.03455	-0.00016	0.13729	-0.12573	0.30324	0.16487
OTHAWARD	-0.00746	0.02580	0.03221	0.02876	0.01925	0.03477	0.45466	0.21088
EMPSPV	0.07656	-0.28055	0.05666	0.28665	0.22153	0.00013	0.32769	0.32640
YRENTER	-0.68717	0.20800	-0.19610	-0.33293	0.00014	0.62637	0.03424	1.05828
GDEENTR	-0.16501	0.34002	-0.13592	0.04551	-0.00499	0.82019	0.04751	0.83839
EDENTER	-0.03050	0.83266	-0.07070	-0.00402	-0.08765	0.33310	-0.03829	0.81937
YRSSVC	0.75356	-0.26152	0.12333	0.07709	-0.04189	-0.56409	-0.01780	0.97766
YRSAGY	0.63350	-0.15191	-0.28088	0.08805	-0.04608	-0.44983	-0.00292	0.71553
YRSMIL	-0.07646	-0.04255	-0.04082	-0.00012	0.65328	0.22747	0.04675	0.49003
TIMESLFT	-0.00768	0.01997	0.16321	0.01485	-0.01476	-0.02236	0.01451	0.02824
YRSI1	0.41462	-0.05997	-0.04592	0.01734	-0.06262	-0.01369	0.06196	0.18586
YRSI2	0.45609	-0.02711	-0.01102	-0.01051	-0.06743	-0.01106	0.05219	0.21638
YRSI3	0.45333	0.01509	0.01927	-0.04275	-0.05545	-0.02165	0.00337	0.21149
YRSI4	0.39842	0.04944	-0.02669	-0.11465	-0.00873	-0.04666	-0.03435	0.17847
TMCHGJOB	-0.29740	-0.13084	0.10459	0.06949	0.05411	0.06837	0.08312	0.13585
HEDLEV	-0.05594	0.93402	0.01309	-0.02482	-0.05358	0.08921	0.00867	0.88721
HONSOC	-0.03485	0.27691	-0.00089	0.04751	-0.07196	0.00603	0.16262	0.11181

factor in the case of most individuals in the upper grades, indicating that executive positions are generally filled from within.

Factor 2—Education

There are positive contributions for "educational level at entry into federal service" and "highest level of education attained" with lower positive loadings for "number of professional and honor society memberships" as well as "entering grade"—an indication that federal executives are well qualified educationally.

Factor 3—Agency Mobility

Positive loadings are present for "number of agencies employed in" with a lower loading for "number of times left federal service." This is an interesting factor in that it suggests something that other statistical profiles have not, namely that while most federal executives have worked in a single agency, mobility has not been a negative feature of some career patterns.

Factor 4—Grade

There is a single positive loading for "present grade." There is a lower negative loading for "year of entry into federal service." There is no correlation between "entry grade" and "present grade." This reflects what is known as the generation gap in government service, with those who entered the service before World War II having entered at lower grades and promotions coming much more slowly than in recent years.

Factor 5—Veteran

There are positive loadings for "veteran preference" and "length of military service" and a lower negative loading for "gender."

Factor 6—Entry

There are positive loadings for "year" and "grade at entry" with a lower loading for "education at entry into federal service"; there are negative loadings for "years of total" and "present agency service." This factor accounts for only 4.8% of variance and probably reflects lateral entry.

Factor 7—Honors

There are positive loadings for "number of offices held in professional societies" and "awards received from other agencies"; lower positive contributions from "number of professional society memberships" and "awards received from present agency" and from "number of employees supervised." The correlation between acknowledgment of merit and expansion of domain suggests that extrovertism is a component of the career structure of the federal executive.

Analysis of Career Structure of Females

The population of females in the Federal Executive Inventory was factored independently (838 cases). Statistical descriptors for the variables for the subset are given. (See Table 7.5.) Results of this study are under analysis in order to study this population independently of the larger universe of the entire Federal Executive Service. However the interest of the present investigation was of women within the context of the executive service, therefore, analytic rotation to simple structure was not performed. Instead the factor pattern of women in the federal executive structure was rotated to maximum

Table 7.5 Statistical Indicators for Women in Federal Executive Service

Variable	Mean	Standard deviation	Cases
YRBIRTH	20.4391	10.2454	838
GRADE	15.1742	0.5087	838
VETPREF	1.0919	0.4175	838
PROFSOC	3.5836	2.1914	538
PROFOFF	1.0459	2.2861	654
NOAGY13	1.2827	0.9203	672
NOAGYTOT	1.6731	1.3187	670
AGYAWRD	1.1411	1.8557	659
OTHAWRD	0.5926	2.4312	653
EMPLSPV	3.4916	1.5173	657
YRENTER	53.0123	10.6438	650
GDEENTR	9.2836	4.7096	603
EDENTER	8.1409	2.2732	674
YRSSVC	13.9626	9.3305	668
YRSAGY	10.9548	8.6741	664
YRSMIL	0.3541	1.8033	658
TIMESLFT	0.2454	0.5186	648
YRS11	2.5090	1.7081	277
YRS12	2.7461	1.8192	319
YRS13	3.4390	2.0030	410
YRS14	3.7345	2.0860	501
TMCHGJOB	0.8128	0.9449	625
HEDLEV	8.4993	1.9441	689
HONSOC	0.8389	1.2183	683

fit with the total FES space, yielding a contextualized factor structure [16]. The new matrix showing the fit of the female career structure in the common space is shown in Table 7.7.

Interpretation of Factors

Factor 1—Service

There are high positive loadings for "years of federal service," "years in present agency," "years in grade 11," "12," "13," "14"; negative loadings for "year of birth," "year entering federal service" with a low negative contribution for "number of times changed job in the last five years." This factor is virtually identical to Factor 1 for the entire universe.

Factor 2—Education

There are high positive loadings for "educational level" with a lower positive loading for "grade at entry" and "membership in professional societies" with a low negative loading for "total years of federal service." This factor also parallels the education factor for the total universe, although the loadings were higher in the female population.

Factor 3—Agency Mobility

The high positive loadings are for "number of agencies employed" and "number of agencies employed in at GS 13 and above" with a very low loading for "times left federal service" and "times changed jobs." This factor, as in the total universe, needs more study. The loadings are sufficiently higher for females to indicate that agency mobility is a more distinct component of career patterns for women then men.

Factor 4—Grade

There is a low positive loading for "grade" and low negative loading for "number of years at grade 12." This factor is much more ambiguous in the female career structure than the entire universe.

Factor 5—Veteran

There are positive loadings for "veterans preference" and "years of military service." Thus, unexpectedly, this factor is as omnipresent in the female career pattern as the male's.

Table 7.6. Simple Structure Factor Matrix—Female

Variable	Factor 1, Service	Factor 2, Education	Factor 3, Agency mobility	Factor 4, Grade	Factor 5, Veteran	Factor 6, Grade at entry	Factor 7, Professionalism	Communality
YRBIRTH	0.32709	-0.31989	-0.25390	0.02414	0.20899	0.20399	0.10215	0.37008
GRADE	-0.04293	-0.10742	0.17420	-0.12527	0.16591	-0.15497	0.18445	0.14498
VETPREF	-0.04994	-0.80302	0.01555	-0.23232	-0.50274	0.09212	0.02795	0.32561
PROFSOC	0.08272	0.26227	0.32420	-0.36023	0.13547	0.17994	-0.06014	0.36484
PROFOFF	-0.04529	-0.01604	0.40741	-0.35440	0.07179	0.11463	0.03658	0.31352
NOAGY13	-0.06335	-0.26752	0.66318	0.20348	-0.02381	-0.08715	0.00633	0.56500
NOAGYTOT	-0.37052	-0.39582	0.60939	0.35297	-0.00895	0.06332	0.02397	0.79457
AGYAWRD	-0.34408	-0.14625	-0.06253	-0.23106	0.10553	0.00308	0.00950	0.20831
OTHAWRD	0.03000	0.01561	0.17306	-0.32002	0.09281	-0.12575	0.02052	0.15835
EMPSPV	-0.17408	-0.17114	0.24046	-0.36338	0.05612	-0.13929	0.00448	0.27203
YRENTER	0.90032	-0.15608	-0.13999	-0.06383	0.01000	-0.13033	-0.00016	0.87569
GREENTR	0.82583	0.24348	0.19422	-0.05768	0.00407	-0.38761	0.00222	0.93259
EDENTER	0.69912	0.57385	0.20800	0.09140	0.00165	0.12707	0.06631	0.89024
YRSSVC	-0.94380	0.25996	0.01413	0.03080	0.03992	0.02081	0.04454	0.96349
YRSAGY	-0.77055	0.41548	-0.15109	-0.07425	0.08015	-0.02415	0.23532	0.85709
YRSMIL	0.00723	-0.10468	0.01705	-0.20911	-0.53255	0.02127	0.15575	0.36335
TIMESLFT	-0.06470	-0.21892	0.14403	0.09912	-0.06832	0.12658	-0.05713	0.10663
YRS11	-0.26472	0.34474	-0.04844	-0.08348	0.00967	-0.00265	-0.11222	0.21093
YRS12	-0.29484	0.33750	0.07541	-0.09392	-0.04123	-0.00978	-0.47636	0.44406
YRS13	-0.25519	0.44458	0.16626	0.14446	-0.09238	-0.18437	0.11917	0.36802
YRS14	-0.16250	0.41811	0.11845	0.14403	-0.03315	-0.10957	0.00951	0.24919
TMCHGJOB	0.08107	-0.45378	0.11859	-0.09307	0.03353	0.04356	-0.11369	0.25116
HEDLEV	0.61077	0.53501	0.24392	0.07496	-0.03244	0.32304	0.04894	0.83220
HONSOC	0.05103	0.03519	0.09256	-0.14471	0.15808	0.16559	0.13465	0.10389

Table 7.7. Female Career Structure (rotated)

Variable	Factor 1, Service	Factor 2, Education	Factor 3, Agency mobility	Factor 4, Grade	Factor 5, Veteran	Factor 6, Grade at entry	Factor 7, Profes-sionalism
YRBIRTH	-0.5629	0.0712	-0.1347	-0.0173	-0.1392	-0.0914	-0.0227
GRADE	-0.0304	0.0076	0.0753	0.3522	0.0035	0.0358	0.1110
VETPREF	0.0052	-0.0260	0.0359	-0.1687	0.5396	-0.0086	0.0540
PROFSOC	0.1621	0.3439	0.0154	-0.0003	-0.0117	0.1256	0.4503
PROFOFF	0.0559	0.1868	0.2002	0.1514	0.1237	0.0503	0.4397
NOAGY13	0.0184	0.0327	0.7102	0.2046	0.0050	0.1291	0.0135
NOAGYTOT	0.0440	-0.1274	0.8375	0.1718	-0.0297	-0.2073	-0.0119
AGYAWRD	-0.0392	-0.2524	-0.0391	0.1451	0.0595	-0.2150	0.2651
OTHAWRD	0.0380	0.0427	-0.0254	0.2022	0.0724	0.1780	0.2754
EMPSPV	0.0335	-0.1401	0.1219	0.2655	0.1617	0.0813	0.3646
YRENTER	-0.6139	0.2756	-0.2362	-0.0592	-0.0245	0.5771	-0.1675
GREENTR	-0.1364	0.4282	-0.1435	0.0996	-0.0591	0.8148	-0.1779
EDENTER	0.0635	0.7835	-0.1299	-0.1829	-0.1508	0.4160	-0.1580
YRSSVC	0.6979	-0.3197	0.0648	0.1344	-0.0022	-0.5768	0.1300
YRSAGY	0.6601	-0.1498	-0.2280	0.2300	0.0284	-0.5354	0.0696
YRSMIL	-0.0357	0.0150	0.0249	-0.0688	-0.5944	0.0156	-0.0410
TIMESLFT	-0.1044	-0.0580	0.2782	-0.0719	0.0358	-0.0856	0.0203
YRS11	0.4009	-0.0370	-0.1487	-0.0788	-0.0408	-0.0782	0.1094
YRS12	0.4916	-0.1755	0.0045	-0.3019	-0.1012	0.0893	0.2470
YRS13	0.5559	0.1026	0.0292	0.1222	0.0132	-0.0165	-0.1759
YRS14	0.4628	0.1077	0.0015	0.0144	-0.0761	0.0158	-0.1286
TMCHGJOB	-0.3606	-0.1588	0.2366	0.0140	0.0426	0.0658	0.1797
HEDLEV	0.0524	0.8127	-0.0476	-0.2818	-0.1110	0.2626	-0.0653
HONSOC	-0.0594	0.2174	-0.0206	0.0963	-0.0336	-0.0840	0.1859

Factor 6—Grade at Entry

There is a high positive loading for "grade at entry" with positive loadings for "year of entry" and "education level at entry." There are negative loadings for "total years of federal service" and "number of years with present agency." Again the loadings on this factor for females is close enough to the universe factor to suspect that they both reflect recent lateral entries. Further study of this factor relative to Factor 2 might provide some additional insights.

Factor 7—Professionalism

There are positive loadings for "number of professional society memberships" and "number of offices held in professional societies" with low positive loadings for "number of employees supervised," "agency awards" and "other awards," though the same variable loaded on this factor as on Factor 7— Honors—of the universe. The loading pattern was sufficiently different from that of the total universe to suggest that this factor is only slightly related to personal recognition in contrast to professional achievement.

Trends for the Future

The study indicates that the movement of women into the higher echelons of the federal hierarchy is not really rapid nor is it quiet. While the total number of women at the executive level of the federal government is not large, the increase is significant. More important, there are now women visible in policy positions who are calling for action. Women are making considerable noise against traditional employment practices that discriminate against them. Evidence of this is the increased attention that major media sources have been directing toward the placing of women in executive positions in the past year.

The executive branch has been moving in a variety of ways to implement the employment of women at higher grades. For instance, in order to facilitate hiring of mature women at higher grades, guidelines have been developed which will allow equating of volunteer work with full-time employment [17].

Agencies have been urged by the Administration to provide women in the Executive Seminar Center and Federal Executive Institute reflects this emphasis (see Table 7.8).

Another small, but positive, event was that 1971 marked the first time in the 23 year history of the Arthur S. Flemming Award for outstanding contributions to government that the recipients were women as well as men.

Despite there having been a grade rollback and a reduction in force during

Table 7.8. Executive Seminar Centers (GS 13–16 Eligible)

Year	Total women	Berkeley	Kings Point	Oak Ridge[a]	Percent of total[b]
1967	28	11	17	0	2.3
1968	31	6	25	0	2.5
1969	30	14	16	0	2.4
1970	31	8	23	0	2.4
1971	53	22	31	0	3.9
1972	117	27	46	44	6.0

Federal Executive Institute (GS 15 and Above Eligible)

Year	Total participants	Women	Percent of total
1969	221	4	1.8
1970	269	4	1.5
1971	266	6	2.3
1972	239	12	5.0

[a]Opened in FY 1972.

[b]Percent of "Total participants."

fiscal 1972, women not only gained in total numbers but they were promoted and appointed to key policy and program positions which heretofore had been the preserve of males. The appointment of a White House staff assistant to work full-time on recruiting women into the public service has made possible the building of a talent bank from which agencies can draw when vacancies occur at executive levels. The Administration has appointed or promoted (career and noncareer) 125 women to high level (GS 16 and above) positions between January 21, 1969 and July 1, 1972. These appointments range widely and include women from a variety of occupational groups. Over half the positions are ones in which this is the first time a woman has held the office. Many of these are in traditionally male areas such as regulatory agencies. Women now head the Federal Maritime Commission and the Tariff Commission. Increasingly women are heading up major research programs in health and science. Women have long been employed in personnel fields, but the last four years has seen a marked increase in the numbers of women who are top administrators for personnel and management in major departments such as Treasury.

Among the departments showing progress both in numbers of women in top positions as well as substantive responsibility for programs are State, Defense, Health, Education, and Welfare, and Labor. An informal survey of departments and executive agencies indicates progress in the GS 15–18 and above range. There are currently 96 women in the top executive levels in the Department of State. Defense has approximately 100 at the top plus five women who are at the Brigadier General-Admiral level of the military.

Traditionally male departments such as Treasury, Agriculture, and Interior have 20, 15, 18 women at the top, respectively. Other executive agencies showing gains are Office of Management and Budget, Library of Congress, and the Veterans Administration. Many departments and agencies are actively recruiting women with specialized skills. An example is Justice's search for women lawyers.

Approximately 20 agencies have filed Affirmative Action Plans with the Civil Service Commission by July of 1972. Twenty-three agencies have appointed or are recruiting at present for full-time directors of the women's program at grade levels GS 13-16. Some 80 smaller agencies have designated someone to coordinate women's programs. Additional positions for fiscal 1973 have been allocated to the Civil Service Commission to allow for careful monitoring of Affirmative Action Programs as called for by the Equal Employment Opportunity Act of 1972.

Of significance for the mobility of women in the career executive service is the fact that in the GS 16 and above group, 50% of current executives will be eligible to retire under existing statutes by 1976 and in the feeder group of GS 15's the number is 48% [18]. If the regulations are liberalized as currently being discussed in legislative proposals, the number of eligibles increases to 62% and 56% in these categories. Thus, there is a potential here for women to move to executive levels without an increase of new positions [19].

Recruitment will be a major factor in ensuring that women are in positions that will allow their competing for these choice positions. The factor analysis of the career structure gives some reason to believe that the hiring, promotion, and reward system for women is frequently based on technical competency while for a man it is based on peer relations and anticipated long-range development.

One of the difficulties in placing women in executive positions has been stereotyped notions holding women unsuitable for top positions as a result of inherent psychological and emotional traits. These myths are being destroyed as a result of research work such as that of Ramey [20]. Management journals are increasingly calling attention to these fallacies [21]. Beliefs based on half-truths and myths have more influence on behavior unfortunately than do statements of fact.

A second problem area in the mobility of women at the executive levels is the attitude of women themselves. The discrimination against women at the higher echelons is of such long standing that at present women tend not to compete for the choice positions. This pessimism is so deep-seated that it extends to the failure to complete the paperwork necessary to be included on lists of referrals. Casual discussion with some of the women presently at the GS 15 and above levels revealed that they had not completed the Executive Inventory Questionnaire. Further questioning revealed that they felt the FES would be useless in furthering their careers. Granted that many males had a similar reaction to the questionnaire, it seemed that the women's rejection has a different basis. The females rejection appeared to be based on the perception of professional discrimination as reported by Tinker in a systematic sampling of women in government [22]. The Tinker study focused on attitudes and perceptions while the present study is limited to empirical data and, therefore, the two studies are not comparable but the same underlying cognitive affects appear present in both studies.

There appears to be sufficient and clear legal and administrative machinery to cope with the problem of sex discrimination in government employment. For instance, all of the recommendations made in the area by the Task Force on the Status of Women of the American Society for Public Administrators at their annual meeting in April 1972 have been or are in the process of being implemented. The problem, thus, lies elsewhere. It is necessary that consciousness of the problem be raised to such a level that even unintentional discrimination can not go unnoticed. This will require diligence and perseverance on the parts of those concerned. Granted that acceptance of women at the top in government seems slow, it appears that recent promotions and appointments of women to policy positions in the federal government are speeding up the process. Although length of service is a major factor in the career structure of the federal executive, the pattern indicates that the system also rewards merit. Perhaps, we are reaching the time when a woman can succeed in the public service if she is perceptive, understanding, ambitious, and highly qualified!

NOTES

1. *Congressional Globe*, 41st Congress, 2d Session, **Vol. XCII**, Part V, p. 4354, 1870. As quoted in *Report of the Committee on Federal Employment*, President's Commission on the Status of Women. Washington, D.C.: GPO, 1963, p. 7.

2. Richard M. Nixon, "Memorandum for the Heads of Executive Departments and Agencies on Women in Government, April 21, 1971."

3. "Women in Government," *USN&WR*, p. 62 (January 17, 1972).

4. A previous study by Shirley D. Patterson, "A Comparison of Some Characteristics of Men and Women Employed at Senior Levels of the Federal Service." Unpublished M.A. Thesis, George Washington University, 1965, was based on a sample of 124 men and 124 women paired for rank and type of job. The questionnaire return was 43 women and 62 men. The data are not comparable to the present study.

5. Bureau of Executive Manpower, United States Civil Service Commission, *Executive Manpower in the Federal Service—January, 1972*. Washington, D.C.: GPO, 1972.

6. For a detailed and complete study of this topic see: Helene Markoff, "The Federal Women's Program," *Pub. Admin. Rev.* **22**, No. 2, pp. 144–151 (Mar./Apr. 1972).

7. It is of interest to note that though the venerable Chairman of the House Judiciary Committee, Emmanuel Celler of New York, proposed a bill to create a Commission on the Status of Women in each Congress from 1946 on, he was defeated in the 1972 primary by a feminist candidate who made much of his opposition to the Equal Rights Amendment.

8. Evelyn Harrison, "The Quiet Revolution," *Civil Ser. Jour.* (Oct./Dec. 1962).

9. *United States Government Organization Manual, 1964–65.* Washington, D.C.: GPO, 1964.

10. *Federal Personnel Manual, 332–15.*

11. See Civil Service Commission OL 273–659. The guidelines will be printed as Appendix A-6 of Federal Personnel Manual 273–73. For General Equal Opportunity Regulations consult FPM Chapter 713.

12. R. J. Rummel, *Applied Factor Analysis.* Evanston, Ill.: Northwestern University Press, 1970.

13. N. H. Nie, D. H. Bent, and C. H. Hull, *Statistical Package for the Social Sciences.* New York, McGraw-Hill, 1970.

14. Bureau of Executive Manpower, U.S. Civil Service Commission, Standard Form 161, November 1967.

15.

Factor	Eigenvalue	Variance (%)	Cumulative %
1	4.55347	18.2	18.2
2	2.56552	10.3	28.5
3	1.90824	7.6	36.1
4	1.65086	6.6	42.7
5	1.37726	5.5	48.2
6	1.19218	4.8	53.0
7	1.10312	4.4	57.4

16. Donald J. Veldman, *Fortran Programming for the Behavioral Sciences.* New York: Holt, Rinehart and Winston, 1967, pp. 237–241. The technique is called RELATE and developed by H. F. Kaiser. The procedure is to arbitrarily equate the origins and factor-vector orientations of the two structures, and then to determine analytically the degree of rotation of the factor axes of one of the structures which will result in a maximum degree of overlap between corresponding test vectors in the two structures. Overall correlation was .91.

17. See Federal Personnel Manual Supplement 337–79, Chapter II, Item 3.

18. U.S. Civil Service Commission, Bureau of Executive Manpower, *Executive Manpower in the Federal Service.* Washington, D.C.: GPO, Jan. 1972, p. 10.

19. Similarly, it has been noted there will be an acute shortage of managers in business within 5 years, particularly in the 35–45 age bracket. See Estill Brechanan "The Growing Opportunities for Women in Management," *Management Review* (Sept. 1968).

20. Estelle Ramey, "Men's Cycles (They Have Them Too, You Know)," *MS,* pp. 8–14 (Spring 1972).

21. Lawrence C. Hackamack, and Alan B. Solid, "The Woman Executive," *Business Horizons,* pp. 89–93 (Apr. 1972).

22. Irene Tinker, "Nonacademic Professional Political Scientists," *American Behavioral Scientist,* **15**, No. 2, pp. 206–212 (Nov./Dec. 1971).

Chapter

8

Ideology and the Law:
Sexism and Supreme Court Decisions

Susan Kaufman Purcell

> . . . the members of the Supreme Court are children of their time, and
> a chronicle of Court doctrine tends to be, in a general way, an intellectual
> history of America.

ROBERT G. McCLOSKEY [1]

The Constitution of the United States is an ambiguous document whose numerous provisions have lent themselves to a variety of conflicting interpretations. In the process of interpretation, the conscious and unconscious personal values and beliefs of the justices, as well as of society in general, come into play. The Constitution that was the basis of the 1896 decision of *Plessy v. Ferguson,* which established the doctrine of "separate but equal" with respect to the Negro race was not, for example, significantly different from the Constitution upon which the Warren Court based its 1954 decision in *Brown v. Board of Education* that "separate" was inherently unequal [2]. What has changed was the attitude of the justices and of the population at large toward Negroes. Racism was no longer a morally and socially acceptable ideology [3] and as a result, the Supreme Court began interpreting the Constitution in such a way as to strike down, rather than uphold, racist laws.

Unfortunately, the same statement cannot be made regarding sexism and Supreme Court decisions. During the past century, the image of the nature, role, functions and interests of woman as reflected in Supreme Court decisions

131

has remained substantially unaltered, with two very recent exceptions, despite the woman's suffrage movement of the late 19th and early 20th century and the current feminist movement. This image of woman is blatantly sexist, for it betrays a belief that men and women have distinctive physical characteristics which determine their respective natures, functions, roles and interests in society, with the implication that the male sex is, and has the right to be, superior [4].

This sexist stereotyping in Supreme Court decisions has had profound negative implications for the status of women in American society. This chapter argues that sexist ideology has served to expand the legal definition of what constitutes "reasonable" discrimination against women to the point where the line between reasonable and arbitrary discrimination has virtually been destroyed. Another way of stating the argument is that in the presence of strong sexist beliefs on the part of most Supreme Court justices, it becomes extremely difficult ever to regard discrimination against women as arbitrary or invidious.

In support of the argument, Part I of this chapter presents an overview of the major Supreme Court decisions affecting the status of American women. These decisions are then compared in Part II with analogous decisions involving other classes of individuals to show how general principles of justice held applicable to others have been systematically declared irrelevant to women. Part III analyzes the legal bases or criteria for discrimination among classes of people under the Constitution of the United States, and Part IV demonstrates how sexist ideology provides a basis for legal discrimination against women. Finally, Part V examines whether a majority of the Supreme Court can be expected in the near future to declare discrimination against women unconstitutional.

An Overview of Supreme Court Decisions on the Status of Women

The Supreme Court decisions which deal with the status of women can be divided into four general categories based on the nature of the question at issue. The first category is comprised of decisions involving the right of women to enter certain professions. The second consists of decisions concerning conditions under which women may labor. The remaining two categories involve decisions regarding citizenship rights, such as the right to vote and to serve on juries, and finally, the issue of education.

Decisions dealing with the right of women to enter certain professions include both the earliest and the most recent Supreme Court decisions. The earliest was the 1872 case of *Bradwell v. The State* [5] in which the Court upheld an Illinois Supreme Court decision denying a license to practice law to women. The Court affirmed that the right to practice law was not one of the privileges and immunities guaranteed to citizens under the 14th Amendment and that the states have the right to regulate who may practice particular professions within their boundaries. A related case arose in 1894, when the Supreme Court, in *In re Lockwood, petitioner* [6], decided that states had the constitutional right to interpret the word "person" in a state statute so as to exclude women. As a result, a Virginia court decision to exclude women from practicing law in that state, despite a Virginia statute granting this right to persons admitted to the bar in other states, was upheld. Perhaps the best known decision in this category is that of *Goesaert v. Cleary* [7]. In this 1948 decision, the Supreme Court upheld a Michigan statute which prohibited women from being bartenders, with the exception of the wives or daughters of male bartenders.

A recent decision involving the issue of entrance of women into particular professions is that of *Phillips v. Martin Marietta Corporation* [8], a 1971 per curiam decision which is the only case to date involving Title VII of the 1964 Civil Rights Act. The Act forbids discrimination on the basis of sex, unless it can be shown that the job requires hiring a person of a particular sex (i.e., that the person's being of a particular sex is a bona fide occupational qualification). The issue before the Court was whether the Martin Marietta Corporation's policy of accepting job applications for certain high level jobs from fathers of preschool children but not from mothers of preschool children constituted discrimination against women. The Court decided that the Martin Marietta Corporation had not sufficiently proved its contention that mothers of preschool children tend to spend more time with them than do fathers of preschool children and, as a result, mothers of such children could not be expected to perform as well on the job as fathers of such children. The Court implied that if the Martin Marietta Corporation could furnish data substantiating its claim that mothers of preschool children spend more time with their offspring, there would be a legal basis for declaring the corporation's discriminatory policy constitutional.

The only decision in this area that challenges job stereotyping on the basis of sex is the June 1973 decision of *Pittsburgh Press v. The Pittsburgh Commission on Human Relations* [9]. Here, the Supreme Court barred the Pittsburgh Press from referring to sex in employment want ads unless the jobs advertised were not subject to the prohibition against sex discrimination in the Human Relations Ordinance of the City of Pittsburgh. The major issue in this case, however, was not the constitutionality of sex discrimination, but whether a prohibition against referring to sex in want ads constituted a violation of the 1st Amendment guarantee of freedom of the press.

The second category of decisions involves those which regulate the conditions under which women may labor. Most of these decisions deal with maximum hours and minimum wage laws. The prototype of the hours regulation cases is *Muller v. Oregon* (1908) [10] in which the Supreme Court upheld an Oregon statute which limited the number of hours of female (but not male) labor to a maximum of 10 per day. Subsequent decisions, such as those of *Riley v. Massachusetts, Bosley v. McLaughlin*, and *Miller v. Wilson* [11], all of which dealt with variations of the hours regulation issue, followed the *Muller* precedent and basically reiterated the Court's original opinion in *Muller*. The 1924 decision of *Radice v. New York* [12] was somewhat different in that the Court upheld the right of a state to prohibit certain kinds of female laborers (specifically, those who worked in restaurants in cities) from working between 10 PM and 6 AM.

The decisions regarding regulation of women's wages are less consistent than those involving hours regulation. In two decisions, *Adkins v. Children's Hospital* (1923) and *Morehead v. N.Y. ex rel Tipaldo* (1936) [13], the Court struck down minimum wage laws which applied only to women in the states and the federal district. These two decisions, however, proved to be temporary aberrations in a long line of discriminatory decisions and were subsequently overturned in the 1937 decision of *West Coast Hotel v. Parrish* [14], when the Supreme Court upheld state minimum wage laws which applied to women and children, but not to men.

A related decision which represents an important departure from tradition is that of *Frontiero and Frontiero v. Richardson* (1973) [15]. In that case, by a vote of eight to one, the Supreme Court invalidated armed services statutes which granted benefits to spouses of male members of the uniformed services while denying such benefits to spouses of female members, unless the latter spouses received over one-half of their support from the female armed services member. The significance of this decision will be discussed in the final section of this chapter.

In the third category of Supreme Court decisions which consists of those involving citizenship rights, the major decision dealing with the issue of voting is *Minor v. Happersett* (1874) [16]. In that decision the Court decided that the right to vote was not one of the privileges and immunities guaranteed to citizens by the 14th Amendment and thereby endowed with an aura of constitutionality, state legislation which deprived female citizens of the franchise. Only in 1920, with the passage of the 19th Amendment, were women granted the right to vote. A related decision is that of *MacKenzie v. Hare* (1915) [17]. Here, the Court upheld a California Supreme Court decision depriving a woman of the right to register (and thereby, to vote) on the grounds that a voter must be a state resident in order to register and vote. The plaintiff, by marrying a foreigner, had lost her residency under California law which did, *and still does*, subscribe to the quaint notion that upon marriage, the identities of husband and wife merge into one, and that the "one" is the husband.

The two Supreme Court decisions involving the right of women to serve on juries also fall into the category of citizenship rights. In *Fay v. New York* (1947) [18] in the process of deciding whether an indictment can be overturned if women were excluded from the jury rendering the indictment, the Court slated that women do not have a constitutional right to serve on juries. A more well-known decision is that of *Hoyt v. Florida*, decided as recently as 1961 [19]. Here, the Court upheld a Florida jury selection process which made males register to obtain an exemption from jury duty while females were automatically exempted unless they registered to be included—a system which obviously resulted in a dramatic underrepresentation of women on juries. The 1971 Supreme Court case of *Reed v. Reed* [20] also belongs in this category, although in some ways it represents a departure from tradition. In that decision the Court ruled that a state law which gave preference to males over females as executors for the estates of persons dying intestate was unconstitutional because no reasonable basis existed for giving preference to males. We will discuss the significance of this case in the final section of this chapter.

Finally, there is the issue of education. There is to date only one Supreme Court decision in this area, and it deals with the issue of sexually segregated public institutions of higher learning. In the 1971 per curiam decision of *Williams v. McNair* [21], the Court summarily affirmed a lower court decision barring males from attending an all female publicly supported college on the ground that there was an all male publicly supported college of equal quality which he could attend.

The Double Standard of Justice in Supreme Court Decisions

The decisions of the Supreme Court have been characterized by a double standard of justice. Laws which have been regarded as unconstitutional infringements upon personal liberties of men have systematically been upheld when they applied to women. Numerous examples can be cited in support of this assertion; however, we will content ourselves here with a few classic illustrations.

As we have seen, the Supreme Court has held it constitutional on several occasions to deprive women of the right to enter certain professions. Yet, when the right of an alien Austrian cook to work in a restaurant was infringed upon, the Court stated: "It requires no argument to show that the right to work for a living in the common occupations of the community is of the very essence of the personal freedom and opportunity that it was the purpose of (the 14th) Amendment to secure [22]."

The double standard of justice is readily apparent when one compares decisions upholding maximum hour laws for women with the Court's opinion

Table 8.1. Major Decisions Involving Sex-Based Discrimination

Year	Decision	Issue
Decisions involving the right of women to enter certain professions		
1872	*Bradwell v. The State*	SC upheld Illinois SC decision to deny license to practice law to women
1894	*In re Lockwood, petitioner*	SC upheld right of states to interpret word *person* in state statute designating who may practice law so as to exclude women
1948	*Goesaert v. Cleary*	SC upheld Michigan statute prohibiting women from being bartenders, excepting wives and daughters of male bartenders
1971	*Phillips v. Martin Marietta Corporation*	Per curiam affirmation tentatively striking down practice of excluding mothers of preschool children from important jobs unless it could be shown that mothers of preschool children spend more time with them than fathers of preschool children
1973	*Pittsburgh Press Co. v. The Pittsburgh Commission on Human Relations*	SC barred Pittsburgh Press from referring to sex in employment want ads unless the jobs advertised are not subject to the prohibition against sex discrimination in the Human Relations Ordinance of Pittsburgh
Decisions involving regulation of conditions under which women may labor		
1908	*Muller v. Oregon*	SC upheld Oregon statute limiting number of hours of female labor to maximum of 10 per day
1923	*Adkins v. The Children's Hospital*	SC struck down minimum wage laws for females in the Federal District
1924	*Radice v. New York*	SC upheld right of state to prohibit females from working in urban restaurants between 10PM and 6AM
1937	*West Coast Hotel v. Parrish*	SC upheld minimum wage laws for women and children
1973	*Frontiero and Frontiero v. Richardson*	SC struck down armed services regulations denying women in the service the same dependents' benefits given men
Decisions involving citizenship rights of women		
1874	*Minor v. Happersett*	SC held right to vote not one of privileges and immunities of citizens, thereby upholding state denial of right to vote to women
1915	*MacKenzie v. Hare*	SC upheld California SC decision depriving woman of right to register

(Continued)

Table 8.1.   (Continued)

Year	Decision	Issue
		since she had lost residency as result of marrying foreigner
1947	*Fay v. New York*	SC held indictment by jury excluding women cannot be overturned since women do not have constitutional right to serve on juries
1961	*Hoyt v. Florida*	SC upheld Florida jury selection process which resulted in gross underrepresentation of women on juries
1971	*Reed v. Reed*	SC overturned Idaho statute giving preference to males over females as executors of estates as arbitrary discrimination on basis of sex
	Decisions involving issue of education	
1971	*Williams v. McNair*	Per curiam SC affirmation upholding lower court decision to deny admission of male to all female public college

in *Lochner v. New York* [23]. In that 1905 decision, the Court struck down a New York law which limited the maximum number of hours a male baker could work to 60 with the words: "Statutes of the nature of that under review, limiting the hours in which grown and intelligent men may labor to earn their living, are mere meddlesome interferences with the rights of the individual." Three years later the Court upheld the constitutionality of a ten hour labor law for women in *Muller v. Oregon*, without overturning *Lochner* as valid precedent [24].

The special way in which Supreme Court justices have thought about women is particularly striking in the case of the jury participation issue. In the 1879 decision of *Strauder v. West Virginia*, the Supreme Court declared that the exclusion of Negroes from juries constituted a denial to them of equal protection and due process under the 14th Amendment. According to the majority opinion of the Court:

the very fact that colored people are singled out and expressly denied by a statute all right to participate in the administration of the law, as jurors, because of their color . . . is practically a brand upon them, affixed by the law, an assertion of their inferiority, and a stimulation to that race prejudice which is an impediment to securing to individuals of the race that equal justice which the law aims to secure to all others.

In the same opinion, however, the justices asserted that their argument did not apply to women, who could constitutionally be excluded from juries since the 14th Amendment, which guaranteed due process and equal protection of the laws, did not refer to sex but only to race [25].

The tradition of nonapplication of general principles regarding the harmful effects or injustices resulting from the exclusion of women from juries was reaffirmed in the 1961 *Hoyt v. Florida* decision. Although the Court realized that Florida's system of requiring men to register for an exemption and women to register for inclusion resulted in a very obvious underrepresentation of the latter on juries, the Court stated that the *Hoyt* case "in no way resembles those involving race or color . . ." since in the *Hoyt* case there was present "neither the unfortunate atmosphere of ethnic or racial prejudices which underlay the situations depicted in (the race cases), nor the long course of discriminatory administrative practice which the statistical showing in each of them evinced [26]. The justices, however, did not consider whether there was present in the *Hoyt* case an "unfortunate atmosphere" of sexual prejudice which, as we shall see, was indeed the situation.

Finally, in the area of education, there is a series of Supreme Court decisions involving racial segregation in publicly supported schools. The 1971 per curiam decision of *Williams v. McNair* which denied a male admission to an all female public college on the ground that there was a school of equal quality for males immediately brings to mind the now thoroughly and justly discredited doctrine of "separate but equal" first enunciated in *Plessy v. Ferguson*. In that 1896 decision, the Court countered the black plaintiff's argument that separate connoted not merely difference but inferiority with the words:

> We consider the underlying fallacy of the plaintiff's argument to consist in the assumption that the enforced separation of the two races stamps the colored race with a badge of inferiority. If this be so, it is not by reason of anything found in the act, but solely because the colored race chooses to put that construction upon it [27].

By 1954, the Supreme Court finally subscribed to Mr. Plessy's perception of the situation and declared that "in the field of public education the doctrine of 'separate but equal' has no place [28]." Apparently the Burger Court decided in 1971 that "separate" was only inherently "unequal" when it applied to race and was a valid approach to cases involving sex-based segregation.

Constitutional Justifications for Sex-Based Discrimination

How is one to account for the different treatment accorded women by the Supreme Court? What, in other words, is the legal reasoning behind discriminatory treatment of women under the Constitution of the United States? The answer lies in an examination of the 14th Amendment, specifically the clause which states that a state shall not "deny to any person within its jurisdiction the equal protection of the laws."

To guarantee to all persons the "equal protection of the laws" does not forbid states from discriminating among categories of individuals. All laws discriminate in some sense simply by identifying and classifying the persons to whom they apply. The important question is therefore what types of legal classifications are prohibited and which are allowed?

In general, in order to uphold a classification, the courts have required that there be a reasonable connection between the classification which a particular law establishes and the public purposes for which the law has been enacted [29]. For example, state laws which require people with poor eyesight to wear eyeglasses when driving an automobile discriminate between people with poor eyesight and those with good eyesight by making only the former wear eyeglasses when driving. This classification of people into groups having good and poor eyesight is considered reasonable since it is related to the purpose of the law, which is to assure the safety of both drivers and pedestrians. A law which required only poor people to wear eyeglasses when driving while exempting the rich from so doing would be considered an unreasonable or arbitrary classification since wealth has nothing to do with the ability to see well.

In most instances of classification or discrimination between classes of people, the burden of proof is upon the plaintiff or the person who allegedly is suffering unreasonable discrimination to show that the classification or discrimination established by the law is arbitrary rather than reasonable. In such cases, the Court's attitude generally is a passive or permissive one—that is, the Court assumes that the classificatory or discriminatory aspects of the law are reasonably connected to the ultimate purposes of the legislation, and it is up to the plaintiff to show otherwise.

There are, however, certain instances in which the situation is reversed and the burden of proof is not on the person allegedly being discriminated against, but rather, on the state to show that it has what is termed a "compelling state interest" in differentiating among classes of individuals. In these instances the Court is said to give strict scrutiny or active review to the statute which is being challenged as unconstitutional.

One kind of situation which has triggered strict scrutiny or active review on the part of the Supreme Court involves what the Court has called fundamental or basic rights. The Court has never made a specific list of so-called fundamental rights which trigger more active review; rather, it has established them on an ad hoc and informal basis in a series of decisions over the past few decades. Constitutional law authorities seem to be in general agreement, however, in regarding as fundamental rights the following: the right to vote, to have children, to practice the religion of one's choice, to associate with persons of one's choosing, to assert familial relationships, to travel, and, to a lesser degree, the right to an education and rights with respect to criminal procedure. Although some of these rights are considered to be more fundamental than others, it has been the practice of the Court to require a state to show that it has a compelling state interest in restricting the fundamental rights of certain classes of individuals while not of others. A state's demonstration that the discrimination is not without some basis in reason is not considered an adequate justification for abridging such fundamental rights.

The other situation which has produced active review or strict scrutiny by the Court involves so-called "suspect classifications." Suspect classifications usually are those which are based on biological or cultural differences among people such as race, lineage, and national origin. As was noted in a recent article on the subject, however, "the invidiousness of a particular classification . . . is not always self-evident. Even when such judgments have been spelled out by the Supreme Court, the basis for the evaluations has remained obscure [30]. Judging from the kinds of classifications which the Court has labeled "suspect," the basis for the Court's decision appears to be a strongly felt belief, shared not only by the justices but also by society at large, that such classification or discrimination is the product of irrational and morally suspect prejudice. Thus, as with cases involving fundamental rights, in those involving suspect classifications the burden of proof is placed upon the state to show that it has a compelling state interest for so discriminating. It is not the responsibility of the person being discriminated against to show that the discrimination is unreasonable. Needless to say, those cases which involve both fundamental interests and suspect classifications, such as those prohibiting Negroes from voting, receive the most active or strict scrutiny.

The answer to our original question of how to account for the different treatment accorded women by the Supreme Court is that a majority of the Court has never declared classifications based on sex to be suspect. Moreover, most of the rights which have been denied women either have not been declared to be fundamental or they have only been declared fundamental with regard to adult males. Thus, neither of the conditions which must be met for a case to trigger strict scrutiny or active review comes into play in cases involving sex-based classifications. As a result, in all cases of alleged discrimination against women which have reached the Supreme Court, the burden of proof has been upon the woman to prove that the discriminatory aspects of the particular law in question have no basis in reason. In view of the Court's traditional reluctance to narrow its definition of what constitutes reasonable discrimination against women, it is not surprising that there have been only two instances during the past one hundred years when the Court declared sex-based discrimination to be unreasonable—the *Reed v. Reed* decision of 1971 and the *Frontiero and Frontiero v. Richardson* decision of 1973.

Sexist Stereotypes in Supreme Court Decisions

Why has a majority of the Supreme Court refused to declare classifications or discrimination among individuals based on sex to be suspect? It clearly is not the result of lack of opportunity to do so. Rather, the answer can be found in an examination of the reasons which the justices themselves have offered in upholding legislation which discriminates on the basis of sex. They can be summarized by one word—sexism. Supreme Court justices have been firm supporters (with very few exceptions) of the idea that woman's unique physiology causes her to have capabilities, interests, goals and functions which are different from those of male citizens. From this unproved and unexamined assumption they have eagerly leapt to the conclusion that virtually any law which recognizes or reinforces these supposedly immutable differences between the sexes is by definition reasonable rather than arbitrary and may therefore be upheld.

The image of woman that emerges from Supreme Court decisions basically conforms to the well-known sexist stereotype of women. First, she is physically weak. Her personality reinforces her physical weakness, for she is a timid creature who cannot stand up for her own interests. Unfortunately, she is also morally weak. The inescapable conclusion is that she needs someone who is physically stronger, psychologically more assertive and morally superior in order to protect her. Luckily for her, there are men, all of whom have been characterized by Supreme Court decisions as having qualities which are the polar opposites of those possessed by women. Thus, men naturally become woman's protector, and women naturally become the dependents of man.

The other aspect of woman's image that appears in Supreme Court decisions is that she has certain functions and roles which she must fulfil in life. A woman can bear children while a man cannot. From this fact, the justices have concluded that a woman must devote her entire life to being a full-time wife, mother and homemaker. Coincidentally, this is what a woman enjoys doing and wishes to do [31]. For most Supreme Court justices, these roles and functions are determined only by woman's distinct physiology, but for a small minority, they are both biologically and divinely, or naturally, determined. Whatever the cause, the result is the same narrow path of motherhood and domesticity. It should also be added that whether because of their roles and functions or their distinctive natures, women are not interested in learning or doing, nor do they need to learn or do, the same kinds of things as men. The resemblance of the Court's sexist image of woman to "the half-truths surrounding the myth of the 'happy slave' " has been pointed out by at least one reputable law journal [32].

Not all the component parts of the stereotyped conception of woman appear in each of the Court decisions. Rather, the decisions reflect the stereotype to varying degrees.

In the case of decisions involving the curtailment of a woman's right to enter certain professions, the rationale used is woman's inferior strength, her supposed functions which are both biologically and naturally determined and, to a lesser degree, her moral weakness. The classic statement appears in the *Bradwell* decision, in which Justice Bradley together with two other justices, concurred with the majority opinion upholding a state's right to exclude women from practicing law for the following reasons:

> the civil law, as well as nature herself, has always recognized a wide difference in the respective spheres and destinies of man and woman. Man is, or should be, woman's protector and defender. The natural and proper timidity and delicacy which belongs to the female sex evidently unfits it for many of the occupations of civil life. The constitution of the family organization, which is founded in the divine ordinance, as well as in the nature of things, indicates the domestic sphere as that which properly belongs to the domain and functions of womanhood. The harmony, not to say identity, of interests and views which belong, or should belong, to the family institution is repugnant to the idea of a woman adopting a distinct and independent career from that of her husband . . . (T)he paramount destiny and mission of woman are to fulfil the noble and benign offices of wife and mother. This is the law of the Creator [33].

Although it might be argued that these views were expressed in 1872 and clearly are no longer subscribed to by the Supreme Court, the 1971 per curiam decision of *Phillips v. Martin Marietta*, while different in style, still supports the notion that if women basically play the role of mothers in society, their exclusion from lucrative high-status jobs can be justified. According to the majority opinion, "(t)he existence of . . . conflicting family relations if demonstrably more relevant to job performance for a woman than for a man, could arguably be a basis for distinction under (Title VII of the 1964 Civil Rights Act)." The justices were saying that if it could be shown that mothers of preschool children spent more time with them than did fathers of preschool children, a company would be justified in excluding the former from consideration for better jobs. Only Justice Thurgood Marshall saw that the Court had "fallen into the trap of assuming that the (Civil Rights) Act permits ancient canards about the proper role of women to be a basis of discrimination" although "Congress . . . sought just the opposite result [34]."

The morality argument forms a salient part of the Court's rationale in the 1948 decision of *Goesaert v. Cleary*. Writing for the majority, Justice Frankfurter blithely stated that "Michigan could, beyond question, forbid all women from working behind a bar" since "bartending by women may . . . give rise to moral and social problems." The Court did not specify what these "problems" might be, but decided that wives or daughters of male bartenders could work in bars since they would be subject to the protective oversight of the male bartender [35].

The decisions between 1908 and 1937 upholding the constitutionality of statutes regulating women's hours and wages while leaving those of men unregulated lean heavily upon the stereotype of women being both weak and the "mothers of the race." The classic argument appears in *Muller v. Oregon:*

> That woman's physical structure and the performance of maternal functions place her at a disadvantage in the struggle for subsistence is obvious. This is especially true when the burdens of motherhood are upon her. Even when they are not . . . continuance for a long time on her feet at work . . . tends to injurious effects upon the body, and as healthy mothers are essential to vigorous offspring, the physical well-being of a woman becomes an object of public interest and care in order to preserve the strength and vigor of the race.

As a result of these differences between woman and man, the Court decided that woman "is properly placed in a class by herself, and legislation designed for her protection may be sustained, even when like legislation is not necessary for men and could not be sustained [36]."

This paternalistic attitude toward woman has been and continues to be hailed as "progressive," since the *Muller* decision established the precedent of maximum hour and minimum wage legislation for women. But even if its intent was progressive, its effect was to increase the cost of female labor relative to male labor, and thus women who had to work found themselves priced out of many jobs. The long range effect of the *Muller* decision was even more disastrous. As Murray and Eastwood have written, "courts generally have been content to parrot the doctrine (of *Muller*) that sex forms the basis of a reasonable classification and to ignore the fact that women vary widely in their activities as individuals [37]." Thus, the language in *Muller* has been cited in a series of decisions to justify not only maximum hours and minimum wage legislation exclusively for women, but also to exclude women from juries, educational institutions, and certain occupations. In this sense, the *Muller* decision is analogous to the *Plessy v. Ferguson* decision, which "grafted a color-caste system onto the amended Constitution, a result achieved by vesting the states, and presumably the national government, with power to classify their citizens and residents on the basis of race [38]."

It should be noted that the only two Court decisions which broke the pattern set by the *Muller* decision are considered retrograde and unprogressive, since they overturned the principle of protective labor legislation. In *Adkins v. Children's Hospital,* decided three years after the passage of the 19th Amendment which enfranchised women, the Court declared:

> (W)e cannot accept the doctrine that women of mature age, sui juris, be or may be subjected to restrictions upon their liberty of contract which could not lawfully be imposed in the case of men under similar circumstances. To do so would be to ignore all the implications to be drawn from the present day trend of legislation, as well as that of common thought and usage, by which woman is accorded emancipation from the old doctrine that she must be given special protection or be subjected to special restraint in her contractual and civil relationships [39].

The primary purpose of the decision, however, was not to do battle for women's rights but rather, to strike down labor legislation which the Court regarded as interfering with the rights of business.

The Supreme Court decisions curtailing the citizenship rights of female citizens, as might be expected, have not relied heavily on the physical weakness aspect of the stereotype but rather on the notion that women have certain roles and functions in society. In the 1947 decision, *Fay v. New York,* the Court declared that "woman jury service has not so become a part of the textual or customary law of the land that one convicted of crime must be set free by this Court if his state has lagged behind what we personally may regard as the most desirable practice in recognizing the rights and obligations of womanhood [40]." In the more recent 1961 decision of *Hoyt v. Florida,* the gross underrepresentation of women on juries was justified by the assertion that "Woman is still regarded as the center of home and family life." This supposedly made it reasonable to uphold a jury selection process which allowed women, but not men, to "be relieved from the civic duty of jury service" unless the woman herself "determines that such service is consistent with her own special responsibilities [41]." Although the Court had an opportunity in 1971 to overturn the *Hoyt* precedent, it refused to avail itself of the opportunity presented by the case of *Alexander v. Louisiana* [42].

The only two cases in which the Court declared discrimination on the basis of sex to be arbitrary rather than reasonable are conspicuously free of any sexist stereotypes regarding woman's nature, role, functions or capabilities. Although the Court recognized in *Reed v. Reed* that the 14th Amendment "does not deny to states the power to treat different classes of persons in different ways," it asserted that a classification "must be reasonable" and "(t)o give a mandatory preference to members of either sex over members of the other, merely to accomplish the elimination of hearings on the merits, is to make (an) arbitrary legislative choice [43]." In the *Frontiero and Frontiero v. Richardson* decision, eight of the justices found the sex-based discrimination of the armed services statutes "invidious" or "unreasonable." Four of these eight descried the "long and unfortunate history of sex discrimination" in the United States and explicitly repudiated the "gross, stereotypical distinctions between the sexes" that appear in the nation's statute books. In the strongest condemnation of sex-based discrimination ever, this four-man plurality concluded that "classifications based upon sex, like classifications based upon race, alienage, or national origin, are inherently suspect and must be subjected to strict judicial scrutiny."

The *Reed* and *Frontiero* cases illustrate that sexist attitudes and reasonable discrimination against women are inextricably related. If one believes that women are inferior, have certain roles, functions and the like, than any law which is based on these beliefs is by definition reasonable. Once the stereotypes are rejected, then laws based on discredited sexist notions are by definition unreasonable or arbitrary.

Although the single case to date regarding the issue of education was decided as recently as 1971, it reflects among the most sexist beliefs of any of the cases so far discussed. The Court's summary per curiam affirmation in *Williams v. McNair* of a lower court decision that separate but equal was an acceptable position regarding the education of men and women was bad enough. Let us accept, for the moment, the notion that separate can ever be equal, (a notion that was repudiated with regard to race in the 1954 *Brown v. Board of Education* decision) and examine the two sexually segregated schools which the Court considered equal. The male college in question offered a full range of liberal arts courses, in addition to courses such as engineering. The all-female college, in contrast, offered mainly courses in stenography typewriting, bookkeeping, drawing, designing, engraving, sewing, dressmaking, millinery art, needlework, cooking, housekeeping and, according to the Code of South Carolina, "other such industrial arts as may be suitable to (the female) sex and conducive to their support and usefulness [44]."

It is difficult to conceive of a parallel decision involving whites and blacks in which the Court would affirm that a white college which taught liberal arts and engineering was essentially equal to a black college which taught courses to prepare blacks for service as janitors, domestic servants, agricultural workers or jazz musicians. In fact, in a case decided prior to the *Brown v. Board of Education* decision, involving a black who was denied admission to the University of Texas law school on the grounds that he could attend a new law school for blacks only, the Court stated:

> whether the University of Texas law school is compared with the original or the new law school for Negroes, we cannot find substantial equality in the educational opportunities offered white and Negro law students by the State. In terms of numbers of faculty, variety of courses and opportunity for specialization, size of the student body, scope of the library . . . and similar activities, the University . . . law school is superior [45].

Apparently, as the poet Eve Merriam has said, "Sex prejudice is the only prejudice now considered socially acceptable [46]."

Prospects for the Future

In 1963, the Committee on Civil and Political Rights of the President's Commission on the Status of Women declared that the principle of equality of rights under the law for both males and females was implicit in both the due process and equal protection clauses of the 14th Amendment and urged "early and definitive court pronouncement, particularly by the U.S. Supreme Court . . . to the end that the principle of equality become firmly established in constitutional doctrine [47]." The best way of giving full recognition to this implicit equality would be to make it explicit by declaring sex a suspect classification. In the 10 years that have passed since 1963, a majority of the Supreme Court has not made such a declaration although, as was noted, in the recent *Frontiero* decision a plurality of the Court stated that sex was indeed a suspect classification. A plurality decision, unfortunately, does not constitute a definitive precedent for the lower courts. As one student of the Supreme Court observed, "because the majority was split, the decision will not be accorded the same deference usually shown high court rulings [48]."

At the time of this writing, it still is not clear whether a majority of the Supreme Court will declare sex a suspect classification in the near future. The few decisions relevant to the issue contain conflicting indications. The strongest bases for optimism are the *Reed* and *Frontiero* decisions of 1971 and 1973 respectively. In unanimously striking down an Idaho law which discriminated on the basis of sex on the grounds that the discrimination was arbitrary and unreasonable, the Court in *Reed* substantially narrowed the definition of what can be considered reasonable sex-based discrimination. The Court could have followed, for example, its approach in the 1961 *Hoyt v. Florida* decision, that is, "it may well have assumed that administering estates would detract in a socially unacceptable manner from a woman's role as the center of family life [49]." In the *Reed* decision, the Court was finally requiring that the discrimination on the basis of sex be rationally related to the purposes of the legislation. In other words, it was retreating from its past cavalier treatment of sex discrimination cases and was now demanding that classifications based on sex conform to the standards applied in cases regarding discrimination against blacks prior to the 1954 *Brown* decision.

In the *Frontiero* case, four of the justices (Powell, Burger, Blackmun, and Stewart) continued to apply this narrow definition of reasonable, while four other justices (Brennan, Douglas, White, and Marshall) further narrowed the definition by declaring that all discrimination based on sex was suspect. The ninth justice (Rehnquist) adhered to the traditional broad definition of reasonable sex-based discrimination.

If one of the five justices who refrained from declaring sex-based discrimination suspect in the *Frontiero* decision should transfer to the more liberal side in a future case, a precedent would be set and the burden of proof in future sex-discrimination cases would fall upon the discriminator rather than upon the object of the discriminatory statute. It is difficult to predict, however, which, if any, of these justices will take this step. It is definitely encouraging that none of the eight justices in the majority took the position that sex-based discrimination is not or could not be considered suspect at some future time. On the other hand, three of the majority justices who refrained from declaring sex-based discrimination suspect did so on the grounds that the states were in the process of debating the proposed Equal Rights Amendment which, if ratified, would have the same effect as a declaration by the Court that discrimination based on sex is suspect. Since the states have until 1979 to ratify the Amendment, it appears doubtful that these three justices will declare sex a suspect classification in the near future. There seems to be little hope that Rehnquist, the lone dissenter in the *Frontiero* decision, will shift his position. It is conceivable that the remaining justice, Stewart, will join with Brennan, Douglas, White, and Marshall in declaring sex-based discrimination suspect, but it is just as conceivable that he will not or that one of the four liberal justices will leave the Court in the near future and be replaced with a more conservative justice.

Should the Supreme Court continue to apply the narrower definition of reasonable discrimination first expressed in the *Reed* decision, many laws which discriminate on the basis of sex would clearly fall. Such a process, however, would be extremely slow, since legislation would be struck down on a case by case basis and no general principle regarding the unconstitutionality of sex-based classifications could be extracted from such a procedure.

The *Reed* and *Frontiero* decisions, furthermore, cannot be considered clear indications of the direction in which the Burger Court is moving. In its per curiam decision of *Williams v. McNair*, the Court upheld the principle of separate but equal in the area of education in a situation in which, as we have seen, the education provided for females was blatantly unequal to that provided for males. And in *Alexander v. Illinois*, a case which provided the Court with an opportunity to reverse the *Hoyt* decision upholding a jury selection process which resulted in gross underrepresentation of women, the Court ignored the sex discrimination issue and dealt only with the race discrimination issue. Both the *Williams* and *Alexander* decisions preceded the *Reed* decision by several months and the *Frontiero* decision by two years and thus could be considered more valid indications of future trends. In a case decided after the *Reed* case, however, that of *Stanley v. Illinois* [50], the Court did not avail itself of the opportunity to declare that an Illinois law which recognized the parental rights of unwed mothers but not of unwed fathers constituted an arbitrary sex-based classification. Instead, it declared the Illinois law unconstitutional on the technicality that it did not give the father a hearing on his fitness as a parent before his children were taken from him. Thus, the recent Supreme Court decisions in the area of sex discrimination are inconclusive regarding the future trend of decisions of the Burger Court.

The January 1973 abortion decision [51] in which the Supreme Court overturned all anti-abortion laws on the ground that they constituted an invasion of a woman's right to privacy under the due process clause of the 14th Amendment, does not substantially change the above conclusion regarding an absence of a clear trend. All of the significant Supreme Court decisions during the past few decades relating to sex-based discrimination have involved the equal protection clause of the 14th Amendment. Although the abortion decision is laudable and represents a great step toward tearing down the barriers prohibiting women from participating in society on a basis equal with that of men, it does not constitute a legal precedent in terms of cases involving an alleged denial of equal protection of the laws. The abortion decision thus has no apparent effect on the efforts to get the Supreme Court to declare sex a suspect classification and to subject legislation which discriminates on the basis of sex to strict scrutiny or active review.

Although the Supreme Court is not compelled to follow trends set by state courts, in some cases an examination of such trends does provide insight into the direction in which the Court itself may ultimately move. The clearest trend in the states is toward an increase in the number of decisions involving alleged sex discrimination, a trend which is also apparent with regard to the Supreme Court. In terms of the direction of the decisions, however, there is once again no unambiguous national trend.

The area in which there is the most activity and the most confusion is employment. Title VII of the 1964 Civil Rights Act prohibited discrimination on the basis of sex by private employers, employment agencies, and unions. By March 1973 it also covered employees of state and local governments and both private and public educational institutions. There are, however, no "specific guides for resolving difficult problems of interpretation—such as the relationship between (its) provisions and various state 'protective' laws [52]." As a result, different states have interpreted the Act's provisions in different ways, some by upholding protective legislation and others by over-turning it [53]. The only Title VII case to reach the Supreme Court to date is that of *Phillips v. Martin Marietta,* and as was noted, the Court's ruling was inconclusive and may have set a precedent which bodes ill for ending sex-based discrimination in employment.

The most spectacular lower court decision to date which has overturned so-called protective legislation is that of *Sail'er Inn v. Kirby* (1971) [54] in which the California Supreme Court declared that a statute forbidding women to work as bartenders violated the 1964 Civil Rights Act, the California Constitution and the 14th Amendment. The opinion is both a model of what the Supreme Court could have said, but did not, in the 1948 analogous case of *Goesaert v. Cleary,* when it upheld a state statute barring most women from bartending, and what the Court should say in the future. In the California decision the Court declared:

Laws which disable women from full participation in the political, business and economic areas are often characterized as 'protective' and beneficial. Those same laws applied to racial or ethnic minorities would readily be recognized as invidious and impermissible. The pedestal upon which women have been placed has all too often, upon closer inspection, been revealed as a cage. We conclude that the sexual classifications are properly treated as suspect, particularly when these classifications are made with respect to employment . . . The state has not only failed to establish a compelling interest served by (the statute forbidding women to be bartenders) but it has failed to establish any interest at all [55].

The *Sail'er Inn* opinion thus is one of the only ones to declare discrimination based on sex to be suspect. In addition, it is the first to recognize explicitly woman's fundamental right to pursue a lawful profession—a right which the Supreme Court has granted to men in general and to male blacks, aliens, and members of minority groups, but has refrained from granting to women. Although it is not clear whether other state courts will follow the reasoning used by the California Court in *Sail'er Inn,* it is interesting that plurality opinion in the 1973 *Frontiero* decision of the U.S. Supreme Court spoke of women having been placed "not on a pedestal, but in a cage [56]."

In the area of citizenship rights, the trend in the states is also far from clear. In the 1966 case of *State v. Hall,* for example, the Mississippi Supreme Court decided that exclusion of women from jury duty is not a denial of protection of the laws. In *White v. Crook*, on the other hand, an Alabama court declared that barring women completely from jury service was a violation of the equal protection clause. In the area of criminal procedure, there does seem to be a trend toward equality in sentencing. In *U.S. ex rel Robinson v. York* and *Commonwealth v. Daniel*, the courts held that a statute providing for longer sentences for women than for men convicted of the same offense was a denial of equal protection [57]. The *York* case was the first lower court decision to apply strict scrutiny in cases involving sex-based discrimination.

In the area of education, there is the already noted Supreme Court per curiam affirmation in which the Court upheld a South Carolina court's decision that a female only admissions policy for a state supported college did not violate the equal protection clause of the 14th Amendment. Here again, however, there is no clear trend, for in another well-known case, *Kirstein v. Rector and Visitors of the University of Virginia* [58], the Court found that the University of Virginia was better than any other state supported school and thus women were being denied admission on the basis of their sex were being denied equal protection of the laws. In this case, however, the lower court refused to consider whether sexually segregated public schools were in general an unconstitutional denial of equal protection.

In view of the absence of a clear trend in the lower courts toward extending the coverage of the equal protection clause to women, and the absence of strong indications that a majority of the Supreme Court will declare classifications based on sex to be suspect in the immediate future, the ratification of the Equal Rights Amendment becomes a necessity. The Amendment, which makes discrimination on the basis of sex unconstitutional, can be considered the functional equivalent of a Supreme Court declaration that sex-based classifications are suspect. Once the Amendment is ratified, the burden of proof will be on the states to show that there is a compelling state interest in upholding legislation which discriminates on the basis of sex, and the Court will have to subject all such legislation to strict scrutiny.

In the aftermath of the 1954 *Brown v. Board of Education* decision, a southern judge wrote:

> We don't know what happens to the brain of man, but we do know that the negro's brain pan seals and hardens quicker than the white man's. We do know that the negro has, in certain instances, elliptical blood cells, which cause disease. We do know that his skull is one-eighth inch thicker, and we do know that he has to have two determiners to have his kinky black hair. We don't know what it takes to make his mind different from our mind. This Supreme Court seeks to set aside all the laws of eugenics and biology! [59]

The southern judge was arguing that there are some real biological differences between whites and blacks, and since no one really knows the implications of such differences, differential treatment of blacks on the basis of their race was reasonable. The Supreme Court's unanimous 1954 decision rejected this reason and gave blacks the benefit of the doubt. No one is arguing that there are no biological differences between the sexes, for such an argument would be patently absurd. In view of the fact, however, that no one really knows to what extent these biological differences, as opposed to societal forces, determine interests, roles, and functions, (and substantial evidence exists that the latter are more important than the former), it is time for a majority of the Supreme Court, at the very least, to withdraw the aura of constitutionality from sexist statutes and give women the benefit of the doubt.

NOTES

1. Robert G. McCloskey, *The American Supreme Court.* Chicago: University of Chicago Press, 1960, p. 182.

2. *Plessy v. Ferguson,* 163 U.S. 537 (1896) and *Brown v. Board of Education of Topeka,* 347 U.S. 483 (1954).

3. William Connolly has defined an ideology as "an integrated set of beliefs about the social and political environment" which "purports to tell us how the system is organized, which desired goals can be promoted, what agencies and channels can most effectively be employed to forward the goals in the given setting and what the required action will cost various groups in the short and long run in terms of status, power, happiness, wealth, and so on. William E. Connolly, *Political Science and Ideology.* New York: Atherton, 1967.

4. This definition of sexism is an elaboration of the one presented by Judith Hole and Ellen Levine, *Rebirth of Feminism.* New York: Quadrangle, 1971, p. 195.

5. *Bradwell v. The State,* 16 Wall. 130 (1872).

6. *In re Lockwood, petitioner,* 154 U.S. 116 (1894).

7. *Goesaert v. Cleary,* 335 U.S. 464 (1948).

8. *Phillips v. Martin Marietta Corporation,* 400 U.S. 542 (1971).

9. *Pittsburgh Press Co., Petitioner, v. The Pittsburgh Commission on Human Relations et al.,* 41 LW 5055 (1973).

10. *Muller v. Oregon,* 208 U.S. 412 (1908).

11. *Riley v. Massachusetts,* 232 U.S. 671 (1914); *Bosley v. McLaughlin,* 236 U.S. 385 (1915); and *Miller v. Wilson,* 236 U.S. 373 (1915).

12. *Radice v. New York,* 264 U.S. 292 (1924).

13. *Adkins v. Children's Hospital,* 261 U.S. 525 (1923) and *Morehead v. New York ex rel Tipaldo,* 298 U.S. 587 (1936).

14. *West Coast Hotel v. Parrish,* 300 U.S. 379 (1937).

15. *Frontiero and Frontiero v. Richardson,* 41 LW 4609 (1973).

16. *Minor v. Happersett,* 88 U.S. (21 Wall.) 162 (1874).

17. *Mackenzie v. Hare,* 239 U.S. 299, 36 S.Ct. 106.

18. *Fay v. New York,* 332 U.S. 261 (1946).

19. *Hoyt v. Florida,* 368 U.S. 57 (1961).

20. *Reed v. Reed*, 404 U.S. 71 (1971).

21. *Williams v. McNair*, 401 U.S. 951 (1971).

22. *Truax v. Reich*, 239 U.S. 33 (1915) quoted in Marguerite Rawalt, "Equal Justice for Women—Update the Constitution," *New York Law Forum*, **17**, p. 533 (1971).

23. *Lochern v. New York*, 198 U.S. 45 (1905).

24. In 1917, in *Bunting v. Oregon*, 243 U.S. 246, the Court declared maximum hour legislation for men constitutional.

25. *Strauder v. West Virginia*, 100 U.S., 308, 310 (1879).

26. *Hoyt v. Florida*, 368 U.S. at 68.

27. *Plessy v. Ferguson*, 163 U.S. at 55.

28. Loren Miller, *The Petitioners: The Story of the Supreme Court of the United States and the Negro.* Cleveland: World, 1967, p. 347.

29. For a more detailed discussion of the following argument see especially, "Sex Discrimination and Equal Protection: Do We Need a Constitutional Amendment?", *Harvard Law Rev.*, **84**, pp. 1499–1524 (Apr. 1971); "Developments in the Law-Equal Protection," *Harvard Law Rev.*, **82**, pp. 1065–1192 (Mar. 1969); "Are Sex-based Classifications Constitutionally Suspect?", *Northwestern University Law Rev.*, **66**, pp. 481–501 (Sept.-Oct. 1971); Barbara Brown, et al., "The Equal Rights Amendment: A Constitutional Basis of Equal Rights for Women," *Yale Law Jour.*, **80** (Apr. 1971), and Mary Eastwood, "The Double Standard of Justice: Women's Rights Under the Constitution," *Valparaiso University Law Rev.*, **5**, p. 296 (Fall 1970).

30. "Developments in the Law-Equal Protection," *op. cit.*, p. 1123.

31. For a perceptive critique of the myth that woman's place is in the home, see Elizabeth Janeway, *Man's World, Woman's Place: A Study in Social Mythology.* New York: Dell, 1971.

32. "Sex Discrimination and Equal Protection: Do We Need a Constitutional Amendment?," *op. cit.*, p. 1507.

33. *Bradwell v. The State*, 16 Wall. at 141 (U.S. 1872). All the decisions quoted in this section, unless otherwise specified, have recently been reprinted in a new and extremely useful reference book by Leo Kanowitz, *Sex Roles in Law and Society: Cases and Materials.* Albuquerque: University of New Mexico Press, 1973.

34. *Supreme Court Reporter*, **91**, No. 8, p. 498 (Feb. 15, 1971).

35. *Goesaert v. Cleary*, 335 U.S. at 466.

36. *Muller v. Oregon*, 208 U.S. at 421, 422.

37. Pauli Murray and Mary O. Eastwood, "Jane Crow and the Law: Sex Discrimination and Title VII," *The George Washington Law Rev.*, **34**, pp. 238–239 (Dec. 1965).

38. Miller, *The Petitioners, op. cit.*, p. 173.

39. *Adkins v. Children's Hospital*, 261 U.S. at 553.

40. *Fay v. New York*, 332 U.S. at 290.

41. *Hoyt v. Florida*, 368 U.S. at 62.

42. In *Alexander v. Louisiana*, 405 U.S. 625 (1972) the Court was asked to overturn a criminal conviction on the grounds that Negro citizens were included on the grand jury list and venire in only token numbers and women were systematically excluded from the grand jury list, venire, and empaneled grand jury. The conviction was set aside on the general grounds of the race exclusion issue and the Court did not deal with the sex discrimination issue.

43. *Supreme Court Reporter*, **92**, No. 4, pp. 253–254 (Dec. 15, 1972).

44. John J. Johnston, Jr. and Charles L. Knapp, "Sex Discrimination by Law: A Study in Judicial Perspective," *New York University Law Rev.*, **46**, pp. 724–725 (October 1971) and Robert A.

Sedler, "The Legal Dimensions of Women's Liberation: An Overview, *Ind. Law Jour.*, **47**, p. 452 (Spring 1972).

45. Miller, *The Petitioners, op. cit.*, p. 339.

46. Quoted in Cynthia Fuchs Epstein, *Woman's Place.* Berkeley and Los Angeles: University of California Press, 1971, p. 34.

47. Cited in Hole and Levine, *Rebirth of Feminism, op. cit.*, p. 195.

48. Linda Mathews, "High Court Takes Major Step Toward Equality of the Sexes," *Los Angeles Times*, pp. 1, 9 (May 15, 1973).

49. Joan M. Krauskopf, "Sex Discrimination—Another Shibboleth Legally Shattered," *Missouri Law Rev.*, **37**, p. 387 (Summer 1972).

50. *Stanley v. Illinois*, 405 (U.S. 645, 649 (1972).

51. *Roe et al. v. Wade, District Attorney of Dallas County*, 410 U.S. 113; *Doe et al. v. Bolton, Attorney General of Georgia et al.*, 410 U.S. 179.

52. Leo Kanowitz, *Women and the Law: The Unfinished Revolution.* Albuquerque: University of New Mexico Press, 1969, p. 106.

53. Cases in the lower courts involve, for example, issues such as the constitutionality of excluding women from certain professions such as wrestling, of weight-lifting, height or weight requirements, and of forced leaves for pregnant women.

54. *Sail'er Inn Inc. v. Kirby*, 5 Cal. 3d 1, 485 P.2d, 529, 95 *Cal. Rptr.* 329 (1971).

55. Cited in Allan D. Spritzer, "Equal Employment Opportunity vs. Protection for Women: A Public Policy Dilemma," *Alabama Law Rev.*, **24**, p. 579 (Summer 1972) and Johnston, Jr. and Knapp, "Sex Discrimination by Law," *op. cit.*, p. 690.

56. *Frontiero and Frontiero v. Richardson*, 41 LW 4611.

57. *State v. Hall*, Miss. 187 So. 2d 861 (Miss. 1966); *White v. Crook*, 251 F. Supp. 401 (N.D. Ala. 1966); *U.S. ex rel. Robinson v. York*, 281 F. Supp. 8 (D. Conn. 1968); and *Commonwealth v. Daniel*, 430 Pa. 642, 243 A. 2d 400 (1968).

58. *Kirstein v. Rector and Visitors of the University of Virginia*, 309 F. Supp. 184 (E.D. Va. 1970).

59. Quoted in Albert P. Blaustein and Clarence Clyde Ferguson, Jr., *Desegregation and the Law: The Meaning and Effect of the School Segregation Cases.* New York: Vintage Books, 1962, p. 141.

Section

3
THE MOVEMENT:
NEW ALTERNATIVES?

Chapter

9

Contemporary Feminism, Consciousness-Raising, and Changing Views of the Political

Nancy McWilliams

(T)he field of politics is and has been, in a significant and radical sense, a created one. The designation of certain activities and arrangements as political, and the characteristic way that we think about them, and the concepts we employ to communicate our observations and reactions—none of these are written into the nature of things.

S. WOLIN [1]

Not long ago, it was commonly observed that at social functions the sexes would frequently segregate, the males often gathering to talk politics and the females to talk "woman talk." Woman talk was understood to be anything but political: the phrase referred to conversations about childrearing, interpersonal relationships, female health problems, sexual confidences, fashion, and other than indisputably nonpolitical topics. Whether or not this stereotypical picture was accurate—and certainly among more highly educated groups it was distorted at best—it is intriguing to recall it and reflect on the redefinition of the political within the last few years. During this time, childrearing, personal relations, gynecology, cultural sexual patterns, contraception, abortion, female consumerism, housework and other traditionally

This paper was originally presented at the Annual Meeting of the American Political Science Association, Washington, D.C., 1972.

feminine preoccupations have become hot political topics. Nowadays, if the sexes segregate at a party, what was once woman talk is often discussed with a political fervor so serious as to astonish male onlookers. What has happened?

As late as 1968 there were very few straws in the academic wind or in the formal literature of political science that suggested we were to see a major resurgence of American feminism, despite the fact that at that time women's protest was already beginning in earnest. Today, few doubt that the movement's long-range effects on our culture will be profound. How is it that we were so unprepared for a political phenomenon of this magnitude? While recognizing that few social scientists have made good prophets, let me suggest that academic unreadiness to deal with the profound political questions raised by radical women was particularly notable.

It will be my contention that our being taken by surprise by the recent explosion of feminist activity is a symptom of some general problems in contemporary academic attitudes about what is "political." I will treat the current women's movement as a kind of case study, hopefully one that can illuminate mass political processes generally and which illustrates the need for a broader definition of politics if we are to understand the dynamics of future social movements.

Specifically, the current feminist movement considered as a case-history political movement highlights two important issues: (a) How do matters previously defined as belonging to the private sphere become recognized as political questions? and (b) What are the implications of the new styles of political activism associated with recently politicized areas? Thus, in the context of examining the women's movement, I am considering the question of political innovation in the areas of both content and process. My sources are primary data from the movement, mostly the writings of contemporary feminists, but also to some extent my personal experiences and impressions [2].

Politicizing the Personal

Our politics begin with our feelings [3].

In 1963, Betty Friedan described a "problem that has no name [4]." Four years later that problem and many others found a name: sexism. Sexism, as Jessie Bernard points out, was an excellent choice of term for a new political movement [5]. Its selection evidenced one of the many lessons that radical women had learned from blacks, namely, that a concern with private actions is not sufficient to confront a problem which, however distinctively its symptoms can be found in individual people, has its roots in the social structure.

Feminists' insistence on defining the difficulties of women as a social problem rather than as individual challenges and "hang-ups" was a startling innovation for the social sciences as well as for society in general. By way of contrast, in Allport's classic book *Prejudice,* the issue of female denigration was limited to a few sentences about the deviant misogynist [6]. And although political scientists have often been sensitive to the tendency of social psychologists and others with less systemic orientations to ignore the institutional bases of attitudes, the social underpinnings of sexist behaviors went unnoticed until radical women forced our attention to them. Myrdal [7], Hacker [8], and a few female psychoanalysts (Thompson [9], Horney [10], Klein [11]) are among the handful of investigators who talked of women's problems as *social issues* before the late 1960s.

The contemporary feminist movement developed simultaneously in two very different milieu: in the quiet of suburbia, where coffee-klatching housewives began discussing Friedan's book, and in the ferment of the early New Left, where activist women began to share their perceptions of a common situation, circulating books like *The Second Sex* [12] and *The Golden Notebook* [13]. In both places, the realizations that one's problems were shared, that individual dissatisfactions had social bases, that private difficulties could be understood as socially caused or aggravated, struck many with the force of a virtual revelation.

Rossi accounts for the awakened feminist consciousness by noting the recent increase in the number of unattached women who could begin to see themselves as a major interest group in the work force, unlike their predecessors in the early 1950s who married young, became mothers early, and had no opportunity to view themselves in any way but as *in relation to* parents, husband, or children [14]. This situation was probably only one factor in a complex social milieu, the consideration of which is beyond the scope of this essay [15]. At any rate, women became aware suddenly and in appreciable numbers that personal questions could be carried beyond the coffee klatch and the psychiatrist to the public arena—that is, that they were essentially political issues.

An exhuberant attitude characterized the first women to liberate themselves from the onus of individualistic attributions of neurosis, guilt, and personal role conflict. The feelings of those who formed the now comparatively conservative National Organization for Women (NOW) differed only in degree, not in kind, from the sentiments that informed Robin Morgan's exhortation:

Let it all hang out. Let it seem bitchy, catty, dykey, frustrated, crazy, Solanisesque, nutty, frigid, ridiculous, bitter, embarrassing, man-hating, libelous, pure, unfair, envious, intuitive, low-down, stupid, petty, liberating [16].

This kind of exhilaration is common in developing movements (or in resurrected ones, in the case of feminism). It characterized abolitionism, prohibition, the labor movement, the civil rights movement, and countless other generic American political ventures. It seems to appear because politicization serves an important psychological function: Self-esteem is increased by participation in a worthy cause. It is a huge emotional leap for an individual when a psychological situation in which he or she suffers the sense of failure to meet a social norm changes to a condition in which there is a dignity as a fellow combatant [17].

Because of the powerful psychological rewards available through politicization, we should expect personal issues always to tend toward public ones. It appears that previously nonpolitical issues will almost inevitably become political whenever two conditions apply: (a) when reality comes to be perceptibly discordant with social myths (in the case of women, thousands were unhappy in the roles of wife, mother, and homemaker which were supposed to provide feminine fulfillment), and (b) when there is the opportunity to compare notes on personal unhappiness. With mass communications, the tendency for private questions to become public ones is obviously enhanced.

A reflection of this process appears in the principle of "the unity of the personal and the political" elucidated in a newsletter of the women's caucus of the New University Conference:

A political being has no exclusively personal problems . . . political activity should not be evaluated apart from personal hangups, interpersonal frictions, grievances, etc. These have roots in political ideology and practice and have important political consequences. Women have learned that their personal problems are not individual or inevitable BUT are generalized, systemic, socially caused and common and they are solving these problems through political action [18].

The relation of the new feminism to the 1960s civil rights movement is interesting in this context. The "We Shall Overcome" era saw the most striking conversion of private to political issues: where one sat on a bus, whom one married, in whose company one ate, where one swam, slept, and urinated, became questions of public policy. Women in SNCC and other radical organizations were expected to see the political nature of private things in relation to blacks but not in relation to themselves. Not surprisingly, they soon made the transfer of outlook [19,20]. Marge Piercy writes of her experience in left-wing politics:

> Once again in the Movement, oppression is becoming something for professionals to remove from certifiably oppressed other people. When I am told day in and day out to shut up because our oppression pales beside the oppression of colonialized peoples and blacks, I remember that half of them are women too . . .
>
> There is much anger here at Movement men, but I know they have been warped and programmed by the same society that has damn near crippled us. My anger is because they have created in the Movement a microcosm of that oppression and are proud of it [21].

With respect to the general tendency of private issues to politicize under certain social conditions, the women's movement differs little from previous social enterprises. There appear to me to be some respects, however, in which contemporary feminism has given American politics a new twist.

One reason that most of us failed to see the new feminism coming, or to take it seriously once it was a clear presence in the political arena, was that politics itself has been construed as inherently male. Conversely, any area which women have dominated has been considered nonpolitical a priori. Thus, for instance, what Jane Addams did in Chicago was not politics but "social work," and Margaret Sanger's crusade was not political but "educational." That contemporary women should describe their condition in explicitly political terms still seems highly peculiar to many.

Another reason may be our cultural tendency to see politics as by definition the interplay of power relationships, and concern with power, in turn, as somehow a masculine attribute. This understanding of the nature of the political pervades American liberal thought and appears even in the writing of present-day feminists: Millett discussing "sexual politics" is basically considering the power gambits between male and female [22], as is Pat Mainardi in exploring the "politics of housework [23]."

A more classical conception of politics is implied in its Greek root *polis;* that is, as the area of shared values and citizenship, in which power relationships are only one feature. Construed this way, politics can easily be seen as "naturally" feminine. Since women have traditionally been reared in this society to be concerned with communal ties, with the understanding of emotional relations, with peacemaking, caretaking, civic propriety and public morals [24,25,26], their political proclivities are obvious. What was needed to turn conventional civic orientations toward feminist activism was the woman-to-woman communication that happened as the suburbs settled into stability and the radical movements of the 1960s got under way.

Personalizing the Political

This is not a movement one "joins." There are no rigid structures or membership cards. The Women's Liberation Movement exists where three or four friends or neighbors decide to meet regularly over coffee and talk about their personal lives. It also exists in the cells of women's jails, on the welfare lines, in the supermarket, the factory, the convent, the farm, the maternity ward, the street-corner, the old ladies' home, the kitchen, the steno pool, the bed. It exists in your mind, and in the political and personal insights that you can contribute to change and shape and help its growth [27].

Having examined innovation in content (how an issue enters the realm of the political) with attention to the particular case of contemporary feminism, let us look at innovations in political process that can be seen in the movement. Here I will note several special features of feminist politics, with the hope that they have useful implications for the study of politics in general.

Consciousness-Raising

One way in which the women's movement differs from prior protests in American history is in its concern with consciousness-raising not as a preliminary to other group activity, but often as the significant political act. Previous movements have utilized consciousness-changing techniques, but mainly as preparation for concerted group action; such methods, for example, were employed by Communists in the 1930s in order to get people into the party, after which they took up other things.

There is some of this kind of *agitprop* in the use of consciousness-raising among feminists, but for many radical women, the practice of sharing experiences and feelings, with the goal of heightened consciousness as women in a particular political environment, is the full extent of their activism. Yet despite the quiet quality of efforts to expand one another's sights, many women consider such activity a revolutionary undertaking.

One reason for the primacy of consciousness-raising among feminists has to do with the nature of the situations in which women feel oppressed. Usually either the woman is isolated or the opponent difficult to confront. It is hardly feasible to take concerted group action against a family, a lover, or a boss; it is equally difficult to take on such elusive oppressors as Madison Avenue or pornographic filmsters. Women rarely find themselves naturally grouped, and each woman must to a great extent fight her battles alone. The support of her sisters may not be available until the rap session next Wednesday.

From these observations about women, we might predict, parenthetically, that whenever persons in a derogated social category are similarly isolated from each other and from their identified oppressors, their political activity will be in this mode. It appears, for instance, that homosexuals have also opted for an approach heavily dependent on consciousness-raising.

A related reason for the emphasis on consciousness-raising in the women's movement is that practical reforms which officially allow women an equal role in various institutions are useless if a great part of the problem lies in women's internalization of the general social denigration of the female. In 1955, Duverger concluded in a UNESCO study of the political role of women that it is

useless to give women a larger part in political life by special reforms. . . . The small part played by women in politics merely reflects and results from the secondary place to which they are still assigned by the customs and attitudes of our society and which their education and training tend to make them accept as the natural order of things. Purely political reforms are effective here only so far as they tend generally to modify this situation, to counteract the effects of habit and tradition, to help women to free themselves from them, and to awaken them to a sense of their own independence. . . . It is probably still more important to fight against the deeply-rooted belief in the natural inferiority of women . . . a particularly serious obstacle because women feel deeply the special characteristics of their sex in this respect [28].

Or as Sally Kempton put it, "It is hard to fight an enemy who has outposts in your head [29]."

Consciousness-raising in the women's movement happens between woman and woman, but also between feminists and the larger society. Again indebted to blacks for an education in the use of symbols, feminists have been particularly attentive to seemingly minor sexist conventions. For this they have frequently been accused of wallowing in the trivial, but it is hard to discount the revolution in public consciousness that has resulted from gestures like affixing the label "This ad oppresses women," sitting-in at all-male bars, insisting on the use of Ms., pointing out the hostility inherent in the catcall, or referring to God as She.

On the question of achieving social change, it can be said that there has always been a contrast between the activist's conviction that the human condition will improve if institutions are changed, and the quietist's insistence that institutional changes are futile without prior alteration of human nature or at least specific individual attitudes [30]. Out of necessity, the women's movement has created something of a synthesis. It has already made certain issues painfully salient to the society in general, and has attempted to effect changes in women's self-perception and attitudes so that each person will be freer to seek the changes appropriate to her situation. Depending on the woman, these may be institutional, interpersonal, or simply intrapsychic.

The Small Group and the Dread of Hierarchy

A common problem in the functioning of a political group is how to encourage independence among members while maintaining sufficient cohesiveness to be effective. Feminists seem to me to have been particularly aware of the dilemmas in this area, probably because developing a sense of oneself as independent and valuable is an especially difficult problem for females [31,32,33,34].

The small group has been the vehicle of choice by which the women's movement pursues common goals, despite the enormous pressures for consolidation and mass operation that this kind of society creates. One reason for this reliance on the small group is, of course, women's greater familiarity with locality and with smaller units of social organization.

But most of the concern with the small group reflects a deliberate, careful attempt by feminists to avoid what they view as negative features of other forms of organization and communication. Some of their concerns are psychological; White and Goode, for instance, emphasize the potential of the small group for developing women's self-esteem, self-respect, and assertiveness [35]. Some stress the appropriateness of small groups for the job of freeing women to use their intellects and to mature in the understanding of things political:

> Often a woman holds the political convictions of her husband, lover, brother, father, or whoever is the essential male figure in her life.
> The small group, however, is a means of ending this confinement. Women whose politics have been unclear or who have been totally uncommitted politically can reach their own individual levels of political awareness through the group experience and ultimately through the entire Women's Liberation Movement. . . . Whether her politics are left or still in the quasi-liberal circle, each woman should be encouraged to express that belief, to learn to "talk politics [36]."

The small group is thus seen as a therapeutic experience and politicizing agent.

In addition, there is in the women's movement an extremely strong distrust of mass communications for their tendency to redefine a movement by what aspects are chosen as newsworthy. Women who came to feminism after developing New Left affiliations had, for example, seen Mark Rudd, whom many considered a minor figure at Columbia originally, catapulted into a major leadership position by the press; they had seen the flower child protest co-opted within a year, as advertising went psychedelic; they had watched the organizers of the Black Panthers trying to deal with self-proclaimed Panther chapters that had nothing but rhetoric in common with the movement's guiding spirits.

Feminists with previous experience in *The Movement* were all too aware of the tendency for publicity to mean distortion, and distortion to mean an influx of sympathizers with whom they had little basic sympathy. Unwilling by temperament to try the yippie technique of turning this intrusive process to their own ends, they worked to refine the rap group as the basic unit of activity. Moreover, the women's movement felt exploitation by the advertising industry had given liberationists a special axe to grind in the case of the mass media. Stambler's statement is illustrative of this position:

> Movement women have always been turned off by the media's tendency to create celebrities and superstars . . .
> It had become an unwritten law for movement women to speak only in pairs and only to women reporters. None of these spokeswomen will claim to be a "leader" since no *one* of them is. Yet the media, tending to gloss over the facts and treat the women's movement with scorn, may lead you to believe otherwise. Usually the movement is poorly represented, often slandered, and frequently made the object of ridicule . . .
> It would be a mistake to believe that there is only one organization known as the Women's Liberation Movement, with a distinct structure, a recognized leader, and one political platform. It would be more precise to envision the movement as a *network of groups* dealing with common causes, each group relatively autonomous yet still dependent upon the larger movement for moral support and a frame or reference [37].

Participatory democracy was an espoused goal in SDS, and many of the above concerns about size and publicity were held by other New Leftists, but in the view of radical women, powerful sexist undercurrents in the movement made democratic communality only a paper ideal [38,39,40]. The observations of radical women about hierarchies of male dominance within Left groups led to their painstaking efforts to avoid somehow duplicating those structures in their own movement.

One sees many attempts to avoid hierarchy in feminist undertakings. The editors of *Liberation Now!* intentionally omitted their names from the anthology's cover [41]. The staff of feminist newsletters is often listed alphabetically, with no identification of position. Sandra and Daryl Bem flipped a coin to see whose name would appear first on a coauthored professional publication [42]. Lot systems and disc systems have been used by feminist groups to prevent a person or group from dominating meetings [43]. The expectation that everyone speak in turn, that no one interrupt a sister, and that all get equal time is a common ground rule of consciousness-raising cells.

As long as consciousness-raising remains the major goal of the women's movement, its anti-hierarchical efforts will probably be practicable. If its main focus becomes formal social institutions, however, its leaderless condition will be a disadvantage. Certainly interest groups which spin off from the movement (e.g., abortion reform groups) must have tighter forms of organization, and already do, but there is a distinction between an interest group and a social movement. Trying to tighten up the movement as a whole with national leaders and large formal organizations would guarantee the worst kind of fragmentation; the ideological splits already apparent in the movement would become unbridgeable.

Feminizing Political Communications

In a sense, the supportive, nonauthoritarian style of movement communication and organization can be considered a uniquely feminine style. Movement women often describe this interpersonal manner as one of the potentially valuable outcomes of an otherwise oppressive socialization, expressing concern to keep it:

> We tend to think of women's ability to deal with each other honestly, to be compassionate, as some sort of innate quality, when really what it comes from is our position in society. As that position changes, and as we begin to see ourselves as entering the mainstream in order to struggle with it, we have to be careful not to lose those qualities as we develop the assertiveness we need [44].

Several now classic experiments in social psychology laboratories have shown that groups tend to develop two kinds of leaders, task specialists whose roles are instrumental to goals, and interpersonal experts with expressive functions [45]. It has also been noted that women more frequently perform the latter role, men the former. The instrumental-expressive distinction has even been suggested in some psychological literature as the main dimension of masculinity-femininity in personality [46].

Although these generalizations about the sexes are far too sweeping, women's expertise in the interpersonal, expressive mode has enriched feminist politics in many ways, both in its inner workings and in relation to the larger society. A male friend of mine has described the difference in style between the women's movement and the male-dominated Left as, "The men tried to batter down the door; the women walked quietly into the living room and remarked, 'You better change your mind.'"

Thus, the traditional feminine interpersonal modes have been productively appropriated by radical women; whether the movement can continue its development largely through these modalities remains to be seen. At any rate, movement women have offered other groups an example of a style which happens in this society to be feminine, but which may be highly effective for future groups also intent on politicizing issues now considered personal.

Concluding Ideas

I suggested early in this essay that the feminist movement as a case study in political innovation might illuminate larger political issues. Perhaps its most obvious implication is that whenever new communication networks develop, private discomforts will tend to politicize. Related to this, we may suspect that when this happens, more personal (feminine) styles will become increasingly politically acceptable [47].

Just to venture one guess in this connection: we might predict that we are very soon to see a movement of the old. Residential patterns are tending to insure communication among the elderly, and certainly they are an unfairly disparaged group in many of the covert ways that women have been (through the youth infatuation of the media, for instance). Grey Lib may seem a bit absurd to most of us now—but then, so did the women's movement at first. Perhaps Simone de Beauvoir, who has recently treated the problems of aging with her familiar sensitivity, has once again indicated what is to come [48].

Finally, a consideration of feminism might call into question certain pluralist assumptions about politics. Taking issue with Bell and Kristol for their argument that politics should be understood in terms of interest groups competing for power [49], Bernard states

> it is hard to think of women and children as interest groups maneuvering "to obtain the greatest amount of public influence and public power . . ." . . . It is hard, too, to think of women in this kind of conflict relationship with families or "the family." Not other "interest groups" but structural arrangements that get in the way of good relationships seem to be more suitable concepts. And this approach assumes some concept of the public interest [50].

I would argue in the same spirit that if politics is regarded only in terms of the conventional model of competition for power, rather than as intrinsically involving values, emotions, and interpersonal experience, a great many political trends will continue to escape academic notice until they are already restructuring our institutions and reformulating our public discourse.

NOTES

1. S. Wolin, *Politics and Vision.* Boston: Little, Brown, 1960, p. 5.

2. I have drawn from earlier, more informal work where possible, for it is there that one can discern most clearly the painstaking formulation of the political goals and means that constitutes my main focus. Some of this material has since its original appearance been collected, anthologized, or integrated into more comprehensive works, but much remains available only in the form of the newsletters of radical groups, underground newspapers, informally circulated pamphlets, and the like. Where source material to which I refer has been collected in more accessible published form, I have referenced it by the newer location for the sake of convenience to the interested reader.

3. San Francisco Redstockings, 1970. Reprinted in B. and T. Roszak, eds., *Masculine/Feminine.* New York: Harper Colophon, 1969, pp. 285–290.

4. B. Friedan, *The Feminine Mystique.* New York: Norton, 1963.

5. J. Bernard, *Women and the Public Interest.* New York: Aldine-Atherton, 1971.

6. Allport, *The Nature of Prejudice.* Garden City, N.Y.: Doubleday Anchor, 1958.

7. G. Myrdal, *An American Dilemma.* New York: Harper, 1941, 1944 (2 vols.).

8. H. Hacker, "Women as a Minority Group," *Social Forces,* **30,** pp. 60–69 (Oct. 1951).

9. C. Thompson in M. Green, ed., *Interpersonal Psychoanalysis,* New York: Basic Books, 1964, pp. 201–343.

10. K. Horney, *Feminine Psychology.* New York: Norton, 1963.

11. V. Klein, "The Feminine Character" in C. Thompson, ed., *An Outline of Psychoanalysis.* Modern Library, 1955, pp. 386–409.

12. S. de Beauvoir, *The Second Sex.* New York: Knopf, 1953.

13. D. Lessing, *The Golden Notebook.* New York: Simon and Schuster, 1962.

14. A. Rossi, "Sex Equality: The Beginning of Ideology," *The Humanist,* **XXXIX,** No. 5, pp. 3–16 (Sept.–Oct., 1969).

15. Briefly, though, other factors sometimes mentioned as clearing the runway for feminist activity include the decline in challenging types of home activities, the fragmentation of communities with solid social supports for women (voluntarism, church work, extended family obligations), the increasing gap between a woman's role and the pursuits toward which she had been liberally educated, the opportunity occasioned by the sexual revolution to compare bedroom encounters, and the new, civil-rights-style popularity of seeing social problems in terms of collective prejudice and oppression.

16. R. Morgan, "Goodbye to All That," in B. and T. Roszak, eds., *Masculine/Feminine.* New York: Harper Colophon, 1969, pp. 241–250. Orig. in *RAT* (New York, Feb. 6, 1970).

17. See also J. Berstein, *et al., Sisters, Brothers, Lovers . . . Listen . . .* Boston: New England Free Press, 1967.

18. New University Conference newsletter, 1970.

19. C. Hayden, *et al.,* "Sex and Caste," *Liberation* (Apr. 1966 and Dec. 1966).

20. J. Mitchell, "The Longest Revolution." *New Left Rev.,* **40** (Nov.–Dec. 1966).

21. M. Piercy, "The Grand Coolie Damn," in R. Morgan, ed., *Sisterhood is Powerful.* New York: Vintage, 1970, pp. 421–438.

22. K. Millett, *Sexual Politics.* New York: Doubleday, 1970.

23. P. Mainardi, "The Politics of Housework," in R. Morgan, ed., *Sisterhood is Powerful.* New York: Vintage, 1970.

24. Erikson, E. "Inner and Outer Space: Reflections on Womanhood," in R. J. Lifton, ed., *The Woman in America.* Boston: Beacon, 1964, pp. 1–26. Orig. in *Daedalus* (Spring 1964).

25. E. Douvan and J. Adelson, *The Adolescent Experience.* New York: Wiley, 1966.

26. J. Bardwick, *Psychology of Women: A Study of Bio-Cultural Conflicts.* New York: Harper & Row, 1971.

27. R. Morgan, *Sisterhood is Powerful.* New York: Vintage, 1970, p. xxxvi.

28. M. Duverger, *The Political Role of Women.* Paris: UNESCO, 1955, p. 130.

29. S. Kempton, "Cutting Loose," *Esquire* (July 1970). Also in *Liberation Now!* New York: Dell, 1971, pp. 39–55.

30. Cf. Orwell writing of Dickens:
[I]t is not at all certain that a merely moral criticism of society may not be just as "revolutionary"—and revolution, after all, means turning things upside down—as the politoco-economic criticism which is fashionable at this moment . . . [T]wo viewpoints are always tenable. The one, how can you improve human nature until you have changed the system? The other, what is the use of changing the system before you have improved human nature? They appeal to different individuals, and they probably show a tendency to alternate in point of time. The moralist and the revolutionary are constantly undermining one another.
G. Orwell, "Charles Dickens" in S. Orwell and I. Angus, *The Collected Essays, Journalism and Letters of George Orwell, Vol. 1, 1920–1940.* New York: Harcourt, Brace & World, 1968.

31. E. Milner, "Effects of Sex Role and Status on the Early Adolescent Personality" in *Genetic Psych. Monographs*, **40**, pp. 231–325 (1949).

32. V. L. Allen and R. S. Crutchfield, "Generalization of Experimentally Reinforced Conformity" in *Jour. Abnormal Soc. Psycho.*, **67**, pp. 326–333 (1963).

33. S. Bem and D. J. Bem, "Case Study of a Nonconscious Ideology: Training the Woman to Know Her Place" in D. J. Bem, ed., *Beliefs, Attitudes, and Human Affairs.* Belmont, Ca.: Brooks/Cole, 1970.

34. E. Maslow, "I Dreamed I Took Myself Seriously in my Maidenform Bra," *Up From Under* (May/June 1970).

35. P. White and S. Goode, "The Small Group in Women's Liberation," *Women: A Journal of Liberation*, **1**, No. 1, pp. 56–57 (Fall 1969).

36. A. Sunshine and J. Gerard, "Small Group: Big Job," *Leviathan*, **2**, No. 1, pp. 20–21 (May 1970).

37. S. Stambler, ed., *Women's Liberation: Blueprint for the Future.* New York, Ace, 1970, pp. 9–10.

38. M. Piercy, "The Grand Coolie Damn," *op. cit.*

39. M. Salo and K. McAfee, "A Caucus-Race and a Long Tale," *Leviathan*, **2**, No. 1, pp. 15–19 (May 1970).

40. B. Jones and J. B. Brown, *Toward a Female Liberation Movement.* Boston: New England Free Press, 1968. Excerpt in B. and T. Roszak, eds., *Masculine/Feminine, op. cit.*

41. *Liberation Now!* New York: Dell, 1971.

42. Bem and Bem, *op. cit.*

43. R. Morgan, ed., *Sisterhood is Powerful, op. cit.*

44. New University Conference newsletter, 1970.

45. R. Bales and P. Slater, "Role Differentiation in Small Decision-Making Units" in T. Parsons et al., *Family, Socialization and Interaction Process.* Glencoe, Ill.: Free Press, 1955.

46. M. M. Johnson, "Sex Role Learning in the Nuclear Family" in *Child Devel.*, **34**, pp. 319–333 (1963).

47. A fascinating comparison of the instrumental-expressive contrast can be made to classical distinctions in political theory between the *rex* and the *dux*. The former by our standards is a more "feminine" sort of leadership, the latter a "masculine" type. Jouvenel has noted the decline in valuation of the *rex* function in modern times; perhaps feminism is restoring it somewhat as an appropriate political style. B. de Jouvenel, *On Power*. New York: Viking, 1949.

48. Other signs have appeared since the original preparation of this article, notably the movement of the Gray Panthers.

49. D. Bell and I. Kristol. Editorial, *The Public Interest*, **1**, No. 1 (Fall 1965).

50. Bernard, *op. cit.*, p. 32. Grant McConnell made a similar argument in *Private Power and American Democracy*, New York: Knopf, 1966.

Chapter

10

Women's and Men's Liberation Groups:
Political Power Within the System and Outside the System

Warren T. Farrell

Typology of Women's and Men's Liberation Groups

Robert Michels documented the iron rule of oligarchy [1]. C. Wright Mills condemned its practice in the American political system [2]. The National Organization for Women (NOW) condemns the exclusion of women from the oligarchy and the radical feminists are trying to organize and defy the iron rule by preventing themselves from developing manifestations of hierarchical patterns of behavior. It is in this latter group that one can begin to see the beginnings of the justification for the hypothesis that women's and men's liberation groups include new forms of pressure groups advocating values distinct from the classical values involved in the acquisition of political power.

A second example of this new form of pressure group is the unique phenomenon of the organization of a group of men seriously considering the forfeiture of the power they already have. These men's groups are variously called Men's Liberation Groups, the Human Alternatives Movement, a Human Liberation Movement or a "group of men in favor of women's liberation." They are attempting to consider not only if their sex has given them an unfair advantage in obtaining power but what subtleties of behavior and attitudes are locking them into these power positions and locking women into their place. Finally they are asking whether the power is a burden they would rather not assume or a corruption of which they would rather

An earlier version of this paper was originally presented at the Annual Meeting of the American Political Science Association, Chicago, 1971.

not be a part. This recognition of the validity of the destructiveness of an accumulation of power is not occurring in a vacuum. The hippie culture's enactment of a life-style with an anti-power bias is a segment of the evolution of a larger anti-power culture which has preceded these men's groups. This anti-power bias assumed an added dimension of legitimacy when distortions of power were made inescapable by the publication of the Pentagon Papers.

The emergence of women's liberation groups in an atmosphere of alienation from power produces a number of conflicting crosscurrents. One is a normal phenomenon of group theory—a group outside of the system attempting to make its presence felt as leverage for a power base within the system. These groups might be considered part of the "pro-power" culture. They include the National Organization for Women (NOW), women's professional caucuses in almost every academic discipline and profession from nursing to law, the Business and Professional Women (BPW), Women's Equity Action League (WEAL), groups of feminists in music and the arts, groups concerned with legislative issues such as New Yorkers for Abortion Law Repeal, and the new National Women's Political Caucus.

Many of these pro-power groups would object to this classification, particularly due to the association of power with abuse of power. Many of these new groups have strongly stated that in a position of power they would use it in a more humane way with opportunities and options available for a broader spectrum of the population [3]. However, the emphasis of these groups is to obtain a place for women in the hierarchy of the academic, professional, artistic, or political worlds. This is power in these respective spheres, and only time will tell whether similarities between men and women include similarities in tendencies toward empire-building and game-playing.

The second of these conflicting currents is unusual in group theory—a group outside of the system organizing to gain the power to have a system without power—that is, a system in which there is no stable power elite. These include groups such as the Feminists, the New York Radical Women (NYRW), groups originating from within the NYRW such as Redstockings and WITCH, plus the New York Radical Feminists (NYRF) and the Stanton-Anthony Brigade [4]. These groups might be considered part of the anti-power culture.

The Psychology of the Anti-Power Groups

Many of these groups have attempted to demonstrate the effect of a system's structure on the psychology of the individual in that system—declaring that capitalism's bias is to produce a competitive, power-seeking and empire-building society and therefore a competitive, power-seeking and empire-building individual. These groups face a fundamental dilemma. On the one hand they are attempting to obtain enough power to stop a system (capitalism) which only recognizes power from its tendencies toward power aggregation. However, in the process of gaining this power they are faced with the prospect of individuals in the new system becoming power hungry themselves.

In other words it is faced with the applicability of its analysis to its own members—that the need to obtain power will mold the individual's psychology to such an extent that once having it she or he will not want to dilute it.

The recognition of this struggle for power, but power in a nonoppressive sense (as contrasted with men's use of power) is illustrated in a portion of the Radical Feminists' Manifesto:

> As radical feminists we recognize that we are engaged in a power struggle with men, and the agent of our oppression is man insofar as he identifies with and carries out the supremacy privileges of the male role. For while we realize that the liberation of women will ultimately mean the liberation of men from the destructive role as oppressor, we have no illusion that men will welcome this liberation without a struggle.

This second current of feminists—the "anti-power culture" feminists—has not been so simple as to allow this contradiction to exist without attempting to eradicate it in practice. Almost all of these groups employ every method possible to rotate leadership and to develop each person's capability at decision-making, a built-in deterrent to a leader's potential for manipulation. At meetings, leaders are either chosen by lot or by rotation, and assignments to projects are made by the same method. One of the functions is to develop self-confidence and a sense of independence through participation in the leadership process.

This system is not dissimilar to the concept of Maximum Feasible Participation developed as a part of the Community Action Programs under the Economic Opportunity Act [5]. Maximum participation was originally seen as a good approach for running a program effectively. Yet one of the few positive results of the program was the method itself—the sense of responsibility and sense of self developed through maximum feasible participation. Evaluators found it impossible to avoid the benefits of this method, yet were constrained from officially weighing the psychic awards of participation in their evaluation of the program.

Women's groups employing a system similar to Maximum Feasible Participation have met with a similar conflict between means and ends. They are often accused by NOW members as accomplishing little in a programmatic sense, and NOW members are often accused of doing little to develop the consciousness and sense of self of women who are not already leaders. Where this latter accusation partially breaks down in practice is that a large amount of work needs to be done. This affords almost anyone with the time to participate an opportunity to build a specialization and through her expertise gain a sense of contributing. One of the characteristics, then, which differentiates a voluntary women's organization from a governmentally sponsored Community Action Program is that in the women's organizations there is no real mutual exclusivity between the participation of one person and another.

The rotation of power may have another psychological effect if Lasswell's hypothesis is correct—that persons with low self-estimates tend to seek power [6]. Rotation may discourage the person who is seeking power just to prove herself or himself worthy since it is no longer a sign of superiority to have obtained power. The willingness of men's liberation groups to opt out of power positions may also indicate a degree of security of self not possessed by the power-seekers. Lasswell's discussion of low self-estimate personality types suggested the transference of attempts to fulfil individual psychological needs to the formal political sphere. It is suggested here that the formal political sphere is only one small way of compensating—that a much more common method might be seeking power over other individuals with whom one is closely associated. This method requires no transference to a different level of manipulation, overcomes fewer barriers, and does not require such favorable circumstances as the right timing or enough money to campaign. A man with a low self-estimate may seek out a woman who defers to him, who offers him much affection, and who props up his moral integrity. These characteristics—affection, deference, and rectitude—are values which Lasswell describes the power-seeker as holding as his highest personal values. The redefinition of power which women's and men's liberation groups are clearly suggesting is a redefinition of its context—the context of personal relationships, of role relations, and family relations.

A further refinement of the sharing of power developed by the radical feminist groups is the division of work into creative and noncreative work with each woman sharing in both types. Exposure to media is recognized as being highly conducive to the creation of stars and the catapulting of a person into power. Media exposure is therefore carefully rotated so that no one meets with the press twice before everyone meets once. One of the Feminists described the system's purpose this way:

> It says that some work is better than other work—but no person is better than any other . . . It also says women—all women—are capable of power—of leadership—but that we no longer want the male values imposed on us—that of hierarchy. It also says that—unless controlled—women—in an anarchic situation—will grab control—and dominate others—become "stars"—cater to the press—and enter into a position they could not have outside the feminist movement—on top [7].

The system of cooperation is also applied to another area in which "stars" are often formed—writing. For example, the Feminists require all written work of individuals to be submitted to the group for approval and correction. The overall purpose is to prevent power from accumulating by cornering a market or specializing. The more of a market one has, the more attached to or possessive of it she or he becomes until another person's entrance into the area is seen as an intrusion rather than a contribution. This begins the process of empire-building. The rotation of all responsibilities is seen as discouraging this. Persons with special talents are utilized as resource persons whose talents may be called upon to contribute to the work of another individual and expand her development.

Consciousness-raising sessions are conducted similarly. There are no leaders; each woman's experience is considered politically relevant (especially in Redstockings) and each woman or sister takes her turn at making a contribution to the topic selected for that evening's consciousness session. The effect is again to build empathy, discourage competition for limelight, and create a feeling of cooperation or sisterhood. These are values antithetical to those characteristic of most groups.

The one political stimulus which the women's consciousness groups encourage, which is common to most groups attempting to obtain leverage within the system, is the development of a political esprit de corps evolving from an understanding of the way they have been used and oppressed. The consciousness groups do engage in an oversimplification of who is the enemy; they often find it necessary to have an enemy, and (almost by definition of holding meetings separately from one of the major candidates for enemy—men) they inevitably distort much of what might be said in his defense. These are all techniques employed by nations, techniques which have classically provided the base of support needed for war and the perception of oppression necessary for sustained fighting against the dominant system.

Relations with Men as Overlapping Membership

The concept of overlapping membership may be helpful in projecting which women and women's groups will be likely in the future to see men as the enemy and which will find it desirable to work with men. Most women have a major overlapping membership, i.e., an intimate relationship with a man. Truman points out that if a person is a member of various groups "the demands and standards" of these groups frequently come into conflict and each conflict has significant implications for the internal affairs of the group [8]. Men fit this category in two ways: their demands and standards are not only made but have the sanction of society's acceptance. For example, if a man's standards involve the woman taking care of the child, society supports this standard.

The second aspect of the threat to women's groups that the overlapping membership with men poses, is the time involved in each membership. The women's group may only consume one evening per week plus a few hours extra in comparison to the two to four evenings per week plus the weekend with the man. This is combined with the uncertainty as to how long the affiliation with the women's group will last and the probability that the relationship with the man preceded the relationship with the group.

The effect of this overlapping membership on the internal affairs of a woman's group is to separate those with the overlapping membership from those without it—or, in effect, to separate the women who are divorced, separated, lesbians, broken-up from men or disinterested in men from the straight or bisexual women involved in present and continuing relationships with men. The resultant difference in outlook is a source of factionalism and division [9] and is doubtless among the reasons the Feminists allow only one-third of their membership to be involved with a man.

One of the additional difficulties of membership in a feminist group while maintaining a relationship with a man is the insecurity which must inevitably develop from the conflict. The woman becomes a "middle woman," taking the arguments of the man to the women's group only to obtain negative sanctions about her decisions and then presenting the arguments from the women's groups to the man only to receive additional negative sanctions of an even more intense nature from the man. If she is already insecure she risks becoming more so unless the women's group is especially cautious about bringing out the best in the woman or unless the man's consciousness is also being raised. It is in this context that the men's consciousness-raising groups discussed below become politically relevant as one mechanism by which internal conflict in the women's groups may be minimized. They are also politically relevant as a mechanism for minimizing the frequency with which the conflict forces a woman to choose between withdrawing from the group or from her relationship with the man or even more significant, losing interest in her own liberation. Lazarsfeld and Korchin [10] discuss these options of forced withdrawal from one of the conflicting groups or loss of interest, either of which, in the case of women's groups, would tend to have a more severe effect on the women's groups than on the men, given what we assume is the more intense relationship with the man.

Feminists' Leadership Rotation and Pressure Group Theory

The leadership rotation system employed by the radical women's groups is particularly relevant and unusual in the light of pressure group theory.

Most pressure groups are primarily educating *leaders* to change the *system.* These groups are educating all their *members* to change *themselves.* Their methods of conducting their own internal affairs are the essence of their political methodology: leaderlessness, rotation of responsibilities, discouragement of "stars," and the monopoly of success by one person. The rotation is combined with the encouragement of each member to see her own experience as a woman as a relevant part of a larger sociological pattern of oppression. The emphasis on membership training rather than leadership training is the key variable.

The Feminists point to a major political strength in this methodology:

> A group operating in this manner has a high survival factor . . . it will not collapse because of its leaders' being picked off by judicial arrests and can't be forced into unwanted channels by a particularly strong member(s) threatening to quit if the group doesn't wish to follow her ideas [11].

Most pressure groups are also fighting to obtain a part of the system—believing that the system is good but its distribution of the goods is poor, that is, "we aren't getting enough of the good system." Most pressure-group theory views the success of a group on the degree to which it can obtain whatever scarce commodity it is seeking. The National Education Association would seek more money for education vis-à-vis defense or medicine. The American Medical Association and Lockheed would define success as more of the distribution of a scarce commodity in its favor (money for medicine or defense) to them.

By contrast, the radical women's groups are asking the system to distribute an entirely different type of goods—human rather than material goods. Their pressure is for a system which encourages rather than distributes—encourages human values such as self-determination rather than distributing goods according to class or sex determination. Their pressure is for a system encouraging cooperation as opposed to competition for a bigger piece of the economic pie. (The assumption implicit here is a relatively stable economic pie, suggesting that as poor persons or women obtain a larger proportion the absolute share of the wealthy will decrease. However, to the extent the overall economy is stimulated by the increased participation of women and the poor the absolute portions for all population segments may become larger.) The concept of lobbying for a larger share of the distribution of a scarce commodity is not a primary input to the system which motivates the radical women's liberation groups. They recognize that if success is possessing a scarce commodity, then persons have a stake in gathering more of it for themselves while others maintain some share as well.

Where success is high on the male hierarchy of values, and where it has been largely through the male hierarchy that we have been measuring the power and influence of pressure groups, it is just this value system and the male hierarchy itself which the radical women's liberation groups are challenging. Where, they ask, are the values of empathy, warmth, cooperation? This returns us to a fundamental dilemma or even contradiction. The dilemma is to attempt to exert pressure for systemic change without employing the kind of pressure to which the system is primed to respond—power. The alternative is moral suasion. If the radical women's liberation groups need to rely on the willingness of power holders to voluntarily give up power because they recognize the injustices of empire-building, they will doubtless be unsuccessful. This was Owen's, Bebel's and Fourier's theory about socialism—that its natural goodness would convince people to adopt it. They found it unworkable in a nation which did not already consider moral values to be superior to material and pragmatic ones.

Ironically, Ti-Grace Atkinson, one of the first leaders of a major women's liberation group to espouse these "outside of the system" or "anti-power culture" values was a former leader of the major "inside the system" women's liberation group—the National Organization for Women (NOW). In 1968, when Ms. Atkinson was president of the New York City Chapter of NOW, she severed her relationship with the organization. Unlike most executives, Ms. Atkinson wanted rotating executive positions to encourage the even distribution and development of leadership potential. She refused to accept the aspect of inevitability implied in the "iron rule of oligarchy," or the sacrifice of equality to gain equality. NOW's position was one of greater concern for accomplishing the goals they had established, asserting that strong executive leadership was only a realistic prerequisite to achieving the goals.

This concept of rotating leadership approaches the heart of pressure group theory. Systematic and frequent rotation of leadership inevitably tends to lead to decreased cohesiveness in a group. Truman points to cohesion as one of the most significant factors in maintaining a group's effectiveness:

Cohesion . . . is a crucial determinant of the effectiveness with which the group may assert its claims. It is a constantly operating influence that limits the activities of a group and its leaders, not only in critical times but as well when a group presents a front of harmonious unity. It is, in fact, the appearance of harmony in a successful group that may mislead the casual observer into treating such a group as a solid, homogeneous unit. A group must approach such a state in some degree if it is to exist at all [12].

Ms. Atkinson's philosophy of refusing to sacrifice the means of equality *among* women for the end of equality *for* women differs with previous practices of pressure groups. Labor unions have invariably fought to gain something for themselves while leaving other workers behind. Groups of workers from one union will protest if they are not receiving more money or benefits than other union workers. This creates a cyclical problem in New York City where sanitation men will strike if policemen or firemen receive an increase in money or benefits. Success is again the distribution of a scarce resource to one group at the expense of the other. It is a division of a group (workers) against members of the same group (workers). Professionals do the same thing in attempting to obtain for their profession a proportionately larger share of a fairly stable amount of government money. More importantly, both professions and unions make every effort to keep their membership exclusive in one way or another. Their success is judged by the failure of others to make it into the union or profession (e.g., the American Medical Association).

The radical feminists are rejecting this entire mode of thinking. If pressure group politics has been defined by men as a description of who gets what, when and how, they are demanding that politics start asking new questions about the "who," "what," "when," and "how":

Who: Not who *does* get but who *should* get.

What: Not *what* they *do* get but what this new "who" *should* get (implying a human rather than material "what").

When: That this new human "what" be received now, that political science not be a valueless description of when and how much of the old "what" was received.

How: That the "how" or means themselves be conducive to the development of equality rather than politics serving merely to perpetuate the iron rule of oligarchy with pressure groups serving as the means by which the oligarchy is rotated.

The National Women's Political Caucus: Pressure Group or Party?

Most of the larger women's liberation groups are not anti-power in orientation. However, they are not necessarily following the guidelines established for the most effective use of pressure groups. It may be said they are striking some middle ground between ideology and the standard criteria for effectiveness. A case of this compromise in effect is the National Women's Political Caucus (NWPC or Caucus).

The NWPC cannot be technically considered a pressure group. It combines some of the characteristics and tactics of a pressure group with those of a political party. Employing some of Schattschneider's criteria for assessing the effectiveness of pressure groups and political parties, we can gain some perspective of what the NWPC is doing to maximize and minimize its potential political effect.

Schattschneider suggests that "pressure politics is a method of short-circuiting the majority . . . there would be no such thing as pressure politics if a shortcut to influence had not been invented. Lobbyists long ago discovered that it is possible to get results by procedures that simply ignore the sovereign majority [13]." He feels this is both what distinguishes pressure groups and provides the basis for their success: "the distinguishing mark of pressure tactics is not merely that *it does not seek to win elections* but that in addition *it does not attempt to persuade a majority* [14]."

The National Women's Political Caucus' strategy totally repudiates Schattschneider's advice to ignore the sovereign majority. It is attempting to make political profit from public support and from an alleged base of 53% of the population—women. While recognizing that not all women will be supporting women candidates (or male candidates who support women's issues), it suggests that in a relatively short period of time women, in general, will be awakened and rally to their support. All women, then, are viewed as a part of their potential membership. At the same time though, the Caucus expects the support of thousands of sympathetic men. If this total projection were accurate, it would be reasonable to expect considerable success for the Caucus in its attempt to gain political strength by appealing to the majority of the people. One suspects, though, that while the absolute number of women and men lending support will be great, the percentage will be less than enough for political success in a winner-take-all system. Millions of women still possess a detachment, apathy or even outright hostility to anything associated with feminism, and the women who could potentially provide the greatest support—the poor, black, and the working class—are so caught in their oppression as to be prevented from gaining a consciousness of it or having the time to do anything if their consciousness is raised. Additionally, the strength of even women supporters is diluted by overlapping membership in other groups in a society generally hostile to women's political strength.

Our analysis to this point of the NWPC's political potential has assumed the validity of Schattschneider's evaluating criteria—that a failure in the attempt to gain majority support will have a detrimental effect on the group's political potential. However, when these criteria are applied in the case of the NWPC they may well be invalid. If the Caucus were to be successful only in putting three to five additional sympathetic candidates into office they would then have gained strong spokespersons for their cause despite their loss of the majority of elections. They would also have gained an ability to guard their interests in different committees, in caucus, and in back room discussions. Each success can be considered that much more ability to apply pressure than the Caucus had previously. The assumption of Schattschneider is congressmen and governmental agencies will act on the *belief* these groups have vast support. The assumption implicit in the NWPC's strategy is that the quality of response will be better if only a part of the vague belief bears fruit in the form of specific representatives clearly elected on the women's rights platform. A few actively working representatives who consistently employ women's rights as a bargaining mechanism provide the same leverage that a few Conservatives in the New York State Assembly provide in extracting agreements in exchange for their support on other issues. This is particularly true of a one-issue candidate, or a candidate willing to give primary attention to women's rights, as might be the case of a woman candidate elected to an almost all-male legislature.

A second characteristic of pressure groups which Schattschneider discusses is an attempt to influence legislative action and the political allocation of resources with the greatest economy of effort, money and public attention. These are again areas in which the NWPC has violated an essential characteristic of a pressure group. While their expenditure of money will be predictably moderate, their expenditure of effort and their exposure to the media and the public has been and is likely to continue to be considerable. Immediately upon the Caucus' formation it consistently made the front pages of newspapers around the country. Unlike the National Organization for Women, which also receives a fair degree of public attention, it was not making an attempt to influence only selected pieces of legislation at selected moments during which it had calculated the greatest amount of potential political impact. However, the Caucus' implicit evaluating criteria may again have been more a focus on ideology—raising the consciousness of the public as to the need and desirability of supporting candidates of a different sex, and therefore of candidates putting a greater value on human priorities.

In a method characteristic of a political party, the National Women's Political Caucus has made a concerted effort to appeal to a bipartisan audience, to moneyed as well as nonmoneyed interests and to women from a broad range within the political spectrum. It is suggesting that what some people would consider a narrow goal—women and women's issues—is in fact a broad goal, broad enough to unite many persons who might otherwise politically disagree. It has brought to its policy council a generally proportional representation of age and racial groups within the population. It has, however, kept men from participating to any significant extent in its formation of policy and stopped short of unity when it conflicts with supporting women racists or women who discriminate against other minorities, including women. The NWPC deviates from a strict definition of a political party in the sense that much of its support goes to candidates who are nominated by the two major parties. While doing this, however, it has emphatically pointed out that it is not beyond nominating its own candidates should the candidates of the major parties fail to be satisfactory, or becoming a real political party should the major political parties be more universally unresponsive. Should the NWPC follow through with either of the two latter plans it will not only be deviating from the distinguishing characteristic of a pressure group—not seeking to win elections—but also deviating from what Schattschneider considers the first rule of successful pressure politics: "to make a noise like the clamor of millions but never permit an investigation of the claims [15]."

Key [16] and Schattschneider both discuss the general inability of pressure groups to deliver votes. Schattschneider feels that one of the major strengths of pressure groups is taking advantage of their own weakness of not being able to put their strength to a test in an election. They can, therefore, make unverifiable claims as to their size of membership ("all women—53% of the population") and influence. He calls this "the method of exaggeration": "exaggeration is the life of pressure politics. The more realistically it can be done the more apt it is to worry timid Congressmen, and that is enough [17]."

The disastrous effects of a pressure group putting its claims for the delivery of votes to a test is illustrated by Schattschneider with the case of Father Coughlin during the election of 1936. Father Coughlin had created the impression of great influence and authority. He was eventually to put up a candidate in the 1936 election. The candidate lost by such a large proportion of the votes that all the claims for Coughlin's Union of Social Justice were severely discredited and the movement largely destroyed [18]. While Schattschneider's criteria may prove correct in the sense that women candidates will win elections in only a small percentage of congressional, state senate and assembly election districts, in those districts where they do run it is suggested their percentage of successes will approach the male candidates' percentage and that the elections they do win will contribute much more to the visibility and success of women's issues.

The National Organization for Women as a Pressure Group

A major women's liberation or rights group which employs many of the standard techniques of pressure groups is NOW. It is the largest and perhaps the most politically effective (in the classical, institutional sense of politics) of the women's liberation or women's rights groups. While it is a volunteer organization and not as well-staffed or financed as a business or professional interest group, it provides its membership with a wide distribution of intelligence concerning effective political pressure points. It gathers information in cooperation with other groups such as the National Women's Party on legislation such as the Equal Rights Amendment. For example, it keeps track of the senators and congressmen supporting and in opposition to both the Equal Rights Amendment and parallel amendments on the state level. Through hundreds of local newsletters it circulates information as to which office holders would be most amenable to pressure and which hold positions such as committee chairpersonships that are most responsible for legislation in question. It encourages its members to write letters and sponsors trips to Washington D.C. and state capitols for direct lobbying. For the Equal Rights Amendment, NOW and other groups prepared packets on how to lobby and distributed information systematically through a number of publications [19].

NOW's response to the radical women's complaints as to the hopelessness of the system and the need to work for a vague but total revolution based on new values, is a focus on specific legislation aiming at implementing at least some of these values. Through its contrasting technique of specialization it focuses on issues such as the more equitable division of property and pension for divorced persons, thus attempting to overcome through legislation some of the disadvantages of the capitalist system's tendency to allow all advantages in the hands of the property owner while giving the man the advantages of property ownership. It tries to reform some of the disadvantages of the present nuclear family by supporting legislation providing for survivorship rights in the case of divorce, the conversion of health and medical insurance to the dependent spouse, the creation of free 24-hour child-care centers and the deduction of child-care expenses from the taxes of working mothers [20].

The judiciary has been a central tool of NOW's efforts as a pressure group. In the case of *Weeks v. Southern Bell,* NOW gave considerable assistance to Lorena Weeks in support of her charge that she was denied promotion on the basis of sex. She was applying for a promotion to switchman (person) with the telephone company. The U.S. Court of Appeals for the 9th Circuit held that the employer had the burden of proving that substantially all women could not perform the job safely and efficiently before promotion could be denied on the basis of sex. The Court awarded $31,000 in back pay, basing the decision on Title VII of the Civil Rights Act of 1964.

The judiciary has responded to pressure by NOW, numerous other women's rights and liberation groups and even some unions [21] to invalidate state protection laws. They have made considerable cracks in the almost solid 100 years of precedent in which women were not included under the jurisdiction of the 14th Amendment. The *Cohen v. Chesterfield County School Board* case, in which the Federal District Court in Richmond held that mandatory maternity leave violated the 14th Amendment's guarantee of equal protection under the law to all persons, was a clear contradiction to the Supreme Court's frequent denial of the 14th Amendment's application to women. Women's rights groups were active in attempts to win the *Cohen v. Chesterfield* case.

The judiciary holds almost infinite potential for use as a political tool by the women's rights groups. If the Supreme Court does apply the 14th Amendment to women it will cover a vast area of discriminatory acts presently under question. The courts' interpretation of the Equal Pay Act of 1963 alone has resulted in more than $30 million in back pay with further application likely to amount well into the billions of dollars. The Wheaton Glass Company case has served as the precedent setter in this area by declaring that equal pay for equal work meant work that was "substantially equal," not necessarily identical.

One of the few possible drawbacks of the judiciary, as far as some women's rights groups may be concerned, is the probability of the elimination of the more favorable aspects of what Nagel and Weitzman term the "paternalistic" treatment now afforded women by courts. It appears women receive favorable court treatment "with regard to being kept out of jail pending trial, not being convicted, and not being sentenced to jail if convicted [22]." However, it seems quite clear that few women's liberation or rights groups are unwilling to trade this paternalistic favoritism for equal rights.

One of the closest groups to NOW in terms of orientation, a group which in fact split off from NOW, is the Women's Equity Action League (WEAL). WEAL has concentrated its energies on discrimination, employment opportunities, and counseling in the field of education. It has worked with NOW in filing complaints against numerous universities, including Harvard, the City University of New York, and the Universities of Maryland and North Carolina. The complaints have been followed by investigations. WEAL has pursued major universities not only for their proportionately greater impact, but because of the pattern of discrimination they have found: the more prestigious universities with higher salaries have fewer women in almost every department [23].

One of the difficulties in assessing the political potential of the women's groups is the difficulty of projecting the outcome of factionalism and splits. For example, those who thought a split with NOW was a sign of weakness in the women's movement did not project the strength which the creation of WEAL would soon add.

Assessing the Political Potential: Factionalism vs. Sisterhood

One of the criteria for evaluating the political potential of a pressure group, movement, or political party is its ability to convince persons that the changes the group is advocating have a high degree of personal relevance. In American politics the economy has more personal relevance than even the war in Southeast Asia; the candidates in both parties, therefore, can agree that it is more likely to be a deciding political issue in 1972 than the war. Here is where the women's groups rank high. Almost all their issues deal directly with the life-style, minds, and bodies of almost every woman and, indirectly with those of almost every man. Abortion is one of the issues which affects almost every woman personally. Few women live without the fear of an unwanted pregnancy at some point and approximately one of four obtain abortions. The support among all women's groups for abortion law repeal is intense. It is an issue which has both united the movement, yet, significantly for its political potential, it has been the source of many divisions.

The unity and the divisiveness were both apparent at the July 1971 Conference of the Women's National Abortion Coalition. While over 1000 women from more than 250 organizations were brought together for the conference, extensive disagreement and bitter accusation were rife. One of the major nonsubstantive disagreements was over access to the political system. The Socialist Worker's Party (SWP) was opposed to the overly legislative approach of the Women's National Abortion Action Campaign, FOCAS (Feminist Organization for Communication, Action, and Service), and of many of the more established groups. The history of the feminist movement appeared to be repeating itself in microcosm with some groups pushing for broader demands such as freedom for sexual expression (implying homosexuality) as part of the principle of a person having control over their own body, and other groups wanting to stick to a few central issues which had a realistic possibility for passage. The latter were necessarily more concerned with immediate access to the system and the former with building a broad social conscience. The history of the feminist movement can offer support to both approaches. The single-issue approach of suffrage did win the vote, but the vote meant little in a stagnant social context. On the other hand the history of the movement constantly witnesses the distraction of women's groups from their original goals with the inevitably resulting factionalism. The significant political question evolving from the abortion conference is whether women, like men, are caught up in the male hierarchy of values—power struggles dressed up as issue differences—or whether the sense of "sisterhood" can take the form of a viable and permanent unifier with a set of less power-seeking priorities attached.

Among the women's groups which are less concerned with access to power directly through the system, the strongest are socialist in orientation. The Socialist Workers Party (SWP) was dominant in the Women's Strike Coalition until they withdrew in mid-1971. Many of the SWP women members who involved themselves in the women's movement have become more devoted to the women's movement than to socialism. However, in almost all the groups to the left of the political spectrum of NOW and WEAL, a substantial percentage of the leadership considers socialism an important prerequisite to women's liberation.

The Socialist Worker's Party considers capitalism a major cause of women's oppression, but does not isolate it as the only cause [24]. It concedes that women's oppression predates capitalism and that even with a socialist revolution, deeply ingrained sexist attitudes would not be eliminated. The contribution of a socialist revolution, its leaders maintain, will be to eliminate the material basis for the exploitation of women. When the profit incentive is lessened the incentive for keeping a class of people who can be hired at low wages to do menial work, such as secretaries or keypunchers, will be lessened.

The SWP recognizes the sexist nature of advertising which it sees as the exploitation of whatever prejudices about sexuality and sex roles exist so as to appeal to the largest number of people. If men like to think of themselves as conquering women and this will sell more cars, no advertiser would suggest the advertisement representing this should be eliminated because it is discouraging equality of the sexes. Advertising and hiring practices in a free enterprise system tend to reinforce whatever prejudices the society already possesses. Capitalists have a direct interest in this reinforcement whereas a government does not and can be free to watch out for the interests of minorities as well as majorities.

Most SWP members recognize that not every socialist government has made use of this freedom to bring greater equality to minorities, but they do feel the socialist track record is considerably better than that of capitalist societies and that the built-in incentive to discriminate is minimized.

The Socialist Worker's Party, somewhat ironically, accuses the Communist Party's position on women's liberation of being reformist and comparable to the position of the National Organization for Women. The Communist Party believes the family can be transformed into a revolutionary force, of which the SWP says, "Theoretically, this is as ludicrous as arguing that the institution of private property can be turned into an instrument for social progress [25]." The SWP considers the Communist Party's support of the election of women to political office to be just as irrelevant and reformist since it is putting them into a system which perpetuates sexism, racism, and the exploitation of workers.

Any assessment of the political potential of the women's liberation movement must consider the ability of lesbian and straight women to work together in the movement and the likelihood of public acceptance or rejection of this alliance. The commitment of lesbian women has already been mentioned as one partially deriving from the fact that their membership is not overlapping with men. Two central points are involved in this so-called "lesbian issue." One is the recognition that role stereotyping and the pressure by society to force people into certain paths (heterosexual) is oppressive to women. Most of the women who have been in the movement with any real commitment agree. The disagreement occurs over what to do about it, which becomes the second issue.

Some of the leaders of the movement, such as Kate Millet and Ti-Grace Atkinson, who were both formerly active in NOW, want the movement to support the goals of the lesbians actively. On the other hand, Betty Friedan and Jacqui Ceballos (1971 President of New York City NOW) have felt that to undertake such a cause would dilute the original goals of NOW and, most importantly, effectively turn off the potential of NOW to reach the millions of women who would be afraid to join a movement identified with lesbianism.

NOW also recognized its particular responsibility as the one organization in the movement most likely to be able to serve as an introduction to women's liberation, as well as its self definition as an action organization bent on legislative goals. The practical achievement of these goals, they felt, meant the maintenance of credibility as well as a total devotion to these goals. It is, of course, debatable whether adding goals of homosexual liberation would have diluted the original aims or would have given the organization a broader base from which to operate.

Perhaps the arguments most relevant to the political potential of the movement are the ones implied by NOW's lack of active support for lesbians: it is likely to alienate too large a segment of the membership. However, this does not consider intensity of alienation and the commitment potential of the alienated. The lack of overlapping membership with the group called "men" has enabled lesbian women to remain particularly committed to women's liberation. As the movement gains more strength and more credibility it is likely that the pressure for active support of lesbian women will increase, not decrease. Historically the issue of "free love" was one that split the early feminists and led to their weakening, a point which highlights the importance of this issue to the current movement.

The organizations in the movement which have received minimal attention in the press, but have perhaps had the greatest impact on a change in the power relationships between the sexes despite or perhaps because of their departure from traditional political forms, are the women's consciousness-raising groups. The private nature of the changes which occur will probably never make it amenable to publicity, but the degree of interest has led to the creation of groups in almost every place where someone was willing to organize them. An appreciation of receptivity to consciousness-raising can be seen by the growth of Entitled, a women's consciousness group in Long Island. The group met for a year and a half by itself. Four of the members decided to form a new group since outsiders had expressed some interest. They casually put a small advertisement in the local paper. Within a week they were inundated with calls. When they organized the phone calls into groups able to arrange meetings, they found enough persons to start new groups every week for a year. As of August 1971, 26 groups were started by these four persons with plans to start a total of 52 groups by the end of the year.

The Problem with Men

While consciousness-raising for women has been employed extensively in almost all the women's groups, consciousness-raising for men has been almost totally neglected. The exclusion of men from the movement to change sex roles is almost exclusively an American phenomenon. In Scandinavia the very concept Americans know as women's liberation is known as a sex-role debate. Scandinavia is also usually credited with considerable progress toward breaking down sex roles. Almost all of the women's liberation groups agree, though, that something very significant needs to be done about men. The Redstockings Manifesto isolates male supremacy as "the oldest, most basic form of domination. All other forms of exploitation and oppression (racism, capitalism, imperialism, etc.) are extensions of male supremacy: men dominate women, a few men dominate the rest . . . [26]." The Socialist Worker's Party and Progressive Labor also view men's attitudes as in need of reform, but feel that man as well as women are in need of liberation from the capitalist system, and as this liberation is achieved the effect will be human liberation.

The methods by which men's attitudes can best change poses still another question and area of disagreement. Many of the women's groups feel men's attitudes will change only when women change their own heads. This partially accounts for the existence of women's consciousness-raising groups with a lack of concern for men's groups. It is reasoned that men have too much at stake to voluntarily forfeit it, and that the nature of what men have been trained to seek—power—builds the type of mental attitude which is unwilling to encourage equality. The inclusion of men in the women's consciousness-raising groups is also viewed as counter-productive to a woman's development of a method of solving her own problems that is not dependent on male help.

These assumptions needed to be put to the test. Can men change and if so under what conditions is the change most likely to occur in a positive direction? Do men need to meet in isolated men's groups in a manner parallel to the women's groups or is it more productive to meet as couples or to rotate among a number of methods?

A few of the highlights of meetings which took place for a year and a half among groups of men and groups of men and women are presented in the following pages to hopefully offer some subjective insight into the approaches which might answer these questions most adequately [27].

Method of Observing Men's Consciousness Groups

The writer was a participant-observer in two continuing men's groups. The purpose of both groups was to raise men's awareness of sex roles and their participation in a power relationship which was keeping women in their place and men in a power position. The bias of both groups was in favor of breaking down sex roles.

Distinctions must be made between the two groups. The first one, the Alternate U. group, was composed almost entirely of politically left or radical men who identified somewhere between the left of the Democratic Party and the Socialist Party. Many of their beliefs concerning equality of women were a logical extension of the equality they proposed for every other portion of society. The men in this group were, on the whole, more initially amenable to a breakdown of sex roles than in the second group. My own consciousness at the outset of this group was lower than it was in the second group and my own participation was one of a participant-observer in a group of equals (no leader). The group lasted 6 months.

My participation in the second group was less detached. I organized the group of men with the same purpose of educating for sex-role breakdown. The group encompassed a much broader cross section of men with a much lower level of initial consciousness. Most of the men were solicited from those attending meetings of NOW (the only women's liberation group meetings to which men are allowed). A couple of the men admitted to being at the meetings as much to pick up a woman as to learn about women's liberation. Others were there at the request of their wives or women friends and had little independent interest in women's or men's liberation. Still others thought if they came the women could benefit from their assistance. With this level of awareness we began a group in September 1970.

The second group was aware from the beginning of both my personal and social science reasons for organizing the group. My personal reasons entailed the desire to overcome my own male chauvinism and understand further the subtleties involved in the maintenance of the sex roles. My social science reasons were to examine the sex roles as a political relationship and discover how much change in the political relationship could occur during once per week meetings over the period of a year.

From a social science perspective my participation in the group was also as an introducer of the experimental variables in a quasi-experiment [28]. From this perspective my function was to expose the group to a set of values, attitudes, and beliefs leading in the direction of the breakdown of sex roles. As a participant-observer I was to observe the effect of this on the group and draw up hypotheses concerning the types of interactions and exposure which appeared to correlate with attitudinal or behavioral change. The number and complexity of the interacting variables plus the desire to minimize the "guinea-pig effect" [29] forced me to observe in a highly subjective and markedly unsystematic manner, although numerous patterns of attitude development and behavior were noted.

From the social science perspective the first group at Alternate U. had more of an effect on my attitudes than I had on theirs. Many of these attitudes became inputs to the second group and are therefore particularly relevant here.

Overcoming Intellectualization: The First Men's Group

When I entered the Alternate U. group, I did so with a feeling of being a "liberated man," meaning to me, at that time, that I was in favor of women's liberation. I came with an intellectual background on the liberation of women and presumed it had relevance to my own liberation or even liberalness. As the group started meeting, all the information I came with ("only 7% of engineers are women," etc.) was not being used. When I did use it, the group continued almost as if I had not spoken. Then I began to notice the difference. They were talking about themselves and their own experiences; I was talking about facts, statistics, trends, generalities—not about me.

Slowly I began to recognize the dimension of political power which extended beyond education, the dimension which demanded an examination of my own personal relationships, the dimension which asked for a change in behavioral patterns in addition to a change in attitudes. The recognition came slowly because statistics appeared to me to be much less refutable than just one person's experience. Statistics were a combination of the experiences of thousands of real people, I had reasoned. However, statistics were the aggregate experience of others, and knowing them demanded nothing of *me* (except a memory).

The political power of changing one's own experience became apparent when I reflected on the powerlessness of the modern church. How many businessmen attend church on Sundays, sit quietly before a sermon on "love thy neighbor," hear the Bible, read and participate in singing a hymn? Then they leave church and "step over thy neighbor" to climb to the top of the corporation during the rest of the week. The modern church, particularly modern Protestant churches and Jewish synagogues, do not ask for *accountability*. A person can act pious on Sunday and ignore the church's teachings during the week. She or he can memorize the tenets of a religion, but never apply them. Historically the Church became less powerful as it demanded less of its members between services. It was most powerful when demands, such as weekly confession, religious education, and living a daily life in accordance with one's religion, were the strongest [30]. The power of the consciousness groups, then, is to get its members to apply a liberated relationship in their own lives. It is not to teach the Bible of women's and men's liberation at its once per week meetings, give psychic rewards to the members who know it best and care less who applies it.

The Alternate U. group had no leader (Alternate U. comes from the name of an avant-garde school in downtown Manhattan whose members identified predominantly as Socialists). Collective responsibility was the group's strength and collective irresponsibility its weakness. Psychologically, the awareness that there was no leader encouraged each of us to speak up when we felt a member was being sexist, or telling his side of the story and leaving out his woman friend's side. A similar psychological awareness, that the entire group might challenge us (rather than just the leader), that our statements were sexist, eventually encouraged us to sidetrack into issues such as "women's liberation and the socialist revolution." A "topic-for-the-week" was safer than getting into a head-on collision with another group member which might lead to the entire group's analyzing that person's consciousness. We had established a system of checks and balances which was so effective that it came into conflict with our need for security and respect from others. We eventually retreated from ourselves rather than face the power we had given others over ourselves. The power of collective responsibility was effective enough to make us seek the comfort of collective irresponsibility. We continued on the "topic for the week" and we were all unconsciously aware of what we had done to ourselves: we were bringing about our own downfall by falling into the trap of which we had been so aware at the outset. At this time I wondered whether men could only take the raising of their own consciousness just so far. We lasted 6 months and experienced many changes, but only marginal ones. I was to find that men by themselves did in fact have this limitation. This eventually led me to experiment with varieties of group experiences, some of which are discussed below.

The Second Group: The Condescending Problem Solver

The second group, in which the men were drawn largely through their direct or indirect affiliation with NOW, began on the same note of intellectualizing their experiences. However, with this group there was also an opportunity to observe some of the men's interactions with NOW members prior to joining the men's group. A typical pattern was the "condescending problem solver." If the women were planning a demonstration inevitably something like the following would erupt: "You girls ought to be more careful about your image. If you want us men to like you and agree with you you should at least have your girls put on dresses when you march. And it's not just convincing the men I'm talking about. Other women too."

The degree of validity in the comment was, of course, irrelevant. The man could not resist "solving" the woman's problem for her. He could not recognize the importance of women reasoning things through independent of male advice, at a meeting held for the purpose of getting women to control their own lives rather than have their lives dependent on a man, be it for his advice, his money, or his love. It was this same point of dependence on men which made his phrase ". . . if you want men to like you" so grating. This male attitude reinforced my feeling of the need for a men's consciousness-raising group. A second basis was the positive attitude of the NOW women toward men.

Most of the men ranged in age between 23 and 40, although one was over 50. More than half were married or had been married, and most were living in some arrangement with women. About one-third had children and a few were from the suburbs of New York City. Politically, almost all of the group was to the left of center, but only a few could be considered radical. Some of the representative patterns of our attitude development are illustrated in the ensuing dialogues and analyses.

Sex Objectification as Exchange of Goods and Services

Sydney (all names are fictitious), a hip-talking graphics designer who had just returned from Europe, expressed his perception of liberated women: "I really like liberated chicks. They are into a lot of things—they're fun to talk to, man. I just got back from Europe and these chicks were really cool. They weren't so hung up and frigid like here."

I was becoming somewhat uneasy at what appeared to be a clouding of the distinction between sexually liberated women and women's liberation. It was not that the men did not recognize that liberated women were also intelligent. It was that the emphasis was on sex and that lip service to the presence of intelligent women appeared unencumbered with an awareness of the complications and obligations accompanying that presence. What was nice about liberated women, the men were saying, was that "you didn't have to go after them, they are not always acting coy. If they want sex, they'll make a pass at you too. That's the way it should be."

We continued, "What's wrong with men treating women as sex objects as long as they are free and liberated to treat you as a sex object too? As long as everyone knows where the relationship is at then no one is using anyone else."

"Yes," a second man agreed, "For example, what's wrong with an orgy, or use of each other as objects if both persons want it?" There was little objection to this "equal" use of each other.

I probably interjected too soon at this point at the expense of seeing where the conversation would take itself. I asked if women might often enter into so-called equal object relationships for other reasons—to attract a man for her ultimate marital security or to obtain his approval. These are also wrong reasons, but the woman is looking for something she has been taught to look for, such as money and security through a man, and is exchanging it for something the man has been encouraged to look for, namely sex. The process and justification that "each wants something" reinforced the traditional role relationship.

The exchange is fair, but it is based on a class difference as determined by sex. For example, the black slave woman would often exchange a sexual relationship with her white master so that her husband would be preserved from a beating or from being sold. Her exchange was fair from the perspective that both were receiving what they wanted, but avoids the unfairness of the original relationship and the predetermination of the original relationship on the basis of sex or color. The sex of the woman places her in a different power relationship to the man than would be true if she had the class advantages of a man and was not really seeking security in exchange for her sex.

This was the first of a number of objections we discussed concerning sex objectification as a reinforcement of traditional role relationships, traditional allocations of power, and traditional exchange of goods and services based upon a predetermined conception of the resources each sex had to offer. Man's basic good is money, and his basic service, security. Women's basic good is her body, and her service, sexual gratification.

The oppressiveness of this exchange was that both the man and the woman are forced into a role which is sexually determined, rather than encouraged to choose among alternative roles. It is a type of oppression similar to the Indian caste system—role determined by birth. Both systems justify this on the basis of the need for "role identity," and role security. Neither gives priority to individual choice, or the "insecurity of freedom." This restriction was still just the first piece of a much larger puzzle in our recognition of the oppressive nature of the sexes' focus on each other as sex objects, or the power of sex objectivism.

A second type of power, which the men in the group often employ and which serves to keep women in their place, is the maintenance of a sex-based *hierarchy of values,* with the assumption that the males' values were superior to the female's. This is reinforced by a technique called *self-listening:* a man listens to a conversation only for the purpose of being able to reply with one of his own experiences, ostensibly as an illustration of the point already made. It is actually a way of telling the person he already knew his or her point and is therefore not learning anything. Most importantly, though, it is a technique for drawing the conversation to his own experiences and encouraging the speaker to focus on him.

An example of self-listening occurred during our first meeting. As the meeting progressed, I noticed Sydney, the graphics designer, sitting on the edge of his seat. His eyes reflected an anxious intensity and he was shaking his head in agreement as each member began a new thought. He seemed to be saying, "I know what you are going to say," and with any pause he would jump in and say it his way, with his own story and elaborations. As the other person was speaking, his own mind was forming his own parallel incidents related to his own experiences.

A few moments later Sydney was explaining how, in the U.S., he was always in the position of bringing women (he was still using "chicks") up to his intellectual level (they knew so little about art, graphics, and design). As I listened further, I could begin to see that this was a fundamental personality trait of a number of the men. Its relevance to women's and men's liberation also became clear. If a woman were to speak, his type of personality would be only half listening, and listening only for the purposes of relating that incident to his own experiences. As soon as his experiences were brought into the conversation, it would begin to revolve around how much the woman knew about *his* world. Inevitably the man would soon be in the position of "bringing her up to my intellectual level."

The man in the group who is unwilling to listen to other men for the values and ideas which they possess, tends also to be unwilling to listen to a woman's contribution except insofar as he can relate it to himself. The problem becomes his inability to understand fully those values which the woman has come to recognize as primary in her life. He unconsciously maintains a hierarchy of values in which masculine values are considered superior to feminine values. The latter might include her ability to empathize with characters in a novel, her desire to work with younger children, her expression of emotions—all female traits which an average man meeting an average woman is likely to find or to look for, and then to devalue. The point is that these female traits could be as important a contribution to the world as masculine traits. The man who believed he was liberated tended to consider his masculine traits as something toward which women should strive and her traits as something which he should understand, tolerate, or be amused by. This process becomes self-defeating for the woman even if she does attempt to develop the man's traits, because until the woman has the confidence that she can make a contribution as a person, as she is, she will be unable to make it in either a woman's or a man's role.

The maintenance of an unconscious hierarchy of values often undermines the consciousness-raising process of a woman whose membership is overlapping with that of her relationship with a man. She is torn between what the group tells her and what the man tells her, which often makes her even more insecure. In most cases, consciousness-raising takes women out of the security of subservience before it offers the security of self.

The longer the group continued, the more annoying the employment of men's values became to all of us. A function the group was able to serve was the observation of these traits as they revealed themselves in the group. Among the traits were dominating, interrupting, condescension, disrespect, aggression, obsession with sex, ego, intellectualization, put-downs, and a lack of empathy, emotion, openness, warmth, and contact with persons as human beings rather than competitors for power and position. These characteristics manifested themselves incessantly in our conversations within the group.

Distinction Among Consciousness Groups, Seminars, and Therapy

In our attempts to assist each other with overcoming these characteristics we had to constantly keep in mind the distinction between a therapy group and a consciousness-raising group. The distinctions are important. A therapy group is led; it can delve into *psychological* explanations as to *why* behavior occurs; it generally teaches one how to *adjust* to the societal norm; the leader is trained to encounter participants on a broad base of problems, and it is assumed that a leader can best help the participants deal with the complications accompanying change. A consciousness-raising group is more specifically focused, dealing predominately with problems resulting from the attempted adjustment to sex roles. Its members encourage each other to question sex roles, rather than to depend on a leader to help them adjust. This process of lay persons supporting each other in change and questioning every behavioral and psychological restriction or sex role has become a major contribution of feminism to therapy, to the point where feminist therapy is a rapidly growing field. In addition, women's consciousness-raising groups are almost entirely supportive rather than encountering in nature; men's groups combine supportiveness through understanding of common socialization experiences with challenging each other to change, using such techniques as "follow through hours" at the start of meetings to see how members have changed since the last session.

Both therapy and consciousness-raising groups focus on the individual and personal problems. For this reason they confront a central problem of masculinity—the difficulty men have in being introspective. Most men are comfortable acknowledging that blacks have problems, that Chicanos, Indians and women have problems, but not that "I have a problem." We find it hard to admit weaknesses, to enter consciousness-raising and therapy, to depend on a group in any way. When we are lost, we cannot ask for advice or even admit that we are lost. In men's groups we have found that we even have difficulty asking for directions when we are lost driving a car.

This difficulty men have in personalizing makes it tempting for men's groups to become issue-oriented seminars. One week we are examining the biology of men and women; the next it is discrimination in employment or education. We emerge more "educated," but not more liberated.

When we do deal with present problems (as opposed to problems we "used to have,"), the meeting often becomes a grudge session: "My problem is my wife." The focus is on women's liberation as a "woman's problem" that is now causing *us* problems; it does not shift to our initiatives or responsibilities in our personal relationships with women. Men's consciousness raising supports other men by sharing the awareness of society's expectations of men, of an understanding of how those expectations become pressures which engender anxieties, and how those anxieties give us feelings of powerlessness which make us fight to be in control. Men support each other by understanding how our personal hangups about masculinity affect our relationships with women, and with other men. If a man has a feeling of sexual inadequacy and cannot talk about it with other men, he will build up a shield of protectiveness and unfeeling coldness which will make him, as so many women complain about men, "hard to love." To the extent a men's group can help men express feelings and a non-defensive openness, they will be establishing the basis for a warmer relationship between the sexes. They will also establish the framework in which women can express feelings and emotions without feeling uniquely "just like a woman." [31]

This feeling of inadequacy is a most basic feeling of powerlessness. It affects power relationships on both a macro and micro level. When a human being or a country feels inadequate in its defenses it builds up walls and cuts off communication to avoid exposing this inadequacy. Men stop communicating with women, as countries stop communicating with potentially threatening countries. Men look instead for something to protect, such as a woman, a role which will enable them to divert their attention from their own weaknesses. On the macro level, countries such as the United States and the U.S.S.R. form protective pacts with weaker countries. NATO, the Warsaw Pact, ANZUS, and SEATO are but a few examples. This need of the weaker country or person for protection, provides an additional justification for the severance of communication with competitive countries or persons, ("if they find out where I'm inadequate, you will suffer too since I protect you").

Perhaps, though, it could be argued men and countries do need to build up these defenses lest they be destroyed, either as individuals or as countries. There is no way to completely argue this point, just as there is no way for a child who is told by his parents "do not leave the house, never cross the street and do not talk to anyone because you might be killed or stabbed by the person you talk to" to assure his parents that is an impossibility. However, the increment of security gained by staying in the house or building defenses must be measured as a value in relation to the increment of freedom, growth, and fullness of life gained by opening oneself to others.

Male Dominance Patterns

A final pattern which recurred in every mixed group was male dominance. At one of our first meetings, a group of the men met with a group of NOW women. One of the women explained an employment problem she had to the mixed group of seven men and seven women. When she finished, the next 20 minutes were spent by all seven men (including myself) giving her advice and asking her questions concerning the nature of her problem. Not one woman offered advice and not one asked even a single question. I remembered the literature of the Redstockings and radical feminists who had condemned the leadership concept because it discouraged so many people from learning to take responsibility and come forth with their ideas. As I saw the men dominate, I remembered how all the men had acknowledged in our men's group that, by dominating, women were frequently prevented from bringing out what they had to offer. There was obviously not a moment's application of this theoretical recognition.

The Feminists had also suggested the distribution of chips, allowing a person to speak for only as many times as she had chips. When the dominant women ran out, the less dominant would have to speak. As I watched this 20 minutes of uninterrupted male dominance with a few men within the group of men clearly dominating the others, the validity of this Feminist concept became more and more clear. Their reasons for limiting their organization, particularly their consciousness groups, to all women also became clearer. Here was a woman coming to a mixed group allegedly to raise her awareness of women's potential and implicitly her own potential for decision-making. The process, though, was serving only to reinforce her image of men as helpers and women as competitors or passive nonhelpers.

Yet what happened in that meeting was also an argument for the validity of combining the groups if only to gain a laboratory experience of how meaningful the theory of male dominance is and how much more difficult it is to change than to reach agreement on the desirability of new attitudes. Both the men and the women could see it happen in a situation which was explicitly designed to handle it, and thus the process became more obvious to both the women and the men present.

At our next meeting of all men, we discussed the importance to the women's liberation movement of what had happened. Equal pay for equal work obviously meant very little if women think of themselves as unable to make contributions in a heterosexual environment. The essence of independence is the ability to ask the type of question which gives one control over her or his own life rather than being dependent on someone else to tell you how to run yourself. If a woman has not trained herself to do this then equal pay for equal work is relevant only for those few exceptions to the rule who are women but have not fallen into this pattern of subservience.

Women's Issues: Impact on Masculine Values

We discussed earlier in this section the distinction between the hierarchy of values women and men possess and the importance for men to open themselves to the positive nature of many of the values in the female hierarchy. We continued by observing some of the negative effects of dominance and other male values on both women and men. We must conclude by recognizing some of the practical difficulties of overcoming these negative effects without a change in some of the basic arrangements within the embryo of our power structure—the family. The issue of child care is fundamental and will serve as an example.

A change in the basic responsibility for child care is a requisite for a change in the attitudes one allows oneself to have about the seeking of power outside of the home. A woman who projects a career interrupted at length by childbearing has a more difficult time imagining herself climbing to the top of the ladder in government, spending the enormous amounts of time it takes running for political office, or working her way to the top of a corporation.

If a man increased his responsibility for child care it would force him to project a year or two respite from "working my way to the top"—a respite into an environment where power games are subservient to love, nurturance, giving, and the constant reminders of the beauty of a child's innocence in a world of contrasts to that innocence. This creates an attitude different from the normal male focus on practicality, and "the real world"—a focus from which man obtains no relief except being drafted into an even crueller world of war. A man is constantly facing maximum exposure to cruelty, hardness and power, an exposure which forces him to adapt to these terms or be nothing. In the adaptation, a vicious circle is completed. Men's reality is the reality of hardness, but this is no more real than the reality of a child's innocence and the increased emphasis on human values which greater amounts of time with that child brings. However, emphasis on human values is not a central part of a man's world now, and a man considers only his world to be the real world. Perhaps the most important political change, which a change in the man's role portends, is the possibility of a change in the balance between values of power and cooperation. It is not until a man lives in a world in which both values are necessary for him to be successful that he will give human values the type of priority which make them a realistic competitor to the values of power and competition. It is at this point, when men are resocialized to women's values as well as women to men's, that access to power will occur in a framework which allocates a meaningful proportion of resources to human priorities.

NOTES

1. Robert Michels, *Political Parties*. New York: Macmillan, 1962.

2. C. Wright Mills, *The Power Elite*. New York: Oxford University Press, 1970.

3. See statements of organizers of the National Women's Political Caucus, *The New York Times* (July 11, 1971 and July 12, 1971).

4. I am indebted to many women friends as a source of information on groups whose meetings I could not personally attend as a male, to the literature published by these groups and to Cellestine Ware's *Woman Power*. New York: Tower, 1970.

5. See Kenneth Clark, *A Relevant War Against Poverty*. New York: Metropolitan Applied Research Center, 1968, especially pp. 106–128 and 231–257.

6. Harold Lasswell, *Power and Personality*. New York: Norton, 1948 and "A Note on Types of Political Personality," *Jour. of Soc. Issues*, **24**, No. 3, pp. 81–91 (1968).

7. Jessica Furie, "The Lot System as a Fundamental of the Feminist Movement," cited in Ware, *Woman Power, op. cit.*

8. David Truman, *The Governmental Process*. New York: Knopf, 1951, p. 157. Obviously Truman did not consider one man a group, but I am suggesting here that this was his short-coming—overlooking the family unit and individual relationship as being politically relevant. See also Muzafer Cherif and Hadley Cantril, *The Psychology of Ego-Involvements*. New York: Wiley, 1947, pp. 5, 290.

9. The implications of the divisions between lesbian and straight women for the movement's political potential is explored on pages 186-187.

10. See Paul F. Lazarsfeld, B. Berelson, and H. Gaudet, *The People's Choice: How The Voter Makes Up His Mind in a Presidential Campaign.* New York: Columbia University Press, 1948, Chap. 6; and Sheldon J. Korchin, *Psychological Variables in the Behavior of Voters,* unpublished Ph.D. dissertation, Harvard University, 1946, cited in D. Truman, *The Governmental Process, op. cit.,* pp. 162-163.

11. Janine Sade, "The History of the Equality Issue in the Contemporary Women's Movement," cited in Cellestine Ware, *Woman Power, op. cit.,* p. 27.

12. Truman, *The Governmental Process, op. cit.,* pp. 159-160.

13. E. E. Schattschneider, *Party Government.* New York: Holt, Rinehart and Winston, 1942, p. 189.

14. *Ibid.*

15. E. E. Schattschneider, *Party Government, op. cit.,* p. 200.

16. V. O. Key, *Politics, Parties and Pressure Groups.* New York: Crowell, 1964, and *Public Opinion and American Democracy.* New York: Knopf, 1964.

17. E. E. Schattschneider, *Party Government, op. cit.,* p. 200.

18. *Ibid.*

19. For example, *NOW Acts.* Los Angeles: NOW Center, and *The Woman Activist.* Falls Church, Va.

20. Some of the relevant legislation in New York State, which NOW's New York City Chapter actively supported in 1971, are bills A-6074 (property division), S-128 (survivorship), A-6821 (insurance), S-176 and A-118 (child care centers), and A-157 (tax deduction for child care).

21. Among the unions testifying before the U.S. Senate Judiciary Committee in favor of the E.R.A. with its provision for invalidating the protective laws, were the United Automobile Workers, the International Union of Electrical Workers, the Butchers and Meat Cutters Union, and the American Federation of Government Employees.

22. See Stuart S. Nagel and Lenore J. Weitzman, "Women as Litigants," to be included in the 1971 Hastings Law Journal Symposium on Women's Rights.

23. See Victoria Schuck's statements and articles in U.S. Congress, House Subcommittee of the Committee on Education and Labor, *Hearings, Discrimination Against Women,* 91st Congress, Second Session, pp. 469-499 (1970).

24. See the report on the women's liberation movement approved by the National Committee of the Socialist Worker's Party at its meeting in New York, February 27-March 1, 1970. Excerpts are in Mary Alice Waters, "Revolutionary Potential of Women's Liberation," *The Militant,* pp. 7-10 (Apr. 3, 1970).

25. *Ibid.*

26. *Ibid.*

27. The subsequent observations are part of a forthcoming book and doctoral dissertation by the author. The book is to be entitled *Beyond Masculinity.* It is scheduled for publication in the Fall 1972, by Norton. The doctoral dissertation is entitled "The Political Potential of Women's Liberation Groups as Indicated by their Ability to Affect a Change in Men's Attitudes."

28. Carl I. Hovland et al., *Experiments on Mass Communication, Vol. III* (Social Science Research Council, Studies in Social Psychology in World War II). Princeton, N.J.: Princeton University Press, 1949; and Arthur Cohen, *Attitude Change and Social Influence.* New York: Basic Books, 1964.

29. Hovland, *Experiments on Mass Communication, op. cit.,* pp. 309–310.

30. In a sense, the Church is a bad example because of its own corruption and abuse of power. To make the consciousness-raising group a large, self-serving institution with its own inflexible doctrine would obviously be a gross error even if it were possible. The analogy is meant to illustrate the effectiveness of accountability.

31. See Warren T. Farrell, "The Resocialization of Men's Attitudes Toward Women's Role in Society," paper presented to the American Political Science Convention held in Los Angeles, September 1970.

Chapter

11

The Tyranny of Structurelessness

Jo Freeman

During the years in which the women's liberation movement has been taking shape, a great emphasis has been placed on what are called leaderless, structureless groups as the main, if not sole, organizational form of the movement. The source of this idea was a natural reaction against the over-structured society in which most of us found ourselves, the inevitable control this gave others over our lives and, the continual elitism of the Left and similar groups among those who were supposedly fighting this overstructuredness.

The idea of *structurelessness*, however, has moved from a healthy counter to these tendencies to becoming a goddess in its own right. The idea is as little-examined as the term is much-used, but it has become an intrinsic and unquestioned part of women's liberation ideology. For the early development of the movement this did not much matter. It early defined its main goal and its main method as consciousness-raising, and the structureless *rap-group* was an excellent means to this end. Its looseness and informality encouraged participation in discussion and the often supportive atmosphere elicited personal insight. If nothing more concrete than personal insight ever resulted from these groups, that did not much matter, because their purpose did not really extend beyond this.

The basic problems didn't appear until individual rap-groups exhausted the virtues of consciousness-raising and decided they wanted to do something more specific. At this point they usually floundered because most groups were unwilling to change their structure when they changed their task. Women had thoroughly accepted the idea of structurelessness without realizing the limitations of its uses. People would try to use the structureless

This article appeared originally in *Berkeley Journal of Sociology*, **17** (1973).

group and the informal conference for purposes for which they were unsuitable, from a blind belief that no other means could possibly be anything but oppressive.

If the movement is to move beyond these elementary stages of development, it will have to disabuse itself of some of its prejudices about organization and structure. There is nothing inherently bad about either of these. They can be and often are misused, but to reject them out of hand because they are misused is to deny ourselves the necessary tools to further development. We need to understand why structurelessness does not work.

Formal and Informal Structures

Contrary to what we would like to believe, there is no such thing as a structureless group. Any group of people of whatever nature, coming together for any length of time, for any purpose, will inevitably structure itself in some fashion. The structure may be flexible, it may vary over time, it may evenly or unevenly distribute tasks, power, and resources over the members of the group. But it will be formed regardless of the abilities, personalities, or intentions of the people involved. The very fact that we are individuals with different talents, predispositions, and backgrounds makes this inevitable. Only if we refused to relate or interact on any basis whatsoever could we approximate structurelessness, and that is not the nature of a human group.

This means that to strive for a structureless group is as useful and as deceptive, as to aim at an *objective* news story, *value free* social science or a *free* economy. A laissez-faire group is about as realistic as a laissez-faire society; the idea becomes a smoke screen for the strong or the lucky to establish unquestioned hegemony over others. This hegemony can be easily established because the idea of structurelessness does not prevent the formation of informal structures, but only formal ones. Similarly, laissez-faire philosophy did not prevent the economically powerful from establishing control over wages, prices, and distribution of goods; it only prevented the government from doing so. Thus, structurelessness becomes a way of masking power, and within the women's movement it is usually most strongly advocated by those who are the most powerful (whether they are conscious of their power or not). The rules of how decisions are made are known only to a few, and awareness of power is curtailed to those who know the rules, as long as the structure of the group is informal. Those who do not know the rules and are not chosen for initiation must remain in confusion, or suffer from paranoid delusions that something is happening of which they are not quite aware.

For everyone to have the opportunity to be involved in a given group and to participate in its activities the structure must be explicit, not implicit. The rules of decision-making must be open and available to everyone, and this can happen only if they are formalized. This is not to say that formalization of a group structure will destroy the informal structure. It usually doesn't. But it does hinder the informal structure from having predominant control and makes available some means of attacking it. Structurelessness is organizationally impossible. We cannot decide whether to have a structured or structureless group; only whether or not to have a formally structured one. Therefore, the word will not be used any longer except to refer to the idea it represents. *Unstructured* will refer to those groups which have not been deliberately structured in a particular manner. *Structured* will refer to those which have. A structured group always has a formal structure, and may also have an informal one. An unstructured group always has an informal, or covert, structure. It is this informal structure, particularly in unstructured groups, which forms the basis for elites.

The Nature of Elitism

Elitist is probably the most abused word in the women's liberation movement. It is used as frequently, and for the same reasons, as *pinko* was used in the fifties. It is never used correctly. Within the movement it commonly refers to individuals, though the personal characteristics and activities of those to whom it is directed may differ widely. An individual, regardless of how well-known that person may be, can never be an elite.

Correctly, an elite refers to a small group of people who have power over a larger group of which they are part, usually without direct responsibility to that larger group, and often without their knowledge or consent. A person becomes an elitist by being part of, or advocating the rule by, such a small group, whether or not that individual is well-known or not known at all. Notoriety is not a definition of an elitist. The most insidious elites are usually run by people not known to the larger public at all. Intelligent elitists are usually smart enough not to allow themselves to become well-known. When they become known, they are watched, and the mask over their power is no longer firmly lodged.

Because elites are informal does not mean they are invisible. At any small-group meeting anyone with a sharp eye and an acute ear can tell who is influencing whom. The members of a friendship group will relate more to each other than to other people. They listen more attentively and interrupt less. They repeat each other's points and give in amiably. The "outs" they tend to ignore or grapple with. The "outs" approval is not necessary for making a decision; however, it is necessary for the "outs" to stay on good terms with the "ins." Of course the lines are not as sharp as I have drawn them. They are nuances of interaction, not prewritten scripts. But they are discernible, and they do have their effect. Once one knows with whom it is important to check before a decision is made, and whose approval is the stamp of acceptance, one knows who is running things.

Elites are not conspiracies. Seldom does a small group of people get together and deliberately try to take over a larger group for its own ends. Elites are nothing more and nothing less than groups of friends who also happen to participate in the same political activities. They would probably maintain their friendship whether or not they were involved in political activities; they would probably be involved in political activities whether or not they maintained their friendships. It is the coincidence of these two phenomena which creates elites in any group and makes them so difficult to break.

These friendship groups function as networks of communication outside any regular channels that may have been set up by a group. If no channels are set up, they function as the only networks of communication. Because people are friends, usually sharing the same values and orientations, because they talk to each other socially and consult with each other when common decisions have to be made, the people involved in these networks have more power in the group than those who don't. And it is a rare group that does not establish some informal networks of communication through the friends that are made in it.

Some groups, depending on their size, may have more than one such informal communications network. Networks may even overlap. When only one such network exists, it is the elite of an otherwise unstructured group, whether the participants in it want to be elitists or not. If it is the only such network in a structured group it may or may not be an elite depending on its composition and the nature of the formal structure. If there are two or more such networks of friends, they may compete for power within the group, thus forming factions, or one may deliberately drop out of the competition leaving the other as the elite. In a structured group, two or more such friendship networks usually compete with each other for formal power. This is often the healthiest situation. The other members are in a position to arbitrate between the two competitors for power, thus enabling them to make demands on the group to whom they give their temporary allegiance.

The inevitably elitist and exclusive nature of informal communication networks of friends is neither a new phenomenon characteristic of the women's movement nor a phenomenon new to women. Such informal relationships have excluded women for centuries from participating in integrated groups of which they were a part. In any profession or organization these networks have created the locker-room mentality and the old-school ties which have effectively prevented women as a group (as well as some men individually) from having equal access to sources of power or social reward. Much of the energy of past women's movements has been directed to having the structures of decision-making and the selection processes *formalized* so that the exclusion of women could be confronted directly. As we all know, these efforts have not prevented the informal male-only networks from discriminating against women, but they have made it more difficult.

Since movement groups have made no concrete decisions about who shall exercise power within them, many different criteria are used around the country. Most criteria are along the lines of traditional female characteristics. For instance, in the early days of the movement, marriage was usually a prerequisite for participation in the informal elite. As women have been traditionally taught, married women relate primarily to each other, and look upon single women as being too threatening to have as close friends. In many cities, this criterion was further refined to include only those women married to New Left men. This standard had more than tradition behind it, however, because New Left men often had access to resources needed by the movement—such as mailing lists, printing presses, contacts and information—and women were used to getting what they needed through men rather than independently. As the movement has changed through time, marriage has become a less universal criterion for effective participation, although all informal elites still establish standards by which only women who possess certain material or personal characteristics may join. The standards frequently include: middle-class background (despite all the rhetoric about relating to the working class), being married, not being married but living with someone, being or pretending to be a lesbian, being between the age of 20 and 30, being college-educated or at least having some college background, being *hip*, not being too hip, holding a certain political line or identification as a radical, having children or at least liking them, not having children, having certain feminine personality characteristics such as being nice, dressing right (whether in the traditional style or the antitraditional style), etc. There are also some characteristics which will almost always tag one as a deviant who should not be related to. They include: being too old, working full time (particularly if one is actively committed to a career), not being nice, and being avowedly single (i.e., neither actively heterosexual nor homosexual).

Other criteria could be included, but they all have common themes. The characteristics prerequisite for participating in the informal elites of the movement, and thus for exercising power, concern one's background, personality or allocation of time. They do not include one's competence, dedication to feminism, talents or potential contribution to the movement. The former are the criteria one usually uses in determining one's friends. The latter are what any movement or organization has to use if it is going to be politically effective.

The criteria of participation may differ from group to group, but the means of becoming a member of the informal elite if one meets those criteria are pretty much the same. The only main difference depends on whether one is in a group from the beginning or joins it after it has begun. If involved from the beginning, it is important to have as many of one's personal friends as possible also join. If no one knows anyone else very well, then one must deliberately form friendships with a select number and establish the informal interaction patterns crucial to the creation of an informal structure. Once the informal patterns are formed they act to maintain themselves. One of the most successful tactics of maintenance is to continuously recruit new people who fit. One joins such an elite much the same way one pledges a sorority. If perceived as a potential addition, one is *rushed* by the members of the informal structure and eventually either dropped or initiated. If the sorority is not politically aware enough to actively engage in this process itself, it can be started by the outsider much the same way one joins any private club. Find a sponsor, i.e., pick some member of the elite who appears to be well-respected within it and actively cultivate that person's friendship. Eventually, she will most likely bring you into the inner circle.

All of these procedures take time. So if one works full time or has a similar major commitment, it is usually impossible to join simply because there are not enough hours left to go to all the meetings and cultivate the personal relationships necessary to have a voice in the decision-making. That is why formal structures of decision-making are a boon to the overworked person. Having an established process for decision-making ensures that everyone can participate in it to some extent.

Although this dissection of the process of elite formation within small groups has been critical in its perspective, it is not made in the belief that these informal structures are inevitably bad—merely inevitable. All groups create informal structures as a result of the interaction patterns among the members. Such informal structures can do very useful things. But only unstructured groups are totally governed by them. When informal elites are combined with a myth of structurelessness, there can be no attempt to put limits on the use of power. It becomes capricious.

This has two potentially negative consequences of which we should be aware. The first is that the informal structure of decision-making will be much like a sorority: one in which people listen to others because they like them, not because they say significant things. As long as the movement does not do significant things this does not much matter. But if its development is not to be arrested at this preliminary stage, it will have to alter this trend. The second is that informal structures have no obligation to be responsible to the group at large. Their power was not given to them, it cannot be taken away. Their influence is not based on what they do for the group; therefore, they cannot be directly influenced by the group. This does not necessarily make informal structures irresponsible. Those who are concerned with maintaining their influence will usually try to be responsible. The group simply cannot compel such responsibility; it is dependent on the interests of the elite.

The Star System

The idea of structurelessness has created the *star* system. We live in a society which expects political groups to make decisions and to select people to articulate those decisions to the public at large. The press and the public do not know how to listen seriously to individual women as women—they want to know how the group feels. Only three techniques have ever been developed for establishing mass group opinion: the vote or referendum, the public opinion survey questionnaire, and the selection of group spokespeople at an appropriate meeting. The women's liberation movement has used none of these to communicate with the public. Neither the movement as a whole nor most of the multitudinous groups within it have established a means of explaining their position on various issues. But the public is conditioned to look for spokespeople.

While it has consciously not chosen spokespeople, the movement has thrown up many women who have caught the public eye for varying reasons. These women represent no particular group or established opinion; they know this and usually say so. But because there are no official spokespeople nor any decision-making body the press can interview when it wants to know the movement's position on a subject, these women are perceived as the spokespeople. Thus, whether they want to or not, whether the movement likes it or not, women of public note are put in the role of spokespeople by default.

This is one main source of the tie that is often felt toward the women who are labeled stars. Because they were not selected by the women in the movement to represent the movement's views, they are resented when the press presumes that they speak for the movement. As long as the movement does not select its own spokeswomen, such women will be placed in that role by the press and the public, regardless of their own desires.

This has certain negative consequences for both the movement and the stars. First, because the movement didn't put them in the role of spokesperson, the movement cannot remove them. The press put them there and only the press can choose not to listen. The press will continue to look to stars as spokeswomen as long as it has no official alternatives to go to for authoritative statements from the movement. The movement has no control in the selection of its representatives to the public as long as it believes that it should have no representatives at all. Second, women put in this position often find themselves viciously attacked by their sisters. This achieves nothing for the movement and is painfully destructive of the individuals involved. Such attacks only result in either the woman leaving the movement entirely—often bitterly alienated—or in her ceasing to feel responsible to her sisters. She may maintain some vaguely defined loyalty to the movement but she is no longer susceptible to pressures from other women in it. One cannot feel responsible to people who have been the source of such pain without being a masochist, and these women are usually too strong to bow to that kind of personal pressure. Thus the backlash to the star system, in effect, encourages the very kind of individualistic nonresponsibility that the movement condemns. By purging a sister as a star, the movement loses whatever control it may have had over the person, who then becomes free to commit all of the individualistic sins of which she has been accused.

Political Impotence

Unstructured groups may be very effective in getting women to talk about their lives; they aren't very good for getting things done. Unless their mode of operation changes, groups flounder at the point where people tire of just talking and want to do something more. Because the larger movement in most cities is as unstructured as individual rap groups, it is not too much more effective than the separate groups at specific tasks. The informal structure is rarely together or in touch with the people enough to operate effectively. So the movement generates much motion and few results. Unfortunately, the consequences of all this motion are not as innocuous as the results, and their victim is the movement itself.

Some groups have turned themselves into local action projects, if they do not involve too many people, and work on a small scale. But this form restricts movement activity to the local level: it cannot be done on the regional or national level. Also, to function well the groups must usually pare themselves down to that informal group of friends who were running things in the first place. This excludes many women from participating. As long as the only way women can participate in the movement is through membership in a small group, the nongregarious are at a distinct disadvantage. As long as friendship groups are the main means of organizational activity, elitism becomes institutionalized.

For those groups which cannot find a local project to devote themselves, the mere act of staying together becomes the reason for their staying together. When a group has no specific task (and consciousness-raising is a task), the people in it turn their energies to controlling others in the group. This is not done so much out of a malicious desire to manipulate others (though sometimes it is) as out of a lack of anything better to do with their talents. Able people with time on their hands and a need to justify their coming together put their efforts into personal control, and spend their time criticizing the personalities of the other members in the group. Infighting and personal power games rule the day. When a group is involved in a task, people learn to get along with others as they are and to subsume personal dislikes for the sake of the larger goal. There are limits placed on the compulsion to remold every person in our image of what they should be.

The end of consciousness-raising leaves people with no place to go and the lack of structure leaves them with no way of getting there. The women in the movement either turn on themselves and their sisters or seek other alternatives of action. There are few alternatives available. Some women just do their own thing. This can lead to a great deal of individual creativity, much of which is useful for the movement, but it is not a viable alternative for most women and certainly does not foster a spirit of cooperative group effort. Other women drift out of the movement entirely because they don't want to develop an individual project and have found no way of discovering, joining or starting group projects that interest them.

Many turn to other political organizations to give them the kind of struc-tured, effective activity that they have not been able to find in the women's movement. Thus, those political organizations which view women's liberation as only one issue among many, find the women's movement a vast recruiting ground for new members. There is no need for such organizations to infiltrate (though this is not precluded). The desire for meaningful political activity generated in women by their becoming part of the women's liberation move-ment is sufficient to make them eager to join other organizations. The movement itself provides no outlets for their new ideas and energies.

The women who join other political organizations while remaining within the women's liberation movement, or who join women's liberation while remaining in other political organizations, in turn become the framework for new informal structures. These friendship networks are based upon their common nonfeminist politics rather than the characteristics discussed earlier; however, the network operates in much the same way. Because these women share common values, ideas and political orientations, they too become informal, unplanned, unselected, unresponsible elites—whether they intend to be so or not.

These new informal elites are often perceived as threats by the old informal elites previously developed within different movement groups. This is a correct perception. Such politically oriented networks are rarely willing to be merely sororities as many of the old ones were, and want to proselytize their political as well as their feminist ideas. This is only natural, but its implications for women's liberation have never been adequately discussed. The old elites are rarely willing to bring such differences of opinion into the open because it would involve exposing the nature of the informal structure of the group. Many of these informal elites have been hiding under the banner of anti-elitism and structurelessness. To effectively counter the competition from another informal structure, they would have to become public and this possibility is fraught with many dangerous implications. Thus, to maintain its own power, it is easier to rationalize the exclusion of the members of the other informal structure by such means as red-baiting, reformist-baiting, lesbian-baiting, or straight-baiting. The only other alternative is to formally structure the group in such a way that the original power structure is institutionalized. This is not always possible. If the informal elites have been well-structured and have exercised a fair amount of power in the past, such a task is feasible. These groups have a history of being somewhat politically effective in the past, as the tightness of the informal structure has proven an adequate substitute for a formal structure. Becoming structured does not alter their operation much, though the institutionalization of the power structure does open it to formal challenge. It is the groups which are in greatest need of structure that are often least capable of creating it. Their informal structures have not been too well-formed and adherence to the ideology of structurelessness makes them reluctant to change tactics. The more unstructured a group is, the more lacking it is in informal structures; the more it adheres to an ideology of structurelessness, the more vulnerable it is to being taken over by a group of political comrades.

Since the movement at large is just as unstructured as most of its constituent groups, it is similarly susceptible to indirect influence. But the phenomenon manifests itself differently. On a local level most groups can operate autonomously, but the only groups that can organize a national activity are nationally organized groups. Thus, it is often the structured feminist organizations that provide national direction for feminist activities, and this direction is determined by the priorities of these organizations. Such groups as NOW, WEAL, and some Left women's caucuses are simply the only organizations capable of mounting a national campaign. The multitude of unstructured women's liberation groups can choose to support or not support the national campaigns, but are incapable of mounting their own. Thus their members become the troops under the leadership of the structured organizations. The avowedly unstructured groups have no way of drawing upon the movement's vast resources to support their priorities. They don't even have a way of deciding what the priorities are.

The more unstructured a movement is, the less control it has over the directions in which it develops and the political actions in which it engages.

This does not mean that its ideas do not spread. Given a certain amount of interest by the media and the appropriateness of social conditions, the ideas will still be diffused widely. But diffusion of ideas does not mean they are implemented; it only means they are talked about. Insofar as they can be applied individually they may be acted on; insofar as they require coordinated political power to be implemented, they will not be.

As long as the women's liberation movement stays dedicated to a form of organization which stresses small, inactive discussion groups among friends, the worst problems of unstructuredness will not be felt. But this style of organization has its limits; it is politically inefficacious, exclusive, and discriminatory against those women who are not or cannot be tied into the friendship networks. Those who do not fit into what already exists because of class, race, occupation, education, parental, or marital status, or personality will inevitably be discouraged from trying to participate. Those who do fit in will develop vested interests in maintaining things as they are.

The informal groups' vested interests will be sustained by the informal structures which exist, and the movement will have no way of determining who shall exercise power within it. If the movement continues to deliberately not select who shall exercise power, it does not thereby abolish power. All it does is abdicate the right to demand that those who do exercise power and influence be responsible for it. If the movement continues to keep power as diffuse as possible because it knows it cannot demand responsibility from those who have it, it does prevent any group or person from totally dominating. But it simultaneously insures that the movement is as ineffective as possible. Some middle ground between domination and ineffectiveness can and must be found.

These problems are coming to a head at this time because the nature of the movement is necessarily changing. Consciousness-raising, as the main function of the women's liberation movement, is becoming obsolete. Due to the intense press publicity of the last two years and the numerous overground books and articles now being circulated, women's liberation has become a household word. Its issues are discussed and informal rap groups are formed by people who have no explicit connection with any movement group. Purely educational work is no longer such an overwhelming need. The movement must go on to other tasks. It now needs to establish its priorities, articulate its goals and pursue its objectives in a coordinated fashion. To do this it must be organized locally, regionally, and nationally.

Principles of Democratic Structuring

Once the movement no longer clings tenaciously to the ideology of structurelessness, it will be free to develop those forms of organization best suited to its healthy functioning. This does not mean that we should go to the other extreme and blindly imitate the traditional forms of organization. But neither should we blindly reject them all. Some of the traditional techniques will prove useful, albeit not perfect; some will give us insights into what we should and should not do to obtain certain ends with minimal costs to the individuals in the movement. Mostly, we will have to experiment with different kinds of structuring and develop a variety of techniques to use for different situations. The lot system is one such idea which has emerged from the movement. It is not applicable to all situations, but is useful in some. Other ideas for structuring are needed. But before we can proceed to experiment intelligently, we must accept the idea that there is nothing inherently bad about structure itself—only its excessive use.

While engaging in this trial-and-error process, there are some principles we can keep in mind that are essential to democratic structuring and are politically effective also:

1. *Delegation* of specific authority to specific individuals for specific tasks by democratic procedures. Letting people assume jobs or tasks by default only means they are not dependably done. If people are selected to do a task, preferably after expressing an interest or willingness to do it, they have made a commitment which cannot so easily be ignored.

2. Requiring all those to whom authority has been delegated to be *responsible* to those who selected them. This is how the group has control over people in positions of authority. Individuals may exercise power, but it is the group that has ultimate say over how the power is exercised.

3. *Distribution* of authority among as many people as is reasonably possible. This prevents monopoly of power and requires those in positions of authority to consult with many others in the process of exercising it. It also gives many people the opportunity to have responsibility for specific tasks and thereby to learn different skills.

4. *Rotation* of tasks among individuals. Responsibilities which are held too long by one person, formally or informally, come to be seen as that person's "property" are not easily relinquished or controlled by the group. Conversely, if tasks are rotated too frequently the individual does not have time to learn her job well and acquire the sense of satisfaction of doing a good job.

5. *Allocation* of tasks along rational criteria. Selecting someone for a position because they are liked by the group, or giving them hard work because they are disliked, serves neither the group nor the person in the long run. Ability, interest, and responsibility have got to be the major concerns in such selection. People should be given an opportunity to learn skills they do not have, but this is best done through some sort of apprenticeship program rather than the sink-or-swim method. Having a responsibility one can't handle well is demoralizing. Conversely, being blacklisted from doing what one can do well does not encourage one to develop one's skills. Women have

been punished for being competent throughout most of human history. The movement does not need to repeat this process.

6. *Diffusion of information* to everyone as frequently as possible. Information is power. Access to information enhances one's power. When an informal network spreads new ideas and information among themselves outside the group, they are already engaged in the process of forming an opinion—without the group participating. The more one knows about how things work, the more politically effective one can be.

7. *Equal access to resources* needed by the group. This is not always perfectly possible, but should be striven for. A member who maintains a monopoly over a needed resource (like a printing press or a darkroom owned by a husband) can unduly influence the use of that resource. Skills and information are also resources. Members' skills can be equitably available only when members are willing to teach what they know to others.

When these principles are applied, they insure that whatever structures are developed by different movement groups will be controlled by and responsible to the group. The group of people in positions of authority will be diffuse, flexible, open, and temporary. They will not be in such an easy position to institutionalize their power because ultimate decisions will be made by the group at large. The group will have the power to determine who shall exercise authority within it.

Part
II
COMPARATIVE PERSPECTIVES

Chapter

12

Women Under Communism

Barbara W. Jancar

The position of women in communist systems is of special interest today when the twin forces of modernization—industrialization and urbanization—have swept away the rigid social pattern of the traditional agricultural community in favor of the rapid growth of cities, and diminished the strength and meaning of extended kinship or patriarchal family ties. Modernization has made it possible for women to free themselves from their dependency role, become economically self-sustaining, and participate in both the formation and distribution of preferred institutional values in a social system [1]. They now have the opportunity to share in the power, the wealth, the education, the recognition, and the responsibility that comes to society's active participants. That they do not yet do so has been the subject of many books written both in this country and abroad [2]. Nowhere in the world have women totally participated in the status revolution which would enable them to take their place as first-class members of the community.

Communist countries are no exception to the general rule. But they are unique when compared to other modernizing and modernized nations in their approach to the question of women. In the first place, in a typology of change processes, communist polities may be defined as coercive in terms of unequal power distribution in the hands of one group of society and the deliberate noncollaborative setting of goals by that one group [3]. The leadership is thus more completely responsible for the formulation, transmission and outcome of policy decisions regarding social change. Second, the communist ideology, as an ideology of progress, has been historically committed to the idea of the total emancipation of all groups in society, including women. One of the chief planks of the first CPSU Program of 1919 was devoted to improving the status of women [4]. Third, a characteristic feature of all communist systems is the planned development of the economy through

217

a centralized planning agent. The ruling group thus has a direct say in the distribution and employment of the labor force.

There is no dispute that, percentagewise, more women are employed in communist countries than anywhere else in the world except possibly Israel. As Table 12.1 indicates, the U.S.S.R. and Eastern Europe have made a conscious effort to draw women into the labor force.

Table 12.1. Share of Women in Total Employment, 1952 and 1967, Eastern Europe and the U.S.S.R.

Country	Percentage	
	1952	1967
Bulgaria	25.8	42.0
Czechoslovakia	37.8	45.5
East Germany	42.7	47.2
Hungary	29.3	39.4
Poland	33.3	37.6
Rumania	26.6	30.5
U.S.S.R.	47.0	50.0

SOURCE: Jerzy Berent, "Some Demographic Aspects of Female Employment in Eastern Europe and the U.S.S.R.," *International Labor Review,* p. 178 (Sept. 1970).

But participation is not synonymous with equality of status and power [5]. Despite over 50 years of communism, women have not yet entered the elite structure of those polities under communist control. Indeed, until recently, they scarcely seemed to be considered subjects worthy of elite recruitment. More significantly, as modernization involves politicization, its progress is dependent to a considerable degree on political inputs and one of its products is the expansion of the political sector [6]. Yet, women are virtually absent from the top political decision-making organs of every communist country. Despite planned efforts to draw women into the labor force and constitutional guarantees of full equality, elite status seems denied to women under communism.

In recent years, the question of why women have not risen to the top of the status pyramid has become a matter of general concern to Western and communist sociologists alike [7]. Some Western experts find the origin of female nonparticipation in high-status careers in the hard facts of (a) the drudgery of housework assigned to most women and (b) the cultural perspectives of families which do not encourage their daughters to full-time careers [8].

While communist sociologists would certainly agree that housework and childrearing keep women from intensive pursuit of high-status careers, they have tended to explain their failure to rise as a product of their passivity towards involvement of any kind. And this passivity has been a source of some embarrassment to regimes which claim to have overcome the bourgeois prejudices and attitudes of the past.

It is clear that there are many factors involved in an explanation of women's low-status position. In setting up a model for the communist experience, I have tried to include factors which would account for the slowness of woman's progress anywhere. These are then applied to the specifics of the communist situation as I understand them. The goal of the model is to present the general indicators in an interactional pattern which, in my opinion, would give the most likely explanation for the condition of women under communism. The model involves four sets of factors: *(a) The environment* denotes the economic level of development, the philosophic orientation and the political system of the country or countries under consideration. *(b) Leadership guidance* involves both the prescribing and promotional functions of the leadership in effecting social change. The prescribing function refers to explicit legislation, party resolutions, and administrative regulations which have as their aim the clarification of social objectives and the justification of the measures taken to reach them. The promotional function concerns the leadership's control and exploitation of mass media and other communications mechanisms to induce public consensus noncoercively as regards the validity of the social objectives currently pursued. *(c) The female self-concept* refers to the internalization by women of various role options, such as the traditional family-childrearing role, the professional role, the political role. *(d) The status of women* is seen as the product of the interaction of the four variables as described in Figure 12.1.

The model hypothesizes that leadership guidance, the female self-concept and the female status position operate within the framework of the economic, philosophic, and political structures of the communist system. The inner part of the circle may be considered the area of political activity, as opposed to the political environment, the operative organization of politics, which determines the rules of political activity. The model indicates that leadership guidance has a direct influence on the female status position (signified by the solid line) and an indirect influence on her self-concept (signified by the dotted line). The interaction between the female self-concept and her status position is also direct, as achievement of any kind brings about a positive redefinition of self, at least to some degree. Both the female self-concept and the female status position react back on the content of leadership guidance; the former again indirectly, the latter, directly, as status is an indicator

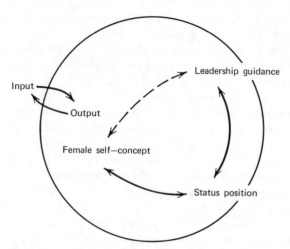

Environment
Economic
Philosophic
Political

Figure 12.1. Interaction model of possible factors involved in woman's status position in communist systems.

of participation in the ruling elite. The environment thus forms the basic frame of reference within which political activity takes place, while the interchange between the three factors within the circle feeds back information to modify the environment.

The model suggests that the basic difference between a communist and noncommunist system in the approach to women's emancipation would be that the former, with its monopoly of power, is organized to coerce change. The latter is more interactional in the change process, in the sense of taking a collaborative attitude toward interests and clients desiring change, but, more often than not, lacking a deliberate all-inclusive plan to effect change. It thus might be expected that communist leaderships would be able to impose change upon the status of any client group, such as women, under their control, with minimum consideration of inputs from the environment. By contrast, less concentration of power would make noncommunist governments more sensitive to environmental input and consequently less able to order change unless developments in the environment are conducive to change.

It is the hypothesis of this chapter that such is not the case. While the leadership may think it is effecting a revolution from above, as Stalin evidently thought, communist leadership guidance as far as women are concerned, appears to be as much a product of environmental forces as is the female self-concept and the female low-status position. Hence, while the Soviet or East European regimes may have thought they had done everything to liberate women, they had in fact done little to change their status. They eagerly sought to give women education and to recruit them into the labor

Table 12.2. Share of Women in Total Employment by Main Economic Sector, 1967, Eastern Europe and the U.S.S.R.

Country	Industry	Con-struction	Transport	Communi-cations	Trade	Public health	Educa-tion	Credit and finance	Agri-culture
Bulgaria	42.6%	12.7%	15.0%	47.7%	50.2%	70.0%	64.7%	62.8%	
Czechoslovakia	42.0	14.7	21.1	60.7	73.6	79.0	62.2	64.0	51.6%
East Germany	41.1	11.2	25.2	66.5	67.6		66.5		
Hungary	40.6	13.8		21.7	59.8		45.4		
Poland	32.0	13.4		18.2	64.9	77.8	66.0	68.7	50.0
Rumania	28.9	7.8	7.5	44.3	42.2	66.4	59.7	49.8	
U.S.S.R.	47.0	28.0	24.0	66.0	74.0	85.0	72.0	75.0	51.0

SOURCE: Jerzy Berent, "Some Demographic Aspects of Female Employment in Eastern Europe and the U.S.S.R.," *Internat. Labor Rev.*, p. 178 (Sept. 1970).

Table 12.3. Share of Women in Total Industrial Employment, by Branch, 1967, Eastern Europe and the U.S.S.R.

Branch of industry	Bulgaria	East Germany	Czechoslovakia	Hungary	Poland	U.S.S.R.
Electricity	11%	40%	24%	21%	17%	29%
Fuel	17	–	12	10	12	–
Ferrous metallurgy	24	21	1	20	16	29
Non-ferrous metallurgy	14		4		18	–
Engineering	25	22	18	33	18	40
Chemicals	42	30	49	38	33	–
Building materials	23	22	11	35	20	36
Cellulose and paper	47	51	–[a]	44	42	47
Glass and ceramics	37	45	43	–	39	–
Textiles	78	70	87	68	64	73
Clothing	83	88	70	78	74	84
Leather	58	66		58	48	64
Printing	59	46	42	52	50	–
Food processing	60	51	59	45	35	55

SOURCE: National statistical yearbooks

[a]Included under printing

force, but had no firm commitment to sharing power and status with them, once they were there. Hence, the paradox between high female participation in the labor force and low participation in the decision-making elites.

The Environmental Inputs

The Economy

With the exception of East Germany and Czechoslovakia, all the present communist countries found themselves in the early stages of industrialization at the onset of communist rule. Technology and capital were at a very low level. What was needed to launch the first Five Year Plans were massive injections of human labor, particularly in China and the U.S.S.R. Because women under the former regimes had had little or no access to education, they were most suited for recruitment into the manual labor force. Women have remained in the physical labor categories in the Soviet Union despite the Soviet claim that educational differences between sexes have now disappeared [9]. Indeed, a striking feature of the pattern of Soviet employment is the number of women doing hard physical labor [10]. The situation is somewhat different in Eastern Europe, but here again, we find women concentrated in agricultural or low white-collar jobs. (See Table 12.2.)

Tables 12.2 and 12.3 also suggest that women are channeled into specific types of jobs. Over two-thirds of the women employed in Eastern Europe and the Soviet Union work in the service sector, specifically in public health and education. When one turns to patterns of female employment in the various branches of industry, he finds women prevailing in the female-type jobs such as textiles, clothing, and to a lesser extent, food processing. On the other hand, there are few women in metallurgy, chemicals, fuel, or electricity.

If one searches further one discovers that even in the areas where women predominate, women will be found in the low-status positions. For example, of 2187 leading positions in the Hungarian industrial enterprises under ministerial jurisdiction, only 144 are occupied by women. 80% of the teachers in primary schools are women, but only 13% of the directors. 68.3% of the workers in the textile industry are female, but only 16% hold leading positions [11]. In the U.S.S.R., women constitute 72% of all MD's, but 93% of all medical workers. 68% of all university professors are women, but 84% of all secondary school teachers [12]. While the educational time lag may be a factor here, the fact remains that women constitute only 23% of the total number of secondary school principals, but 54% of all primary school principals [13].

It has to be understood that lower-status jobs mean lower pay. Perhaps

Table 12.4. Wage Scales for Men and
Women in Hungary, 1970

Wage scale	Percentage	
(forints[a] per month)	Men	Women
Less than 800	0.7	32.2
1,000–1,500	13.0	44.6
1,500–2,000	33.0	10.4
2,000–2,500	27.6	9.0
2,500–3,000	13.6	2.4
Over 3,000	12.1	1.4

SOURCE: Speech of Central Committee Secretary, Arpad Pullai, to the 18–19 of February 1970 session of the HSWP CC, as reported in *Magyar Hirlap* (February 20, 1970).

[a]30 forints = $1.05.

nowhere have official statistics made so clear the wage discrimination against women as in Hungary as is shown in Table 12.4 [14].

The existence of women's jobs, as this pattern would suggest, indicates that less competitive positions and therefore less status-valuable positions more readily assimilate women than do the more competitive, higher status posts. Several economic reasons can be offered to explain this phenomenon. The first has already been suggested: the educational time lag. But this is no longer operative in the industrialized countries of East Germany, Czechoslovakia, and the Soviet Union. A second and even more important factor, because it is persistent, is the generally lower activity rates of women with families and particularly large families than unmarried women or men. (See Table 12.5.)

The negative correlation between the employability of a married woman and the number of children she has is quite obvious in this table. However, in his article on the demographic aspects of the question in Eastern Europe, Berent argues that when you consider female employment on the average, this correlation substantially weakens [15]. Moreover, the number of dependent children has virtually no effect whatsoever in the rural areas as is suggested by the higher Polish and Hungarian rates. When the figures are broken down by class of worker, one discovers that the number of children has the highest effect on employability among white-collar workers [16]. It seems clear that the economic factors of industrialization and urbanization tend to set up a conflict between childbearing and employment more generally in higher level factory or institutional settings.

It is not merely childbearing that operates against women moving into elite status careers. While women in every industrializing and industrialized country have had to bear almost the total burden of housework, in communist

Table 12.5.   Female Employment Rates by Age, Marital Status, Number of Children in Czechoslovakia, East Germany, Hungary, and Poland, 1968

Age of women	All women	All married women	No children	5 children
Czechoslovakia				
17–19	62.9%	43.2%	83.2%	—
25–29	53.7	48.9	84.9	21.4%
35–39	63.3	60.3	74.3	40.4
45–49	64.3	59.9	64.7	41.7
55–59	42.5	44.5	41.0	—
East Germany				
18–20	84.4		92.2	—
25–29	65.4		90.8	35.2
35–39	70.5		81.0	48.3
45–49	68.1		83.0	44.9
55–59				
Hungary				
15–19		37.5	44.2	—
25–29		43.5	63.3	18.5
35–39		45.6	57.6	30.6
45–49		42.0	51.9	31.1
55–59		26.4	35.8	19.2
Poland				
15–17	33.3	40.3	43.8	—
25–29	63.8	58.1	76.1	53.3
35–39	68.5	63.9	70.4	66.3
45–49	72.0	65.6	64.3	72.1
55–59	71.4	62.2	60.9	60.0

SOURCE: Jerzy Berent, "Some Demographic Aspects of Female Employment in Eastern Europe and the U.S.S.R.," *Internat. Labor Rev.,* pp. 185–188 (Sept. 1970).

countries this burden becomes even heavier because of the sheer amount of physical time it takes to get the housework done. The more children, the more work that has to be done at home [17].

And where the husband can come home and relax, the wife has to perform her wifely duties of shopping, washing, and the education of the children.

Table 12.6.   Division of Work Performed in the Home by Husband and Wife, East Germany

Type of work	Wife	Husband	Other
Meal preparation	84.2%	6.8%	12.0%
House cleaning	78.8	12.5	9.0
Laundry	89.7	2.9	7.4
Shopping	76.5	11.8	11.7
Miscellaneous	56.9	33.3	9.8

SOURCE: *Der Morgen* (East Berlin) (September 22, 1968)

In 1968, East German sociologists published the results of an extensive survey which showed that women spent an average of 47.6 hours per week on housework, of which 15.4 hours were spent on the preparation of meals alone. The report also showed that even though 74% of the husbands interviewed were helping their wives at home, the women were still doing most of the work. See Table 12.6.

Perhaps the most significant of the survey findings was the revelation that the average weekly free time for the East German man was 37.1 hours as opposed to 26.6 hours for his frau, while the nonworking woman had on the average 10 hours more free time than her working sister [18]. Statistics could be given from every communist country to reveal a similar problem. Goode's statement that women can never improve their situation as long as they are the chief housekeepers, holds especially true for the communist regimes. Because of the burdens of home, women prefer to work where and when it is most convenient in terms of their families. A survey made of a Moscow working district by Soviet sociologist Dr. Zoia Iankova, found that 95% of the questionees preferred to work the first shift of the day in order to be at home with the children when they returned from school [19].

Thus, the very demands of a modernizing society bring new pressures in the shape of competition at work, the need for trained skills, while at the same time increasing rather than decreasing a woman's responsibility at home.

Philosophy

This environment includes what Bernard had identified as society's crescive or nonwritten rules imbedded in family structure and tradition [20].

Of consideration in the identification of changing patterns in the family structure of communist polities are three main factors: (a) the disintegration of the extended family and/or patriarchal family system, (b) the degree to which women have secured equality in the home, and (c) the impact of divorce and abortion on family life.

It must be noted that extended kinship families are specific mainly to the Near East and Far East. Their rigid hierarchical structure never existed in Europe. The breakup of this family pattern into the conjugal family, the prototype for industrialized societies, demanded large inputs by the leaderships of China and Soviet Central Asia, as it constituted an integral part of the traditional fabric of societal organization in these areas. The principal aim of the ruling regimes was to shift loyalty from the family to the party and state. This shift was not accomplished without resistance. The strength of the old family pattern is evident in Soviet Central Asia by reports in the Soviet press regarding the continuance of such customs as bride price. As late as the 1960s, fathers customarily took their girls out of school at the age of 12 or 13 to marry them off [21]. As large families were considered evidence of a Moslem male's virility, they were easily socialized into a dependency childrearing role within the family.

The restructuring of the family in China began with the Chinese Revolution of 1912, but the old ways are still widespread. Myrdal's *Report from A Chinese Village* is full of instances of the survival of traditional family patterns, especially among the older generation. Many peasants, for example, prefer the old practice of a purchase marriage, where they marry off their daughter for a price equal to what it costs to bring her up. Again, the centuries-old tradition of male dominance in the household has not been wiped out in the short time the Communists have been in power. In the peasant village, men, especially the older men, are accepted as rulers of the household, and their wives consider themselves just women [22]. Perhaps the most important survival of the old family system has been the deference and respect traditionally paid to the aged. Significantly, there has been no government campaign against the elders. Rather, there has been some attempt to define the relationship of young to old in the new democratic, united family. Emphasized in this context is not only filial piety in the sense of respect for the aged, but the younger generation's duty to care for their parents. The newer liberated position of women, the Chinese regime has been careful to stress, does not mean their absence from the household. Rather, every housewife should consider it a patriotic duty to feed the old, teach the young, and make every member of the family feel comfortable [23]. Such teachings by the government are indicative of the deep roots of the modern Chinese family in old China.

In Eastern Europe and the western part of the Soviet Union, family life has been that of the traditional Western family. Kinship ties have been strong, and patriarchalism the predominant family form. Contrary to the Asian experience, the conjugal family evolved in the West long before industrialization. Consequently, there was no need for any communist regime to break up the intricate network of extended family relationships for the sake of modernization as there was in China and Soviet Central Asia. The main focus of Soviet and East European concern has been factor (*b*), the degree to which women have secured equality in the home. My own personal observations based on visits to Soviet and East European families is that the man is still regarded the head of the household. My views are supported by a survey conducted on 595 working families in Leningrad by Soviet sociologist, A. L. Pimenova. In the survey sample, 69% of the female respondents indicated that the husband or some other male member of the family was head of the household although the percentage indicating acceptance of the traditional patriarchal arrangement tended to decrease with the age of the couple [24].

The situation in the U.S.S.R. and Eastern Europe as regards equality within the home should not be considered identical. The Soviet leaders have consistently been conservative in their outlook on women, and particularly on their own wives. It should not be forgotten that Lenin refused to condone free love, and that Stalin reinstated a marriage ceremony and put restrictions on divorce. The "latest Soviet Principles on Marriage and the Family" stress the importance of marriage almost in religious terms, insisting on a 1-month waiting period before a marriage can be finalized [25]. In addition, the Soviet leaders have traditionally kept their wives out of the public view, and none of them with the exception of Lenin's wife, Nadezhda Krupskaia, ever actively participated in public life.

The East European leaders have been more progressive in their attitudes towards their wives. Mme. Fucik is a member of the Czechoslovak CC. Bulgarian Politbureau member Zhivko Zhivkov's wife, Nadya Zhivkova, was secretary of the Bulgarian Central Council of Trade Unions and is now a full member of the BCP CC. And even in *kirche, kuchen,* and *kinder* East Germany, First Secretary Erich Honecker has seen fit to give his wife, Margot Honecker, the Ministry of Public Education. A possible explanation for the East Central European attitude is that all the countries of East Central Europe had greater contact with Western Europe in the inter-war period than did the Soviet Union and thus their leaders were more exposed to Western ideas than were their Soviet counterparts. Another factor is, of course, the continuing impact of Russia's rural past upon the present leaders, who are but recently removed from the peasant village. According to the 1970 census, only one-fourth of today's urban population was born in the city. Even more important, in my opinion, is the strain of puritanism which appears time and time again throughout Russian literature in such heroines as Pushkin's Tat'iana and Tolstoi's Natasha, and which also pervades Soviet communism. A study of attitudes on premarital sex at Leningrad University, for example, indicated the continued existence of a double standard of sexual values. Men were more likely to have premarital relations with someone other than their wife-to-be and women were less likely to condemn them because they did so [26]. The survival of a Victorian moral code for both rulers and ruled alike in the Soviet Union means an environment where woman's place is in the home as a subordinate to her husband.

Divorce would seem to be both a blessing and a curse to a woman born in the communist system. On the one hand it has symbolized, particularly in China and Soviet Central Asia, the long-delayed freedom of women to

Table 12.7.   Divorces per Thousand Population 1970
for Selected Countries

Country	Rate
U.S.A.	2.90
U.S.S.R.	2.60
Hungary	2.20
Czechoslovakia	1.70
East Germany	1.70
West Germany	1.40
Bulgaria	1.10
Poland	1.05
France and U.K.	0.60
Rumania	0.39

SOURCES: *Vestnik statistiki*, No. 12, p. 86 (1971). *Statistical Abstract of U.S.A.*, p. 60 (1970). East European Statistical Yearbooks.

choose their husbands and to be liberated from the tyranny of a marriage situation where no divorce was possible. As can be seen from Table 12.7, the divorce rate in the Soviet Union and Eastern Europe has been rising sharply in recent years and now compares with the U.S. There are no comparable divorce statistics for China.

The pattern of divorce in the Soviet Union has been of special concern to the leadership. In terms of divorce totals, the rate has almost doubled in the last 10 years with 636,000 registered in 1970 in a country reckoned to have 60 to 70 million families. *Literaturnaia gazeta* indicated that these figures might be on the low side as not all divorces are registered [27]. In China, also, the divorce rate has risen during the course of communist rule, as a consequence of the Chinese government's adoption of a fairly permissive attitude toward freedom of choice. As might have been expected, about two-third of the applications for divorce have come from couples married less than one year, and in the majority of cases women have taken the initiative [28]. The increase in divorce has troubled all the communist regimes as it is indicative of growing instability in the family unit. Until the state can totally take over the childrearing functions and the care of the elderly, the family will continue to be what the Soviet principles term, "the core societal cell."

The rise in the divorce rate has been accompanied by an increase in abortions and a decline in the birth rate. It is highly significant that the 1970 U.S.S.R. census showed even the more tradition-oriented Moslem families of Central Asia now average 1.5 children per family [29]. The problem of abortions has become especially critical in Czechoslovakia with a 1969 abortion rate of 56.6 abortions per 100 live births [30]. To remedy the situation, the Soviet-modeled commissions which consider applications for abortions, became much tougher in granting permission for the operation [31]. In October 1971, the Czech Minister of Labor and Social Affairs, Emilian Hamernik, published an article calling for a "more suitable moral and political climate" and for more instruction in parenthood [32]. In Rumania, abortions were so numerous that the government reintroduced a ban on them [33], while in Poland, voices have been heard demanding a revision of the Polish abortion law [34].

It is doubtful that any communist government will adopt a policy toward women which would encourage the dissolution of the family and a drop in the birthrate. Thus, the demographic problem is a crucial factor operating in favor of maintaining an ideological-cultural environment which encourages the preservation of a strong family unit.

These considerations lead to the second aspect of the philosophic tradition, the promotion of the old concept of the female role. In most societies, femininity has been associated with dependency and submission, but female conformance to these characteristics has tended to vary from culture to culture. In Moslem Central Asia and in Confucian China, for instance, women were completely excluded from public life. The situation was not the same in Eastern Europe and European Russia where women were highly visible outside the home. While they had few legal rights, they enjoyed greater freedom, particularly in the last century, than their Asian sisters ever did. In his study of the Soviet family, Geiger points out that the peasant woman in old rural Russia often merely maintained the myth of male dominance in the household, while in fact, she controlled the purse strings and made most of the important decisions [35]. The pattern held true for East European peasant families as well. Even today, as Table 12.2 indicates, women tend to be found in those areas which require the handling of money, such as the restaurant business or in credit and finance. Because the Western family never developed along strict hierarchical lines, where every member from great-grandfather on down to the youngest son had special duties and obligations in the family structure, Western women had more freedom and status in the household than did women in the East. Upper-class women in particular, in Eastern Europe and European Russia, had considerable influence on their husband's careers through their maintenance of the social conventions.

However, in no culture was it considered proper that women go out to work in a career, or enter a profession. Those who did were considered very daring. In fact, women, from intellectual backgrounds such as Aleksandra Kollontai, Rosa Luxembourg, or Elena Stasova, were embracing communism for much the same reason and at the same time as their British and American counterparts were fighting for their political rights. But the female Bolshevik movement never reached the wide mass of peasant women, which might have given it real political strength [36].

This view of woman's place has carried over into communist rule and permeates all strata of communist society. One Soviet survey found that most of the male respondents preferred their wives not to work (74%), while 64% of the female respondents rationalized their working by saying they felt their jobs strengthened their home life [37]. In Hungary, Central Committee Secretary Arpad Pullai attributed the survival of the concept of the traditional female role to "centuries-old Weltanshaung," which could not be erased by legal measures and resolutions alone [38].

In summation, emphasis on the family and the persistence of the traditional concept of the female role can be seen as responsible for a critical amount of the input from the environment into the political sphere for communist systems, where women are conditioned to act from habit. When habit informs the behavior of any group, it cannot hope to influence or exercise power.

The Political Structure

Table 12.8 provides data on the participation of women in the ruling bodies of the communist parties and governments of Eastern Europe and the Soviet Union. The statistics indicate a correspondingly low level of female participation in the leading party and government institutions as in the economy. Only four of eight countries have women on the Politbureau, the most important decision-making organ in the communist system. Of 416 possible high-governmental positions, only 13 are filled by women. The communist political world is a man's world.

As far as recruitment of women into the party is concerned, only East Germany can claim success with a 45% representation. Female membership in the CzCP had fallen off well before 1968, and has not come back since. The Soviet party leaders launched an all out recruitment campaign prior to the 24th Party Congress and were delighted when they finally increased female representation to 22.9% [39]. None of the other parties can boast over 30%, although the percentage of women in the total population is much higher.

The question that immediately comes to mind is how to account for the apparent political passivity of women in communist countries. One possible explanation is that offered by Volgyes. He argues that the present emphasis in East European and Soviet socialization is on the decrease of political participation to minimal levels [40]. If such is indeed the case, then the leadership will not be encouraging women to enter the political structure. It would be sufficient to have token amounts of female participation in the party and government at the lowest levels. The rather equal percentages

Table 12.8. Participation of Women in the Politbureau and Government of the U.S.S.R. and East European Communist Countries, 1972

Country	Politbureau		Government		
	Number of women	Total	Number of women	Total	Position held
Albania	1	17	1	26[a]	Deputy Chairman, People's Assembly
Bulgaria CP	1	17	1	41	Ministry of Justice[b]
CSSR	0	13	1	25	Chairman of the Federal Assembly of People
Slovak CP	1	11			
Czech government			0	16	
Slovak government			0	19	
East Germany	1	23	4	86	3 members of State Council, Ministry of Public Education, Ministry of Light Industry
Hungary	1	13	1	32	Ministry of Light Industry
Poland	0	15	1	51	Member, State Council
Rumania	0	9	3	49	Deputy Chairman of the National Assembly, Ministry of Education and Instruction, Minister of Finance
U.S.S.R.	0	22	1	71	Ministry of Culture

SOURCE: *Radio Free Europe Research Paper*, November 23, 1972 (mimeographed).

[a]These figures refer to all the national ministerial posts, membership in the state councils, and the chairmanships of the national assemblies.

[b]A woman lost her position as Minister of Light Industry last year.

of female membership in the national parties and local government organs in the East European countries and the U.S.S.R. suggest that such might have been the regime's objective.

Another explanation is that offered by Mandel. The situation of women in the communist countries, so the argument goes, has so improved under communist rule that their very passivity attests to the success of the communist achievement. The same argument, of course, could be made with equal validity in the case of the American Negro around 1900. A third explanation which holds more relevance for Eastern Europe is a fundamental antipathy to the regime on the part of most of the populations of the East European countries, particularly in Poland, Hungary, and Czechoslovakia, which have had recent experiences of direct Soviet intervention. But this explanation cannot be applied to the Soviet Union with the same consistency.

A more comprehensive reason would be the enormous sacrifices which high participation in the communist political environment demands of the power-seeking aspirant. It has already been seen how women in communist systems prefer the less demanding and less prestigious jobs in order to have the time to spend with and on their families. Given a philosophic environment which encourages a traditional concept of the female role, women are less apt to be motivated to compete in the ruthless political arena where a wrong decision or ill-timed action would have strong negative results. Thus, the tough demands of upward political mobility in terms of time and competition would seem to discourage women in communist regimes from the active pursuit of a high-level political career. As a consequence, the input from the political environment into the area of interaction between the leadership and the female population must perforce be male oriented, since there is not a sufficiently strong female participation at the highest levels of decision-making to speak for women's interests.

Leadership Guidance

Leadership guidance involves actions taken by the communist ruling groups in response to the inputs from the environment, to modify the existing situation of a client group, in this case, women. In determining an appropriate response, the regimes have to assess the relative value of the various demands coming to them from the economy, the philosophic tradition, and the political structure. Communist leadership response to the position of women may conveniently be divided into two time periods: the post-revolutionary phase, when the objective was to break up time-honored social patterns, and bring women out of the home into the economy; the present maintenance phase, where the regime is combining its various options to maintain itself firmly in power and promote economic development. The performance of the prescribing and promoting functions varies both with the different time periods and with the stage of economic development of the country concerned.

The Prescribing Function

The postrevolutionary phase is characterized in all communist regimes by the pursuit of labor and marriage policies designed to mobilize women into the work force and loosen their ties with the home. Included in an official program would be party resolutions and laws pertaining to the secularization of marriage and divorce; laws establishing the working conditions of female employment and providing for the setting up of kindergartens and child care centers; and party directives urging female activism. Following the Russian Revolution, when the nation was in the stage of economic takeoff, the regime had a very relaxed policy toward marriage and did much to bring women into the economic and political world. Marriage and divorce were made very easy [41]. When women seemed to be hesitant to try the world of work, the regime substituted quotas for women in vocational schools. In 1924, a woman foreman occasioned much publicity as there was a question at the time whether women were suited to such jobs. In 1939, the regime began to encourage women into the engineering field by an open admission policy into engineering institutes. Thanks to the Soviet state, Moslem women were able for the first time to appear in public without veils in 1920, despite the protests of outraged Uzbek husbands [42]. With the collectivization of agriculture, another Moslem custom, bride price, was forced out of existence because there were no longer bridegrooms who owned sheep enough to pay.

By the Second World War, the patriarchal family pattern had substantially weakened and family life further deteriorated in the course of the struggle. To restore family stability, and to encourage the birth rate, the divorce law of 1944 was passed, which made divorce very difficult. Women in the meantime had started to penetrate the upper echelons of the educational system, but their progress was impeded by quotas favoring the admission of veterans over women. Even now, although the need to balance women and men in higher education has diminished, the discriminatory policy has not been abandoned [43].

In China, the post revolutionary phase has been symbolized by the commune. In contrast to the Soviet leadership, which attempted only the modification of the patriarchal family, the Chinese have gone so far as to try to break up the family altogether. The commune may have been Mao's view of the ideal living unit for a communist industrial society. One reason for such regimentation was, of course, economic. It released huge untapped labor reserves into the economy. By 1959, reports were published proclaiming the organization of women into "street factories," street production units, and mess halls [44]. The ideological focus of the communes was the creation of a situation where men would not have to give up their time-honored prerogatives by participating in housework, but women who were not heavily involved in childrearing would be free to work because of the existence of communal dining halls, nurseries, and kindergartens. The aim was the elimination of the second shift.

Tradition and the lack of facilities have proved stronger than government edict. The considerable objection to the commune system seems to have been a strong factor in subsequent public endorsement of the continuance of the family as a unit.

During the maintenance phase, the postrevolutionary objectives have been secured, and the communist leaderships can then turn to the solution of the more glaring of the unsolved problems of the first time period. In the Soviet Union, the regime has made a conscious effort to promote women to higher status positions. In 1968, for example, 25% of all those promoted to associate professor were women [45]. In addition, the government has passed numerous laws directed at the further improvement of female working conditions such as those allowing a woman a year off from work to have a child, and raising the allowances for large families. Great effort has been made to expand the number of kindergartens, although these are still far from sufficient to meet the demand [46]. These efforts give some indication of the force of the environmental pressures on the leadership. The Moslem areas have given the Soviet leaders particular cause for concern as they have required the most extensive social changes, and have responded only slowly to them. By 1970, the CPSU evidently felt this failure to be of sufficient proportions to require the Central Asian Parties to pass resolutions to increase the activism of Central Asian women [47].

The East European regimes have been most innovative in the maintenance phase. All the East European countries have adopted marriage and labor legislation similar to that in the Soviet Union. In addition, to help overcome the problem of the second shift, Hungary has instituted a free Saturday for women [48]. In East Germany, the government has followed its communist neighbors in increasing the number of correspondence courses [49].

The Promoting Function

The foregoing brief catalogue of the more significant pieces of communist legislation must be seen within the context of the regimes' promoting function. What needs to be investigated is the relationship between the message, as enacted into law, and the way it is transmitted to the population. Even in an authoritarian society, legal rules will not provide equality unless the message of equality is also transmitted. Space does not permit a full examination of the socialization of women under the various communist countries, but a cursory study suggests that the leaderships are conveying a message, not of equality, but of the value of the traditional female role, and the propriety of female employment in a few limited fields. If one reads *Pravda, Literaturnaia gazeta,* or an East European periodical, he cannot help but be struck by the number of photographs of female dancers and young happy peasant girls. Film and ballet stars are glamorized, and one rarely reads about a collective farm chairman or a leading female engineer. More often than not, in photos of industry, there is a woman standing in the background, the helpmate of the virile male foreman in the foreground. In Soviet and East European films, women are frequently portrayed as doctors or lawyers, seldom as scientists. The traditional female role is further buttressed by the communist regimes' official recognition of motherhood in awards such as "Heroine Mother [50]." Even the more liberal novels like Aksenov's *Ticket to the Stars* celebrate traditional romance. And while Soviet literature has moved from the adoration of socialist motherhood to criticism of the sterility of Soviet officialdom's neobourgeois marital habits [51], there has been only one short novel, to the best of my knowledge, which has attempted to describe the plight of Soviet women caught between the demands of work and family [52]. Not surprisingly, its author is a woman. As all publication in the Soviet Union needs to pass the censor, it must be assumed that the image of women presented in the mass media and literature is one the leadership wants transmitted. One has to go all the way to China to find a ballet like "The Red Detachment of Women."

The inputs from the environment upon leadership guidance would seem substantial. The concern for the falling birth rate in Rumania, the Soviet Union, Poland, and Czechoslovakia was directly responsible for such varied responses as the rescinding of the abortion law (although this apparently did not help the situation in Rumania) and the official reluctance to provide too much leniency in the matter of divorce expressed in the 1968 Soviet "Principles on Marriage and the Family." The competitive demands of industrialization and the political system are also critical factors. In their structure of priorities, women play a minor role in the economic and political transformation of society required by the process of modernization. In its focus on problems of greater urgency, leadership guidance consigns women to their traditional childrearing functions and assigns their professional role to second place.

The Female Self-Concept

A cross-national survey of female attitudes toward family, job orientation, place of work, relationship of self to work colleagues, etc., would be a useful tool, if it could be freely administered, to determine how women under communism actually see themselves, given their environment and the rather conservative posture of leadership guidance. Failing such a possibility, the researcher must rely on sociological studies from the countries under consideration, always bearing in mind that whatever is published reflects official policy.

Studies and press reports offer some clues for a starting point for an investigation. One survey in particular is worth comment. It was made of a team of 13 workers at the Siberian Scientific Center at Akademgorod over a 3-year period. The object of the survey was to find out how the women and men of this highly educated group perceived themselves in relation to their colleagues. The survey discovered that the women team members generally saw themselves in the role of colleague or subordinate. Only 23% saw themselves as managers [53]. Again, in an otherwise fine study of the relationship between a woman's work and home life, the researcher, Dr. Zoia Iankova, argues for education for women on the grounds of its improving the home situation [54], rather than on the basis of career advancement. A Polish study reported that women were discouraged from seeking promotion because of male hostility toward women in administrative positions [55]. An East German broadcast indicated that one-third of all East German women were working part time because of family demands [56]. In a campaign promoting full-time work for women, a *Neues Deutschland* interview with three women revealed that the reason for their return was because the children were now grown [57].

When these reports are compared with the findings of Table 12.5 relating to female activity and the number of children, it would seem women under communism are still being conditioned to identify themselves primarily in the traditional subordinate role. On the other hand, the data on divorce and abortion would suggest that the meaning of this role is being modified to include a greater personal freedom of choice. The franker tone of the more recent women's meetings in the communist countries, and their stress on the problems confronting women rather than on the successes communism has won for them, can mean that women in East Europe and the U.S.S.R. are becoming conscious of their position and are beginning to seek ways to change it. The women's gatherings in Eastern Europe seem particularly open and candid in this respect [58]. But even the sociological studies in the Soviet Union make no attempt to hide the problems of crowded living, the difficulties of the long work week, and the hostility a woman can incur on the job [59]. It must be remembered that the demographic balance has only recently reasserted itself in the U.S.S.R. For over 20 years, the Soviet woman has had to face stiff competition to get a man [60] and femininity naturally has been identified with her success in marriage and family.

On balance, the traditional role continues to have priority in the female self-concept primarily again, as was the case with leadership guidance, because of the force of environmental pressures. Women's identification with the home and family carries over to their self-concept in a subordinate role at work. Their experience of inferiority in the job situation reinforces their reluctance to engage themselves in the economic and political environments in order to overturn the traditional patterns of male-female behavior in the home. The regimes can work towards the goal of communal dining rooms and kindergartens for every child, but it is highly doubtful anyone really sees these as a solution. Indeed, Iankova's study mentioned earlier, suggests that women higher up the social ladder do not want their children in kindergarten, that enrollment in kindergarten is associated with low status. The traditional image of the Victorian lady is apparently still an appealing one. At a recent international congress held in Moscow, one Soviet woman with an advanced degree was reported as telling an American sister that she thought the greatest freedom might lie in *not working at all* [61].

The influence of leadership guidance on the female self-concept cannot be ignored. In its promotion of equality, communist officialdom has been ambivalent, or more accurately, uncommitted. On the one hand, the regimes have encouraged women to take an active interest in pursuing high status careers where male resentment appears the most severe. On the other, they have sponsored the message of the value of the traditional female role. For women living under the communist system, the continuation of self-identification with this role means their expectation to change their status position must perforce remain low.

The foregoing analysis of a model for the study of women under communism suggests some guidelines for the further investigation of the problem.

1. Leadership capabilities in a coercive type of modernizing process, are limited. Governments have to select priorities. These must involve economic development, social transformation to the extent necessary to promote this development, and the maintenance of power to effect additional increases in leadership capabilities. To realize these objectives, communist ruling groups had to break up the traditional family structures and mobilize women into the work world, but needed to give little attention to revolutionizing the female status.

2. The more traditional a society, the greater the role leadership guidance can play in its social and economic transformation. The only communist leadership which evidently believed a radical approach to the question of women was essential to the modernization process was the Chinese. It was no accident that the communes were aimed at the complete destruction of the traditional Confucian family. The Soviet attack on the Moslem family in Central Asia comes somewhat under this category as well. In Western Russia and Eastern Europe, where the family had already evolved into the

conjugal limited kinship form, strong government direction was unnecessary. Hence, the leaderships in these countries could respond to the economic and political demands of modernization without mounting an all-out assault on traditional values. Such a policy reinforced their power position by securing a certain measure of male popular support.

3. Caught between this interaction between the environment and leadership capability, the behavior of women under communism has tended to be determined by habit and acquiescence to established cultural patterns. As a consequence, they have been unable to exercise any real power. Groups which rise to elite status expect to derive some advantage from their new position. The evidence suggests that women in the communist systems as yet see little advantage to be gained by a change in status which might replace their traditional role.

The model would seem applicable, with modifications, to the problem of women in other areas of the world and to problems of minority groups as well. Its suggestion that direct leadership intervention can have as negative an influence as the failure of governments to take action opens up the whole area of the definition of goals in the modernizing process and the need for all sectors of society to participate in the formulation of these goals. Such participation by definition is absent in communist societies.

NOTES

1. In his value-institution model of social change, Harold Lasswell defines development as growth towards the goal of widespread participation in all preferred values which have been formulated in institutional terms. In his definition, value refers not only to wealth, but power, respect, enlightenment, skill, well-being, affection, rectitude. In other words, the term value refers to every major category thought to exist in the social process. Harold Lasswell, "Toward a General Theory of Directed Value Accumulation and Institutional Development," *Comparative Theories of Social Change*. Ann Arbor, Michigan: Foundation for Research on Human Behavior, 1966, pp. 12–50.

2. See, for example, William J. Goode, *World Revolution and Family Patterns*. New York: Free Press of Glencoe, 1963; Jessie Bernard, *Women and the Public Interest*. New York: Aldine-Atherton, 1971, as well as her shorter paper, "The Status of Women in Modern Patterns of Culture," *The Annals of the American Academy of Political and Social Science*, Thorsten Sellen, ed., *375*, pp. 3–14 (January 1968); Elizabeth Fulkner Baker, *Technology and Woman's Work*. New York: Columbia University Press, 1964; and Cynthia Fuchs Epstein, *Woman's Place, Options and Limits in Professional Careers*. Berkeley, Ca.: University of California Press, 1970.

3. For a discussion of a possible typology of change processes, see Warren G. Bennis, "Applying Behavioral Science for Organizational Change," *Comparative Theories, op. cit.*, p. 303ff.

4. For the text of the 1919 Program, see *The USSR and the Future: An Analysis of the New Program of the CPSU*. Leonard Schapiro, ed. New York: Praeger, 1963.

5. For a detailed survey of the Soviet case, see Barbara Jancar, "Women and Soviet Politics," a paper presented at the 1972 meeting of the American Political Science Association.

6. Karl Deutsch holds that modernization *is* politicization and places high priority on the role of the political sector in effecting economic and social change. Karl Deutsch, *Comparative Theories, op. cit.,* pp. 61–64.

7. In the U.S.A. in 1968, for example, women represented only 15.2% of all managers, officials, and proprietors. U.S. Department of Labor, *1969 Handbook on Women Workers.* Washington, D.C.; GPO, 1969, p. 92. By contrast, Soviet women constituted only 6% of all enterprise directors for the same year. *Zhenshchiny i deti v SSSR.* Moscow: Statistika, 1969, p. 68.

8. Goode, *World Revolution and Family Patterns, op. cit.,* p. 369; Matina Horner argues that women are not motivated to status achievement because they have been conditioned to view success as a masculine characteristic. Consequently, they fear to succeed lest they lose what they have been conditioned to see as their femininity. Matina S. Horner, "Femininity and Successful Achievement: A Basic Inconsistency" in Judith M. Bardwick, *et al., Feminine Personality and Conflict.* Belmont, Ca.: Brooks/Cole, 1970, pp. 45–72. And Betty Friedan vituperates against the feminine mystique of the 1950s which encouraged women to believe that self-fulfillment could only be found in having children and staying home. Betty Friedan, *The Feminine Mystique.* New York: Norton, 1966.

9. "Report of the U.S.S.R. Council of Ministers' Central Statistical Administration: The Population of Our Country," *Pravda* (April 17, 1971).

10. For a discussion of Soviet criticism of the prevalence of women in physical labor jobs, see Lotta Lennon, "Women in the USSR," *Problems of Communism,* pp. 52–53 (July/Aug. 1971).

11. Data based on Central Committee Secretary, Arpad Pullai's speech to the 18–19 February 1970 session of the HSWP CC, as reported in *Magyar Hirlap* (February 20, 1970).

12. *Zhenshchiny i deti, op. cit.,* pp. 98, 100.

13. *Ibid.,* p. 73.

14. Equal pay has been apparently such a rarity in China that the press plays up instances when it has been achieved. Goode, *World Revolution and Family Patterns, op. cit.,* p. 305.

15. Jerzy Berent, "Some Demographic Aspects of Employment in Eastern Europe and the U.S.S.R.," *Internat. Labor Rev.,* p. 178 (Sept. 1970).

16. In Czechoslovakia, for example, 72.7% of all female cooperative farm workers with more than five children were employed in 1961, while only 37.5% of all female employees with the same number of children were employed. Zdenek Jurecek, "Diferencni plodnost podle vysledku scitani lidu z r. 1961, Part 2," in *Demografie* (Prague), No. 3, p. 213.

17.
Expenditure on Nonworking Time (in hours per week) by Women in Gorkey Relative to the Number of Children

	Number of children			
Type of work	0	1	3	5 and over
Work time	49.1%	49.0%	48.5%	47.5%
Time for sleep and meals	62.8	60.2	58.1	59.1
Time for sleep	50.0	47.0	44.3	45.4
Housework and cleaning	28.1	43.8	48.5	52.4
Leisure time activities	11.4	5.6	3.9	4.3
Culture and education	16.6	9.4	8.0	4.7

SOURCE: G. A. Slecarev, "Voprosy organizatsii truda i byta zhenshchin i rasshirennoe vosproizvodstvo naseleniia," *Sotsial'nye issledovaniia.* Moscow: Izdatel'stvo "Nauka," 1965, p. 159.

18. *Der Morgan* (East Berlin), (September 22, 1968).

19. Z. A. Iankova, "OSemeino-bytovykh roliakh rabotaishchei zhenshchiny," *Sotsial'nye issledovaniia, No. 4.* Moscow: Izdatel'stvo "Nauka," 1970, p. 81.

20. Jessie Bernard, "The Status of Women," *op. cit.,* p. 5.

21. See Richard Pipes, "Assimilation and Muslims: A Case Study," *Soviet Society a Book of Readings,* Alex Inkeles and H. Kent Geiger, eds. Boston: Houghton Mifflin, 1961, pp. 588–607.

22. J. Myrdal, *Report from a Chinese Village.* New York: Signet, 1965, pp. 252–257.

23. For a good study of the Chinese family, although somewhat dated, see Goode, *World Revolution and Family Patterns, op. cit.,* pp. 230–270.

24. A. L. Pimenova, "Novyi byt i stanovlenie vnutricemeinogo ravenstva," *Sotsial'nye issledovaniia, No. 7.* Moscow: Izdatel'stvo "Nauka," 1971, p. 38ff.

25. For the text of the Principles of Marriage and the Family, see *Izvestia* (September 28, 1968).

26. S. I. Golod, "Sociological Problems of Sexual Morality," Publication of the Philosophical Faculty, Leningrad University, 1968, as translated in *Sov. Rev.,* **XI**, No. 2, pp. 136–137 (Summer 1970).

27. *Literaturnaia gazeta* (September 3, 1970).

28. As reported by Goode, *World Revolution and Family Patterns, op. cit.,* p. 317.

29. Statistics derived from 1970 U.S.S.R. published in *Pravda* (April 17, 1971).

30. *Statisticka rocenka CSSR, 1970,* p. 102.

31. Under Order No. 162/62, the abortion committees were composed of a chairman (who had to be district national committee deputy), a member of the regional population commission, and one doctor. This gave officials the majority and ensured party control.

32. *Narodni vybori,* No. 42 (October 21, 1971).

33. The decree was dated October 1, 1966 and published in *Scanteia* (October 2, 1966).

34. See *Kultura* (August 29, 1971) and *Zycie Warszawy* (September 9, 1971).

35. H. Kent Geiger, *The Family in Soviet Russia.* Cambridge, Mass: Harvard University Press, 1968, Chap. 11.

36. At the 1907 All-Russian Congress of the RSDP (Bolshevik), 45 out of the 1000 delegates were women, of which one was a peasant. At the First Duma, bourgeois women managed to get 9000 signatures for woman's suffrage. George Mandel, "Soviet Women and Their Self-Image," *Science and Society,* **XXXV**, No. 3., p. 288 (Fall 1971).

37. *Literaturnaia gazeta,* No. 29 (September 22, 1971).

38. *Magyar Hirlap* (October 30, 1971).

39. I. Kapitonov, "Some Questions of Party Building in the Light of the 24th Party Congress," *Kommunist,* No. 3, p. 35 (February 1972).

40. Ivan Volgyes, "Political Socialization in Eastern Europe: A Comparative Framework," prepared for delivery at the 1972 annual meeting of the American Political Science Association, Washington, D.C., September 5–9. See especially p. 6ff.

41. For a discussion of marriage and family legislation during this period, see John N. Hazard and Isaac Shapiro, *The Soviet Legal System, Part III, Legal Relations Between Soviet Citizens* (Parker School Studies in Foreign and Comparative Law). Dobbs Ferry, N.Y.: Oceana, 1962, pp. 99–135.

42. For a more detailed account of Soviet official actions with regard to women in the early days of the Soviet Union, see Mandel, "Soviet Women," *op. cit.,* p. 289ff.

43. The percentage of women studying in higher and specialized schools reached its peak of

41% during the war, fell off to 23% in 1956, and is now at 48%. Norton B. Dodge, *Women in the Soviet Union: Their Role in Economic, Scientific and Technical Development.* Baltimore: Johns Hopkins Press, 1966, pp. 135–136, and *Vestnik statistiki*, 1971.

44. As reported in Goode, *World Revolution and Family Patterns, op. cit.*, p. 301.

45. Mandel, "Soviet Women," *op. cit.*, p. 292.

46. The appropriate resolution was passed at the 24th Party Congress. The USSR has spent a good deal of money on grants to mothers of large families. From 1940 to 1969, federal budget expenditures in this area rose from 123 million rubles to 438 million rubles. As regards preschool facilities, Soviet kindergartens and other institutions are equipped to take care of approximately half the nation's 20.6 million children. (*Zhenshchiny i deti, op. cit.*, pp. 76, 81.)

47. See, for example, the Uzbek Party resolution to promote women to higher positions and increase their party mindedness in *Literaturnaia gazeta* (May 27, 1970).

48. *Magyar Hirlap* (October 30, 1972).

49. As a special encouragement to women to enter higher education, the East German government, in 1967, initiated special courses for women for which they can qualify through their places of work. Should they not have the proper entrance prerequisites, it is the task of the enterprise educational system to see that they attain them. *Frankfurter Allgemeine Zeitung* (November 8, 1969).

50. Between 1950 and 1959, the number of awards rose to 94,000. *Zhenshchiny v SSSR, op. cit.*, p. 76.

51. For an excellent discussion of the way women have been presented in Soviet literature, see Vera Dunham's, *The Role and Status of Women in the Soviet Union*, Donald R. Brown, ed. New York: Teachers College Press, 1968.

52. Natal'ia Baranskaia, "Nedelia kak nedelia," *Novyi mir*, No. 11, pp. 23–55 (November 1969).

53. V. N. Shubkin, G. M. Kochetov, "Rukovoditel', kollega, podchinennyi," *Sotsial'nye issledovaniia, No. 2.* Moscow: Izdatel'stvo "Nauka," 1968, p. 153.

54. Dr. Iankova's research was reported in *Nedelia*, No. 18, p. 20 (April 24–30, 1972).

55. As reported in *Literaturnaia gazeta* (September 22, 1971).

56. Reported in a commentary by Christa Weiss on "Professional Women in the GDR," Radio GDR (February 1, 1972).

57. *Neues Deutschland* (February 6, 1972).

58. I am referring specifically to the Women's League Congress held in Warsaw on November 17–18, 1970 and the Hungarian National Woman's Conference held in Budapest on October 29–30, 1971.

59. Male collective farmers have been reported as resistant to the idea of female tractor drivers, the prestigious job on the Soviet kolkhoz. *Pravda* (August 19, 1971). As a result it has been very hard to recruit women for training. In 1970, women comprised only 0.3% of the tractor-mechanizers. *Vestnik statistiki*, No. 4, p. 93 (1971).

60. A particularly poignant example of the Soviet girl student's fate is given in Solzhenitsyn's *The First Circle*. New York: Harper and Row, 1968.

61. *The New York Times* (December 31, 1972).

Chapter

13

Modernization Theory and Sex Roles in Critical Perspective:

The Case of the Soviet Union

Gail Warshofsky Lapidus

The term *modernization* conjures up a multiplicity of images associated with the vast transformation of the economies, societies, and polities of the Western world in the past few centuries. For economists it suggests the broad technological and organizational changes associated with industrialization which have enhanced man's mastery over the natural environment. For sociologists, it evokes the process of structural differentiation which has altered patterns of social organization and the distribution of social roles at all levels of the social system. To political scientists, it entails egalitarianism and democratization: an expanded definition of citizenship, widened political participation, and the enhancement of institutional capacity associated with nation-building. For students of all disciplines it evokes a vast transformation in human values, perceptions, and behavior, indeed a revolution in character and personality.

Studies of this far-reaching process of change have not, for the most part, directly concerned themselves with its consequences for the position and roles of women [1]. However, certain assumptions are implicit, if not always explicit, in the literature. The process of modernization necessarily entails certain changes in the role of women within the family, economy, and polity. The separation of household from employment and the growing degree of geographical and social mobility, fundamentally alter the role of the family, divesting it of its once important economic, educational and placement functions, and of its extended kinship solidarities; thereby reducing it to a

An earlier version of this paper was presented at the Annual Meeting of the Western Political Science Association, San Diego, 1973.

243

highly specialized nuclear unit largely devoted to emotional gratification, reproduction, and early socialization of children. The development of modern industry and trade disrupts traditional patterns of division of labor, creating more differentiated and complex economic institutions, and allocating roles to women as well as men on the basis of achievement-oriented, rather than ascriptive, norms. The democratization of political life extends the privileges and responsibilities of citizenship to women on a basis of equality with men, while changes in the structure and scope of political authority and efforts to institutionalize political responsiveness create new avenues for greater political participation.

The evaluation of these changes, however, has provoked widespread controversy. Are the consequences of modernization essentially liberating for women or do they diminish the possibilities of self-fulfillment? Contradictory answers have been offered; apotheoses of social progress vie with the romantic idealization of the past. The current literature expresses an ambivalence reminiscent of earlier intellectual responses to the consequences of industrialization [2].

For some writers, the consequences of modernization are essentially liberating. The variety and complexity of modern life bring enhanced personal and social freedom, new possibilities of choice among various life styles, and wider opportunities for self-expression in public as well as private realms. The emphasis on mobility, achievement, and equality enhances possibilities of choice for women as well as men. The more modern a society, the wider the range of options it offers to all its members [3].

But a contradictory, more pessimistic evaluation of the implications of modernity for women's roles can also be found in the literature [4]. Changes in the structure of the family have demeaned and impoverished traditional feminine roles without offering meaningful new ones in their place. Where women once found status and authority in mediating relationships within the extended family, and where the management of households required important economic and political skills, the breakup of the traditional family has narrowed the scope of women's activities. Women have ceased to be fully productive members of society whose status derives from their economic productivity, but have become objects of conspicuous consumption, valued for expressive rather than instrumental roles [5].

The entry of women into the industrial economy and into political roles has occurred in ways that largely confine their contribution to the least rewarding positions at the bottom of the hierarchy of status and responsibility. Although modernization has encouraged the entry of women into the industrial labor force in large numbers, they typically occupy low-paid and often marginal positions. They predominate as relatively unskilled laborers or are concentrated at the lower levels of administrative work and in the paraprofessions, holding jobs rather than pursuing careers. Few women are found in the more prestigious realms of the business world or of the professions [6]. In public life, they have played a largely passive role, politically mobilizable for certain purposes at certain times, but without aspiring to leadership and power [7].

From this perspective, modernization destroys the comparatively undifferentiated distribution of sex roles which presumably prevails in traditional societies, creating new public roles almost exclusively for men while relegating women to more confined and less satisfying social functions. Because of their overriding concern with productivity, and with the enhancement of economic and political capacity, modernizing societies are essentially hostile to a fundamental redefinition of values, roles, and capacities, a redefinition which awaits the postmodern society.

The whole process of modernization, then, vastly intensifies the social strain experienced by women by confronting them with contradictory imperatives. The ideology of modernity, with its emphasis on freedom, equality and achievement as supreme and universal norms, and on competitive, instrumental personality traits, collides with pervasive cultural norms, supported by social realities, which transmit conflicting images of ideal feminine roles and attributes.

These contrasting views of the consequences of modernization for women's roles reflect divergent concerns as well as different values in appraising the outcomes of long-term social change. But they reflect, as well, more basic conceptual problems which broadly underly the study of modernization.

The studies of social change which have proliferated in the past two decades have shared a conceptual framework centered about the antithesis between tradition and modernity. These studies have described the process of change in essentially evolutionary terms, as a process of structural differentiation during which entire societies make the transition from an essentially static and uniform tradition to a relatively homogeneous modernity largely defined by the experiences of England and the United States. They have also treated modernization as a systemic process, in which change in one or more sectors induces interrelated changes in all other segments of the social system [8]. These evolutionary and systemic assumptions, the legacy of the imagery of 19th century biological sciences, have distorted the analysis of social change more generally and of its effects on women's roles as well.

A number of recent studies have suggested that this orientation involves a gross oversimplification and distortion of the process of change which occurred in the West [9]. First, the juxtaposition of terms like tradition and modernity may be a useful analytical tool when they are conceived as ideal types, a point of departure from which to analyze empirical social institutions. However, the terms have come to be confused with the social reality itself.

Secondly, the systemic, evolutionary approach to change implies a degree of uniformity and homogeneity, horizontally, vertically, and over time which is questioned by all empirical investigations. The process of modernization was a relatively natural, spontaneous sequence of developments only in England. Once industrialization had begun, other societies came to view this development as a model to be imitated consciously, using the power of the state to create functional equivalents of the social processes which had occurred in the natural course of events in the pioneering society.

The pattern of Russian development, for example, is but one striking instance of the importance of "international emulation, governmental initiative, nationalism and the diffusion of ideas [10]" in more backward societies for whom modernization is less a spontaneous pattern of internal evolution than a politically-directed process selectively adapting elements of foreign experience and recombining them with selected elements of the national tradition. Indeed, it was Lenin who made this point quite explicitly in responding to the Menshevik and Marxian view which insisted on "the necessary prerequisites of political change," when he argued that no one had ever been able to demonstrate the necessary sequential relationship between economic, political, and social change [11]. The proper course was to seize power first, and then to utilize control of political institutions to alter the economy, social system, and values of Russian society.

While economic, social, and political changes are not entirely unrelated and asystemic, previous conceptions have perhaps over-exaggerated the interconnection between change in various social subsystems, and treated them as largely the consequences of changes in economic organization. Less attention has been devoted to the wider variety of sequences and combinations which are possible, and particularly to the ways in which the forms of social change may be shaped by cultural norms, by political institutions and processes or by ideological commitments. Moreover, both the nature and the rate of change in different sectors will be different for different groups and strata within a society, and more differentiated models and hypotheses need to be developed to illuminate this area.

Finally, the whole conception of modernization as an evolutionary process of increasing social differentiation has come to be seen as itself an oversimplification of a complex process. Social differentiation entails new mechanisms of integration as well, and, as Smelser has persuasively argued, modernization involves a "contrapuntal interplay" between social differentiation on the one hand, and "integration which unites differentiated structures on a new basis [12]." The implications of this perspective are profound for it introduces important descriptive as well as evaluative ambiguities in the analysis of social change. Modernization has brought about diverse and varied configurations of roles for both men and women, in which are joined both new opportunities and new costs.

The pattern of Soviet development is a particularly illuminating illustration of these larger theoretical considerations and their implications for the study of sex roles [13]. As a revolutionary government which committed itself to a total transformation of social values and institutions, including the family, and as an authoritarian regime able to mobilize enormous resources to implement its preferences, the U.S.S.R. conducted what may be viewed as a vast experiment in social engineering to alter deeply rooted attitudes and patterns of behavior. As an avowedly socialist society which insists upon the connection between the institution of private property and the subordination of women, it offers a setting in which to examine the effect of basic economic changes upon the position and role of women. And as a developing society which has rapidly moved from relative backwardness to industrial maturity it offers the opportunity to look at both the possibilities and the limitations of planned, institutional change.

The Soviet pattern of development and its impact on the role of women in economic, political, and family life consequently deserves detailed analysis, for it has important implications for both the conceptual treatment of modernization and sex roles and for empirical comparative studies. It brings into sharp focus the inadequacies of theories of role change which rely on the static dichotomies of tradition and modernity, and on the evolutionary and systemic imagery of classical modernization theory.

Analyses of the effects of modernization on sex roles founder on the complexities of conceptualizing the process of social change. The view that social change involves a transition from a static and uniform tradition to a homogeneous modernity has, as we have seen, been widely criticized. Tradition and modernity are neither mutually exclusive nor are they composed of functionally interdependent attributes [14]. Not only are there a variety of traditions, modernity is itself diverse. The few attempts which have been made to define the meaning of either tradition or modernity for sex roles have done violence to the variety of historical experience without offering conceptual precision or clarity. Modernity in particular has been used in a variety of ways, and its descriptive function entangled with a normative one.

The relationship of modernity to sex roles has been conceived in a variety of ways. For analytical purposes four distinct approaches can be identified. The first, elaborated most completely in the work of Parsons [15], argues that modernization entails an increasing differentiation of sex roles. Although its rationale is functionalist, deriving from the specialization of roles inherent in small group behavior, the functional rationale merges into biological determinism when the differentiation between instrumental and expressive roles is assigned ascriptively within the family on the basis of sex, and extended to children as well as to adults. Parsons argues that the process of development, far from erasing this natural differentiation, actually intensifies it. As the process of economic development reduces the diffuse character of economic activity it makes the occupational role of the father more central, and accentuates his instrumental functions in mediating the relationship of the family to the outside world. At the same time, the decline of kinship groups and the increasing responsibility for the socialization of children which devolves upon the nuclear family intensifies the salience of the expressive role of the mother. Differentiation between male and female roles increases not only in the public sphere but also within the family, and even at the level of personality itself, where the imagery of fission permeates functionalist definitions of masculinity and femininity. Male and female roles, then, are conceived in this first approach as differentiated and complementary.

A sharply contrasting perspective attacks the extreme differentiation of sex roles as dysfunctional for modern societies, and offers the image of androgyny in its place [16]. This approach anticipates a movement away from sexual polarization as societies develop, toward a world in which individual roles and personal behavior are more freely chosen. It envisages the equal participation of both men and women in the full range of public, as well as familial, activities, and the opportunity for both to move freely between instrumental and expressive roles. At the level of personality, differentiated and complementary definitions of masculinity and femininity are replaced by new cultural norms permitting a more flexible and varied range of self-expression for both men and women. Distinctively male or female attributes merge into essentially human ones. Thus, the process of development is seen as one which entails fundamental and simultaneous redefinition of both male and female roles in ways that expand the possibilities of each.

A third approach is essentially assimilationist [17]. It views the subordinate status of women as the legacy of a more primitive stage of social development, and sees the process of modernization as one of democratization in which economic, legal, and political equality is gradually extended to ever wider circles of man and womankind. This view, most eloquently expressed by John Stuart Mill, asserts that "every step in the progress of civilization has . . . been marked by a nearer approach to equality in the condition of the sexes; and if they are still far from being equal, the hindrance is not now in the difference of physical strength, but in artificial feelings and prejudices [18]." It calls for the elimination of laws and social constraints which inhibit full freedom for women and calls, in effect, for a policy of laissez-faire in which individual liberty and social competition will define women's future roles in the larger society. This approach denies the desirability of extensive role differentiation in the wider society or within marriage. It also rejects the image of androgyny, however, defending a residual division of labor within the family [19]. Unlike the first two approaches, which involve a reciprocity in the definition of roles, the assimilationist strategy is essentially unilateral. It envisions a partial redefinition of women's roles without a correspondingly fundamental alteration in those of men.

A final definition of modernity for sex roles, somewhat different in character from the previous three, is the pluralist one [20]. It has no single image of the ideal relation between the sexes, but envisions a society in which men and women choose from among a variety of possible options in the absence of social constraints or sanctions. A society is defined as modern in terms of the diverse opportunities it offers to all its members. This is an approach which embraces all three of the others as possible individual solutions, but gives far less emphasis than they to the power of cultural norms and socialization in shaping societal roles and the close interrelationship between personality and culture.

This typology suggests a new perspective from which to view the emergence of feminism in 19th century Europe. In its broadest sense, feminism represented an extension of liberal individualism to the realm of sex roles. It reflected the development of an intellectual critique of theories of sexual differentiation based upon biological or physiological determinism. The character and role of women, feminist theorists argued, were not given by nature but were shaped by convention. Changed economic, legal, and social arrangements could significantly alter the position and roles of women. The further evolution of feminism as a political movement, however, was shaped by the conflict between pluralist, assimilationist, and androgynous strategies, a conflict which assumed a particularly acute form in the Russian revolutionary movement.

The emergence of the woman question in 19th century Russia in the decades following the Crimean War was one dimension of a broader movement for social and political emancipation which agitated the educated Russian elite. The early discussions of the nature and role of women, largely shaped by European currents of thought, occurred in a setting inhospitable to egalitarian premises, and focused less upon political and social issues than upon reforms of marriage and education. But as the intelligentsia became increasingly radical toward the end of the century, and divided in its political strategy, similar cleavages occurred within feminist circles. Where earlier writers had emphasized education as the key to women's emancipation, the growing socialist movement, influenced by the writings of Marx and Engels, came to view economic arrangements as decisive.

But despite its more radical approach to social change, and its emphasis on revolution rather than reform, Marxism shared with liberalism an assimilationist strategy [21]. Sex roles are shaped by economic organization. The subordination of women in the bourgeois family is, Marx and Engels argued, a consequence of its economic functions, the accumulation and transmission of private property. Emotional ties are distorted in order to serve economic interests. The abolition of private property would divest the family of extraneous functions and would permit the development of genuinely egalitarian relationships between the sexes based entirely upon emotional gratification. Moreover, Marx and Engels insisted that economic independence alone could provide the basis for full sexual equality. Where Mill had called for a reform of property laws to assure the economic independence of women, Marx and Engels viewed their participation in the labor force to be essential. Where Mill believed women should be capable of supporting themselves, the socialists urged that they do so in fact. The socialist society of the future would make this possible by accepting as a communal responsibility the tasks of childrearing and housekeeping formerly performed within the individual household. This meant, however, that the emancipation of women would occur as a consequence not of the reciprocal redefinition of both male and female roles, but rather of the reallocation of functions between the family and the society at large.

Thus Marxism rejected pluralism as a solution to the problem of women's roles in a modern society. It called for the extension of economic, legal, and political rights to women, and the replacement of authoritarian family relationships with egalitarian ones. These changes would occur as a consequence of a fundamental political and economic revolution; the Marxian emphasis on class conflict precluded a strategy which would emphasize the solidarity of women as a social entity, or separate reform from revolution.

Although this approach was essentially assimilationist, it was possible, as more radical feminists within the Social Democratic movement did, to see in the Marxian formula a description of future sex roles as androgynous, and to insist on a political strategy which gave priority to the emancipation of women rather than subordinating it entirely to the achievement of more general political objectives [22]. In the novels of a leading Bolshevik feminist, Alexandra Kollontai, for example, one finds heroes and heroines without specifically masculine or feminine traits whose identities are merged in the figure of the party activist [23]. Others of the Party left envisioned the imminent "withering away of the family" and with it the evaporation of all functions which had traditionally been the special concern of women [24]. Apart from the task of childbearing itself, women's roles and activities would be identical with men's.

These expectations were disappointed in the aftermath of the Russian revolution, when radical visions of social reconstruction were abandoned. At the same time a vast effort was made to assimilate women into new economic, political, and family roles. The consequences of this effort have disappointed writers whose criteria of modernity are either pluralism or androgyny. Nevertheless, it should be clear at the outset that the Soviet leadership never accepted these goals as its own.

In the first years of the Soviet regime a variety of decrees and codes were promulgated which expressed a new concept of women's position and role in the larger society. Citizenship was for the first time defined in egalitarian and universal terms, and women were granted full legal, civic, and political rights. New economic rights and opportunities were also conferred upon women as a consequence of the revolution, providing a juridical foundation for economic independence. All restrictions upon women's freedom of movement were abolished, far-reaching changes in property relationships weakened the role of the family as an economic unit and the dominant position of the father within it, while other laws gave women equal rights to hold land, to act as heads of households, and later, to be paid as individuals, rather than as part of a household, for collective farm labor. Efforts to encourage the entry of women into the labor force were buttressed by protective labor, social, and maternal legislation based upon the most progressive European models. Legal arrangements were supplemented by financial inducements, and by efforts to provide child care facilities for the children of working mothers.

The importance of education in developing the capacities of women to perform new economic and political roles was not overlooked. Literacy was seen by Lenin as the fundamental requirement for political communication and real participation. "A man who can neither read nor write," Lenin insisted, "is outside politics: he must first learn the ABC, without which there can be no such thing as politics, but merely rumors, gossip, fairy tales and prejudices [25]." Massive campaigns to achieve adult literacy and political literacy were directed to millions beyond the reach of formal educational institutions. For the education of the younger generation, new decrees established a unified, coeducational, ladder system to provide a universal and equal educational experience to children of all classes and both sexes in order to prepare them for full participation in everyday social and political life. Technical and professional schools were opened to women and fixed quotas assigned to them to facilitate their entry into more specialized occupational roles.

In the realm of family law, early Soviet legislation was equally revolutionary. A series of decrees attempted to weaken the legal and religious basis of the traditional family by removing restrictions upon marriage, divorce and abortion, and by obliterating the distinction between legitimate and illegitimate children.

While these new legal arrangements were a source of both pride and propaganda, changes in economic patterns were considered to be of decisive significance. The entry of women into the labor force in large numbers was viewed as the necessary and almost sufficient condition of their emancipation. With the family largely divested of its economic functions and circumscribed in its ability to transmit property as a result of new inheritance laws, and with women contributing an important share of the household income, a decisive change in the relationship of the sexes was thought to be assured and the full equality of women only a matter of time.

The pattern of social change in the Soviet Union, however, does not in fact reveal a unilinear evolution toward increasing equality. Many of the achievements of the first decade of Soviet power were reversed under Stalin, while in other areas progress came to a halt. The effort to draw women into new economic roles, for example, has taken a somewhat uneven course. While the Soviet regime explicitly undertook to increase the number of women in the industrial labor force for ideological and political reasons, the pace and timing of this development was uneven and, especially after 1928, reflected economic and demographic needs more than a concern with emancipation. The periods in which women entered the labor force in greatest numbers were periods of severe manpower shortages. The economic demands of Stalinist development policies and the financial pressures faced by Soviet families as a consequence of larger social developments required the massive entry of women into the industrial labor force without much regard for personal preferences. In even the most recent opinion surveys, material need was cited by working women as a far more central motivation in their employment than "broadening of horizons" or "civic satisfaction [26]." Similarly, a rising concern with the decline of the birth rate has led Soviet demographers to propose the partial withdrawal of married women from the labor force as a solution.

The pattern of participation of Soviet women in the labor force, by economic area and by level of skill, also raises questions about the adequacy of evolutionary models. In the Soviet Union, as in other industrial societies, women tend to cluster in what have been traditionally women's fields, or in semiskilled and clerical work. The occupations in which they predominate are usually low in status and in pay, and even in these fields the proportion of women declines at higher levels of responsibility [27]. They are found less frequently in the more prestigious professions and in managerial and executive capacities [28]. The Soviet situation differs in several important ways from that found in the United States, with a far higher proportion of women performing unskilled agricultural labor on the one hand, and skilled technical, engineering, and scientific work on the other. Nevertheless, while industrialization has expanded the range of opportunities available to women through the creation of entirely new fields and occupations, there is a tendency for occupations which were female at an earlier time to remain so [29].

Evolutionary models of development are even less applicable to analyses of the nature and extent of changes in the political roles of Soviet women. On the one hand, there has been a clear and dramatic increase in the rates of female political participation. Particularly in the late 1920s and early 1930s the proportion of women voting in elections and participating in the work of soviets and governmental executive committees at all levels increased rapidly [30]. This pattern is less true at higher levels of leadership, where the small number of women in high executive positions within the governmental apparatus contrasts strikingly with their active role in local civic affairs.

Moreover, the limited role of women within the Communist party, the most significant indicator of the extent to which women are engaged in professional political careers, both reflects and accentuates their wider situation. As a result of intensive recruitment efforts the proportion of women in the party rose from 8% in 1922 to 16.5% in 1934, and from 17% in 1945 to 20.7% in 1950. It has remained stable at this level for over two decades, with the current proportion at 22.6%. Moreover, women are largely absent from the leadership of the party. Only one woman has ever been a member of the powerful Politburo, and the proportion of women on the Central Committee has never risen above 5%. Indeed, the proportion of women in the party leadership was greater in the prerevolutionary period than it has been at any time since then [31].

Finally, if we follow the course of Soviet family law and policy, here too, no clear evolutionary pattern of development emerges. The radical legislation of the early years reflected a view of the family as the embodiment of tradition and the carrier of counter-revolutionary values. By the mid-1930s a dramatic change had taken place in Soviet views. No longer was the destruction of the family viewed as the inevitable and desirable consequence of economic and political change. The family was now considered the bulwark of the social system, and its new importance was reflected in legislation designed to encourage marital stability, procreation, and the proper upbringing of children. Motherhood and domesticity were glorified, and even housework—once so harshly stigmatized by Lenin—was now to be considered "socially useful labor." New definitions of femininity were superimposed on older norms of work and civic duty, while images of male and female roles took on increasingly differentiated features. Recent proposals to encourage a rise in the birth rate by paying women to retire from the labor force to raise children would strengthen this tendency further, even as they enhanced the options available to Soviet women.

In surveying the changing roles of Soviet women since 1917, we find that a partial assimilation to male roles has occurred in the economy and polity. Levels of female participation in both the industrial labor force and in the political system have increased enormously. If women have been successfully mobilized for these purposes, they have not, however, achieved substantial equality in roles which involve managerial or political authority. Nor have they been freed from primary responsibility for family affairs, where no significant redefinition of male and female roles has occurred. Evolutionary models of development are inadequate to describe this complex pattern of social change.

Nor are systemic models of great utility in analyzing Soviet development patterns. Economic, political, and family roles have changed in different ways in response to different forces. The period of greatest political mobilization was one in which relatively little change occurred in economic roles, while the entry of women into the industrial labor force on a large scale has been compatible with sharply variant policies toward the family. Neither have changes in economic organization been decisive for the broader patterning of women's roles. The economic independence of women, however far-reaching its consequences in other respects, has not dramatically transformed the structure of status and authority in economic and political life nor has it radically altered cultural definitions of male and female roles outside the work arena. Thus, the very success of Leninism as a strategy for politically forced development calls into question Marxian models of social change which stress its evolutionary and systemic character. The Soviet experience suggests that the character of the development process, rather than the fact of development per se, is decisive in shaping women's roles. Cultural norms and political choices and capabilities become more significant than socioeconomic determinants. Both the desire and the capability to alter existing societal arrangements become central.

Precisely because the character, goals, and capabilities of the political system are of such importance, the process of change is complex. In the short run, at least, the timing, sequence, and direction of change in different sectors may take different forms. The Soviet pattern illuminates the degree to which societies are segmentary rather than systemic, and suggests the variety of amalgams which may emerge.

NOTES

1. See, however, Esther Boserup, *Woman's Role in Economic Development.* New York: St. Martin's, 1970, and William J. Goode, *World Revolution and Family Patterns.* Glencoe, Ill.: Free Press, 1963.

2. The ambivalent response to industrialization is examined in Adam Ulam, *The Unfinished Revolution*. New York: Vintage, 1960, and in Reinhard Bendix, "Tradition and Modernity Reconsidered," *Comparative Studies in Society and History*, IX, 3 (April 1967).

3. For this definition of modernity, see Constantina Safilios-Rothschild, "A Cross-Cultural Examination of Women's Marital, Educational and Occupational Options," *Acta Sociologica*, XIV, Nos. 1–2, pp. 96–113 (1971).

4. Boserup, *Woman's Role, op. cit.*; Cynthia Epstein, *Woman's Place*. Berkeley: 1971; Richard Sennett, *Families Against the City*. Cambridge: Harvard University Press, 1970; Dean Knudsen, "The Declining Status of Women: Popular Myths and the Failure of Functionalist Thought." *Social Forces* 48, pp. 183–193 (December); Renate Bridenthaler, "Beyond Kinder, Küche, Kirche; Weimer Women at Work," *Central European History*, VI, 2, pp. 148–166 (June 1973).

5. Thorstein Veblen, *The Theory of the Leisure Class*. New York: Mentor, 1963; Talcott Parsons and Robert Bales, *Family, Socialization and the Interaction Process*. Glencoe, Ill.: Free Press, 1955.

6. For extended treatment of the role of women in the U.S. labor force, see Valerie Oppenheimer, "The Sex-Labelling of Jobs," *Industrial Relations*, VII, 3, pp. 219–234 (May 1968); Cynthia Epstein, *Woman's Place, op. cit.*; Robert Smuts, *Women and Work in America*. New York: Schocken, 1971. A comparative analysis is offered in Harold Wilensky, "Women's Work: Economic Growth, Ideology, Structure," *Industrial Relations*, VII, No. 3, pp. 235–48 (May 1968).

7. Kirsten Amundsen, *Silenced Majority*. Englewood Cliffs, N.J.: Prentice-Hall, 1971; Martin Gruberg, *Women in American Politics*. Oshkosh, Wis.: Academia, 1968.

8. This general approach is characteristic of a large number of studies, including Daniel Lerner, *The Passing of Traditional Society*. Glencoe, Ill.: Free Press, 1964; Walt Rostow, *The Stages of Economic Growth*. Cambridge: Harvard University Press, 1960; C. E. Black, *The Dynamics of Modernization*. New York: Harper and Row, 1966. Marxism is, of course, a classic example of this perspective; its implications are captured vividly in Marx's statement that "the country that is more developed industrially only shows, to the less developed, the image of its own future."

9. For an extensive analysis and critique of the intellectual traditions underlying this perspective see Reinhard Bendix, "Tradition and Modernity Reconsidered," *op. cit.*, and Dean C. Tipps, "Modernization Theory and the Comparative Study of Societies: A Critical Perspective," *Comparative Studies in Society and History*, XV, 2, pp. 199–226 (March 1973).

10. Reinhard Bendix, "Tradition and Modernity Reconsidered," *op. cit.* This argument is also developed at length by Alexander Gerschenkron in *Economic Backwardness in Historical Perspective*. Cambridge, Belknap Press, 1966.

11. V. I. Lenin, *Sochineniya*, 2nd ed., Vol. XXVII, pp. 398–401.

12. Neil Smelser, *The Sociology of Economic Life*. Englewood Cliffs, N.J.: Prentice-Hall, 1963, p. 110.

13. For a more extended treatment, see the author's *Changing Roles of Soviet Women*. New York: Praeger, in press.

14. Dean C. Tipps, "Modernization Theory," *op. cit.*

15. Talcott Parsons and Robert Bales, *Family, Socialization and the Interaction Process, op. cit.*

16. Alice Rossi, "Equality Between the Sexes: An Immodest Proposal," *Daedalus*, pp. 607–652 (Spring 1964). Carolyn Heilbrun, *Toward a Recognition of Androgyny*. New York: Knopf, 1973, suggests that androgyny represents not a developmental outcome but an ongoing human ideal, traceable across civilizations and centuries. This approach permeates the radical feminist literature; its implications are expressed in fictional form in the novels of Alexandra Kollontai.

17. For a classic statement of this approach, see John Stuart Mill, "The Subjection of Women," in Alice Rossi, ed., *Essays on Sex Equality*. Chicago: University of Chicago Press, 1970, pp. 123–242.

18. John Stuart Mill and Harriet Taylor, "The Enfranchisement of Women," *Essays on Sex Equality*, *op. cit.*, p. 73.

19. Mill argues, for example, that while all women should be capable of supporting themselves, married women should not seek employment outside the home. Their proper function is not to support life, but to "adorn and beautify" it. "The Enfranchisement of Women," *op. cit.*, p. 75.

20. Constantina Safilios-Rothschild, "A Cross-Cultural Examination," *op. cit.*

21. See, in particular, Frederick Engels, *The Origins of the Family, Private Property and the State*. New York: International, 1942; Karl Marx and Friedrich Engels, *The Communist Manifesto*. New York: New York Labor News, 1948; Karl Marx, *Capital*, Vol. I, New York, 1947, pp. 239–240, 390–391, 495–496, and August Bebel, *Women Under Socialism*. New York: Schocken Books, 1971.

22. This strategy was explicitly criticized by Lenin, who insisted that the activities of women Communists draw a clear and ineradicable line between Bolshevism and feminism. See Clara Zetkin, *Lenin on the Woman Question*. New York: International, 1927, pp. 54, 62, 68.

23. See, for example, the novels *Free Love*. London, 1932; *A Great Love*. New York, 1929; and *Red Love*. New York, 1927.

24. These views are described at greater length in H. Kent Geiger, *The Family in Soviet Russia*. Cambridge: Harvard University Press, 1968.

25. Lenin's own approach to the emancipation of women was less influenced by the egalitarian individualism of either Marxism or feminism than by a unique awareness of its potential for enhancing the economic and political capacities of the Soviet system.

26. G. B. Osipova and J. Szczepanski, eds., *Sotsialnye problemy truda i proizvodstva*. Moscow, 1969, pp. 444, 456.

27. For a more extended treatment, see Norton Dodge, *Women in the Soviet Economy*. Baltimore: Johns Hopkins Press, 1965.

28. *Ibid.*

29. This is true of professions like medicine and teaching, of industrial sectors such as the textile industry, and of employment in white-collar jobs.

30. Statistics are given in T. Woody, *New Minds; New Men*. New York: Macmillan, 1932.

31. For statistics on female membership in the Communist party from 1922 to 1967 see T. H. Rigby, *The Communist Party Membership in the USSR, 1917–1967*. Princeton, N.J.: Princeton University Press, 1968, p. 361.

Chapter

14
A Marxist Analysis of Women and Capitalism

Temma Kaplan

A Marxist critique of the situation of women in contemporary capitalist society includes an historical analysis of changes in women's position which accompanied the transition from feudalism to capitalism, the most fundamental social and economic change in modern history; consideration of the relation of women's oppression to social class under capitalism; and discussion of the potential socialism offers for genuine women's liberation which is impossible under capitalism.

Marxist analysis is not limited to narrow economic investigation but recognizes the organization of production as the basis on which social, political, and psychological structures ultimately rest. Particularly important are the questions of social class structure—who owns what—and the matter of surplus distribution—who gets what of the total production after subsistence.

The industrial revolution had the potential to abolish the scarcity that previously dominated the life of most people, of radically increasing the social surplus and distributing it more equally. Furthermore, industrialization and automation reduce the need for repetitive, drudging human labor, thereby promoting the liberation of women and men from uncreative work itself. But, while industrialization could free people, historically the opposite has often occurred.

The transition from feudalism to capitalism was accompanied by a movement from near self-sufficiency to dependence on a market, a trend which upset the previous relationship of women to production. Capitalism was progressive insofar as it destroyed feudal servitude, but it also reduced, then abolished, communal rights, replacing them with privileges for the few who owned property and tools. Whereas in the transitional period, women's work

257

had included gardening on open land, grazing a sheep or cow on common lands, setting pigs free to forage in communal oak forests, and gleaning, all these privileges were abolished when capitalist notions of private property prevailed and common lands were removed from the public domain.

Early capitalism deprived women of productive capacity, Clark argues in *Working Life of Women in the Seventeenth Century* [1]. While most women had been responsible for manufacturing cheese, beer, bacon, woolen yarn, cloth, and clothing, and for otherwise contributing labor necessary to their family's subsistence, capitalist enclosures of common lands, on which they were basically squatters prevented them from raising a sheep for wool, a pig for pork, or having a garden. Increasingly their work was concerned with sewing woolen cloth bought on the market and preparing food purchased with their husbands' wages [2].

Men and women's market-oriented labor—that is, work for other people, outside the home—paid for in money wages under capitalism, came to be defined as productive work; housewives' domestic tasks, since they did not yield money wages, were not considered work at all.

This pattern of capitalist relations was already well established in the West when steam and waterpowered machines were introduced to cloth manufacturing in the 18th century [3]. Industrialization might have liberated all people from scarcity, but capitalist priorities eliminated the possibility of rational, democratic distribution of the surplus, dividing it instead primarily between consumption for the elite and reinvestment [4].

Profit, and the need for ever increasing profit, is an essential part of capitalism and cannot be reformed out of the system. Because in early capitalist society, functions which did not create profit were not performed, it eventually became clear that the social unrest which resulted threatened the capitalist order itself. Thus there arose the capitalist welfare state which created in the public service sector the institutions to meet human needs which could not be satisfied through the profit mechanism: social security, health insurance, public transportation, sanitation, and public education, to name only a few.

Services which do not create profit or which create less profit than industrial production, however, tend to be impoverished and inadequate in capitalist societies. Urban mass transportation, public health and child care, public education all operate—if they exist at all—at inefficient levels, recognized as unsatisfactory by practically everyone, but their limited profitability precludes improving them to the level of private transportation, elite medical and child care, or private education.

A part of capitalist economy, seldom recognized as such, is the work performed by housewives, especially when they are not employed as wage earners. They raise children and train them to become obedient workers; as consumers, they provide a vast market for industrial production. Cooking and cleaning for workers is economically necessary for the capitalist who might have to pay for it himself if it were not performed by workers' wives for no wages.

Defining human production, repair, and maintenance as nonproductive labor, as it is under capitalism, means that the employer is able to make the worker pay for it out of his or her own pocket. In this way, capitalists' profit is increased, male and female workers are further exploited, and the family plays an integral role in sustaining the employers' rate of profit.

Capitalist needs for family service may be one reason why early factory inspectors in England were shocked to discover that working mothers, many of whom had been employed since they themselves were infants, could not sew, cook, clean house, or care for their own children [5]. The introduction of protective legislation for women must then be seen against the background of capitalist needs for unpaid social services, performed by women, nonwhite men, and old people.

Feminist capitalism might exploit the labor of men, bar them from power, make them believe that the interests of female capitalists are their own, but it is still capitalism and thus places profit above social needs. Even female controlled capitalism could not liberate all women, let alone all people, from the degradation associated with powerlessness and exploitation. Introduction of women into the upper echelons of capitalist circles usually means allowing an elite group of women—the wives, sisters, and daughters of male capitalists—to exploit other women and men.

Industry creates the precondition for socialism, but equitable distribution of surplus is impossible under a system in which ownership of property gives a small percentage of the population control over most goods. So long as profits for this group are more important than democratic and rational allocation of the surplus—including high quality health and child care for all—there is no possibility of genuine women's liberation.

The issue of women's liberation to a certain extent turns upon the distinction between exploitation and oppression. If one works, one creates value and profit for someone; exploitation exists when that labor is not adequately remunerated proportionally to the cost of reproducing it with food, clothing, shelter, leisure, and intellectual growth, as well as a percentage of the profit. An individual is not exploited if he or she does no work. If a person lacks control, especially if that person is dominated by another who makes most of the major decisions about a person's activities and thoughts, the person in the power of the other is oppressed.

Under almost all social systems, women's oppression is associated with psychological repression and socialization, the process by which people learn political and social attitudes. Here it is important to remember that what we consider the prevailing attitude toward women is almost always the attitude of ruling-class men to their women. Through the media, through sex-role education in the schools, and through social organization, this idea permeates down to all women and men, including the working class. The ideal of wife and mother supported by the husband's labor is a ruling-class ideal, imitated and elaborated by the working class, who often pride themselves in the fact that the men can support their wives in return for their subordination to their husbands in the home.

What ruling-class men get from such a system is assurance of a legitimate heir to inherit their property and a domestic social system which mirrors their powers in the larger economy and society. Working-class men get the deference, respect, and psychological gratification which they do not get from their work. The ideals of femininity, motherhood, and courtesy toward women in capitalist society transcend class and help to mask the larger issue, lack of creative, meaningful work for men or women.

Women who work outside their homes are not only oppressed, they are also generally exploited. In England and the U.S., the industrial revolution provided jobs for women and children who were paid lower wages than men; females were employed in mills and mines. Early capitalism needed the cheap labor of single, working-class women who toiled as domestic servants, miners, or mill girls to support themselves and their families. Because they were willing to work for less than men, they were often the sole breadwinners in their parents' households when higher paying jobs for men were not available.

In 19th century England and the U.S., white married women seldom worked outside their houses after marriage, so long as their husbands were alive. But at the turn of the century in the U.S. almost one-third of black female wage earners were married [6]. The trend in 20th century capitalism has been to force married women into the labor market to support their families' living standards.

Until recently, the total female workforce was relatively small. Married white women in the U.S. remained at home except in wartime, when they replaced men in all the productive sectors of the economy. Since the Second World War, throughout the industrial world, women, including married women, have become a major part of the labor force. Taking the U.S. as a primary example of this trend, according to the 1970 census, 40% of all women over the age of 14 work outside their homes [7]. Still more interesting is the fact that 25% of all married women with children under six work; and among blacks, 50% of women with preschool children are permanently in the workforce. 30% of the entire female population are gainfully employed and 42% of the total workforce are women [8].

Similar situations prevail in Japan where 39% of all women work outside their home while 51% of all workers are women [9]; in the Federal Republic of Germany, where 44% of all employees are women and 30% of all women work [10]; in Sweden, where 44% of all wage earners are female while 30% of all women are employed outside their homes [11]; and in the United Kingdom, where 47% of all salaried employees are women and 33% of all females are gainfully employed [12].

If we take the situation of women in the contemporary U.S. as an example of the condition of women under advanced capitalism, we notice that most women are in the lowest paying, least desirable work. Since the Second World War, women have entered the labor force as clerks, secretaries for state, county, and municipal governments, telephone operators, hospital workers, and food handlers (72% of all waiters and waitresses, cooks and bartenders are women) [13]. Women are 55% of all service workers and 93% of all domestic servants [14]. In 1966, 32% of all female wage earners were clerical workers of whom 87% were white [15]. In Japan and Germany, where a larger proportion of the female workforce is employed in factories, this figure is reduced somewhat [16].

The number of married women who work because they must, has increased all over the capitalist world. Older women and married women account for the greatest increase in the female workforce because the so-called middle-class male worker can no longer put food on his family's table without the additional income provided by his wife—despite the ideology which maintains that she ought not work.

Single parent households, usually headed by women, account for the largest proportion of welfare families in the U.S. because it now takes two incomes to support a family [17]. Long viewed as pocket money, women's salaries, which generally are two-thirds those of men doing comparable work, are necessary for the subsistence of a middle-class family. In the U.S., where the average worker is under 30, it is significant that 48% of women between the ages of 45 and 65 were in the labor force in 1970 [18]. One imagines that most older women work because they cannot afford to live otherwise.

The fault is not with women but with capitalism. Few workers, male or female, democratically participate in decisions concerning their work; few are encouraged to perform their jobs in a creative way; few are rewarded for improving their product. Any critique of capitalism must include a political challenge to feminists to show that increasing women's participation in undemocratic, wasteful, monopolistic corporations will improve the human condition of women or men.

The issue is not whether underdeveloped countries, trying to industrialize under socialist political forms, have solved the problems of women, but whether the advanced industrial capitalist countries have done the job. Marxists and other critics of capitalism argue that socialism will not necessarily bring women's equality in a democratically controlled economy—not unless women actively participate in building socialism and struggle for power alongside their political class allies. But through democratic workers' controls, through equitable patterns of distribution and consumption, and by placing social values above individual competition and profit, a real socialist state establishes the precondition for the emancipation of women and of all people.

Among the socialist states, China probably has gone farther to improve the situation of women than any other, but it had farther to go. The divorce law, an integral part of Chinese social policy in the early 1950s, broke the chains of bondage which had enslaved Chinese women to their families. But women under capitalism generally have divorce rights. Where China has moved toward real improvement in the condition of women among other people has been in its recognition of the value of social production and its willingness to allocate rather scarce resources to this sector. Attempts in the Great Leap Forward to collectivize kitchens and break up families seem to have failed, at least temporarily, but the system of vast, high-quality child care centers, hospitals, and homes for the aged seems to have succeeded.

Because capitalists have distributed the benefits of industrialization unequally and irrationally, capitalism must be replaced by a system with different priorities. Any criticism of women's role in capitalist society must take into account the promise of industrialization and how limited the rewards have been for most workers. Compared to the potential it has for setting all people free from poorly remunerated and repetitive, often degrading work, industrialization under capitalism has not fulfilled its promise.

Because of their special dual role as members of the labor force and as unpaid housewives and mothers, most working women may be a crucial group in the transformation from capitalism to socialism. In advanced capitalist society, housewives perform a great deal of the socially necessary labor. Sweden takes this into account and pays housewives a salary. The Chase Manhattan Bank estimates that the average American housewife works 99 hours a week despite labor-saving devices.

Working mothers have the additional worry and expense of hiring outsiders to watch their children. Since the state in most capitalist societies does not provide child care for children under six unless they are on welfare, their care becomes the private expense of working mothers. In a society which assigns priority according to the possibility of financial profit, working class child care ranks low.

As the capitalist nations move in the direction of monopoly capitalism, preferring to sell fewer items at higher prices rather than compete for larger shares of the market, and as a result of automation, there will be fewer and fewer jobs in industry and manufacturing. In Japan and the U.S., only 26% of the wage earning population were engaged in industrial production and manufacturing in 1971 [19]. 36% of the present Japanese industrial working class are female [20].

In most advanced capitalist states, the service sector is growing rapidly, and here the importance of women can be seen. By 1970, 31% of all working people in the U.S. were engaged in service occupations, including work in gas, electric, water, and public sanitation companies. Of these, 55% were women [21]. In Japan, where only 18% of workers are associated with the service sector, roughly 40% of these are female [22]. The figures for the United Kingdom, the German Federal Republic, and Sweden are comparable.

Work in the service sector, production of goods and services for human needs, is valued less than production of material goods under capitalism; hence, everyone associated with the service sector—largely women and minority men in the U.S.—are even more powerless and underpaid than industrial workers. Capitalism did not create the division of labor according to sex but it benefits from its continuation. Unpaid childrearing and housework give women low status because, under capitalism, social position is associated with wealth. Women generally do the same work publicly for low wages that they do privately for no pay at all.

Most women in capitalist society are socialized to be charitable, selfless, conscious of other's needs, and considerate, and it is neither socially useful nor ultimately productive to make women more individualistic and competitive. In fact, socialist societies face the task of training men to develop traits we generally associate with females under capitalism.

Women's dual role provides us with an image of what relations might be like under socialism in a country which has already industrialized. Women's unique position in the economy of advanced capitalist nations amply suits them to share leadership positions with men in creating the new society. This is not to argue that women are better than men or that oppression and exploitation ennobles one, but it is to make the point that women, especially in the U.S., comprise the majority of workers in the largest single sector of the economy, the service industries. They therefore constitute a crucial power base.

For Marxists, the key to political action and to revolution is not only the existence of exploitation, but the social experience that makes political organization possible (Marx believed this was factory labor) plus location in a crucial area of the economy. In advanced industrial countries, where women nearly dominate the service sector and play an important role in the industrial sector, women are gaining the experience that makes future revolutionary political action possible. The potential socialist movement of women, organized on the basis of their social class exploitation, must be sharply distinguished from the feminist strategy of organizing women of all social classes around their oppression in relation to men.

It is unlikely that women can or would be organized separately from working-class men under capitalism. The issue is only whether they will share equally in political power. Since they already perform tasks necessary to preserve society, we can speculate that they are more conscious of or could be more easily persuaded to recognize the need for social services than men. Of course, women can not make the revolution alone, but it can not be made without them.

Just as feudalism contained the seed of capitalism, so too, welfare capitalism contains the seed of socialism in the service sector. The expertise of those engaged in promoting human needs, the physical plant now devoted to serving those needs for a profit, and the human insight gained from experiencing the contradiction between degrading, low-paying work in the service sector and the vast potential of industrial society, may contribute to restructuring the priorities under socialism.

For nearly a century feminists and Marxists have argued that the only way to emancipate women is to throw them into the labor market. Freeing women from economic dependence, according to the feminists, or from the handicraft production of the household, according to the Marxists, is a precondition for women's liberation. Feminists have called for increased job training for women, for quotas enabling women to enter executive positions in corporations, government, and the university, and for the resocialization of women to teach them to compete, win, and dominate happily.

Marxists pose the issue differently. Since Engel's *The Origin of the Family, Private Property and the State,* they have argued that women's entrance into the labor force would help them to overcome the individualism, narrowness of vision, and petty productive activity of housewives. Work in the public sector of the economy would mold the working woman into a potentially class-conscious proletarian who would cease to be an isolated wife and mother.

Later Marxists have argued that the demand for increased female participation in the labor force would heighten male and female consciousness about the inability of monopoly capitalism in the U.S., for example, to provide enough jobs for men or women. If the hidden unemployment of housewives who would work to bring up their family's living standard if work were available were added to the invisible unemployment of black, Chicano, Asian, and native-American men who do not appear on unemployment rolls in the U.S. because they have despaired of finding jobs, some have estimated that unemployment in the U.S. would now be as high as 20% of the adult labor force. The immediate result of this reduction in job possibilities proportional to people on the labor market will inevitably be increased competition for the jobs which do exist—and concommitantly, increased racism and increased sexism—unless workers are organized around a principle antagonistic to competition for drudging work.

What such high unemployment in the U.S. indicates is that, increasingly, automation and cybernetics are advanced enough so that, if social conditions and political priorities were changed, full employment combined with a 2–3 day workweek (for a full week's salary, of course) would be feasible. The fantasy of the film, "A Nous la Liberte" of machines working while laborers played chess, made beautiful objects, played with children, and communed with nature, would be a possibility.

Marxists view human nature as creative, active, and productive; therefore they oppose work which is stultifying or limiting and seek for all people the fullest expression of their creative ability. If profit were abolished, the surplus from socialized industry could be redistributed more equitably to pay for good, free public transportation, child care centers, communal kitchens, comprehensive medical care, high quality schools; and a portion could be reinvested to further improve the productive capacity of industry.

Perhaps we should stress Jancar's quotation from a Soviet woman who argued that "the greatest freedom might lie in not working at all [23]." Contemporary white American feminists are often surprised when black women sneer at demands that all women be allowed to work. Most single, working-class women, whatever their color, have always been in the labor force and do not find it liberating. The idea that work outside the home makes one free must seem absurd to anyone who has done meaningless office or factory drudgery for low pay, as most women do.

Creation of imaginative work, democratic decision-making, social equality, and the end of waste and competition are socialist goals for men and for women. The establishment of socialism in an advanced industrial country creates the potential, though not the certainty, of achieving them.

NOTES

1. Alice Clark, *Working Life of Women in the Seventeenth Century.* London: Cass, 1919, reprint 1968; for a discussion of women's multiple activities see Natalie Z. Davis, "Women in the Labor Force in Early Modern Europe," paper given at the AHA-PCB conference, August, 1972. Available from the author.

2. Ivy Pinchbeck, *Women Workers in the Industrial Revolution, 1750–1850.* London: Cass, 1930 reprint, 1969, pp. 84–110, 183–281.

3. There has been an unfortunate tendency among contemporary social historians to romanticize preindustrial European society and to ignore the fact that the agricultural revolution, not the industrial revolution, was largely responsible for the development of capitalist relations, which were well-established by the time mechanized industry came in. An excellent corrective to these errors can be found in Elizabeth Fox Genovese's "The Many Faces of Moral Economy: A Contribution to a Debate," *Past and Present,* **58,** pp. 161–167 (February, 1973).

4. Maurice Dobb, *Papers on Capitalism, Development, and Planning.* New York: International. 1970, pp. 56–59.

5. Margaret Hewitt contends this in *Wives and Mothers in Victorian Industry.* London: Routledge, 1957).

6. Mary White Ovington, *Half a Man: The Status of the Negro in New York.* New York: Schocken, 1967, p. 144.

7. News of the 19th U.S. Census, *U.S. Department of Commerce News,* Press Release (Nov. 1971).

8. *1971 Year Book of Labour Statistics.* Geneva: International Labour Office, p. 25.

9. *Ibid.,* p. 29.

10. *Ibid.,* p. 35.

11. *Ibid.,* p. 39.

12. *Ibid.,* p. 40; see also Viola Klein, *Employment of Special Groups: Women Workers.* Paris: O.E.C.D., 1965; and *Labor Developments Abroad, Employment of Women in Seven European Countries Analyzed.* Washington, D.C.: GPO, 1970.

13. U.S. Department of Labor, *1965 Handbook on Women Workers.* Washington, D.C.: GPO, 1966, p. 87.

14. U.S. Department of Labor, *Underutilization of Women Workers.* Washington, D.C.: GPO, 1966, p. 13.

15. *1965 Handbook, op. cit.,* p. 87.

16. *1971 Year Book, op. cit.,* pp. 218–219, 250–251.

17. *U.S. Department of Commerce News* (Dec. 1971).

18. *Ibid.* (Nov. 1971).

19. *1971 Year Book, op. cit.,* pp. 88–89, 102–103.

20. *Ibid.*

21. *Ibid.,* pp. 88–89.

22. *Ibid.,* pp. 102–103.

23. See p. 238, this volume.

Chapter
15

The Mobilization of Women
in Allende's Chile

Elsa M. Chaney

Today all over the world we observe the paradox of nations striving to become modern, yet maintaining one-half their populations on the periphery of the enterprise. Whether the effort to bring about social, economic and political change is called "development," "liberation from dependency," or "class struggle" makes no difference. Women participate only marginally, and they are virtually excluded from the ranks of the decision-makers [1].

Nowhere is woman's absence more marked than in government. Summing up the findings of a detailed assessment of women's participation in political life around the world, Menon points out that "a prime minister here or a judge there or a few ambassadors in relatively minor stations" do not indicate that women have been successful in politics. Even in socialist countries which have made special efforts to involve women, she says, "the results, strangely enough, have been identical [2]."

In a few countries—Italy and Chile under the influence of the Christian Democrats are the best examples—women wield a certain political power at the polls [3]. In electoral politics, the gap between proportions of men and women voters has been narrowing in most countries; women form one-third to nearly one-half the electorate in many nations. (Women represented 56% of the electorate in Chile at the time of the last nationwide elections—the congressional contests of March 1973.) Increased participation in elections has not, however, opened the way for women's greater participation in political leadership anywhere in the world. As many surveys have demonstrated, the act of voting often is not regarded as political, but the civic

An earlier version of this article was presented as a paper at the 1972 Southern Political Science Association Meeting, Atlanta, Georgia. The author also wishes to thank members of Columbia University's faculty-graduate student Latin American Seminar for helpful comments.

267

duty of every citizen. Thus women now routinely vote in many cultures where women in political office still are exceptional. The participation of women in electoral politics must therefore be analyzed as a phenomenon distinct from their assumption of political leadership roles.

The government of Socialist Salvador Allende in Chile offers a fascinating case study of the difficulties in mobilizing women for social and political change at both the voter and the leadership levels. By mid-1973, Allende's regime clearly had to win substantial increases in women's electoral support to survive, yet daily demonstrated that it had little idea how to go about the task. Moreover, Allende had failed to recruit women to the leadership ranks of his government.

Nowhere else in the world have events conspired to make women's political participation so vital an issue as in Chile. Since women's votes are tallied and reported separately from men's votes, no government can have any illusions as to where it stands with either sex. Allende has reminded the men of Unidad Popular (Popular Unity, the governing coalition) on many occasions of "all the elections we lost because of the women's vote." He always tells the men that it is "our fault, because we haven't found out how to reach the consciousness and heart of the woman [4]." There is "still prejudice among the men of Unidad Popular," he has said, "a political machismo which denies to woman the equal rights she has [5]."

Allende indeed has fared badly at the hands of women, these *hacedoras de presidentes*, the makers of presidents, as the popular phrase has it. Women voted in national elections for the first time in 1952, casting 23% of the ballots; their votes did not affect the outcome. In 1958, however, the women's votes jumped to 35% of the total, and they gave the conservative candidate, Jorge Alessandri, a 33,000 vote plurality. If women had not voted in that election, Salvador Allende would have won with the 18,000 votes the men gave him over Alessandri. (The decision still would have had to go to the Congress, as it did in 1970, since no candidate would have won a majority in the popular vote.)

Twelve years later, Allende was duly elected, but he came into office with hardly a popular mandate: only 36.4% of the total vote, and a slim 39,000 lead over his nearest rival, again Alessandri. Moreover, while winning nearly 153,000 more of the male vote than Alessandri, Allende lagged almost 114,000 behind him in the women's column. Today, after 3 years in office, Allende has gained only a little ground with the mass of women in the electorate; 700,000 women voted for candidates of his party in the recent congressional elections, but 1 million women cast their ballots for the opposition [6].

During his first years in office, Allende frequently asserted that his revolution would not succeed unless it incorporated women at all levels of responsibility. His statements showed that he was quite aware of Chilean women's well-documented conservative tendencies within each social class. He often tried to quiet the fears of women by asserting that his revolution would be "creative and not identified with violence"; that it signified "moral achievement, generosity, a spirit of sacrifice and dedication to achieve a new life for all Chileans within the framework of the nation's free institutions [7]."

Yet in spite of many allusions to women's importance, Allende moved slowly to increase their role in his government. Only after 2 years in office did he appoint a woman to cabinet-level position; Mireya Baltra, a Communist and official of the Centro Unico de Trabajadores, Chile's largest trade union organization, assumed the post of Minister of Labor and Social Welfare, but she lasted only a few months. There is a pool of outstanding Communist and Socialist women militants in Chile, yet only one other high appointive post has gone to a woman. Carmen Gloria Aguayo, a member of the Movimiento de Accion Popular Unitaria (MAPU), heads Desarrollo Social (Social Development), the successor agency to Frei's Popular Promotion. Sra. Aguayo's agency links the nominally autonomous neighborhood councils and mothers' centers (Juntas de Vecinos and Centros de Madres). If a projected Ministry of Family Protection becomes a reality, these mass-based organizations will form its basic units.

The President rightly complained that men did not properly esteem the talents and capabilities of women, yet he often revealed his own narrow vision of what women could contribute, always articulated in terms of their role as mothers or potential mothers. He was fond of using an image which he said came from his own experience as a medical doctor: "el binomio madre-niño," literally, the mother-child in one being. Often he returned to this theme:

> When I say 'woman,' I always think of the woman-mother. . . . When I talk of the woman, I refer to her in her function in the nuclear family . . . the child is the prolongation of the woman who in essence is born to be a mother [8].

Projects to mobilize women invariably were cast in a "feminine" mold, and none had materialized after 2 years of Allende's administration. A ministry of the Family was the scheme Allende most often talked about in his speeches to women. By mid-1973 the bill for its creation has been allowed to languish 2 years in a parliamentary committee with no political pressure applied to bring it to a vote. Even if the new ministry were to be inaugurated, however, the effort appears to this observer as an attempt to create a sufficient number of appropriate, but marginal, posts for women so that important ministerial slots need not be wasted on them.

A new law requiring every government agency and private enterprise employing more than 20 women to provide nursery care went unfinanced and unenforced; again and again the President apologized that there just was not enough money. Another of Allende's favorite ideas—to recruit girls between the ages of 16 and 21 for 3 months' obligatory *Servicio Femenino*—would not assign them projects according to their talents and training, but would use them in hospitals, social welfare centers and as the 120,000 auxiliaries needed to set up day nurseries and kindergartens. These tasks would be distributed on a strict feminine-masculine basis; the single, young woman would learn fundamental things for her own future, the President said, and she would be "linked to babies and children . . . learn to prepare bottles, change diapers, warm the food. . . . How fine it would be if these girls could help the children get off and on the buses, *while a trained man drives the bus* [9]."

Allende's speeches were full of projects to include housewives in social security provisions, to allow women to retire at an earlier age "because of the biological inequality between the man and the woman [10], to distribute more free schoolbooks, to equalize family allowances among workers, white-collar employees, and government functionaries. Yet he rarely talked of more equal professional opportunities for women or more equal distribution of leadership responsibilites. On one occasion, he could not remember how many congresswomen Chile had [11]. Like a good father, and often in a manner revealing his own intimate knowledge of the Chilean reality, he would scold the men for their treatment of their women—but the remedy appeared to rest exclusively in the men's hands and to consist in their becoming more aware of the woman's needs and educating her:

> In this country there are thousands and thousands of women who never have worked and have no possibilities of doing so. And the result is, whether the husband earns a little or a fair sum, he never gives her a bit of money to go to the movies, to buy a new dress . . . the wives run around disheveled; they don't go to the beauty shop, they aren't able to buy a lipstick, they don't have money to go to the dentist.
>
> Men have the obligation of understanding the woman and of making themselves understood . . . you all go to the demonstrations alone, you don't ever bring along your wives. You go home and you don't talk to them. You never say, "Look here, Comrade Allende has declared such and such, etc." You don't dialogue with the woman [12].

Many speculations might be offered on the reasons behind the failure of the Allende government to move ahead on projects related to women. In justice it must be recognized that many of the proposals were far too costly to implement. Moreover, Allende could realistically promise more jobs to women only in the distant future. Meanwhile, some resources had been channeled to the mothers' centers to buy materials and foster what essentially was *cottage industry*—knitting, embroidery and crocheting of articles destined for an undetermined export market. A project to create 10,000 knitters was characterized by Sra. Aguayo in an interview in the summer of 1972 as "frankly an intermediate step, a stop-gap to put a little money into the hands of women in the marginal districts until jobs can be created for them."

Other reasons suggest themselves. Perhaps there was lack of conviction that gaining women's support, outside the electoral sphere, really deserved top priority. By mid-1973 Chile faced many urgent problems: food shortages, high inflation, miners' strikes and falling copper prices, lack of foreign exchange. Perhaps there simply was no attention to spare for solving the woman problem.

Or perhaps there was an underlying fear to see women mobilized at all. The famous march of the empty pots organized by middle-class women to protest food shortages in late 1971 had reverberated around the world. All through the waning months of 1972 women were beating their pots again in the *barrio alto* (the middle and upper-middle class districts of Providencia and Los Condes in Santiago). Women of the Right, encouraged by their success, were busy organizing a movement across party lines, *Poder Femenino* (Feminine Power), to shore up the opposition forces and to "fight for our homes and families." Perhaps there was an unspoken distrust that women, even of the Left, could be controlled—and a disinclination to facilitate their mobilization.

There was also the persistence of *machismo*, and the tendency of males, whatever their political ideology, to define woman in terms of the "hot chick"—the chorus girl of the BIM BAM BUM (a burlesque house in Santiago), as Bambirra, Marxist analyst, recently observed [13]. She accuses the leftist press in particular of diffusing systematically the symbol of the *mujer-objecto*, the woman as sex object, and points to the persistence of traditional institutions and values in relation to woman which, she says, leftist organizations "are not in fact even worried about, much less making any effort to overcome through the communications media they control [14]."

The most casual perusal of the leftist press confirms Bambirra's contentions. Illustrated comic books, published by Unidad Popular (particularly *Firme*), picture leggy women militants, their fantastically exaggerated breasts encased in tight sweaters, and wearing the briefest of skirts. Leftist publications routinely carry cheesecake; this reaches truly grotesque levels as in a recent issue of a leftist youth magazine, *Ramona*, printed at Editorial Quimantu, the government publishing house, and listing males as both director and editor. This particular issue proclaims 1972 as the decisive year of the woman, and illustrates the theme with a photo of a shapely, naked girl, draped in the Chilean flag [15].

> For the working class woman, her day begins at dawn and ends late at night. . . . Beyond the incredibly-long working hours, Chilean women are victims of a [male] chauvinist culture that pervades both left and right. The most popular leftist newspapers invariably feature a partially nude woman on the front page. . . . This astonishing lack of concern persists in the face of one clear fact: the inability of the Chilean left to win the woman's vote, including the vote of the working class woman. . . . We doubt that the left will change its policy with regard to the organization of women before a major confrontation with the right [16].

The preceding report on women in contemporary Chile has been presented almost entirely from the masculine point of view: the difficulties perceived by males of the Left as they grope with the problem of women's involvement in the Chilean revolution. What do the women have to say about the kind of feminine image male leaders project as they speak and write of the female potential? Do they accept their inferior status within the Left and the feminine cast to all the projects for their progress and betterment?

On a recent visit to Chile, I talked with many women of the Left, Center, and Right, most of whom had been my interviewees in a study of 167 women in political office in Peru and Chile in 1967—the final years of the Belaúnde and Frei regimes. Whatever their political sympathy, Chilean women feel *postergadas*—that their interests have been too long postponed. One militant socialist, on a committee to plan a world congress of women from socialist countries, confided that the government had not given a single *escudo* to pay the rent on their two postage-stamp sized offices. "We even have to raise the money to pay the electricity and stationery bills ourselves," she said. "The government talks a lot, but we are not given any practical help."

Although they complain about the lack of resources, there is little doubt that the feminine leaders of Unidad Popular support enthusiastically the projects this government has proposed for women. Women *politicas*, whatever their party, always have worked in a feminine style of politics in Chile; they are as deeply influenced by the traditional image of woman as their menfolk. The world of work, professions and government is divided into masculine and feminine sectors; even those women who cross the boundaries and prepare for a masculine-stereotyped profession (of which politics certainly is one) feel constrained to exercise it in a feminine way. Hernández Parker, one of Chile's leading political writers, has described the political style of Chile's women politicians, whether of the Left or the Right:

The woman constitutes a 'political world' apart from the male. . . .When the woman speaks in the *poblaciones* [marginal settlements around the cities] or in the countryside, she does so in language of the heart. In Parliament—and with the sole exceptions of Maria de la Cruz [Partido Nacional, conservative-liberal coalition] and Carmen Lazo [Communist], who are as spectacular and combative as the men—they fulfill their role in another style.

Whether they are called Ines Enriquez or Graciela Lacoste, Maria Maluenda or Laura Allende [Radical, Christian Democrat, Communist and Socialist, respectively], they are the untiring 'ants,' valiant and tender. The men will be preoccupied with problems as abstract as constitutional reforms. The women are fighting for kindergartens, for drinking water in the *poblaciones*, for day care centers [17].

Traditional images of woman's proper activity still are very strong in Latin America. Among my most interesting findings in the survey of women leaders mentioned above was that when women do enter professions or government, they (and the men) almost invariably consider their intervention as an extension of their family role to the arena of public affairs. Many envision women's offices (to use descriptions originated by Parsons to characterize current male-female role images [18]) in terms of the nurturant and affectional tasks society assigns to women, rather than in terms of the instrumental male role which is more aggressive, active and achievement-oriented.

Bunster thinks that professional women in her country, Chile, approach their jobs in a style quite different from what she perceives as the North American woman's attitude:

What happens is that we extend matrimonial roles to work. . . . [W]e tend to treat the man as a mother would, and not as if he were the husband, the lover or the colleague. The Chilean is a *mamá* who approves, sanctions, corrects, quite different from the North American environment where professional relations are marked by the sense of competition [19].

A woman official thus often sees herself as a kind of *supermadre*, tending the needs of her big family in the larger *casa* of the municipality or even the nation. My own study showed that such an attitude was correlated with a conservative outlook and an ambivalent attitude toward change on the part of many women leaders. Historically, the image of the active woman as *supermadre* has prevented all but a few women from joining the vanguard of movements advocating profound political or social reform.

It is important to note here, as many observers have done, that women in Chile have made some remarkable advances. They form nearly one-half the university population and 22% of the workforce—a high figure for Latin America. As early as 1939 the Peruvian Aprista leader, Magda Portal, exiled in Santiago, wrote admiringly of their progress in comparison to those in the rest of "colonial and semi-colonial" Latin America, and particularly in her own country [20]. In Chile, traditional attitudes are changing to some extent, permitting a notable group of Chilean professional women, bureaucrats, and politicians to come forward in numbers not equalled in any countries with the possible exceptions of Sweden, Yugoslavia and the Soviet Union.

Even in these countries, however, few women have assumed top policy positions, and the totals shrink to insignificance when compared to males in leadership roles, especially at the higher policy-making levels.

How are we to account for women's virtual absence from the councils of decision makers in every country? What theories might be advanced to explain women's inferior status and lack of participation in the vital areas of national life—not only in the "New Chile," but all over the globe?

Certainly we cannot complain that modernizing nations lack philosophical guidance on the emancipation of woman. Whether our model of modernity is built on the liberal values of the West or on Marxist philosophy, we identify a cloistered place for women with traditional society and an emancipated place with modern society. In the West, serfs are emancipated and feudal privilege ends. Women's rights become the logical extension of the claims to individual liberty and autonomy which undergird the whole process of transformation in the West over the past two centuries. In the socialist state, there is no ideological basis for denying equal rights to one-half the toilers because of their sex. Lenin returned again and again to the notion that mere legal equality is only a first step; it is not "bourgeois feminism," he said, to suggest that women must form their own organizations to achieve complete emancipation because "the building of socialism will begin only when we have achieved the complete equality of women and undertake the new work together [21]."

Despite the logic of their ideologies, however, in neither East nor West has woman reached equality. If we define emancipation to mean equal access for women—in law and in fact—to responsible roles in political, economic, and social life, then it is obvious that women are not emancipated even in developed societies, whatever the type of regime or the nature of its guiding ideology. Marxist women scholars [22] are beginning to join their bourgeois sisters in noting that expanded opportunities in the labor force do not bring about an automatic expansion of women's liberty even in socialist societies.

This situation leads us to ask what is holding women back. Before we can answer this question with any certainty, we may need to devise entirely new frameworks and theoretical concepts to deal with the data of women's behavior. Women in most societies do not, for example, fit any of the current models through which political scientists attempt to analyze the phenomena of politics. They are not an elite; they do not, as a group, seek power; they do not form coalitions to bargain with other power contenders. Women are so unorganized and ill-defined as a group and command so few political resources that to regard them as forming an interest group in the same sense as industrial laborers, the military, or landowners would be misleading. Nor does a simple economic/class explanation of women's inferior position appear adequate. The three Marxist women analysts mentioned above no longer accept such a thesis, nor expect (as the men appear to believe) that women will be available for full political and intellectual participation in the revolution as soon as they can be drawn into socially productive work. They all agree that doing productive work outside the home is the precondition for changing women's status, but they insist that obstacles in the sociocultural superstructure must be directly attacked if women are to be free.

Many current attempts at explanation of women's inferior status are based upon sociological concepts; they prove equally unsatisfactory because they imply that all women are uniformly oppressed. Countries vary dramatically on the ranges of options they offer women, and even within countries, regions, and cities, there are great gaps between the privileged and the poor. Women as women therefore cannot be classed as marginals; neither are they outcastes nor second-class citizens, although substantial numbers of women may form part of all these groups in a given country.

Women are not a caste, because by definition caste fixes forever a person's position in society. A woman is an outcaste not because of her sex, but because of her birth. If her father is lower caste, she will inherit his status in exactly the same way as her brother. She may not marry into a higher caste and many opportunities are closed to her, not simply because she is female (her brother lives under the same restrictions), but because of the limitations imposed by the caste system.

Nor are women a class; rather, they are attached to and derive their position from a significant male. They share the honors, prerequisites, and class position of the men upon whom they depend, acquiring more status if father or husband is upwardly mobile, and losing status if the significant males in their lives fail to maintain their class position. Historically, women never were able to improve their position through their own brains and effort, but only through marrying upward, just as they lost status by marrying downward. In traditional societies, it is true, the situation of the male was not much different; yet as modernization began to break up the stratified class system, only the males achieved mobility.

Not all women are by any means marginals. Rossi, in a landmark article on woman's emancipation, points out that women are the only group which lives on intimate terms with their oppressors and are accorded a nominal status equality [23]. No other type of social inequality, whether racial, class, religious, or ethnic permits representatives of the unequal group to live in closer association than with members of their own groups.

Although Rossi does not mention the comparison specifically, my own objection to the "woman as nigger" parallel—often drawn by feminists in the U.S.—lies here. No other members of a minority group except women are taken into the house of their oppressors as their nominal equals, to share their tables and their beds. Perhaps in even greater degree, the Spanish tradition of *caballerosidad* gives honor and respect to the upper and middle-class woman (in public if not always in private). In the lower classes, where the Moorish tradition still holds and where the woman walks along the street behind the man and eats what is left after the men finish their meal, the parallel to a slave status may be more accurate.

What must be noted is that from the most "in," to the most "out," from the most marginal to the most integrated, from the highest to the lowest caste or class, women are discriminated against not only by all the men and women of higher groups, castes and classes, but by the men of their own status as well. Thus the woman of the highest status suffers unequal treatment at the hands of at least one group of significant males: her own father, uncles, brothers, and husband. Conversely, as Fidel Castro has pointed out, the woman of the working class is in a desperate situation not entirely explained by her class status: she is not only oppressed (as also are the males of her class) by all the men and women of the classes above her; she is exploited and depreciated by the men of her own class as well [24].

An alternate explanation which may be more valid because it accounts more completely for the inferiority of women in every caste and class is the fact that for centuries only one approved role was open to women: motherhood. Whatever her social position, the woman's major validation lay in producing children. The woman who married and failed to achieve motherhood was pitied; the woman who did not marry was despised. Because she broke the link in the generations, in many societies the single woman's life was counted a waste, and her very existence became a tragic burden to herself and to her family.

One can readily comprehend why motherhood was woman's only possible option in the early centuries of humankind's existence. Women had little choice but to passively receive children up to nature's biological limit. Moreover, demographic realities demonstrated the wisdom of bearing many children as a guarantee of seeing some survive to adulthood so they could provide for parents in their old age. Certainly it is nonsense to demean women's role in primitive society; in terms of humankind's long fight for survival, she performed essential tasks. Not only was it her exclusive role to bear children, but she made important contributions as food gatherer and cultivator. Yet her life was quite unlike that of the male because of her motherhood vocation. For most women, their adult lives coincided with the span of their fertility, and bearing children literally wore them out. In peasant societies, women's work role became more equal to the man's; as societies modernized, however, many of women's tasks were taken away from her—and never did she share an equal authority with the male either in or outside the walls of the home.

The male was never limited in the same way. His life may have been brutish and short, but in earlier societies the role of fatherhood probably was even less significant than it later became. Certainly not then nor later did anyone suggest that fatherhood was the only possible role for a man. The male from earliest times combined and subordinated his fatherhood role to the hunt, to war, and to politics. Very early, man was occupied in trades and professions which by their nature set up competition, differentiation, drive to excel, and necessity to organize. Meanwhile, women remained isolated in their individual families or clans, often guarded to guarantee the legitimate paternity of sons. The tasks of motherhood were by their nature hidden, unspectacular, unchanging, unconnected with any power nexus. If all women were destined for motherhood, then no special distinction was possible to women except to become outstanding mothers or to seek a surrogate motherhood in a womanly profession.

As a consequence, when the woman begins to move out to the larger society, the boundaries and style of her participation are profoundly influenced by her classic role as mother and preserver of the race. Most women go into fields analogous to the tasks they perform in the home, preeminently education and the welfare of women and children. But women do not improve their inferior position very much by turning professional. Feminine fields are neither prestigious nor powerful because they are associated with the hidden, unspectacular tasks of birth and nurture, tasks which males never have deemed important.

Nothing is more natural than that women's first ventures into public life should have been put in the framework of their traditional vocation as wives and mothers and should emphasize moral values. What is remarkable is that the horizons of influential women so often still are confined exclusively to these feminine interests.

At this stage of research, we do not know to what extent men act as gatekeepers, excluding women from policy positions, and to what degree women's exclusion is self-imposed by their own ideas on spheres proper to women officials. As Lane observes, quite aside from women's primary responsibility for the young in most cultures and their consequent preoccupation with the training of the next generation, there is some evidence that the custody of moral values often is bestowed as a consolation prize for exclusion from other activities more highly valued in a society [25]. In this respect,

Latin American women differ only in degree from other Western women. Summarizing what we know about the political behavior of women, Lane comments:

> A moralizing political orientation of women arising from maternal responsibilities, exclusion from more socially valued areas of activity, and narrow orbits, tends to focus female political attention upon persons and peripheral "reform" issues [26].

The ideal, in a world without traditions and prejudices, certainly would be that men and women would fill posts in government and elsewhere for which their talents and training prepared them, without any special note being taken of their sex. Men and women would dedicate themselves to primary and secondary institutions as their own particular capacities and bents dictated. Men would serve in child welfare without (as is the case now in Latin America) casting doubts on their virility, and women would be engineers or administrators without being considered *marimachos*—castrating females. The ideal justly asks: Why should not both men and women, according to their own desires, concern themselves with improving the lot of the woman, the child, the old, the sick, the juvenile delinquent—and with planning, industrialization, balance of payments, inflation, monetary reform, agricultural development, and outer space?

But the ideal world is not yet, and tradition has designated (or stereotyped, if you will) certain areas of life and concern as feminine. So far, only a few women have shown any inclination to venture very far beyond these feminine boundaries, either in their professional or political life, and only a few men have indicated that they are willing to see many women engage in masculine tasks, especially at the command echelons. In my own view, it is the enduring image of the *supermadre* which may best account for women's style of participation, not only in Chile but in many other cultures as well. We badly need to explore the consequences of such a definition of women's role, particularly its implications for the mobilization of women in programs, agencies, parties, and movements dedicated to political and social change.

NOTES

1. Recently the United Nations Commission on the Status of Women asked government and private organizations for their views on the role women might play in social and economic development. Replies from 77 countries and 36 nongovernmental agencies showed that even where women are active professionally, their level of responsibility is low except in certain sectors of the social field traditionally considered suitable for women. Their participation in

higher planning bodies related to innovation and social change is practically nonexistent. According to the survey, there is growing awareness all over the world that women's role is changing and should change, yet "only a few countries have come fully to grips with the problem or are ready or able to embark upon new avenues." United Nations, *Participation of Women in the Economic and Social Life of Their Countries.* New York: U.N. Commission on the Status of Women, 1970, pp. 3–4.

2. Lakshmi Menon, "From Constitutional Recognition to Public Office," *The Annals of the American Academy*, **CCCLXXV** (Jan. 1968).

3. Chile, today a country of about 10 million people, has enjoyed more than 100 years of constitutional life, and presidents have followed one another in orderly succession with only two short episodes of dictatorship and army intervention. With a 70% literacy rate *America en Cifras, Situacion Cultural.* Washington, D.C.: OAS, 1971, pp. 10–11, the electorate in Chile has broadened since 1925 to include most of those eligible to vote. Political analysts agree that Chilean elections, in contrast to those in most other Latin American countries, are free, honest, and meaningful. Chileans like to picture themselves as the Englishmen of South America; they patterned their institutions on the British parliamentary model. There is a high degree of political consciousness in all classes and a deep-grained respect for the country's democratic traditions. In 1970, in this unusual setting, Chileans chose as President the Marxist coalition candidate of six leftist parties to succeed Christian Democrat Eduardo Frei Montalva.

4. Salvador A. Allende Gossens, *La historia que estamos escribiendo: el presidente Allende en Antofagasta.* Santiago: Consejeria de Difusion de la Presidencia de la Republica, 1972, p. 178.

5. *Ibid.*, p. 105.

6. All figures in preceding paragraphs rounded to nearest thousand. The increase in the women's vote from 30.5% for Unidad Popular in 1970 to 41.2% in 1973 may be accounted for partially by the fact that 18 to 21-year-olds were voting in large numbers for the first time; difficulties over registration in the 1971 municipal elections prevented many young people from exercising their francise at the earlier date. Election figures are all taken from Direccion del Registro Electoral, mimeographed official election returns.

7. Salvador A. Allende Gossens, *El Pueblo debe origanizarse . . . y actuar: el presidente Allende en Concepcion.* Santiago: Consejeria de Difusion de la Presidencia de la Republica, 1972, pp. 196–197.

8. Allende, *La historia, op. cit.*, p. 204.

9. *Ibid.*, p. 204.

10. *Ibid.*, p. 180.

11. Allende, *El Pueblo, op. cit.*, p. 107.

12. Allende, *La Historia, op. cit.*, pp. 105–106.

13. Vania Bambirra, "La mujer chilena en la transicion al socialismo," *Punto Final*, suplemento, No. 133, p. 7 (22 de junio 1971).

14. Bambirra, "La mujer chilena," *op. cit.*, pp. 7–8.

15. "1972: decisivo para la mujer chilena," *Ramona*, **I**, No. 22 (28 de marzo 1972).

16. Patricia Garrett and Adam Schesch, "Chile: Social Revolution vs. Bureaucratic Reform," *Cardinal Monday*, **LXXXII**, No. 106, p. 4 (Feb. 28, 1972).

17. Luis Hernandez Parker, "La mujer en politica," *Revista del Domingo de El Mercurio*, p. 11 (26 de marzo 1967).

18. Talcott Parsons and Robert A. Bales, *Family, Socialization and Interaction Process.* Glencoe, Ill.: The Free Press, 1956.

19. Ximena Bunster, "El nuevo y eterno femenino," *Ercilla*, **XXIV**, No. 1740, p. 40 (23a 29 de octubre 1968).

20. Magda Portal, *Flora Tristan, la precusora.* Lima: Ediciones Paginas Libres, 1945, p. 10.

21. V. I. Lenin, *The Emancipation of Women: From the Writings of V. I. Lenin.* New York: International, 1934, pp. 111, 69.

22. Margaret Benson, "The Political Economy of Women's Liberation," *Monthly Review,* 21 (Sept. 1969); Juliet Mitchell, "Women: the Longest Revolution," *New Left Rev.,* No. 40 (Nov./Dec. 1966); Bambirra, "La mujer chilena," *op. cit.*

23. Alice S. Rossi, "Equality Between the Sexes: an Immodest Proposal," in *The Woman in America,* Robert Jay Lifton, ed. Boston: Beacon, 1965, pp. 101–102.

24. Fidel Castro, "Women's Liberation: The Revolution Within a Revolution," *Women and the Cuban Revolution.* New York: Pathfinder, 1966, p. 7.

25. Robert A. Lane, *Political Life: Why and How People Get Involved in Politics.* New York: Free Press, 1959, p. 212.

26. Lane, *Political Life, op. cit.,* p. 216.

Chapter

16

Changing the Political Role of Women:
A Costa Rican Case Study

JoAnn Aviel

New questions are being raised and old ones reformulated about the role
of women, as well as about the role of schools in society. Do schools perpetuate inequality? Can progressive educational policies be used to promote
social justice and a new set of social values? Can and should role differentiation between men and women be eliminated? What is the effect of modernization on the role of women? These questions have most often been raised
by different individuals: revisionist educational historians, on the one hand,
and the new feminist writers, on the other. However, there are important
linkages between these questions which need to be explored by empirical
case studies. This particular study reports on an unique opportunity to
compare the effects of two different educational policies on women—one
a traditional policy similar to that followed in the 19th century U.S. and
one a progressive policy similar to that introduced in the early 20th century
U.S. by John Dewey and his followers.

Unlike the gradual, unsystematic adoption of progressivist policies in the
U.S., policy-makers in one small Latin American state decided to implement
educational reform throughout the secondary school system systematically
one year at a time. This study was thus able to compare two different
educational policies by surveying the last class to graduate under the traditional program with the first to do so under the reform program one year
later. The reform program was heavily influenced by the progressivist educational philosophy and programs of the U.S.

While Costa Rica is most certainly not the U.S., in spite of the efforts

An earlier version of this paper was presented at the Annual Meeting of the American Political
Science Association, Washington, D.C., 1972.

of some of its citizens—as well as some North American advisors—to remodel its educational system in the image of the U.S., the study of the immediate results of these policies should shed some light on the role of the schools and the role of women not only in the U.S. and Costa Rica but in other countries as well.

Costa Rica is a Central American nation of some 1.5 million people. Since the Revolution of 1948 the presidency has alternated peacefully between the National Liberation Party and the coalition of parties formed in opposition to it. A strong Legislative Assembly and an independent judicial branch serve as checks on the President. In 1948 the military was abolished, though a police force does exist. Fitzgibbon's survey of Latin American specialists in 1955 and 1960 ranked Costa Rica second only to Uruguay in an evaluation of the democratic attainment of Latin American countries [1]. Costa Rica continues to be evaluated highly today because, while class distinctions do exist, they are less rigid than in most other Latin American countries due to relatively open educational opportunities and relatively equitable distribution of land. In Needler's ranking of Latin American countries, Costa Rica ranked third on an economic development index based on life expectancy [2]. However, Costa Rica has serious demographic, social, and economic problems. As a result of an average annual population growth rate of 3.7% between 1950 and 1962, per capita income grew at only 1.6%. Although in the past decade the growth rate has been lowered to 2.7%, the Costa Rican population is still a very young one with 45.7% of the population aged 14 or younger [3]. There is an inequitable distribution of income, as illustrated by the fact that in the capital city 41.6% of families earn less than $22 a month with per capita income being approximately $425 [4].

Katz's description of the rise of public education in mid-19th century U.S. can also be applied to the rise of public high school education in Costa Rica.

> Only a very small minority of the community's children even began high school, and most of them left before graduation. It was wealthy, prestigious community leaders concerned with economic development and social integration, as well as middle-class parents concerned with mobility and educational expense, who formed the nucleus of high school promoters [5].

Discussion on the need for educational reform could be dated back to 1934. The constitution of 1948 introduced some changes, the most important of which was making secondary education free for all. Each administration introduced some changes but gave other government programs more priority. In fact, one Minister of Education during the administration of President Otilio Ulate (1949–1953) was believed to have held the following views: "the poor should not go to secondary schools because they have to work" and "if poor girls went to high schools, there would be no one willing to work as a servant [6]." Nevertheless, the secondary school system expanded rapidly from four public secondary schools in 1941, to 16 in 1950, to 61 in 1966. This increase has more than kept pace with the population increase. However, there is a high drop-out rate with only 7.98% of those who started their education in 1955 finishing secondary school in 1965 [7]. The economic system, especially the public administration, has supplied jobs to the majority of those leaving high school and incapable of entering the university. Costa Rica still has need for unskilled workers but seasonal unemployment is a problem among the working classes who have dropped out of elementary school [8].

In deciding to reform the educational system Costa Rican policymakers declared their concern for modernizing what they considered to be a democratic political system by increasing "a spirit of political community and of participation and responsibility [9]." Almost all definitions of political modernization and development include, either implicitly or explicitly, a concern with the political system's capacity to deal with expanding participation. Eisenstadt states, for example, that modernization ". . . is characterized by the continuous spreading of political power to more groups in the society—ultimately to all adult citizens [10]." In most societies, the participation of women in politics has lagged behind that of men. Even in developed societies their participation has differed from that of men because role differentiation has not been eliminated. Neither those concerned with the reform of education in Costa Rica or progressivist reformers in the U.S., nor most reformers in other areas of the world were concerned especially with the role of women. However, in defining a democratic system they emphasized efficient participation by each member in society without reference to the sex of the member. By efficient, of course, was meant a form of participation which would not upset the stability of the society.

The Ministry of Education stated that "This participation presupposed social sensibility, cooperation and tolerance and a grouping of abilities, habits and attitudes whose formation is the responsibility of the school [11]." An important objective of the reform movement was the expansion of the secondary school system to include not just the children of the elite but also those of the masses. The reformers argued that in order to complete its function of recruiting the masses for participation in the political system, the school needed to assume some of the duties of political socialization for all which had previously been assumed by the families of the upper class [12]. This emphasis on participation by all had important repercussions on the role of women: increasing their participation in school and the community, as well as resulting in some attitudinal change.

As in the progressive educational movement in the U.S., Costa Rican reformers stressed "the incorporation of the experience of the child into the development of the curriculum, the softening of pedagogy, the breaking down of barriers between subjects, and the active participation of the learner." They also "saw education as the key to social uplift [13]." The traditional secondary curriculum in Costa Rica had divided time between fundamental subjects (Spanish, Mathematics, Natural Sciences, Physics, Chemistry, English, French, History, History and Geography of Costa Rica, Civic Education, Cosmography, Psychology, Literature, and general Geography) which represented 87% of the students' schedule, and special subjects (music, drawing and manual work, and physical education) which represented 13% of his time. In the reform program the sciences and the social studies were each integrated. Social skill was made the core of the new program, with more emphasis placed on contemporary history, institutions, and problems. Now academic subjects represented only 63.5% of the student's schedule. (Spanish, Social Studies, Science, Mathematics, Psychology, English, and French). In Costa Rica, as in the U.S., the reform program emphasized activites intended to accomplish what was considered to be the new function of political socialization, now assigned to the high school. Of course the school had played a role in political socialization of elites before. The traditional activities of musical and physical education remained, while exploratory activities, library and laboratory, student orientation, group and democratic formation activities were added to account for 36.5% of the student's time. The reform program envisaged great differences in teaching methods. In the traditional program all that was necessary was that the student be able to answer questions, usually through memorizing material which the teacher had previously dictated. Now, in all subject fields, individual investigation and group discussion were to be emphasized. Teachers were to use a greater variety of methods, including audiovisual aids, visits to local institutions, interviews with community leaders, directed study, and small groups.

The elaboration and implementation of the reform plan showed the results of the often frustrating search for consensus felt necessary by the policymakers. The objectives stated in the reform plan were very general. This was partly due to a desire to smooth over differences between teachers, administrators, government officials, and citizens, all of whom participated in discussions about the program under the guidance of the administrators, and partly due to the lack of importance attached to clear and detailed objectives whose results could be tested and evaluated. The plan was approved by the Superior Council of Education in 1957, but a new President was elected who responded to the concerns of teachers and administrators for the improvement of the professional preparation of teachers before implementing the new plan. Thus 7 years and another election passed before a President from the same political party which had initially approved the plan began to implement it in 1964, a year at a time. The first class to have completed the full reform program did not graduate until 1968.

In order to evaluate the effects of this reform program, teachers, school administrators, Ministry of Education officials, and various political leaders were interviewed. Textbooks, teaching units, and Ministry of Education internal correspondence and correspondence with the schools were collected and analyzed. After analyzing these objectives and methods, a questionnaire was developed to test the results of the reform program. Two surveys were then taken of 5th year students (final year of secondary school). Students in the first sample were the last to experience the full traditional curriculum program, while those in the second sample taken a year later were the first to complete 5 years' experience of the reform program. Approximately 15% of the total enrollment in public secondary schools were tested. Out of 39 public day schools, 10 were selected: five in the central urban region and five in the provinces. The same schools were used in both surveys. In each school, approximately 50% of the 5th year students were chosen randomly [14].

The selection process resulted in a sample composed of 50.7% male and 49.3% female students in the traditional program, and 51.2% male and 48.8% female in the reform program. These figures correspond to data derived from other sources which state that 48% of students from 15 to 19 years are women. It is important to note that the percentage of women college students is nearly the same—44% [15]. Unlike many developing countries, Costa Rican women have approximately equal educational opportunities. However, in Costa Rica only a small percentage of both sexes have the opportunity to attend secondary school. In 1964, only 18% of the population between 14 and 19 years of age were so enrolled [16]. Nevertheless, the situation is improving. In this sample, 12% had fathers who had completed three years or less of primary schooling, with 33% having completed from 4-6 years of schooling, and only 6–10% having attended university. In contrast, Daniel Goldrich found in his study of elite youth in one private school that 42% had fathers who had attended university [17]. These public secondary school students compose an important group which can either represent the interests of their lower-class origins, be co-opted into the elite, or serve as mediators between the elite and the rest of the population.

Survey Results

This study demonstrated that the school can play a particularly important role in the political socialization of women. The introduction of a program of educational and political modernization affected women students even more than men. While certain of the results may be unique to the Costa Rican situation, most seem comparable to the results of studies carried on in other countries. The school environment in most countries is probably the most egalitarian of all in which the female student is likely to find herself either in the present or the future. In Costa Rica approximately half the secondary teachers are women. Women can be found as high school principals, university professors, and in important posts in the Ministry of Education, although men do dominate these positions [18]. In Costa Rica, women comprise about 42% of the bazaar and service occupations, but only 25% of the modern occupations such as in the professions and industry. The majority of Costa Rican women devote themselves to the home. Only 18.2% of women are economically active, most likely due to the high birthrate and the attitudes which caused it [19]. Women have had to choose between marriage and the accompanying large family and a career. This situation may be changing as the birthrate is presently decreasing.

The announced objectives of the reform program placed a major emphasis on increasing participation. However, teachers and administrators, as members of the middle class and as practitioners and students of the more traditional methods, were all committed or skilled in increasing participation and leadership opportunities. The Almond and Verba study showed that the amount of participation in the classroom was highest in those countries which rates highest in the extent of democracy, as well as in the participation of women in politics—with the U.S. ranking first, followed by Great Britain, Germany, Italy, and Mexico—but without demonstrating the causal relationship. They also suggested that school participation has the greatest effect upon the political competence of those who for other reasons would be expected to be less politically competent, and this judgment would seem to apply to women [20].

Survey results indicated that students in the Costa Rican reform program responded to efforts of teachers and officials by participating more actively in their classes than had those in the traditional program. Female participation in classes other than social studies increased to almost equal that of males. The fact that their participation in social studies classes was still lower than that of males may be due to traditionally lower interest of women in politics. Women students also expressed less interest in talking with their teachers about political, social, or economic problems. Nevertheless, many more were willing to do so in the reform program than in the traditional program. In attempting to evaluate the success of the endeavor to establish a more democratic school environment, students were asked questions about their relations with teachers and administrators. In response to questions of whether students would talk with a teacher or administrator they felt had not treated them fairly, male students expressed more willingness to discuss their treatment than did females. However, the difference did narrow

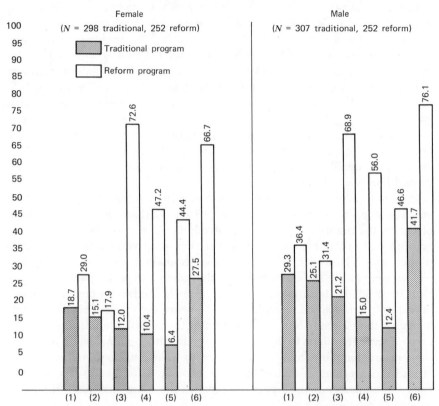

Figure 16.1. Participation in school. Percentage participating more than once in (1) classes, (2) social studies classes, (3) school meetings, (4) talks with professors over unfair treatment, (5) talks with administrators over unfair treatment, (6) talks with professors about politics.

in the reform program. The framers of the reform program emphasized the importance of participation in clubs and student government and scheduled regular meetings of these groups in contrast to the traditional program's infrequent calling of school assemblies. The change in the participation of female students was great. In the reform program there was greater participation by females than by males, whereas in the traditional program more males than females had participated in such activities. The traditional program appears to have reinforced the traditional differences in the roles society assigned to the sexes. The reform program's emphasis on participation by all seemed to help to change these roles. However, the process is a gradual one. While participation of women often increased to a greater degree than that of men, in all but participation in school meetings, male participation remained higher, as can be seen in Figure 16.1.

Female students consistently expressed a more positive attitude toward school than did male students. While a majority in both programs felt that school experience did not help much to resolve the problem of real life, more females than males felt that school was useful. Females expressed greater concern than males that secondary education be made obligatory, although the difference was less in the reform program. If, as studies in the U.S. indicate, length of time in school corresponds to income and thus rewards go to those with the best aptitude for school, why are not women better rewarded? This aptitude for school is probably not rewarded economically because of persistent role differentiation which determines entry into certain occupations, usually lower paid than others, as well as to traditional attitudes toward family planning.

In the reform program, more females than males felt that class participation was valuable and should be increased. This relationship was the reverse of that in the traditional program, probably because now that females were encouraged to participate more they had more positive feelings toward class participation. However, in social studies courses in the reform program, women were more satisfied with the existing amount of participation in classes than those in the traditional program. Female students were much more in favor of participation in student governments and clubs. Female students increased their already higher estimation of the school administration's concern for student opinion in the reform program, although males also increased their regard for the administration. Due to more recent participation and attitudes concerning feminine behavior, women most likely expected less from the administration. Figure 16.2 shows the more positive attitudes of women to school.

The reasons for these more positive attitudes of women are complex. Although feminine participation rose in the reform program, it was still below that of males in all except participation in clubs. Among those who participated most and had the most contact with the administration, there was a higher percentage who felt that the administration did not take student opinion into account. To increase favorable feelings toward the system, the participation must be considered favorably by those in authority, otherwise disillusionment increases among the most active. School administrators who voiced the official encouragement of student participation were still more accustomed and sometimes more committed to the traditional, more authoritarian practices.

Although the focus of this study is on the school's role in the political socialization of female students, the role of the family and peer group must also be considered. While the exact nature of the interaction between these various agents of socialization cannot be detailed, some idea of their relative importance can be ascertained. The school reform program influenced females even more than males in their relationship with the family and the peer group. For example, more females than males chose the social studies professor as the best source of advice on politics, and this percentage rose in the reform program, with the family declining in importance. It is interesting to note that a majority of all students in the public schools surveyed chose the social studies professor in contrast to the 70% or more of male students in Goldrich's sample of a private elite school who chose a family member [21].

As the policy-makers intended, the school does indeed seem to have assumed some of the duties of political socialization for the most recent entrants into the political system, which the families of the upper class assume for their members. Discussion of politics within the family did increase in the reform program, especially for females. Females in Costa Rica are traditionally

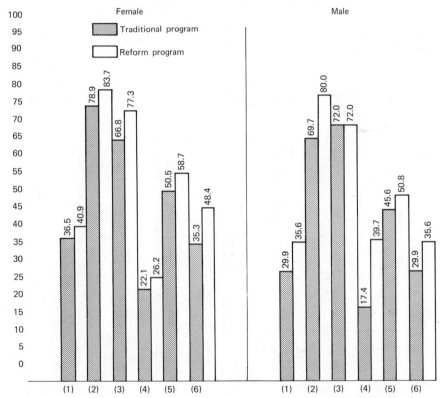

Figure 16.2. Attitudes toward school. Percentage expressing favorable attitude toward (1) usefulness of school, (2) compulsory secondary education, (3) participation in class, (4) participation in social studies class, (5) participation in student government and clubs, (6) school administration's regard for student opinion.

required to spend more time within the family circle than males of this age group, so the family may be more important to female than to male students. A much greater percentage of females in the traditional program reported agreement with parents' political party preferences than did males. However, the difference between the sexes narrowed in the reform program with women now being more ready to disagree and men more likely to agree than in the traditional program.

While the peer group ranked lower as a source for advice on politics for both sexes than either the school or the family, it rose in importance

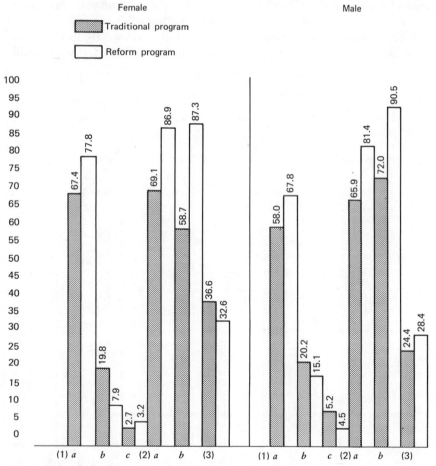

Figure 16.3.   Influence of family and friends. (1) Percentage choosing as source for advice on politics (*a*) social studies professor or counselor, (*b*) family, (*c*) friends. (2) Percentage discussing politics more than once with (*a*) family, (*b*) friends. (3) Percentage agreeing to vote for parents' political party.

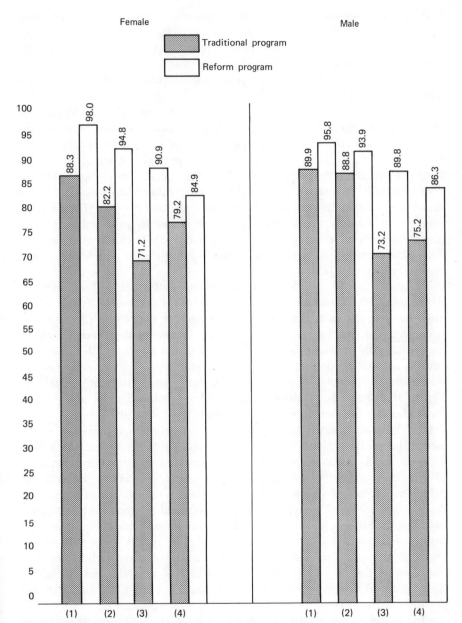

Figure 16.4. Exposure to the media. Percentage reporting occasional to daily exposure to (1) newspaper articles on national problems, (2) newspaper articles on international problems, (3) political programs on radio and television, (4) political articles in magazines or books.

in the reform program. In the traditional program, females discussed politics more with family than with the peer group, while males did the reverse. The percentage of women reporting frequent political conversation with friends more than doubled in the reform program, but since the percentage of men also increased, the female percentage remained below that of the male (Figure 16.3).

It is likely that these changes are indicators of future changes in the role of the family in political socialization. With women increasing their participatory skills and interests in politics, events in the polity will be increasingly transmitted into the family via both marriage partners. Almond and Verba suggested that this is the pattern followed in the U.S., thus resulting in political discussion which is more frequent and reciprocal rather than male-dominated as in the other countries studied—Germany, Italy, and Mexico. They further suggest that a family that is open to reciprocal discussion of political issues provides a type of political socialization that enables children to develop within the family itself a sense of political competence which is essential to the civic culture [22].

The media can be considered as another agency for political socialization whose role in the formation of political attitudes is acknowledged but whose importance is disputed. Since a basic objective of the reform program was to encourage students to keep informed by reading newspapers and periodicals and by listening to news programs, contact with the media will be considered here as a result of politicization. In the reform program exposure to the media greatly increased for all students, but particularly for females, as Figure 16.4 indicates. However more males continued to be daily users, thus indicating the time necessary to eradicate traditional attitudes and habits.

In addition to stressing more participation in school and more use of the media, the reform program stressed participation in the community, whether urban or rural. As a result, there was a great increase in the percentage of students working on community improvement projects or social work. A higher percentage of females than males in the reform program reported doing community work daily, while in the traditional program the relationship had been the reverse. However, a higher percentage of males report participation of some kind even if infrequent. Similar results were obtained in regard to the extent of contacts with government officials, such as deputies (members of the Legislative Assembly), municipal officials, and officials of the Ministry of Education, with a higher percentage of females being among the most active. These results suggest that the women who depart from the traditional norms tend to involve themselves in active participation in the community much more so than did males. Those studied were still secondary students and the real test will come after they leave school with its positive emphasis on participation. Figure 16.5 indicates that overall participation of women is still less than that of men.

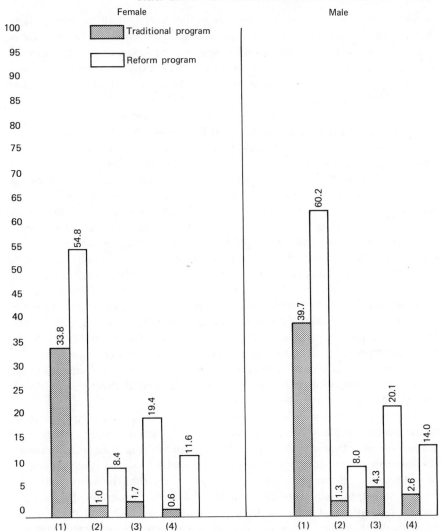

Figure 16.5. Community participation. Percentage reporting occasional to daily (1) participation in community projects or social work, (2) contact with deputies, (3) contact with municipal officials, (4) contact with Ministry of Education officials.

An important objective of the political socialization program was to foster attitudes favorable to democracy and to the Costa Rican political system, which was assumed to be a good example of democracy. It was also expected to increase the student's own competence in that system. At the same time, students were to develop a more realistic and independent understanding of politics and of contemporary problems. These objectives are somewhat contradictory and thus it is not surprising that the results of the reform program were not always in the direction anticipated by the policy-makers—more independent investigation and participation infused by a more positive attitude to the political system. Different teachers continued to apply their individual interpretation of these directives, some stressing independent discussion and some indoctrination. A lack of books limited independent research.

Before being able to participate independently, a person must have a feeling of personal competence and a belief in the possibility of success. Women and men differed in their estimation of their chances to achieve success in their personal life as distinct from that of politics. Whereas in the traditional program women expressed more optimism about their chances for personal success than they did their chances for political success, the relationship was reversed in the reform program. Male attitudes remained similar in both programs. They expressed more confidence in obtaining the success they desired in life rather than politics. In both programs, there was an especially high percentage who were uncertain about their political future, with women being more uncertain than men. In the reform program, women were definitely more confident than men in achieving the political success they desired, probably because they desired less. An important cause for the different response of men and women appears to be the higher degree of male self-confidence concerning their understanding of politics. While the reform program decreased the amount of self-confidence expressed by both sexes, the difference between the sexes increased. Female students' increased participation with men may have increased their doubts about their own relative competence.

There was much less difference between the sexes in their high estimation of the average student's political competence. It is interesting to note that while the percentage of females in the two programs remained approximately the same in their estimation of student competence, a greater percentage of males in the reform program were likely to agree that the average student was incompetent than were those in the traditional program. Likewise, a greater percentage of males in both programs were critical of the average citizen's competence. Since the percentage of females remained constant while that of males rose, the difference between the sexes increased in the reform program. The similarities between the sexes were greater than their differences—the majority of both gave a high rating to the political competence of the average student and a low rating to that of the average citizen. While these responses seem undemocratic, the attitudes could be expected because in their 5th year of secondary school, they had already received more education than the average citizen in Costa Rica. The differences between the sexes, while interesting, are difficult to explain. Females' own lack of self-confidence may make them more ready to trust in the competence

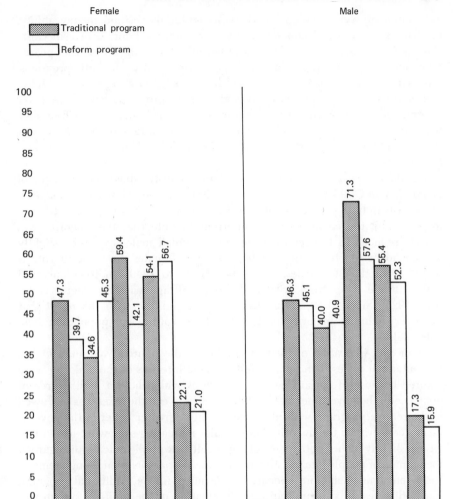

Figure 16.6. Attitudes affecting political competence. Percentage expressing confidence in (1) obtaining success in life, (2) obtaining political influence, (3) understanding the principal problems of the country, (4) the political competence of the average student, (5) the political competence of the majority of people.

of others. Figure 16.6 summarizes these differences in attitudes affecting political competence.

The higher regard of women for the average student and average citizen is similar to their higher regard for the school system and the administration. Likewise, women consistently expressed a more positive evaluation of the Costa Rican political system than did males, especially in the reform program.

When students were asked to consider whether family position, money, ability, hard work, or political contacts were most important for success in Costa Rica, a greater percentage of females than males in both programs appeared to believe in the existence of equality of opportunity. In both programs, a higher percentage of females than of males assigned importance to ability and hard work. The majority of students in both programs ranked the party program as the most important factor for political success in Costa Rica with ability second, money third, and family position ranking last. However, the percentage doing so was highest in the traditional program and highest for females.

The data indicates that females are more idealistic about the existence of democracy in Costa Rica, or perhaps just less realistic. However, a majority of students in both programs felt that the vote was the most important factor in governing the country. It is important to note that this majority was greatly reduced in the reform program, in which males expressed slightly less confidence in the vote than females. For females the right to vote is more recent than for males, dating back only to 1949. Indirect universal male suffrage dates from 1889 and direct suffrage with the secret ballot from 1925. Since 1959, voting has been compulsory, with the result that the overwhelming majority of the country's voting age population does vote [23].

In another indication of their evaluation of the political system, a higher percentage of males than females felt that the interests of the majority were ignored because of certain persons or groups which hold a high degree of influence in the government. The difference between the sexes was narrowed in the reform program, with males indicating a greater belief in the government's concern for the majority and females indicating somewhat less. Likewise, a slightly higher percentage of males felt that public officials disregarded the opinion of people like the student or student's parents even though females had been somewhat more alienated than males in the traditional program. For both sexes in both programs, the evaluation of the political system was thus somewhat contradictory. A majority felt both that the vote was the most important factor in governing the country and that the interests of the majority were ignored. The percentage of students believing the government affected daily life also decreased, especially for males. The reform program thus increased a negative evaluation of the political system in spite of the desires of the Costa Rican policy-makers, as can be seen in Figure 16.7.

An essential aspect of the reform program was to insure respect for democratic institutions and methods through formal teaching and participation in student government and clubs. However, as could be expected from their more negative evaluation of the political system, reform students expressed slightly less support for democratic methods than did those in the traditional

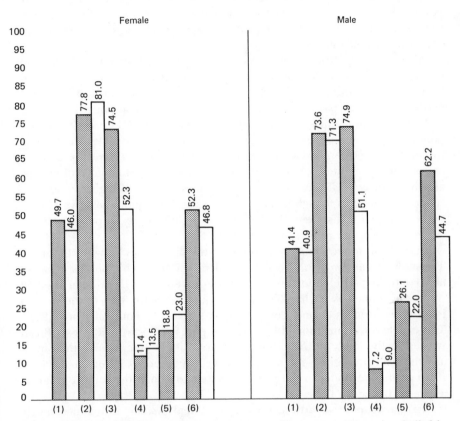

Figure 16.7. Evaluation of the political system. Percentage expressing belief in (1) ability and hard work being most important for success in life, (2) ability and the party program being most important for political success, (3) the vote as most important in deciding how the country is governed, (4) interests of the majority being upheld by the government, (5) public officials being concerned about what people think, (6) government's effect on daily life.

program. The majority of students in both programs were against the use of violence to resolve political or social problems. However, in the reform program the percentage of females expressing support for violence more than doubled to 11.1%, while that of males increased only slightly to 6.0%.

While a majority of students in the traditional program felt that elections should never be postponed, this majority was reduced especially by males. Women appeared more willing to protect their more recently acquired right to vote. Unlike the situation in many other Latin American countries, elections have rarely been postponed. Since 1889, the democratic pattern prevailed, except for the Tinoco dictatorship from 1917 to 1919 and the 1940 period which culminated in the successful 1948 civil war against the administration in power which had cancelled a narrow electoral victory by the opposition candidate.

One aspect of political socialization encouraged by policy-makers in most countries is the promotion of respect for government laws and a willingness to contribute to the political system. The majority of students in both programs objected to paying taxes if they could avoid it although there was a slightly greater appreciation of the necessity of taxation in the reform program. A much higher percentage of females than of males was willing to avoid paying taxes. In Costa Rica about 57% of the government's revenues come from indirect taxes, which fall hardest on those least capable of paying, although, since 1954, those with large incomes have paid higher taxes [24]. It appears that even though males expressed somewhat more negative evaluation of the political system, they expressed slightly more support for democratic methods, as can be seen in Figure 16.8.

It is difficult to ascertain the reasons for the differences between the sexes. The study of *The American Voter* concluded that although "moralistic values about citizen participation in democratic government have been bred in women as in men, what has been less adequately transmitted to the woman is a sense of some personal competence vis-a-vis the political world [25]." This conclusion seems to hold true only in part for Costa Rica. Costa Rican women in this study do have less sense of political competence than men, and the reform program only increased these differences. Women also hold more positive attitudes to the political system although the reform program appeared to reduce these.

Their more positive attitudes to the political system do not necessarily mean that females in Costa Rica will be more consistent supporters of the status quo or of morality in politics. In the reform program a higher percentage of females than males were willing to use violence and to avoid paying taxes, although they were less willing to postpone elections. These results differ from some of the studies comparing female and male attitudes in the U.S. Hess and Torney, for example, found that girls more frequently reported that the most important duty of the adult citizen is to obey laws and that girls see the legal authorities as more responsive than do boys [26]. In Costa Rica the alienation of females from public officials remained constant in both programs, with that of males lower in the traditional program but increasing to only slightly higher than females in the reform program. It is difficult to explain the reasons for these differences. The results themselves are not consistent. Female experience in participating in school and commu-

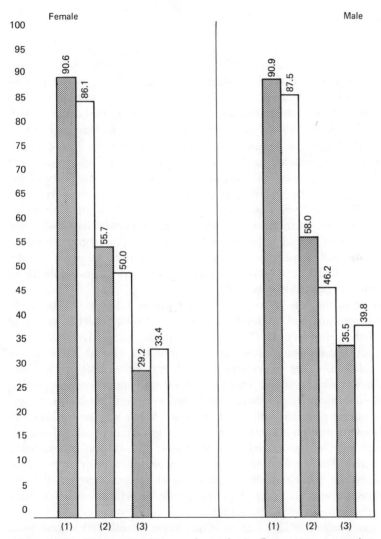

Figure 16.8. Respect for democratic methods. Percentage expressing belief in (1) not using violence to resolve political or social problems, (2) not postponing elections for any reason, (3) paying taxes.

nity is more recent than that of males and thus a smaller percentage may have grown disenchanted with the results. While they may be more willing to accept the ideas of others about the political system, they may not be as familiar with nor supportive of the methods advocated.

Conclusion

The Costa Rican reform program succeeded in increasing the participation of female students both inside and outside school and contributed to narrowing the difference between female and male attitudes and skills. However, neither inequality nor role differentiation between men and women were eliminated since men who always had participated more also increased their participation. Whether these students, and in particular women, will lead in bringing about political chance can be ascertained only through some future survey when they have participated in and become a part of the adult world. It seems likely that while men will continue to constitute the majority of the political leadership in the country, there will be an increasing percentage of women. While they will contribute a certain amount of stability to the political system through their more optimistic assessment of its capabilities, and more egalitarian attitudes, they cannot be counted upon to give automatic support. While still small, there is an even higher percentage of females than males who feel that it may at times be necessary to use violence to resolve social and political problems.

This change in the role of women was not planned, but it will certainly contribute to the political modernization of Costa Rica, which was one of the goals of the reformers. In Costa Rica, as in the rest of Latin America, the major political influence of women has been felt through their role in educating children, either informally in the home, since most are not employed, or in the school system. Increasing their skill and interest in participation and contemporary political, social, and economic problems, as was done in the reform program, will affect this role. While women traditionally have not been very active directly in politics or government administration, some change may be introduced in these areas. The reform program has recruited female leaders who in some cases were even more active than men. Thus, while the Costa Rican educational reform program did not directly focus on women or their political role, it will nevertheless have resulted in changing their political role.

Costa Rican leaders, as U.S. leaders before them, manifested a good sense of timing in introducing progressivist reform. They expanded secondary education to include children of working-class parents who had not previously had the opportunity of such education and introduced a civic education program to prepare students for participation in the political system while they still composed a relatively small percentage of their respective age group. Although Lasch cited evidence that in the U.S. "the school does not function in any direct and conscious way as the principal agency of indoctrination, discipline, or social control [27]," the results from this study of the Costa Rican reform program indicate that the school can play an important role in these areas. Costa Rican reformers succeeded in greatly increasing participation in the school and the community, discussion of politics with family and friends, and exposure to the media. It was more difficult to change attitudes in the direction they desired. Favorable attitudes toward school increased, but feelings of political competence, a positive evaluation of the political system, and respect for democratic methods all decreased in the reform program. The differences indicated by this study between those who had been educated under the reform program and those who had experienced the traditional program are all the more striking since both groups of students had lived in much the same environment: the same Ministry officials and school administrators, often the same instructors, and with considerable social contact between students in the different programs in the first years of the reform program.

Political conservatives and revolutionaries alike can criticize the Costa Rican reform program as they have criticized the progressivist reform movement in the U.S. The conservatives can criticize it for increasing dissent while at the same time increasing the students' skill in participating and for not maintaining different roles and attitudes for men and women. However, as Rustow states, "Only by means of dissension can democracy become a learning and a problem-solving process. . . . Only through continual expression of disagreement by sharply rivaling groups can political participation be maximized and political equality thus approximated [28]."

Revolutionaries can criticize the program for not encouraging more independent thinking and dissent, and for decreasing student feeling of political competence. Women among them can criticize the program for not eliminating differences between men and women. In their attempt to moderate between the two extremes the policy-makers seem to have leaned in the direction of the conservatives; this is to be expected, for no regime is eager to displace itself voluntarily or to place obstacles in the way of its functioning. In Costa Rica as in the U.S. "The common school's mission was to maintain and transmit the values considered necessary to prevent political, social, or economic upheaval [29]." If role differentiation was not eliminated, this also can be expected as traditional attitudes regarding men and women persist in even the most modernized of countries, and in some cases are even accentuated through diminishing the status accorded to the traditional roles of women.

What happened to Costa Rican women as a result of this reform program has happened to women and other new entrants into the political system in other areas of the world. The quotation from Eisenstadt in the introduction of this paper needs to be modified. It is true, as he states, that modernization is indeed characterized by the spread of political power to more groups in society and ultimately to all adult citizens. However this spread has not eliminated differences between groups. As Greer states,

> While American social institutions seem to have permitted talented individuals to rise up the ladder of power, it is quite fallacious to believe that those institutions have allowed the same room for movement to underprivileged groups seeking to share power with those groups comfortably lodged in positions of power [30].

The progressivist reform movement in the U.S., as in Costa Rica, stressed equal opportunities to participate in new programs of political modernization. These resulted in raising the skills and changing the attitudes of the previously excluded or underprivileged elements so that leaders could arise among them. However since the traditional participants—in this study, males—also increased their skills and changed certain attitudes, as a group they remain in command even though the gap in skills and attitudes between them and the new entrants—women—diminishes. Educational reform can thus prove useful to policy-makers who wish to modernize while still maintaining the legitimacy of the political system. However, broader social reform is needed if new entrants to the political system, such as women, are to reach a position of equality.

NOTES

1. Russell H. Fitzgibbon and Kenneth F. Johnson, "Measurement of Latin American Political Change," Robert Tomasek, ed., *Latin American Politics, 24 Studies of the Contemporary Scene.* New York: Doubleday, 1966, p. 10.

2. Martin C. Needler, *Political Development in Latin America: Instability, Violence and Evolutionary Change.* New York: Random House, 1968, p. 90.

3. Charles F. Denton, *Patterns of Costa Rican Politics.* Boston: Allyn and Bacon, 1971, p. 1 and Costa Rica, Ministerio de Educacion Publica, *Planeamiento del Desarrollo Educativo—Diagnostico.* San Jose, 1971, pp. 7–11.

4. *Ibid.,* pp. 21–22.

5. Michael B. Katz, *Class, Bureaucracy, and Schools.* New York: Praeger, 1971, pp. 42–43.

6. Isaac F. Azofeifa, "Problematica de la Segunda Ensenanza," *Revista de la Universidad de Costa Rica,* pp. 142–143 (junio de 1954).

7. Rafael Cortes, *Centros de Educacion de Costa Rica.* San Jose: Ministerio de Educacion, 1966, p. 18.

8. Denton, *Costa Rican Politics, op. cit.,* p. 6.

9. Jose Figueres, *Cartas a un Ciudadano*. San Jose: Imprenta Nacional, 1956, p. 30.

10. S. N. Eisenstadt, "Education and Political Development," Don C. Piper and Taylor Cole, eds., *Post-primary Education and Political and Economic Development*. Durham, N.C.: Duke University Press, 1964, p. 31.

11. Costa Rica, Ministerio de Educacion, Inspeccion General de Ensenanza Media, *Boletin de la Reforma*, No. 1, p. 31.

12. Oscar Zavala Nunez, *Informe General del Seminario de Profesores de Estudios Sociales*. San Jose; Ministerio de Educacion, 1958, pp. 21, 28.

13. Katz, *Class, Bureaucracy, and Schools, op. cit.*, p. 117.

14. For a more complete analysis of the reform program, and the surveys undertaken, see my "Political Modernization through Educational Reform: A Costa Rican Case Study," unpublished PH.D. dissertation, Fletcher School of Law and Diplomacy, Tufts University, 1971.

15. Ester Boserup, *Woman's Role in Economic Development*. London: Allen and Unwin, 1970, p. 120.

16. John F. Helwig, "Guidance Services in Costa Rican Secondary Schools: An Overview," unpublished monograph, 1968, p. 1.

17. Daniel Goldrich, *Sons of the Establishment, Elite Youth in Panama and Costa Rica*. Chicago: Rand-McNally, 1966, pp. 17–18.

18. Feliz Hernandez Andrino, *Caracteristicas del Personal Docente y Administrativo de los Establecimientos Oficiales, Semioficiales y Particulares de Educación Media de la República de Costa Rica*. Guatemala City: Instituto de Investigaciónes y Mejoramiento Educativo, 1965, p. 2.

19. Boserup, *Woman's Role, op. cit.*, pp. 177, 250.

20. Gabriel Almond and Sidney Verba, *The Civic Culture, Political Attitudes and Democracy in Five Nations*. Princeton, N.J.: Princeton University Press, 1963, pp. 353–357.

21. Goldrich, *Sons of the Establishment, op. cit.*, p. 19.

22. Almond and Verba, *The Civic Culture, op. cit.*, pp. 389–399.

23. Harry Kantor, *Patterns of Politics and Political Systems in Latin America*. Chicago: Rand-McNally, 1969, pp. 205–206.

24. *Ibid.*, p. 221.

25. Angus Campbell, et al., *The American Voter*. Ann Arbor, Mich.: Survey Research Center, University of Michigan, 1960, p. 491.

26. Robert D. Hess and Judith V. Torney, *The Development of Political Attitudes in Children*. Chicago: Aldine, 1967, pp. 179–181.

27. Christopher Lasch, "Inequality and Education," *New York Review of Books*, p. 19 (May 17, 1973).

28. Dankwart A. Rustow, *A World of Nations, Problems of Political Modernization*. Washington, D.C.: Brookings Institutions, 1967, p. 234.

29. Colin Greer, *The Great School Legend: A Revisionist Interpretation of American Public Education*. New York: Basic Books, 1972, p. 74.

30. *Ibid.*, p. 26.

Chapter

17

Memsahib, Militante, Femme Libre:
Political and Apolitical Styles of
Modern African Women

Judith Van Allen

African women today are not for the most part in politics. More accurately,
they are between politics. Those who had opportunities for political power
and autonomy in traditional societies have largely lost that power and autonomy under the impact of colonialism and what Westerners call modernization. But they have not gained power in modern political institutions, nor
autonomy in modern urban social and economic life.

African women are not caught between modern Western values, which
would emancipate them, and traditional values, which limit and confine them.
Their position is, rather, the result of a complex interaction between African
traditions and Western influence, both in the early colonial period and in
the current period of continued African economic dependence on the developed countries. A survey of women's position and political activity in each
of the countries of independent black Africa is impossible here. But a sense
of what politics may mean to increasing numbers of African women can
be gained by describing briefly the impact of colonialism and modernization
on African women, and then focusing on three types of responses women
are now making to the dislocations produced by that impact.

Traditional Politics and Colonialism [1]

There was tremendous variation in the political structures of traditional
African societies, but for our purposes two rough categories are useful:

An earlier version of this paper was presented at the Annual Meeting of the Western Political
Science Association, San Diego, 1973.

hierarchical societies headed by (often divine) rulers, and stateless societies in which political functions were diffuse and widely shared. While most African traditional societies are patrilineal; women have exercised power and exerted influence in both matrilineal and patrilineal societies as queens, queen mothers, sisters of the king, priestesses and military leaders, and have been revered as founders of cities and of states [2]. In stateless societies, many formal and informal groupings of people made decisions about the running of the community, and, in many of these societies, women participated in this process with men or dealt with matters which concerned them in their own meetings. In hierarchical societies, individual women had power over both men and women. In stateless societies, groups of women might exercise power over other women, or, less often, over men—for example, by collectively harassing a wife-beater until he apologized and gave his wife a present [3]. But common to more societies was the existence of an area of female autonomy—a sphere of life, usually centered around women's economic lives as farmers or traders—in which they governed themselves collectively, without male interference.

Even in hierarchically ordered societies, ordinary women might have much economic independence, as women in most agricultural societies shared a common pattern of rights and responsibilities. They had the major responsibility for feeding themselves and their children, but whatever profits were left from farming and trading were their own. In East Africa, women were primarily farmers, trading usually only to sell surplus produce. In West Africa, women were, and are, vociferous traders, spending half or more of their time trading surplus produce, prepared foods, and small domestic and imported goods, in some cases becoming *big women* who deal in thousands of dollars worth of goods [4].

It is, therefore, misleading to think of women in traditional African societies as either powerful and autonomous or not powerful and autonomous. It is much more fruitful to picture them as having multiple roles, as has been argued by Mbilinyi in discussing Tanzanian women [5]. In each society a woman had many roles, each defined by its *alter* (the other person involved) and by the situational context. A woman might have authority over her son, power over men when acting collectively and publicly with other women, and autonomy in planning her farming and trading, yet be deferential and obedient to her mother-in-law, her husband, and other in-laws in personal relationships within the compound.

The most servile and deferential female role was usually that of wife. There is no presumption in African traditions of conjugal emotional intimacy or equality. Strong emotional bonds are expected to exist not between husbands and wives, but among members of same-sex groups—for example, kinsmen or kinswomen, members of men's or women's associations. The only exception is the bond between mother and son: "Mother is the only woman you can trust," and a son may be "my husband, my brother, my father, my all-in-all [6]." He is also expected to be the support of his mother in her old age, as all a daughter's earnings will belong to her husband's lineage [7].

Sexual warfare is often explicit and institutionalized in traditional societies in a way in which it is not in Western societies today. Our battle of the sexes is a joke used to trivialize intersex hostility, and the battle is commonly thought of as one between an individual man and an individual woman, who, despite the battle, are more closely bound to each other than to anyone else. Traditionally in Africa, however, there has been a strong sexual class consciousness: women as a group versus men as a group. The conflict has been expressed in proverbs and parables, and institutionalized in rituals and organizations which each sex uses to protect itself against the other. Men's secret societies have used threats, beatings (in the past, beatings to death) and other terror tactics to keep women in their place, and women's societies have protected and passed down to girl initiates female mysteries, including the use of charms to control men [8]. Although secret societies are found mainly in West Africa, the existence and tactics of sexual warfare have traditionally existed throughout the continent.

The effect of colonialism and modernization has not been to mediate or to soften this conflict through the introduction of egalitarian and individ-ualistic norms, as much of the literature on modernization would suggest. The effect has been, rather, to intensify the conflict, to deepen the contra-diction between women and men by weakening and destroying the more powerful and autonomous female roles while very visibly improving the economic, social, and political opportunities and status of African men.

Colonial administrators gave no recognition to the socioeconomic or politi-cal status of women: They "sought spokes*men* or head*men* [9]." Diffused political functions were centralized into more modern political institutions, under the control of colonial administrators and African men. Mission educa-tion and a European language soon came to be the requisite for prestige and for political and economic power, and girls were, and are, sent to school much less often than boys. Even when sent to school, girls, unlike boys, still must do their house and farm chores, and they are often not taught the same subject as boys. Colonial girls' "training homes" taught some domestic science and the Bible in the vernacular. Girls' education continues to be oriented toward teaching them to be better housekeepers and mothers, and thus continues to put them at a disadvantage in modern economic, social and political life [10].

Women have been further disadvantaged in agricultural training, despite their responsibility for 60–80% of current agricultural labor. Western male technical experts' bias against women as farmers has resulted in men's being trained in new techniques and the use of new equipment (in some cases, even when the men had never farmed before), while women have been left to grow their own and their children's food with their traditional hoes and digging sticks. Some agricultural training is now being made available to women in a few countries, but generally women remain disadvantaged, as male-controlled cash cropping erodes their traditional economic independence by reducing women's wealth relative to that of men. The agricultural workload is greatly increased for women whose husbands and sons migrate to cities or to plantations and mines to work, but there is no increase in such women's economic independence. The men retain the right to the sale of cash crops, even if their wives have planted, weeded, and harvested them. The women have less time to produce crops or goods to sell and less time to spend in social, economic, or political activities [11].

When married women move to urban areas, their economic independence is further reduced. They are separated from their farms, there are few opportunities for them to earn money which are compatible with the household and childrearing duties for which they remain responsible, and they are isolated from other women and from community life in a way in which they were not in the extended-family environment of the village.

In West Africa many uneducated urban wives continue active trading. Although for most of them profits may be low, their trading does provide a life with other women outside the home, and market women's organizations continue the tradition of women collectively protecting their own interests, most notably in Ghana and Nigeria [12]. For women elsewhere, however, who traditionally traded only surplus farm produce, the move to town destroys their economic independence. Their identity comes to be based not on a wide range of activities in family, marketplace, and community, but on their sexual and domestic roles, and they become socially, psychologically, economically, and politically dependent on their husbands, as they lack the money, the education, the skills and the experience to deal with the modern urban world on their own [13].

Then processes of colonialism and modernization thus deepen the contradictions in women's lives and their perceptions of the contradictions between what is happening to them and what is happening to African men. The rural wife faces a heavier workload with no increased reward, and she must still feed her children from her farm while watching men get agricultural training denied to her. The urban wife still feels responsible for feeding her children, but finds few ways to earn money. Even if she has some education, she will find most jobs closed to her because she is a woman. Her youth in the village and her schooling will very likely have produced expectations of married life which conflict with the social isolation in which she finds herself, and with her husband's demands not only for deference but for all of her time to be organized around their private family life. She will see him leave the home for his social, economic, and political life with other men, while he expects her to stay home so that she is there whenever he chooses to return [14]. Education itself, even a few years of it, lessens women's ignorance of the possibility that things could be different. Education, along with the promises of the nationalist movements of freedom, equality, and dignity for all, has increased women's expectations at the same time that, in many ways, their position has been worsening.

Men, enjoying differential benefits in their favor, are generally unreceptive or hostile to changes in marriage and property laws, to female access to education and jobs, and, on the whole, to women's entrance into modern social, economic, and political life. In many places there seems to be a significant difference between female and male acceptance of new ideas which benefit women, and this, together with women's rising expectations and relative deprivations, suggests the possibility of the radicalization and mobilization of women and their confrontation with men [15]. The potential for such political mobilization, and for possible male responses to it, can perhaps be inferred from an examination of the situations, attitudes, and actions of three categories of African women: those we are calling the *memsahib*, the *militante* and the *femme libre*.

Femmes Libres but Not Free Women

Perhaps 75–80% of urban African women have come to town with their husbands, having been married in the village or, in the case of some highly educated men and women, having met and married overseas. The 20–25% of urban women who are unmarried are often pictured in the optimist modernization literature as the prototype of the new, free urban African woman [16]. But recent examinations of their situation suggest that they reveal the difficulties and limitations for women who try to improve their status by individual action.

The desire to lead a more independent life—to escape the traditional controls of kinsmen, an arranged marriage, and the physical toil of rural life—attracts young women to towns. But without education, they find few ways of making a living open to them: there are only limited openings in semiskilled factory work, petty trading, illicit brewing, and prostitution, or some combination thereof. Even women with some education find most jobs closed to them, as preference is given to men [17]. Prostitution or liaisons with a series of men may provide a life of less physical toil than in the village, and since men outnumber women in urban areas by two or more to one, such a life is always possible—for a young woman. But even though prostitution is more respectable in most African cities than in the West, it can hardly be regarded as a fully chosen occupation when there are not other jobs. Most prostitutes soon have children to support, and as their incomes depend on maintaining their sexual attractiveness, they face a future of increasing financial insecurity [18].

This class of unmarried women—prostitutes, workers, traders—with few exceptions, live male-dependent and economically precarious lives. As workers and as women they are subject to exploitation because of their economic and social marginality. There are indications that for many their continued unmarried status is not a reflection of their preferences, but only of men's negative attitudes toward them as potential wives—both urban and rural men generally see all unmarried town women as prostitutes, or *femmes libres* [19], whether they are or not. Town women are for pleasure—to be used, but not to be taken seriously, except as traps for innocent men from whom they may try to extort money by becoming pregnant [20].

These women provide an important service for the economic system and for the men—"a refuge from the impersonality of urban and industrial life"— but the myth that they are free and independent obscures their victimization and "furnishes alibis for those who, at base, seek to elude the problems of the difficult integration of women into the new African society [21]." The vulnerability of these women is further indicated by the verbal and physical attacks on town women in East Africa for un-African dress and demeanor. Wipper suggests that their powerlessness and marginality make these women easy scapegoats for anti-Western feeling and for male hostility to changes in women's traditional status [22].

To the extent that these women participate in market women's organizations or in prostitutes' unions, as some do in West Africa, they have some opportunity for collective political protection of their interests [23]. But their situation illustrates the illusory nature for African women of an individual path to independence common in Western societies: the gaining of respectable independence by going to the big city and finding a job. To the African man, the unmarried urban woman is a *femme libre*, and while the term has, as Bernard puts it, "the merit of suggesting that liberty is not the lot of married women [24]," it does not mean that the *femme libre* is in fact a free and equal person in modern urban life. Female freedom and independence seem, in modernizing Africa as in traditional African societies, to be dependent upon some form of collective female action.

Memsahib: Equal Rights within the Bourgeoisie

For Africa, modernization is not a culturally neutral process, with certain societal changes occurring inevitably as a result of the introduction of modern technology, industrialization, and urbanization. Theorists of modernization, who write as though this were so, simply ignore the fact most African modernization is Westernization, the transfer to Africa of a specifically Western, capitalist, class-stratified socioeconomic structure. The kind of development fostered serves the needs of foreign capital, not those of the mass of Africans. It produces a small African elite—an African bourgeoisie— whose incomes are hundreds of times that of the ordinary African peasant and whose interests are allied with those of foreign capital, not with those of the other 95% of Africans [25].

This pattern produces several results politically relevant for women. The most visible result to Westerners is the presence of African women in important positions in United Nations delegations. The first woman elected president of the General Assembly and the first woman to preside over the Security Council were Africans, and many African women have served in high positions in other U.N. bodies [26]. But the positions of these elite women do not reflect the general status of women in their countries. These women come from wealthy and prominent or ruling families, whether of traditional chiefs or nationalist leaders. They are highly visible, but very few in number, and in most African countries, there was no significant female political presence—no members of parliament or cabinet ministers—even before the majority of African civilian nationalist governments were replaced by military juntas [27].

Educated women would seem to be the key to the mobilization of African women. They are in a position to see the pattern of relative deprivation of women, compared to men, and the contradiction between the promises of the nationalist movements and what has actually been done legally and economically to aid women; they could articulate women's grievances and propose the possibility of change to the masses of women. However, the cultural domination of the West seems to work against this route to change. Many educated urban African wives belong to women's associations. However, the associations do not challenge the subordinate and dependent position of women, but help their members to acquire the wifely skills of Western "ladies" and then to pass those skills on to the less privileged urban wives. Women's clubs teach their members how to serve tea, sew fashionable dresses, set the table European style, choose jewelry and wigs, and sit gracefully in a tight skirt. Educated women then pass on these skills, along with some instruction in modern hygiene and baby care methods, to uneducated women. The associations of female producers of traditional society have become associations of female consumers, and community life is largely replaced by social climbing [28].

A few educated women, however, work actively for women's rights in several African countries, as part of their women's association activities. In Kenya, for example, during the last few years, a small group of elite women has been speaking and writing on issues that affect women, organizing lobbying and educational efforts to raise women's status and campaigning for political office on a platform of women's rights. While the leaders say that rural women "responded quickly to the opportunity to form their own associations," the movement—a network of clubs and organizations—remains basically urban and more relevant to literate women [29]. The clubs provide the usual homemaking, hygiene, and infant care instruction, which does not lead to political participation or economic independence. Much of the leaders' notion of equal rights is essentially bourgeois: greater access to education, including higher education, and access to jobs and political office for those with the educational qualifications. Their goals in reforming marriage and property laws have somewhat wider relevance, but still do not touch the more than 80% of Kenyan women who are illiterate and who live most of their lives under customary law.

The efforts of these elite women are hampered, and their concepts of equality themselves conditioned, by the commitment of Kenya's ruling party to a capitalist form of development and the party's lack of commitment to any change in traditional sex roles, despite rhetoric about equality. Kenya is a one-party state. If the party wanted women elected to office, women would be elected: the first woman was elected to the legislature in 1969, and women candidates face ridicule and harassment when they speak. Despite agitation by women's organizations, reform laws have not been passed. In fact, in June 1969, the legislature abolished the law requiring a man to contribute to the support of his illegitimate children. In Kenya, as elsewhere in East Africa, women have been criticized by high officials and assaulted and harassed on the street for dressing and acting in un-African ways—an echo of the terrorist activities of traditional men's societies to keep women in their place [30].

With this kind of male opposition, a great deal of female solidarity and determination is needed, and the polarization between the urban elite and the rural peasantry works against that solidarity. The politics of the ruling party would seem to be a major block to the mobilization of Kenyan women, even though two of their stated goals—changing the norms of female deference and reducing women's physical workload—would benefit rural, illiterate women. Even here, their most radical goal—changing the norms of defer-ence—is affected by the bourgeois ideology which accompanies Kenya's capitalist development pattern. The idea of some elite women, that African men should address African women as *memsahib*—the Swahili term of respect used in addressing European women—clearly indicates their Western-oriented status consciousness [31]. Equality becomes being as good as European women, and the goal becomes to extend titles of status to more women, rather than to do away with titles and other indications of status altogether.

Militantes, Ujamaa and Black Detachments of Women

As long as Western-controlled development is not successfully challenged, equality for African women would mean only that elite women would be more nearly equal to elite men and peasant women would be more nearly equal to peasant men. With access to agricultural training, a peasant woman could produce cash crops and make 1/235 as much income as an elite woman who became a member of the government [32]. Three attempts to challenge Western hegemony suggest that commitment of nationalist party leadership to the emancipation of women is the most significant factor in initiating changes in the status of women, but that a strong women's organization may well be needed to protect and consolidate women's gains.

In Guinea, the ruling party under the leadership of Sekou Toure has involved women on a significant scale since the beginning of the nationalist movement; "the women support the Party, and the Party supports the women [33]." Rules of the Parti Democratique de Guinee (PDG) require certain percentages of female representation at local, sectional, regional, and national levels. The PDG, in an attempt to combat elitism, adopted a policy of putting party loyalty before education as a qualification for party position. Women's relative disadvantage in access to education thus did not cut them off from political participation and leadership in Guinea, as it did in most other places. Many women, literate and illiterate, urban and rural, have become *militantes*, the lowest cadre level; women occupy positions of authority throughout the country, from the central government and administration to presidencies of local councils; many have challenged men for positions of leadership within the Party itself [34]. In 1968, 20 of the 75 deputies on the PDG slate (27%), elected to the National Assembly for 5-year terms, were women. Women were at that time 16% of the regional deputies. These percentages are remarkable for any country, but perhaps even more significant, though a lower percentage, is the women members of the central policy-making body of the PDG—almost 12%, more than twice the female percentages on the Soviet and Chinese Central Committees. Toure, in 1968, said that one of every 15 Guinean women had some position of public responsibility [35].

The *militantes* have led in challenging traditions which subordinate or restrict women. Toure has supported them, and they him, but they have also managed to protect their gains against male opposition within the PDG. Toure has had a long commitment to equality for women. His speeches refer to women as one of the two most oppressed groups in Guinea (peasants being the other), and to the contradiction between men and women as one of the basic contradictions in society. He led both in the organization of women in the Party and in the passage of reform legislation. Guinea has one of the strongest reformed marriage and divorce laws, and is reported actually to enforce its provisions fairly effectively [36]. Toure has long opposed polygamy, and in January 1968, at the first Congress of Women (women previously having been organized only as sections of the PDG), polygamy was abolished by a resolution which later became a government decree. This occurred despite the reported lack of general support because the resolution was carried by a faction of *militantes emancipees* and was "the will of the President [37]."

The power of the organized women is indicated by a 1964 dispute. Male backlash had led the party leadership to abolish the separate women's sections in the villages because they were provoking strife in the family and in local party organizations as women pushed for changes in relations between the sexes. By acting collectively, the women were able to impose their claims on Toure, and on the Party, and the women's sections were reestablished and gained in strength [38].

The PDG initiated the organization of women, but the Guinean women's organization, uniting urban and rural, educated and illiterate women dedicated to improving the general position of all women, has developed a dynamic and a strength of its own. Thus, the interests of women seem to be firmly in their own hands and not subject to the whims or passing political concerns of a male party elite. This gives Guinean women two distinct but related kinds of power and autonomy: the ability to protect their own interests as they define them at the time (more conventional interests, perhaps, as wives and mothers); and the ability to redefine their own interests, roles, obligations, and goals as their ideas change and develop over time.

Guinea has had economic troubles since 1958, when she was the only former French colony to vote not to remain in the French community and the French did their best to make successful independence impossible. She has not succeeded in developing independently and has, for several years, moved toward a rapprochement with Western capital. Class distinctions have not disappeared, and despite some reductions of salaries of government officials, there is still a significant distance between elite and peasants. Development plans calling for human investment have not been successfully implemented [39]. Nonetheless, PDG's attempts to draw cadres from all levels of the population does work against urban/rural polarization and enables activist women to develop a strong organization which both benefits them and provides an important base of support for the Party.

In Tanzania the ruling party has been more successful in maintaining its independence from foreign capital, in pursuing at least some rural, labor-intensive development which benefits ordinary peasants, and in checking the aggrandizement of the elite, thereby reducing the urban/rural, elite/peasantry polarization which characterizes Africa. However, the Party has not had a strong commitment to improving the status of women, despite the principles on which Tanzania's socialist society is to be based. The general ideology proclaimed by President Julius Nyerere ("Equality and respect for human dignity, sharing of the resources which are produced by our efforts, work by everyone and exploitation by none [40]") is affected by Nyerere's concept of what socialism means in Tanzania—*ujamaa*. *Ujamaa*, or "familyhood" in Swahili, reinforces traditional family roles and female status. While reforms have been made in the marriage and divorce laws, including the provision of some rights of inheritance for widows, the effects are expected to be limited by male political, economic, and social dominance [41]. Attacks on town women have occurred in Tanzania as well as in Kenya and Malawi, and the Party has not moved to stop these attacks, nor to make any special appeals to female support.

In Tanzania, women in the national women's organization work both for legislative reforms and for the extension of education and agricultural training (as well as the more conventional homemaking skills) to more women. The educated Tanzanian woman, however, seems to face a double battle: on the one hand, to convince the male party leadership that it should take women seriously as a base of support for a democratic socialist, rather than capitalist, development; on the other, to raise female consciousness and organize women with or without the help of the Party. Tanzania, then, may provide a test of the possibility of women themselves initiating changes in their status by building their own movement, which could then force the ruling party to take strong action to bring about changes in men's attitudes and behavior toward women. In the words of Mbilinyi:

> while engaged in [the] national struggle, [women] must be conscious of the peculiar contradictions of their own lives and act to remove them *at the same time.* In doing so, women will be "saving" their daughters and sisters and awakening them to the realisation of their own true abilities and potentialities. Women cannot expect anyone else to do this for them. Their future rests in themselves [42].

None of the independent African countries had to engage in a war of liberation to gain its independence, none went through a social revolution at the time of independence. Rather, independence meant the filling of governmental posts, formerly held by a colonial elite, with the educated African minority which then became the new African elite. The few African leaders who have tried, or are trying, to bring about social revolution and socialist development find themselves in opposition to much of that elite, and they lack the support of a mass movement whose consciousness has been developed by years of protracted struggle.

China's path of labor-intensive rural-based development seems to these leaders more relevant than Western models to Africa which has 75–80%

of her population in the rural sector. But without a war of liberation, such as the Chinese fought, to serve as a crucible for rapid and intense changes in consciousness, each change becomes a much greater struggle in itself. Changes which are seen by the (male) party leadership as threats to the building of mass support are postponed. If the party leadership, as in Guinea, sees women as an important base of support from the beginning, then a women's movement can grow as the party grows, and can protect its gains even in the face of male opposition. When that does not happen, as in our examples from Kenya and Tanzania, women who want to make changes find themselves faced with a preemptive backlash, prior to any significant, widespread change in women's status.

However, there are wars of liberation going on in Africa, and in two of the most successful ones—against continued Portuguese colonialism in Mozambique and in Guinea-Bissau—we can see some of the possibilities for radical changes in sex roles within a guerrilla movement [43]. Liberation movements have existed for more than a decade in the Portuguese colonies, and today FRELIMO (Mozambique Liberation Front) and PAIGC (Party for the Independence of Guinea and Cape Verde) each control large areas of land in which they operate schools, courts, markets, and hospitals while they continue guerrilla warfare against the Portuguese. As well as working to break down tribal barriers and to form a national consciousness, these movements are also making efforts to change traditional ideas about women's—and men's—roles.

In FRELIMO and PAIGC, as in Guinea, these efforts seem to have been initiated by male party leaders. In October 1966, the FRELIMO Central Committee decided that women should be trained in political and military skills in order "to take a more active part in the struggle for national liberation, at all levels [44]." The first group of women trained became the basis of the women's detachment of FRELIMO. Members of the women's detachment fight both on the front lines and in defense of liberated areas, and work in the Department of Security guarding against enemy infiltration. Women also play a key role in mobilization and political education, "by developing the political understanding of the war" among both men and women [45]. Members of the women's detachment also perform duties more conventionally female in Western terms: running the FRELIMO orphanage, working in health centers, teaching in primary schools and adult literacy classes, in the latter case performing also the political function of overcoming prejudices against education for women. According to a political commissar of the women's detachment, once the basic level of political understanding and literacy education has been reached, the women "work at the next level of encouraging even more active participation by inviting [women] to follow our example, to leave their homes and train as fighters, nurses, teachers . . ."—thereby continually increasing the size of the women's detachment [46].

In addition to encouraging women to do tasks formerly considered men's work, FRELIMO tries to break down the sexual division of work itself. Male as well as female soldiers cook, take care of children, and do planting, weeding, and harvesting as well as the traditional male farming tasks of clearing fields and other heavier work [47].

In PAIGC, also, women have been given political and military training, although apparently in fewer numbers. Although in these liberation movements, women fighting or acting in party positions are few compared to the number of men, their impact is reportedly far out of proportion to their numbers. They provide for both men and women the new experience of interacting with "confident and capable female militants who are themselves the best examples of what they are propounding [48]." The significance of the party in providing legitimacy for women acting in nontraditional ways is indicated by the statement of a woman serving as chief political commissar for PAIGC's Southern Front that she has found no handicap in being a woman among traditionally patriarchal tribes: "They accept me as a party authority and directives given through me are always carried out [49]."

Liberation movements—if committed to changes in women's status—thus seem to offer the possibility for radical changes in both women's and men's roles which would break down the male-female contradiction. But only the victory of these movements will show whether the changes are deep and permanent, or whether women will be pressured back into the kitchen and nursery as has happened after some other successful revolutions and wars of national liberation. The need for women to be able to protect their own gains seems as great in postrevolutionary societies as in any others [50].

Conclusion

The processes of modernization can be expected to continue to produce dislocations in the status of African women and to deepen the contradictions in women's lives, not because anyone intends this to happen, not because it is the unplanned result of development which serves the needs of foreign capital and "does not measure [the] human cost [51]." Women's status is not inevitably raised by modernization, nor by nationalist struggles for independence or anticolonial guerrilla wars. It is raised only by the conscious, organized efforts of women, and of male leadership in nationalist parties, movements, and liberation armies. The conditions for the mobilization and radicalization of African women can be expected to continue to develop. But whether male African leaders will recognize that potential is problematic; it is much more a question of the values of particular individual men than of historical forces. In the absence of strong agitation by women, significant increases in women's status and political power and autonomy seem unlikely. In many different settings, the experiences of African women support Mbilinyi's words: "Women cannot expect anyone else to do this for them. Their future rests in themselves."

NOTES

1. There are wide variations among African traditional societies, and generalizations about them will necessarily be rough and have exceptions. The area covered in this essay is sub-Saharan Africa, excluding white-dominated territories except when discussing guerrilla movements. Most African traditional societies are agricultural, and it is the position of women in such societies with which we will be concerned. From 75% to 80% of the African population continues to live and work wholly or primarily in the rural sector.

2. Annie Le Beuf, "The Role of Women in the Political Organization of African Societies," in Denise Paulme ed., *Women of Tropical Africa*. Berkeley: University of California Press, 1963, pp. 94–6.

3. Judith Van Allen, " 'Sitting on a Man': Colonialism and the Lost Political Institutions of Igbo Women," *Canadian Journal of African Studies*, **6**, No. 2, pp. 169–71 (1972); Paulme, *Women of Tropical Africa, op. cit.*

4. Marjorie Mbilinyi, "The 'New Woman' and Traditional Norms in Tanzania," *The Journal of Modern African Studies*, **10**, No. 1, p. 66 (1972); Paulme, *Women of Tropical Africa, op. cit.*, p. 6; Ester Boserup, *Woman's Role in Economic Development*. St. Martin's, 1970, pp. 45–51.

5. Mbilinyi, "The 'New Woman,' " *op. cit.*, pp. 59–60, following W. N. Goodenough, "Rethinking 'Status' and 'Role': toward a general model of the cultural organization of social relationships," in M. Banton, ed., *The Relevance of Models for Social Anthropology*. London: African Studies Association, 1965, p. 4.

6. Monique Gessain, "Coniagui Women (Guinea)," in Paulme, *Women of Tropical Africa, op. cit.*, p. 28; Ama Ata Aidoo, *No Sweetness Here*. New York: Anchor, 1972, p. 77.

7. Marjorie Mbilinyi, "The State of Women in Tanzania," *Canadian Journal of African Studies*, **6**, No. 2, p. 375 (1972).

8. Iris Andreski, *Old Wives' Tales: Life Stories of African Women*. Schocken, 1970, pp. 57–72, and *passim*, for Ibibio women's memories of women being killed by the men's secret society.

9. Mbilinyi, "The 'New Woman'," *op. cit.*, p. 61.

10. *Ibid.*, p. 67; Van Allen, " 'Sitting on a Man,' " *op. cit.*, pp. 171–2; Boserup, *Woman's Role, op. cit.*, pp. 211–25; United Nations Commission on the Status of Women, "Resources Available to Member States for the Advancement of Women," 1966. Much African education continues to be in the hands of voluntary agencies, who carry on the mission tradition.

11. United Nations, Economic Commission for Africa, Human Resources Development Division, Addis Ababa, Ethiopia, "Women: The Neglected Human Resource for African Development," *Canadian Journal of African Studies*, **6**, No. 2, pp. 359–68 (1972); Boserup, *Woman's Role, op. cit.*, pp. 34, 53–63, 78–9, 85–6, 167–72; and Mbilinyi, "The 'New Woman," *op. cit.*, emphasize women's increased workloads when males migrate, and point out that women do many chores once considered men's work, but men will rarely do women's work. Melvin L. Perlman, "The Changing Status and Role of Women in Toro (Western Uganda)," *Cahiers d'Etudes Africaines*,

No. 24, **6,** No. 4 (1966), found increased freedom, particularly sexual freedom. Robert A. Le Vine, "Sex Roles and Economic Change in Africa," *Ethnology* (April 1966), studied societies with a high rate of labor migration and found that "labor migration has not resulted in a drastic restructuring of sex-role norms in these rural communities but rather in an accentuation of traditional tendencies (p. 188)."

12. Tanya Baker, *Women Elites in Western Nigeria,* unpublished ms., Dept. of Social Anthropology, Edinburgh University, cited by Kenneth Little, "Voluntary Associations and Social Mobility," *Canadian Journal of African Studies,* **6,** No. 2, 1972, p. 283; Suzanne Comhaire-Sylvain, "Associations on the Basis of Origin in Lagos, Nigeria," *Amer. Catholic Sociological Rev.,* **11,** pp. 183–4; Henry L. Bretton, "Political Influence in Southern Nigeria," in Herbert J. Spiro, ed., *Africa: The Primacy of Politics.* New York: Random House, 1966, p. 61; Miranda Greenstreet, "Social Change and Ghanaian Women," *Canadian Journal of African Studies,* **6,** No. 2, pp. 353–4 (1972); Dorothy Dee Vallenga, "Attempts to Change the Marriage Laws in Ghana and the Ivory Coast," in Philip Foster and Aristide R. Zolberg, eds., *Ghana and the Ivory Coast: Perspectives on Modernization.* Chicago: University of Chicago Press, 1971.

13. See, for example, Guy Bernard, "Conjugalite et role de la femme a Kinshasa," *Canadian Journal of African Studies,* **6,** No. 2, 1972; Josef Gugler, "The Second Sex in Town," *Canadian Journal of African Studies,* **6,** No. 2, 1972; Mbilinyi, "The 'New Woman,' " *op. cit.;* Alf Schwarz, "Illusion d'une emancipation et alienation reelle de l'ouvriere zairoise," *Canadian Journal of African Studies,* **6,** No. 2 (1972).

14. Boserup, *Woman's Role, op. cit.,* Parts II and III, *passim;* Bernard, "Conjugalite et role," *op. cit.,* pp. 267–73; Gugler, "The Second Sex in Town," *op. cit.,* pp. 295–9.

15. Bernard, "Conjugalite et role," *op. cit.,* p. 270; Perlman, "The Changing Status and Role," *op. cit.,* says that one result of this male-female difference is that women who refuse domination are likely to end up as divorcees; A. W. Southall and Peter Gutkind, *Townsmen in the Making.* Kampala: 1957, pp. 62, 73; Audrey Wipper, "African Women, Fashion, and Scapegoating," *Canadian Journal of African Studies,* **6,** No. 2, pp. 338–46 (1972); Rene Dumont, *False Start in Africa,* 2nd ed. New York: Praeger, 1969, pp. 228–9.

16. Useful discussions and critiques of the optimist viewpoint, which claims that urban life and modernization in general are highly beneficial to women, can be found in Schwarz, "Illusion d'une emancipation," *op. cit.,* and in Wipper, "African Women," *op. cit.*

17. Boserup, *Woman's Role, op. cit.,* Parts II and III, *passim.* Sex is an even greater hindrance than race in the countries with white settler populations; in Kenya and South Africa, Asian men (Indians, for the most part) hold more administrative positions than European women. pp. 149–50.

18. Women in towns form a wide variety of extramarital relationships with men, from prostitution, which provides the woman's entire livelihood and involves no relationship with the men beyond the sexual act, to what is called concubinage—temporary cohabitation. Courtesans are prostitutes whose high level of sophistication, beauty and fashionable wardrobe give them significant control over their social relationships and high social status. Little, "Voluntary Associations," *op. cit.,* pp. 283–7. In this article, *prostitutes* is used loosely to cover all women who derive a substantial part of their income in this way. Cyprian Ekwensi, *Jagua Nana.* New York: Fawcett, 1969, strikingly conveys the fragility of such a woman's economics and sense of identity.

19. The term originated as a legal classification in the Belgian Congo, where *femmes libres* were women who qualified for residence in the African townships in their own right. It now means prostitutes and courtesans. A colonial legal term for town women first became a synonym for prostitute, and now has become a label for the ever-increasing numbers of town women who are not prostitutes. Schwarz, "Illusion d'une emancipation," *op. cit.,* pp. 201–3; Boserup,

Woman's Role, op. cit., pp. 99–102, 157; Wipper, "African Women," *op. cit.,* p. 339, reports that this view is so prevalent that, in 1964, a Kenyan cabinet member addressing the East African Women's Seminar, admonished his audience that, "It is necessary that we should change our attitude towards them, and discard the assumption that an unmarried girl in town is a prostitute; she may well be pursuing a very honourable calling."

20. Le Vine, "Sex Roles," *op. cit.,* pp. 191–2, reports the emergence in Eastern Nigeria of an anti-town woman pamphlet literature, and the theme of the scheming, licentious town women is common in novels by African men. For a contrasting picture by an African woman writer, see Aidoo, *No Sweetness Here, op. cit.* Debates on laws requiring men to contribute to the support of illegitimate children also reveal these attitudes, as reported for Kenya (where an all-male legislature abolished the requirement) in Wipper, "African Women," *op. cit.,* and for Ghana in Vallenga, "Attempts to Change," *op. cit.*

21. Schwarz, "Illusion d'une emancipation," *op. cit.,* p. 212.

22. Wipper, "African Women," *op. cit.* Her interpretation is supported by Mbilinyi, "The 'New Woman,' " *op. cit.,* p. 69, who points out that if attacks on miniskirts and other female Western fashions were part of a "progressive attempt to affirm the African identity of women"—as the men involved claim—"the leaders of the anti-mini movement would be women. They would be shouting, not only for longer skirts, but also for a reaffirmation of the economic autonomy of women and the need to restructure the developing economy to give them a place in nation building," p. 69.

23. Little, "Voluntary Associations," *op. cit.,* pp. 283–7; Bretton, "Political Influence," *op. cit.*

24. Bernard, "Conjugalite et role," *op. cit.* My translation.

25. See, for example, Giovanni Arrighi and John S. Saul, "Socialism and Economic Development in Tropical Africa," *Monthly Review* (May 1969); Glyn Hughes, "Preconditions of Socialist Development in Africa," *Monthly Review* (May 1970); Edwin A. Brett, "Dependency and Development: Some Problems Involved in the Analysis of Change in Colonial Africa," *Cahiers d'Études Africains, No. 44,* **11,** No. 4 (1971); David Horowitz, ed., *The Corporations and the Cold War.* New York: Monthly Review Press, 1970; Tamas Szentes, *The Political Economy of Underdevelopment.* Budapest: Hungarian Academy of Sciences, 1971; Dumont, *False Start, op. cit.*

26. Angie Brooks of Liberia was elected General Assembly president in 1969. Jeanne Martin Cisse of Guinea became Guinea's permanent representative to the Security Council in 1972. The chair rotates among permanent representatives. Cisse's prominence is a more accurate reflection of her country, but Guinea is the exception, as described below.

27. Carol P. Hoffer, "Mende and Sherbro Women in High Office," *Canadian Journal of African Studies,* **6,** No. 2 (1972), describes women traditional chiefs in Sierra Leone who became influential in nationalist government. One served as Minister Without Portfolio, and another was a civilian advisor to the military junta which ruled Sierra Leone in the mid-1960s. Kenya President Jomo Kenyatta's daughter's position as mayor of Nairobi does not reflect women's status in Kenya, although Margaret Kenyatta herself is now involved in efforts to gain equal rights for all women. A. Wipper, "Equal Rights for Women in Kenya?" *Journal of Modern African Studies,* **9,** No. 3 (1971), describes the privileged background of prominent Kenyan women. Women's insignificant impact on Kenya politics is described by Alwyn R. Rouyer, "Political Recruitment and Political Change in Kenya," paper presented at the Western Political Science Association meeting, 1973, p. 7.

28. *Educated,* following Little, "Voluntary Associations," *op. cit.,* is used to mean completion of secondary school at least; *literate* usually means the completion of several years of schooling. Female illiteracy in Africa runs higher than 90%, and up to 98% in rural Africa. Education women are a tiny minority—less than 1%—of all women. The civilizing function of women's

clubs is described—approvingly—by Little, "Voluntary Associations," *op. cit.* and Little, *West African Urbanization: A Study of Voluntary Associations in Social Change.* Cambridge: Cambridge University Press, 1965, pp. 70–1, 79–80, 136–7, 158–60.

29. Wipper, "Equal Rights," *op. cit.* Some form of women's organization exists in most countries, although they vary greatly in the degree to which they pursue women's economic, social and political rights as well as teach literacy, homemaking, hygiene and baby care. See, for example, Perlman, "The Changing Status," *op. cit.* (Uganda); Vallenga, "Attempts to Change," *op. cit.* (Ghana); Wipper, "African Women," *op. cit.* (East Africa generally); Little, "Voluntary Associations," *op. cit.*

30. Wipper, "Equal Rights," *op. cit.,* and "African Women," *op. cit.*

31. *Memsahib* as a title for African women would reverse the deference hierarchy, requiring male deference toward women. It is ironic that deference of manners toward women is one of the norms attacked by Western women in their campaign for equality.

32. Dumont, *False Start, op. cit.,* describes a salary range of one to 235 in the Congo, contrasting it with China's range of one to six, or one to four in the communes, pp. 288–9. He estimates, p. 81, that a legislator earns, in 1½ months as much as a peasant does in a lifetime.

33. Claude Riviere, "La promotion de la femme guineenne," *Cahiers d'Etudes Africaines, No. 31,* **8,** No. 3, p. 406 (1968).

34. Victor D. Du Bois, "The Problems of Independence," West African Series, V. 8, Washington, D.C.: American Universities Field Staff Reports Service; Riviere (1968), "La promotion," *op. cit.*

35. Riviere (1968), "La promotion," *op. cit.,* p. 423; V. D. Du Bois, "Guinea," in James S. Coleman and Carl G. Rosburg, Jr., eds., *Political Parties and National Integration in Tropical Africa.* Berkeley: University of California Press, 1964, pp. 190, 198–9, 202 ff.; Robert Donaldson and Derek Waller, "Stages and Change in Revolutionary Elites: A Comparative Analysis of the 1956 Party Central Committees in China and the USSR," *Sage Professional Papers in Comparative Politics,* **1,** p. 630 (1970); Gaíl Lapidus, "Modernization Theory and Sex Roles: A Critical Perspective," in this volume.

36. Riviere, "La promotion," *op. cit.,* pp. 409–16; provisions include a higher minimum age for marriage than other countries' reform laws (17 for girls); wives' freedom from having to repay bridewealth in order to obtain divorces; property inheritances for widows; and fathers' responsibility to contribute to the support of illegitimate children.

37. *Ibid.,* p. 413.

38. *Ibid.,* p. 423.

39. C. Riviere, "Les mécanisms de constitution d'une bourgeoisie commerçante en République de Guinée," *Cahiers d'Études Africaines, No. 43,* **11,** No. 3 (1971); Dumont, *False Start, op. cit.,* praises Guinean efforts to reduce salaries and promote honesty, in the course of analyzing "the failure of socialism in Guinea," pp. 86, 244–55. The view that agricultural labor is demeaning for the literate, or for all men because it is women's work, contributes to the failure of human investment development schemes on the Chinese model, pp. 230–2, 251–5.

40. Julius J. K. Nyerere, "Education for Self-Reliance," 1967, reprinted in *Ujamaa/Essays on Socialism.* New York: Oxford University Press, 1972. Patrick McGowan and Patrick Bolland, *The Political and Social Elite of Tanzania: An Analysis of Social Background Factors.* Syracuse, N.Y.: Syracuse University, 1971, p. 53, put female representation among the elite in the 1960s as between 4 and 5%.

41. Mbilinyi, "The 'New Woman,' " *op. cit.,* p. 68.

42. *Ibid.,* p. 72. Mbilinyi is on the faculty of the University of Dar es Salaam, Tanzania.

43. Information was not available on women's roles in other liberation movements. Discussing only two should not be taken to imply anything about women's position in the others.

44. Josina Machel, "The Role of Women in the Revolution," *Mozambique Revolution*, 1970, reprinted in Carol Bengelsdorf and Elsa Roberts, eds., *Building Freedom: Mozambique's FRE-LIMO*. Cambridge, Mass.: Africa Research Group, 1971, pp. 14–5. Machel was "a political commissar . . . , head of the section of social affairs of FRELIMO and a fighter on the front line"; she died in April 1971, from illness, at the age of 25.

45. *Ibid.*, p. 15.

46. *Ibid.*

47. This process is described and pictured in *A Luta Continua*, a film produced and directed by Robert Fletcher and Robert Van Lierop, which describes FRELIMO's actions in the liberated zones from a sympathetic point of view (distributed by TriContinental Films, P. O. Box 4430, Berkeley, Calif. 94702).

48. Machel, "The Role of Woman," *op. cit.*

49. Barbara Cornwall, *The Bush Rebels*. New York: Holt, Rinehart and Winston, 1972, p. 193. The political commissar, Carmen Pereira, was a bourgeois townswoman, a member of the very small privileged group of educated Africans in Bissau. In 1962, she fled to Senegal to escape the Portuguese security police, and in 1966, when the war escalated, she went with the soldiers into the Guinea bush.

50. See, for example, Lapidus, "Modernization Theory," *op. cit.*

51. Schwarz, "Illusion d'une emancipation," *op. cit.*, p. 212.

Chapter

18

The Politics of Cultural Liberation

Kay Boals

This article presents a model for the study of the dialectic between culturally dominant and culturally oppressed groups and applies that model to one case: that of male-female relations in an Algeria still caught in the dialectic of colonizer and colonized. Culturally oppressed groups means, for example, women in male-dominated and masculine-value-oriented societies, blacks in white America, homosexuals in straight society, and colonized peoples in colonial and postcolonial societies. The major similarity among these otherwise diverse cases is that all involve a kind of dominance by one group over another which is both external and internal. The dominance, in other words, is not merely technological or economic or military; it is also emotional, cultural, and psychological, producing in the dominated a pervasive sense of inferiority and insecurity [1]. As one feminist recently noted, "it is hard to fight an enemy who has outposts in your head [2]." Thus an essential part of liberation from domination involves coming to terms with those outposts.

The process of self-liberation with which we shall be concerned simultaneously involves both individuals and groups. For one thing, although it takes place within the psyches of individuals, it is absolutely central to political analysis, if only because it is the crucible out of which all reformist and revolutionary movements arise. For another, although it is necessarily an individual process, it is one which cannot be successfully completed by individuals in isolation since it is their identity as members of a (usually ascriptive) group which is under attack. What has been discussed so far are obvious similarities among various culturally oppressed groups. We shall

An earlier version of this paper was presented at the Annual Meeting of the American Political Science Association, Washington, D.C., 1972.

try in the body of this paper to suggest that there are additional similarities in the process of psychic liberation.

Comparisons among culturally oppressed groups are, of course, not new. The term *nigger*, for example, has been applied to women and to students to describe their positions vis-a-vis males and professors, respectively. Similarly, *woman* and *faggot* have become generalized terms of opprobrium when used among certain males, and the two terms convey similar meanings [3]. On a rather different level, comparisons are also frequent both by observers and participants. Thus NOW (The National Organization for Women) has long been referred to as the NAACP of the women's movement, and a group of older feminists call themselves the Gray Panthers. Less specifically, comparison is also made in common parlance when people speak of the black movement being ahead of the women's movement, or of gay liberation as beginning to catch up with the earlier feminist and black movements. So far, however, such comparisons have been unsystematic, largely intuitive, and the bases on which they rested remained implicit and perhaps unconscious. The contribution of this paper will be to provide a framework of process-oriented stages in terms of which fruitful comparisons can be made [4].

At this point it might be useful to discuss briefly the uses and limitations of the kind of conceptual approach I have adopted. Clearly there is much to be said against this approach. It neglects not only a good deal of uniqueness, richness of detail, and empirical complexity, but also some very real differences among the various groups to which it purports to apply. (The *mix* of psychic and economic oppression is rather different from case to case, for example.) Moreover, we do not yet have for any of these groups the kind of detailed monographic work which must precede all attempts to generalize and compare at a high level of abstraction. Indeed, black-white relations, male-female relations, and the like became subjects for serious scholarly study in the U.S. only very recently—very much as an outgrowth of the changes currently underway in the consciousness and political visibility of blacks, women, and gays.

In contrast to those who say that theorizing must await the collection of masses of detailed, noncomparative studies, I believe that it is precisely at the present, initial stage that conceptual frameworks are of particular importance in orienting thinking and research efforts. They provide a preliminary mapping of the area to be explored; like a map they indicate which paths are likely to be main highways and which may be dead-ends or meandering bypaths. They do not provide exhaustive descriptions or analyses of every inch of terrain, but they do give a sense of the whole, while at the same time providing a context within which more limited and detailed studies can be placed [5]. It is this modest and yet at the same time indispensable function that the framework presented in this article attempts to perform.

There is one further preliminary problem: namely, the problem of method of presentation. The framework to be presented did not, of course, emerge de novo as a deductive system to be applied to empirical reality; it emerged as a result of reading and research done over a period of years [6]. I shall first present the general framework, using illustrative examples drawn from a number of sources, and then apply it to attitudes toward male-female relations in post-independence Algeria. A variety of problems will be discussed in order to present empirical material of intrinsic interest and to illustrate the application of the proposed framework to specific problems.

Part I

The proposed framework for the study of the politics of cultural liberation is composed of six stages of types of consciousness. The question of relationships among the various stages will be left for later consideration.

The first of these stages is *traditional* consciousness. Its most important characteristic is an unquestioning acceptance of the way of life of one's own group as the only possible way for that group to live. In some cases, as in the case of Islamic traditional culture, it is characterized by a calm conviction of superiority over others and a sense of being at the center of the cosmos [7]. In others, however, including male-female and homosexual-straight society relationships, the element of unquestioning acceptance, which is the hallmark of traditional consciousness, may be present even in the face of very strong cultural misogyny or contempt for homosexuals. Traditional consciousness is also often linked to a religious belief about the proper station in life of various individuals and groups—an attitude which has disappeared to such an extent in contemporary America that we too easily forget the degree to which it was once all-pervasive in most societies.

A number of examples could be cited to illustrate what is meant by traditional consciousness. One telling instance is cited by Rama Mehta in *The Western Educated Hindu Woman,* a study of 50 Indian women who were in their 20s at the time of Indian independence [8]. The fathers of these women were in the Indian civil service and the women themselves were educated in missionary secondary schools and had attained at least the B.A. in Indian colleges and universities. Their mothers, however, were almost entirely uneducated, spoke only the language of their own province and knew almost no English, remained devout Hindus, and continued both to practice the daily religious rituals and to try to bring up their children, especially their daughters, according to traditional Hindu ideas of modesty, reticence, submissiveness to male domination, and sacrifice of individual personal growth and development in the interests of family harmony and filial respect. Their mothers, the respondents reported, were not at all embarrassed at their poor English or their unfamiliarity with British manners and ideas, nor did they take the British and Anglicized Indian way of life as a threat or challenge to themselves. Rather, they were so firmly convinced of the unquestionable rightness and morality of their own way of doing things that the British way was not even seen as a possible alternative.

Another example of traditional consciousness at its best is given by Smith in his discussion in *Islam and Modern History* of al-Khidr Husayn, the first editor of the journal of al Azhar, Egypt's religious university [9]. According to Smith, what distinguishes this editor from his successor (whom we shall meet below) is his clear distinction between the Muslim community as it actually exists and the ideal Islam to which that community must continue to aspire. Neither romantic nor nostalgic, he focuses on what needs to be done to make the community a better embodiment of the Koranic ideal and is not hesitant to point out existing defects. Two things are crucial: his firm conviction that the Islamic ideal is the direction in which to move, and his commitment to judging the community in terms of standards and criteria derived from that ideal rather than by criteria external to it. Although writing in the 1930s he apparently remained essentially unaffected by the British occupation [10].

In this respect he differed profoundly from many who came under colonial domination in various regions of the world. To the extent that colonialism went hand-in-hand with a cultural domination that challenged the previously accepted way of life of the indigenous society it was instrumental in generating new kinds of consciousness in response. One of these was what might be called traditionalist consciousness. The essential characteristic that differentiates it from traditional consciousness (although not, as we shall see, from other forms) is that the sense of unquestioning acceptance of the traditional way of life is irrevocably gone and in its place is a will to believe without the capacity to do so. In the Islamic community, for example, to use Geertz's terms, religiousness is replaced by religious-mindedness [11]. Put somewhat differently, faith becomes ideology [12]. In the process, there develops an increasingly strident defensiveness. Moreover, the ideology is of a very particular kind, reflecting the situation from which it arose: namely that of being threatened by a culturally potent other. The traditionalist continues to reaffirm the criteria of judgment of his own traditional culture or religion but he is unable to do so with internal conviction. There is thus a strong internal incoherence between emotions and thinking, between what one would like to believe and what one knows in one's bones.

In Rama Mehta's study of Hindu women, traditionalist consciousness appears clearly in the respondents themselves (although as we saw above, their mothers were traditional). Many of the respondents, for example, asserted their belief in the desirability of the extended family or subcaste affiliations or teaching their daughters to be women in the traditional style, but their own education and life-style made it both psychologically and practically difficult for them to do so in any consistent or convincing way, and they definitely saw the Western life-style as a threat and challenge to their own [13].

The parallel in this country would be those women who assert with increasing shrillness and defensiveness the superiority of the wife-and-mother-only role against the felt threat of feminist challenges. A woman with traditional consciousness would not be similarly defensive, because she would not see the feminist point of view as a threat in the first place. It is, in general, fairly easy to discriminate between traditional and traditionalist consciousness by focusing on the tone of assertions. It can also be done by content, however, since traditionalists are already in the position of arguing primarily against something (i.e., the external cultural threat), whereas traditional individuals do not take a comparative stance.

What is more difficult is to make distinctions, in concrete cases, between traditionalist and reformist consciousness, a point we shall return to in the context of discussing reformist consciousness. This difficulty can be seen to some degree in the case of the second editor of the al Azhar journal discussed by Smith. For the moment, however, we shall be concerned only with his differences from his traditional predecessor. Whereas his predecessor focused on serving God and saw Islam as a transcendent ideal toward which the Muslim needed to strive, the second editor's emphasis was on serving Islam, and Islam conceived, not as ideal, but in terms of the actual historical community. This emphasis reflects the fact that he is writing with an eye to refuting attacks and judgments based on standards external to Islam. In so doing, he himself takes over some of those standards, and indeed often quotes Western scholars to make his points. As Smith points out:

> In a strict sense, even, such apologetic is more appropriate for non-Muslim consumption.

> In fact, a fanciful case could be made out that these writings are really functioning for readers who in the most profound, most religious sense are not Muslim; rather are men who, religiously ex-Muslim, are (or want to be) proud of their heritage, and desperately need reassurance in a hostile world. They believe (or want to believe) ardently in Islam and delight to see it defended. A true Muslim, however, is not a man who believes in Islam—especially Islam in history; but one who believes in God and is committed to the revelation through His Prophet. The latter is here sufficiently admired. But commitment is missing [14].

Traditionalism is by no means the only possible response when traditional consciousness is undermined by having to come to terms with a culturally potent other, although it is presumably the most widespread initial reaction. An alternative adopted by some is what might be called assimilationist consciousness [15]. The essence of assimilationist consciousness is the attempt to close the gap created by the destruction of traditional consciousness by identifying oneself, wholly and completely, with the dominant culture. It is primarily, although not necessarily, an attempt to find an individual solution to the problem by disassociating oneself from the culturally subordinate group to which one originally belonged. Examples would be what one author calls *loophole women,* that is, those who feel they have made it as individuals to status and acceptance in the male world [16], colonized *evolues* who immerse themselves in the colonizer's culture, homosexuals who try to pass in the straight world, and blacks who believe their individual talents and achievements will be sufficient to overcome racial prejudice. Inevitably, attempts at individual assimilation are accompanied, not only by rejection of identification with one's own culturally oppressed group, but also by contempt for that group as a whole and for individuals within who do not assimilate successfully. There is, of course, an implicit self-denigration in this contempt, particularly where ascriptive groups based on race or sex or culture are concerned, but this may not be consciously recognized.

Nor is the assimilationist stance sufficient to overcome internal incoherence within the individual. It may well please an assimilationist-minded woman to be told that she thinks like a man, but such compliments provide only temporary reassurance that one has made it into the dominant group and any trace of what may be interpreted by others as typically female behavior may be sufficient to destroy the always precarious acceptance. Moreover—and more importantly—it is doubtful whether the stigma of being female or black or colonized will be so entirely forgotten as to permit full acceptance in the first place.

Partly for this reason, perhaps, some individuals develop a second version of assimilationist consciousness which focuses on assimilating the culturally dominated group itself to the dominant culture rather than on individuals' disengagement from their initial group. This type of assimilationist consciousness can be seen among those feminists who hold that achievement of desirable forms of male-female relations requires elimination of all differences that are group differences. It assumes that the culturally dominant group already has the pattern of behavior or way of life that ought to characterize everyone. Therefore, the solution to the problem of overcoming cultural domination is seen in terms of the culturally dominated group's need to take on that already existing way of life. It may well be the case that some of these behavior patterns would be useful and desirable, but the important point here is that they are advocated more because they are part of the culturally dominant life-style than on their own merits. It is thus not surprising that form and substance are often confused or that some things come to be desired simply because they are associated with the dominant culture [17].

In group-oriented as in individually focused assimilationism, one's own culture is rejected in toto in favor of that of the culturally dominant group. There is no attempt to harmonize the two; there is a dichotomy whereby whatever belongs to the dominant culture is modern or civilized or otherwise desirable, while whatever belongs to the dominated culture is backward or uncivilized or otherwise undesirable. Thus it is easy to distinguish assimilationist consciousness from both traditional and traditionalist consciousness. It is also quite easy to distinguish it from the next form of consciousness to be discussed: reformist consciousness.

The essence of reformist consciousness is the attempt to take over from the dominant culture aspects which are felt to be valuable to the self and to ground those aspects in one's own tradition or culture. This process involves a reinterpretation of that tradition or culture in order to read back into its past the genesis of ideas which have been absorbed from the dominant culture. In the Islamic case, the choosing of the caliph by community leaders is reinterpreted to demonstrate the democratic nature of Islam; Koranic verses about the position of women are given a new reading to demonstrate Islam's superiority in the realm of male-female relations; the religious tax is advocated as a socialist system offering the golden mean between communism and capitalism, etc., and it is conveniently (or genuinely) forgotten that no one ever saw them that way before.

The problem of the extent to which the forgetting is convenient rather than genuine is one which needs further exploration. I would suspect that it is a mixture of both. The reformists are in a situation, in this respect, more difficult than that faced by traditional individuals. Given the commitment of the traditional individual to the transcendent ideal of his own culture, he can easily afford to reinterpret that tradition rather broadly in the light of changing circumstances. The reformist, however, is in a different position, since he must show that what he advocates has long been part of his own culture and is firmly rooted there, when in fact that is usually not the case. It is not hard to see that, in such a dilemma, one's desire to succeed would promote easy distortion of the tradition, distortion which is probably both conscious and unconscious.

It was mentioned above, in discussing traditionalist consciousness, that there were sufficient similarities to reformist consciousness to make the application of the concepts difficult in certain concrete cases. What the two have in common is that individuals having both kinds of consciousness are led by their interaction with the dominant culture to distort their own tradition, to judge it by standards external to itself, and to attempt to demonstrate its superiority to the dominant culture. In both cases, moreover, a similar kind of defensiveness is likely to be found, as is a similar unwillingness to abandon their tradition in the face of new problems. The differences between the two are nonetheless profound, however, and can most easily be discussed in terms of the fundamental viewpoint from which each speaks. One gets the impression from Smith's earlier-cited discussion of the traditionalist editor of the Azhar journal that the traditionalist is out to defend and affirm his own tradition or culture at any price, using any arguments that come to hand, however subversive to that tradition they may turn out to be. What he is not interested in doing is changing that tradition or reforming it. The reformist, by contrast, is not so much concerned to defend the tradition as he is to change and reform it by a process of incorporation. In the interaction between his own tradition and the dominant culture, the traditionalist stands squarely in the camp of his own tradition, firing broadsides in the direction of the other, whereas the reformist may want to place himself within his own tradition but in fact has a foot in both camps. This being the case, the reformist's tone is often rather less strident than that of the traditionalist. His attitude toward aspects of the dominant culture is "yes, that is good, but we already have it ourselves when our tradition is properly interpreted," whereas that of the traditionalist is "no, that is not good, and what we already have ourselves is far better."

Another alternative which has similarities to both traditionalist and reformist consciousness (and especially to the latter) is what might be called revolutionary consciousness. Those with revolutionary consciousness polarize much more strongly against the colonizer than do reformists and have a much more cynical or skeptical view of the dominant culture, tending to see and to highlight its negative aspects. At the same time they carry the remythologizing of traditional culture even further than do reformists and develop a much more explicit ideology about the need for self-liberation from cultural oppression. The essence of revolutionary consciousness, then, might be seen as a dual process of demystification of the dominant other and a simultaneous remythologizing of one's own tradition.

In particular, that tradition is remythologized in terms of finding within it episodes and periods of heroic resistance to the dominant culture, episodes which are then interpreted in terms of their own ideology of struggle against the oppressor. For example, among colonized peoples revolutionary consciousness often takes the form of making the idea of the nation and, specifically, of nationalist (rather than merely xenophobic or traditional) resistance to the colonizer retroactive to precolonial times, and the entire colonial period is searched for evidence of revolutionary activity. A similar process can be seen in the emphasis among American blacks on slave revolts and uprisings and among feminists on reinterpretations of female behavior patterns like indirectness or (seeming) submissiveness as strategies of power rather than as signs of subordination.

The revolutionary attitude toward the dominant culture is that that culture purports to be superior but in fact is full of hypocrisy, lies, and exploitation. Thus there is nothing to be taken over because there is nothing worth taking. Whatever is needed can be found in the revolutionary's own culture once that culture is in fact rediscovered. Rediscovery is vitally necessary, however, since the dominant culture has tended to suppress and distort its most positive aspects and to hide them from view.

What the revolutionary seeks in the past, then, is quite different from what either the traditionalist or the reformist looks for, as is the viewpoint from which he seeks it. This process of demystification of the other and retroactive mythologizing about the self is absolutely central to the creation of a new community, a new consciousness, and a new society. It is thus a crucial stage in the process of self-liberation and a fascinating one to explore. Its predominant tone tends to be a mixture of rage and exaltation, of fury at the way one's consciousness has been distorted by internalized self-images of inferiority and backwardness and joy, relief, and enthusiasm as self and other are reinterpreted in ways that give the self a new sense of potential and worth.

But if this is the case, why then are there six rather than only five stages in the process of self-liberation? Why is revolutionary consciousness not sufficient to complete the process? There are several answers to be given. First of all, the revolutionary is still caught in a polarized dialectic with the still-dominant other. This can be seen, inter alia, from the strength of the need to debunk and demystify. Revolutionary consciousness is thus still engaged in a process of dethroning—it is not yet free to go its own way. Moreover, there is still a large element of defensiveness and touchiness present, often accompanied by a chip-on-the-shoulder attitude to the world. In addition, a very rigidly held ideology operates to explain the world in terms of rather simplistic and emotionally charged categories. One example among many is the so-called *prowoman line* developed by some American feminists in the 1970s. According to this view, expressed in slogans like "women are messed over, not messed up," there is nothing wrong with any woman except that she is being oppressed. All women are innocent and all men guilty. This kind of ideology may well be an emotional necessity at a particular stage in the process of self-liberation, but it hardly reflects completion of that process. What de Beauvoir says about women in *The Second Sex* applies equally well to revolutionaries in other oppressed groups:

> By aspiring to clear-sightedness women writers are doing the cause of women a great service; but—usually without realizing it—they are still too concerned with serving this cause to assume the disinterested attitude toward the universe that opens the widest horizons. When they have removed the veils of illusion and deception, they think they have done enough; but this negative audacity

leaves us still faced by an enigma, for the truth itself is ambiguity, abyss, mystery: once stated, it must be thoughtfully reconsidered, re-created. It is all very well not to be duped, but at that point all else begins [18].

What begins at that point is what I would call modernizing consciousness, a kind of consciousness which would feel genuinely free to forge new combinations of personality traits, life-styles, and ways of being without the need either to imitate the model of the European or white or male other or to refrain from seeming to do so; without the need either deliberately to perpetuate previous forms of one's blackness or femaleness or Arabness or else to reject anything having a resemblance to those forms; and without the need for approval by or fear of being judged by the male or white or European other. The quote from de Beauvoir expresses beautifully the gap that exists between this kind of consciousness and the best that any culturally oppressed group qua group has been able to achieve so far.

What makes it seem like a nonutopian possibility for groups in the future, however, is that one can find examples of individual blacks or women or homosexuals or formerly colonized people who seem to have achieved it. But even if that were not the case, it would still be necessary to discuss modernizing consciousness in considering the process of self-liberation from cultural domination, since it can be shown that genuine liberation is possible only on that basis. None of the other kinds of consciousness we have discussed heal the wound caused by the destruction of traditional consciousness. Only modernizing consciousness allows the individual to have that disinterested attitude toward the universe that opens the widest horizons and does not place ideological obstacles in the way of perception. Only modernizing consciousness allows the individual to affirm his ascriptive group identity without shame or defensiveness, while at the same time leaving him or her free to develop new ways of being that are relevant to contemporary problems.

Thus, the conceptual framework presented in this paper is composed of six stages, each of which represents a qualitatively different kind of consciousness in relationship to the problem of cultural liberation. The first, traditional consciousness, is that stage which is in a sense prior to the whole process. It is a stage in which liberation from cultural domination has not yet become problematic for the dominated group, either because the relationship of cultural domination has not yet been established or because it is so accepted as the way things are that it is not perceived as subject to change. Similarly, the sixth stage, that of modernizing consciousness, represents successful liberation. The other four stages—traditionalist, assimilationist, reformist, and revolutionary—are all partial and inadequate attempts to come to grips with the problem of perceived and internalized cultural domination. Their common characteristic is a kind of strident defensiveness and anxious touchiness foreign to the self-assurance and sense of self of both traditional and modernizing individuals. To say that the middle four stages are partial, inadequate, and emotively defensive, however, is not to suggest that all of them can be dispensed with along the way or that it is possible to step straight from traditional to modernizing consciousness. I know of no case in which that has occurred. Moreover, it is highly improbable on all sorts of grounds. It is as though both individuals and cultures are obliged to pass through a period of crisis, anguish, and psychic incoherence, once traditional consciousness has been destroyed, before coming once again to a sense of wholeness and connectedness within and without. As one Muslim theologian wrote concerning the shattering of the glass of traditional faith: "That is a breaking that cannot be mended, and a separating that cannot be united by any sewing or putting together, except it be melted in the fire and given another new form [19]."

Yet, while it is probably true that there is no possibility of skipping directly from traditional to modernizing consciousness, that does not mean that every individual in a given society passes through all six stages in relation to every aspect of cultural oppression. This is especially the case once the process of cultural domination and liberation is already underway in a society. First of all, the starting point of an individual who grows up in a group already subject to cultural domination by another group may well not be traditional. That is, he may grow up without ever having experienced the sense of security and unquestioning acceptance of the ways of one's own group that is the hallmark of traditional consciousness. Moreover, not all individuals or groups manage to achieve modernizing consciousness and remain stuck in one or another less productive dialectic between self and other. Furthermore, some individuals may remain traditional while others become traditionalists and still others opt for an assimilationist stance. Thus it is likely that, at various times, the group in question will display a range of responses, conceivably ranging from traditional individuals to those with modernizing consciousness. As we shall see, that is certainly the case in the example we shall be considering, namely, male-female relations in contemporary Algeria.

Part II

In contrast to other areas of life, traditional patterns of male-female relations in Algeria were relatively little disrupted by French colonialism. Even though (like other areas of life) they became politicized in the context of the dialectic between colonizer and colonized, the patterns themselves continued to function without much change. Both for this reason and because it was an area of life into which the colonizer could not penetrate directly, the realm of male-female relations and the family became a bastion and a refuge. It was also the one area in which the colonized male could freely dominate others without being himself dominated in turn by the colonizer. Moreover, the family during the colonial period continued to be the major institution of socialization into Muslim culture, especially since much of this socialization was done by women who themselves led very restricted lives that did not bring them into contact with the dominant culture. For both of these reasons, because it was less subject to direct disruption and because it offered a haven from colonial domination, the family perpetuated traditional patterns of male-female relations and traditional consciousness about those relations.

Nonetheless, traditional consciousness in this realm was undermined by the interaction with the dominant other for two major reasons: first, it was clear that the traditional Muslim patterns of male-female relations (including polygamy, very early marriage, easy divorce for the man, and the veil) elicited contempt and derision from the colonizer, making some justification of those patterns to the self increasingly necessary, and, second, because it was those patterns, especially polygamy, which were cited by the French as the major reason why Algerians could not be granted French citizenship and political participation. There is also a third reason whose weight is more difficult to assess: the effects of Algerian exposure to French patterns of male-female relations. There is no doubt that Algerians were shocked by and strongly disapproved of some of the freedoms available to French women, however, it seems clear that, at least in some circles, there was an attraction as well.

Whatever the relative weight of the various factors, they operated jointly to undermine the major aspect of traditional consciousness: its unquestioning acceptance of traditional patterns as the only possible way to do things [20]. Traditional consciousness was probably replaced by traditionalist consciousness for most of the population in the first instance, but other patterns emerged as well. Among males, assimilationist consciousness was least evident; indeed, it is not at all clear that unmixed assimilationist consciousness developed at all even among those *evolues* who so eagerly embraced other aspects of French civilization. There was some intermarriage between *evolues* and European women, but the education and social level of the women was often below that of their husbands, a fact which would tend to make easier the perpetuation of male dominance within the household. Reformist consciousness was rather more prevalent, although perhaps not as much in this as in other realms of life. It was typically a position advocated by men, leading Tillion to remark that in Muslim countries feminism is a male affair [21]. Reformist consciousness is certainly not feminist in any very far-reaching sense and her remark is thus misleading. She is nonetheless right in saying that in many Muslim countries the theoretical arguments in favor of reforming Muslim practice in the realm of male-female relations were advanced by men: Emir Khalid in Algeria [22], Qasim Amin in Egypt, and Tahar al-Haddad in Tunisia, for example. This is not surprising given men's greater access to education and contact with the culture of the colonizer. It is also not surprising that men should be the main representatives of reformist consciousness for two additional reasons: first, reformist consciousness is by its very nature most likely to be found among those who have been thoroughly educated in Islamic law and culture and at the same time exposed to Western influence. Such education was normally open only to men. Second, reformist consciousness, by wanting to purify the tradition, takes that tradition very seriously as something of value to be reinterpreted for modern life. It is thus concerned with male-female relations, not directly and in themselves, but rather as they reflect the (rightly interpreted and purified) Koranic prescriptions for relationships between the sexes. Women, by contrast, have tended to be more directly concerned with male-female relations in and of themselves in terms of the possibilities of freedom and self-expressions they permit to women.

Algerian male revolutionary consciousness toward male-female relations does not share the concern of reformist consciousness with purifying or reinterpreting the tradition. Instead emphasis is placed, not on the content of the tradition, but rather on its function as a symbol of identity and pride vis-a-vis the dominant culture. What this meant in practice in relation to male-female relations was that the revolutionaries lauded women and the family for having preserved and passed on the Algerian cultural heritage, accused the French of having tried to corrupt and undermine that heritage, and stressed the need to build a modern society on Islamic bases or along Arabo-Islamic lines as part of the revolutionary desire to break the deeply ingrained equation of European with modern and Algerian or Muslim with backward. This pull in two opposed directions—toward reassertion of the (remythologized) tradition, on the one hand, and toward the creation of a modern, developed society on the other—is at the heart of the revolutionary's dilemma, a dilemma that has proved to be particularly painful in the realm of male-female relations.

The differences among Algerian males in terms of kinds of consciousness can be illustrated in brief compass by discussing the changing meaning of a single symbol, namely, the veil. For the traditional Muslim the veil symbolizes feminine modesty, women as sexual threat and temptation, as weak and amoral, and as impure and dangerous to man. It functions as part of the internal nexus of symbols, customs, and patterns of behavior that operate within the traditional Islamic system. For the traditionalist that meaning remains, but added to it is the defensive assertion of the traditional way of life against colonialist inroads. It thus comes to function as part of the dialectic between self and other. For those of assimilationist consciousness it is equally part of that dialectic, but is seen as a symbol of backwardness and degradation of women and as something to be eliminated in favor of European styles of dress. For the reformist the emphasis is once again on the meaning and function of the veil within the Muslim community, and the tendency is to retain it while fundamentally reinterpreting its meaning. Instead of stressing women's untrustworthiness and dangerous sexuality (and therewith the veil's function as a protection for men), the reformist stresses respect for women and the freedom it gives them from unwelcome advances (and therewith its function as a protection for women). Since this reinterpretation takes place in the context of reformist discussions of Islam's provision for appropriate equality between the sexes, it seems clear that it reflects the attempt to incorporate into Islam a modified version of Western ideology on male-female relations. Thus, for traditionalist, assimilationist, and reformist alike the veil as a symbol becomes politicized as part of the dialectic of cultural domination. At the same time, however, its traditional complex of connotations is reacted to and either approved, disapproved, or modified through reinterpretation. For the revolutionary, however, the traditional meaning of the veil tends to be forgotten or submerged, and only its function as a symbol of cultural separateness and integrity is stressed.

But so far we have spoken primarily of Algerian males. What of the women? How did they respond to the undermining of traditional consciousness? Here two things are crucial for understanding the different response of women. First, it must be recognized that women experience more repression, restriction, and denial of opportunity and less freedom, dominance, and status under the traditional Muslim system of male-female relations than do men. Thus they have less reason for commitment to the tradition and more reason to want to change it. Secondly, whereas male-female relations are only one aspect of the Algerian man's life, they both shape the totality of the woman's life and constitute a far larger proportion of it. Thus, male-female relations are in a sense of more direct and immediate relevance to women, and whatever dissatisfactions they entail are likely to be more deeply experienced by them.

The differences to be found between male and female responses are not surprising when viewed from this perspective. In the most general terms they could be expressed as follows: the overall consciousness of Algerian males is traditionalist, and very few show any signs of being willing to give up the privileged position associated with traditional male dominance. There is a sense of nostalgia and of affection for the traditional patterns. Nonetheless, on some problems (education of girls, for example), nontraditionalist policies may be adopted by individuals or groups (including the government) for one or both of two reasons: first, because considerations relevant to concerns other than male-female relations take primacy (the desire for cadres for economic development, for example), or, second, because the incompatibility between the specific action (educating a daughter, marrying an educated girl) and the perpetuation of traditionalist patterns of male-female relations is not clearly recognized. There is some desire to have one's cake and eat it too by taking some of the benefits offered by changing the traditional patterns, but great resistance to giving up the perceived benefits to males inherent in those patterns. Where consciousness is not traditionalist it tends to be at best reformist.

By contrast, the primary concern of a growing number of Algerian females is probably to escape from particular aspects of the traditional patterns that restrict their lives and curb their freedom. They want to be allowed to continue their education instead of being withdrawn from school when they reach puberty, to have a say in choosing their husbands rather than being married off by their parents, they want to have some freedom to come and go, and some, in addition, want the opportunity to work at a career or job that will provide some measure of independence and some contact with the modern world [23]. What they aspire to corresponds more closely to patterns of male-female relations in European than in traditional Muslim culture. But their outlook is not primarily oriented to the dialectic between Muslim and European culture or to adopting European models. Rather it is oriented to the internal dialectic between themselves and Algerian males.

What complicates the situation, however, is that the dialectic between Algeria and Europe continues to operate and creates an ambivalence or uncertainty with respect to action for change. To cite only one example of this kind of ambivalence, the woman committed to building a modern society on Arabo-Islamic bases as part of the revolutionary dialectic with the European other, may feel vulnerable to charges that she is betraying the Algerian heritage or aping Frenchwomen if she tries to change the patterns of male-female relations that operate in her life. The situation for most Algerian males is one in which they would like to maintain traditional patterns of male-female relations, but are forced by the need to build a modern society to move reluctantly and, in part, unconsciously toward modifying those patterns. For a growing number of Algerian women the situation is one in which they are eager to change the traditional patterns, but are somewhat inhibited in doing so by the internal psychic ambivalence created by the desire to affirm the Algerian heritage and culture.

Let us now see how the general schema we have presented can be applied to a series of concrete problems in the realm of male-female relations. In the area of political rights women were granted full legal and formal equality with men in voting, party membership, and candidacy for office. Thus they attained, on the formal plane, rights which it took European and American women decades of bitter struggle to attain. In actual practice, however, a variety of obstacles continue to exist. Given the novelty of such political participation for women, a good deal of active propaganda and encouragement by the government and party would have been necessary to foster female involvement. While some efforts have been made in this direction, they were rather limited in scope [24]. At the same time, some males, particularly those in the lower echelons of the party, have refused to let women join local party cells, telling them to go instead to the women's organization, the *Union Nationale des Femmes Algeriennes* (referred to hereafter as UNFA) [25]. Another indication of women's difficulty in achieving actual equality in political participation, of course, is their gross underrepresentation in the government, the parliament, and the higher party cadres, as well as the generally subservient and acquiescent role played by UNFA vis-a-vis the government. Nonetheless, the formal commitment to equality is of great symbolic importance and should not be underrated. It appears to stem from two major sources, neither of which are directly oriented to male-female relations: first, the crucial role played by women during the struggle for independence and, second, (and probably more importantly) the fact the granting of equal political rights to citizens of both sexes had by 1962 become part of the fundamental concept of a modern polity.

In terms of economic rights and opportunities women have been affected by a combination of traditionalist views about women's place being in the home and, perhaps more importantly, by the staggering rate of unemployment in postindependence Algeria. The position of most men, including President Haouri Boumedienne in his speech on International Women's Day in 1966, has been that men should receive first priority in jobs. Many of the women active in UNFA and the party have sharply disagreed, however, as can be seen from the fact that part of the audience left during Boumedienne's speech to show their disapproval of what he had said [26]. Since it is the case that the war of independence left many women widowed and needing to support themselves and their children, the suggestion that priority in jobs be given to men clearly reflects male prejudice rather than being simply a rational priority derived from objective conditions [27]. Traditionalist prejudice is even more strongly rooted outside governmental circles. Men typically do not want their wives to work and try to restrict their daughters to jobs that do not bring them into contact with men [28].

The area of education is perhaps the one in which the government has taken the most modernizing position, devoting a great deal of the national budget to education and getting large numbers of girls into the schools [29]. Government and party leaders have also sharply attacked those who have objected to girls' participation in gymnastics and other athletic activities [30]. This attitude to education can perhaps be explained on two main grounds: first, the regime recognizes the necessity and desirability of educating the next generation in order to create a modern society, and, second, at least at the level of primary school (where the major push has been undertaken) girls have not yet reached the age where complications arise concerning puberty, marriage, and the like. Education is thus a prime case in which the government acts indirectly to change male-female relations because of its dedication to social change in other respects.

In that sense, political rights, economic opportunities, and access to education can be grouped together as areas which are perceived both as only indirectly related to male-female relations and as areas in which the goals of development and modernity dictate the according of greater (if not yet equal rights to women.

The case is quite different, however, when we come to matters that touch more directly on male-female relations both inside and outside the context of the family. These matters are also what might be called women's issues since they are of particular importance to women as well as being relevant to the society as a whole. Whereas political rights, economic opportunities, and access to education affect women's possibilities for autonomy and self-development profoundly but at a further remove, these matters are part of the intimate substance of interpersonal relations between the sexes. Three of them will be considered here: dress, marriage and divorce law, and birth control.

The matter of dress has been of great symbolic importance in postindependence Algeria. Many letters to the editor have taken sides for or against clothing associated with European fashions, in particular the miniskirt [31]. Here, in contrast to the Tunisian government which has encouraged women to unveil and to adopt modern dress, the Algerian government, particularly since the overthrow of Ben Bella in 1965, has tended to take a conservative position on the issue. Thus in his speech to the first National Congress of UNFA, President Boumedienne referred to the "false problem of the suppression of the veil" only in order to urge his listeners to transcend this merely formal problem. Algerian women, he assured them, already had all of their rights, and the veil was neither here nor there [32]. His regime failed to show an equal neutrality on the other side, however, and in 1967 the police rounded up girls whose skirts were considered to be too short and painted their legs with mercurochrome from the knee to the skirt hem [33]. What is at stake here clearly goes very deep, as controversies in our own society over hair length, unisex, and the like indicate. Dress is a very important expression of attitude and life-style, and it is thus not surprising that it has received attention from would-be revolutionary leadership in a number of cases—Turkey and China, for example. The position of the Algerian leadership on this issue is indicative of their underlying attitudes. Those attitudes would seem to be a combination of revolutionary puritanism, conservative morality, and a suspicion of female emancipation in this realm.

Similar attitudes have been shown on the question of reform of the code of family law concerning marriage and divorce. The project for a new law that was circulated in 1967 has been extensively analyzed in a book by M'Rabet [34]. The project, while making certain modifications in traditional Islamic marriage and divorce law, remains squarely within the traditional Islamic cadre in its overall orientation and major provisions. Thus, for example, polygamy is not prohibited but merely made more difficult; a woman must still have a matrimonial tutor who consents to her marriage for her; divorce is still much easier for the man than for the woman, although its traditional arbitrariness is sharply curbed; and the man is explicitly recognized as the head of the family. In that capacity his wife is legally bound to show him both deference and obedience. While in the political, economic, and educational realms the obstacles to women's emancipation are private and social rather than public and legal, in the realm of marriage and divorce the law itself perpetuates a situation of grave inequality and disadvantage for the woman. This realm, like that of dress, seems to be an area in which no overriding reasons intervene to prevent the expression of male traditionalism.

The area of birth control and family planning would at first sight seem to fit this pattern, but in fact it apparently does not. Very little has been done in the way of developing family planning services in Algeria; indeed, there was not even any discussion of the subject during the first few years after independence. Since 1965 there have been cautious discussions and a few model clinics have been set up, but no large-scale program has been undertaken. This inaction occurred in the face of a rate of population increase that is one of the highest in the world, in a country in which unemployment, lack of educational facilities, and the like mean that not even the existing population can be accommodated without massive emigration to France [35]. The reason for the inaction is apparently not to be found in Muslim traditionalism, however, but rather in the anti-Malthusian orientation typical of Marxists. According to this view, the problem is not to limit population; it is to develop the productive resources of the country. An example of how this view affects official Algerian attitudes toward family planning can be seen in a speech given by Dr. Nefissa Laliam, the President of UNFA and herself a physician. The first part of her speech is a compelling presentation of all of the reasons why family planning would seem to be highly necessary and desirable in the Algerian context. Having made this convincing case, however, she then goes on to say that no decision about the necessity for planning can be made until investigations into the potential productive resources of the country have been completed [36]. Thus in this area it is modern ideology rather than traditionalist prejudice which is the major obstacle to providing women with control over their own reproductivity—a sine qua non of genuine liberation.

This example demonstrates the necessity of investigating the particular factors operating in each case rather than assuming that they can be deduced from a general framework of categories or from generalizations about the overall orientation of particular groups or individuals. Nonetheless, the framework proposed in this paper does serve an important function in helping to clarify the nature of what is at stake in particular problem areas by connecting them to the more general ideological context in which they take place.

Conclusion

This paper has attempted to do two things: to present a general framework for the analysis of the dialectic between self and other in situations of cultural domination, and to analyze the situation with regard to male-female relations in postindependence Algeria, in terms of the general orientation of males and females and in terms of governmental and individual positions on a range of important problems. In no sense was either of the two done exhaustively, nor indeed was that the purpose of the enterprise. The purpose was rather to indicate briefly some of what can be done with such a framework in the hope that others will be encouraged to undertake their own investigations along these lines. The framework I have presented is certainly in need of further refinement and development. Indeed, it may even turn out to be unworkable as a general model when tested against a wider universe of cases. But even if that turns out to be the case, the framework will have served a useful purpose if it stimulates further work on the problem of the politics of cultural liberation.

NOTES

1. The lengths to which this sense of inferiority can go were brought to my attention recently in a conversation with Badi Foster, a Ph.D. candidate at Princeton, whose work on Morocco will add much to our knowledge of the problem of cultural identity. In Morocco, he pointed out, whatever is European in dress, in life-style, and the like is considered civilized, whereas whatever is Moroccan is thought of as savage or uncivilized.

2. Sally Kempton, "Cutting Loose," *Esquire*, p. 57, July 1970.

3. For example, Naomi Weisstein, "Woman as Nigger," *Psychology Today* (Oct. 1969). Charles J. Levy, "ARUN as Faggots: Inverted Warfare in Vietnam," *"Trans-Action,* **8,** No. 12, pp. 18–27 (October 1971).

4. As I have discovered since initially developing the framework presented in this article, others have used terms similar to those I thought I was coining. For example, David Gordon speaks in *The Passing of French Algeria.* London: Oxford University Press, 1966, p. 21, of assimilationists and traditionalists. What others have not done to my knowledge, however, is to develop these

concepts in the context of a comparative, process-oriented study of the development of political consciousness that includes women, blacks, and homosexuals, as well as colonized peoples.

5. There is, moreover, some doubt as to whether general theory ever emerges from masses of monographic literature in the way that those who urge the postponement of generalizing apparently assume. It seems at least as likely that trees will function to obscure the forest as that tree-by-tree perusal will eventually constellate it. Research in Gestalt psychology lends support to the view that the perception of meaningful wholes is a primary rather than secondary perceptual process.

6. See my "Algeria: A Case Study of the Requirements of Revolutionary Transformation," *Proceedings of the 1967 Princeton University Conference on North Africa*, forthcoming; and "The Liberation of Women in Tunisia, Algeria, and Egypt," a paper prepared for presentation to the 1971 Annual Meetings of the Middle East Studies Association. A preliminary sketch of the framework presented in the present paper was set forth in my "The Politics of Cultural Liberation: A Comparative Study of Algerian Nationalism and American Feminism," a paper prepared for presentation to the HEW-sponsored Institute, Women: Crisis in Higher Education, Pittsburgh, June 1971.

7. For further discussion of this point see Joseph Campbell, *The Masks of God: Occidental Mythology*. New York: Viking Press, 1964.

8. Rama Mehta, *The Western Educated Hindu Woman*. New York: Asia Publishing House, 1970, pp. 16–32.

9. Wilfred C. Smith, *Islam and Modern History*. New York: Mentor, 1957, pp. 127–37.

10. For additional examples see Elizabeth Fernea, *Guests of the Sheik: An Ethnograph of an Iraqi Village*. New York: Doubleday-Anchor Books, 1969.

11. See Clifford Geertz, *Islam Observed: Religious Development in Morocco and Indonesia*. New Haven: Yale University Press, 1968, e.g., pp. 17–19.

12. This terminology comes from Manfred Halpern, a colleague from whose work on modernization I have learned much of relevance to the present theme. Indeed, those who know Halpern's work will have no trouble seeing the types of consciousness proposed in this paper as relevant to Halpern's discussion of Emanation in his forthcoming book, *The Dialectics of Transformation in Politics, Personality and History*.

13. Halpern, *The Dialectics of Transformation*, op. cit., pp. 137–61.

14. *Ibid.*, p. 151.

15. Perhaps this is as good a place as any to mention briefly the enormous problems raised by the structure of our language for discussions of this kind. People do not adopt a particular kind of consciousness—least of all by surveying the range of choices and picking the one they want. Rather, there is a large component of unconscious unintendedness. It would thus be more accurate in some ways to speak of *finding oneself with* rather than *adopting* a kind of consciousness. Consciousness is itself a term that is difficult to use sensibly and consistently, and there is always the danger that it will come to be used (or at least sound as though it is being used) as a pseudo-explanatory label rather than as a concept that illuminates the relationship between the individual and his world. (To say, for example, that so-and-so did such-and-such because he has traditionalist consciousness sounds, on one level, like an essentialist pseudo-explanation, although it may well be at the same time a useful shorthand.) I have certainly not been able to avoid these problems in the present article (and indeed it may not be possible to do so entirely). I need therefore to beg the reader's indulgence and hope that I have been able nonetheless to communicate my meaning in spite of linguistic obstacles.

16. See Carolyn Bird, *Born Female: The High Cost of Keeping Women Down*. New York: McKay, 1970.

17. This is particularly true in matters of dress, personal appearance, and the like, and can

be seen, for example, in the adoption by American blacks of this persuasion of white standards of beauty (straightening hair, dying skin, etc.), as well as in the adoption among formerly colonized peoples of the miniskirt. The important point, of course, is not what is done, but in what spirit and for what motives it is done.

18. Simone de Beauvoir, *The Second Sex.* New York: Knopf, 1968, pp. 709–10.

19. Al Ghazzali, *Al Munqidh min al-dalal (Preservation from Error),* cited by Manfred Halpern, *The Politics of Social Change in the Middle East and North Africa.* Princeton, N.J.: Princeton University Press, 1963, p. 31.

20. I know of no material which would shed light on at what stage or under what circumstances traditional consciousness about male-female relations began to give way. It is certainly clear in the postindependence period, however, that traditional consciousness has been thoroughly undermined.

21. Germaine Tillion, *Le Harem et les Cousins.* Paris: Editions du Seuil, 1966, p. 211 n. 1. She makes this remark in the context of discussing the support for traditional patterns given by older Algerian women who have finally achieved a position of some power, status, and dominance within the traditional system.

22. J. P. Charnay, *La Vie Musulmane en Algerie d'Apres la Jurisprudence de la Premiere Moitie du XXe Siecle.* Paris: Presses Universitaires de France, 1965, p. 64 n. 1.

23. Abundant evidence for this assertion is provided by Fadela M'Rabet in her accounts of girls' desire for education, attempts to avoid arranged marriages, and longing for greater freedom and contact with the world. *Les Algeriennes.* Paris: Librairie Francois Maspero, 1967, pp. 81–112.

24. See the article by Nefissa Bensaadi, "La femme doit remplir son devoir de citoyenne," *El Moudjahid* (May 24, 1969).

25. For illuminating examples of this obstructionism see M'Rabet, *Les Algeriennes, op. cit.,* pp. 235–37.

26. David Gordon, *Women of Algeria: An Essay on Change.* Cambridge, Mass: Harvard University Press, 1968, p. 77.

27. For a discussion of women in the labor force see M'Rabet, *Les Algeriennes, op. cit.,* pp. 144–64.

28. See Flora Lewis, "No Revolution for the Woman of Algiers," *The New York Times Magazine* (Oct. 29, 1967).

29. For statistics see M'Rabet, *Les Algeriennes, op. cit.,* pp. 168–93.

30. Gordon, *Women of Algeria, op. cit.,* pp. 76–77.

31. For examples see M'Rabet, *Les Algeriennes, op. cit.,* pp. 27–29.

32. *UNFA, Bulletin Interieur,* report on the first UNFA National Congress held on 19–23 Nov. 1966, p. 4.

33. Lewis, "No Revolution," *op. cit.,* p. 28.

34. See M'Rabet, *Les Algeriennes, op. cit.,* pp. 241–80.

35. For figures see *ibid.,* pp. 208–19.

36. Nefissa Laliam, "Le Planning Familial," a speech given to UNFA in Algiers on April 14, 1968 and printed by UNFA.

Bibliography

Mary Cornelia Porter

None of the occupations which manage a city belongs to women because they are women or to men because they are men, for natural capacities are distributed similarly among both sexes.

PLATO [1]

It has been a freakish aspect of American political science which both as theory and descriptive thinking tends . . . to thought of the male only as a factor in the state . . . Nearly all the textbooks on government, . . . beyond reporting that women now have the vote in the United States, . . . pay little or no attention to what women have done with the vote, to their political agitations, to their work in government as administrators and judges.

MARY BEARD [2]

The bibliography, selective rather than definitive, is meant to serve a dual purpose. First, it should provide evidence that women's studies are a legitimate scholarly pursuit and have a valid place in the political science curriculum. As a professional as well as general interest in female political participation increases, Mary Beard's indictment loses much of its sting. She would have been pleased.

Second, the bibliography represents a preliminary effort to impose some order upon, and supply a frame of reference for, the existing and the rapidly growing body of literature—academic, journalistic and popular, concerned with women and politics. That which has been listed might be described in this way. (a) Research, some if it as yet unpublished, which is consciously directed toward exploring, defining, and understanding the political aspects of the status of women. This would include, for example, papers which have been presented at the last few annual meetings of the American Political Science Association (some of which appear in this volume), and publications such as Gruberg's *Women in Politics* and Lamson's *Few are Chosen*. On

343

the whole, the titles of the works themselves reveal what should fall within this category. (*b*) Published works about women, but not primarily about politics, which illuminate facets of political life. Examples would be the Lash books about Eleanor Roosevelt; biographies of Emma Goldman, Mary Lease, Margaret Sanger and Ida Tarbell, and the depiction (Smith, *When the Cheering Stopped*) of Mrs. Woodrow Wilson as acting President during her husband's long and incapacitating illness. (*b*) Political studies, only peripherally concerned with women, but which illustrate their political, legal, economic, or social status. Among these would be Engels's treatise on capitalism, *Origins of the Family, Private Property and the State;* Odegaard's pioneering and classical case study of a pressure group, *The Story of the Anti-Saloon League;* Mason's account, in "The Case of the Overworked Laundress," of the development and judicial acceptance of the "Brandeis brief" and along with it, of the principles of sociological jurisprudence; and histories of the activities of the Women's International League for Peace and Freedom in which Jane Addams was a moving force.

The headings under which the material is listed have been determined by what is available and by a concern to stay within the parameters of what is political [3]. While some works might be more properly assigned to the other branches of the social sciences or the humanities, they have been included because they relate to politics. So, while Bird's *Born Female* is devoted to women's economic status, the problems discussed do, of necessity, raise questions of public policy. And while *Mont St. Michel and Chartres* (art, religion, medieval history) and "The Liberation of Men and Women" (philosophy, psychology, economics, education) are widely divergent in other ways, Adams, Drews, and Lipson all suggest that women are, or could be, a humanizing element in political life, unwilling (or less willing, perhaps, than men) to utilize power for destructive ends.

The bibliography itself is characterized by three factors. The first, and most obvious, is the meagerness in some, and the richness in other, areas. (What, indeed, is there to say about women and the American presidency?) However, as the literature continues to expand, we should expect to see more studies under the other headings, Political Anthropology, for instance, and International Relations.

The reasons for the heavy concentration of material under other headings are self-explanatory, and need only passing mention. Since Marx and Marxists made connections between economic and political exploitation on the one hand, and sexism on the other, they have provided an analysis of sexual oppression which has been refined by the theoreticians of the so-called radical feminist movement [4]. The listings under Legal Status of Women, which are merely representative of a burgeoning literature, attest to women's inequality in the eyes of the law and efforts made, with varying degrees of success, to seek redress in legislatures and the courts. And, since it is in state and local government and politics that women have participated most actively and experienced (thus far) the greatest electoral success, this continues to be a fruitful field of investigation.

A second characteristic of the material presented in the bibliography is that much of the recent research employs the tools of the political scientists' trade and draws upon earlier studies and ideas. A veritable storehouse of information and data, gathering dust for all these years, has been subject to analyses which have provided fresh insights into the campaigns for women's suffrage (Grimes, *The Puritan Ethic and Women's Suffrage;* Morgan, *Suffragists and Democrats).* The work of the Survey Research Center of the University of Michigan [5] has been expanded to indicate that another look should be taken at female voting patterns—as the educational levels of women rise, so does their political participation (Lansing, "Sex Differences in Voting and Activism"). The Center's concept of political efficacy has been utilized to study the political attitudes of a group of young mothers (Lynn and Flora, "Child-bearing and Political Participation"); and to identify the factors which, from early childhood on, motivated Congresswomen Green and Hanson to pursue their successful political careers (Rosenberg, "Political Efficacy and Sex Roles"). Students of political socialization have noted that boys are more politicized than girls [6]. However, a Seattle project suggests that if children were questioned about micro rather than macropolitics, we might discover that girls are more sensitive (than boys to the) power relationships of home, school, and neighborhood. Then, perhaps, it will be possible to lay to rest the tired myths about women's political interests and abilities (Iglitzin, "Sex Typing and Politicization in Children's Attitudes"). Some work signifies that the status of women may be useful as a unit for the comparative analysis of given political systems—much in the way that the electoral, legislative, or societal arrangements of various countries are compared (Boals, "A Comparative Study of the Development of Political Consciousness"; Milburn, "Cross-National Comparison of Women's Legal Status") [7]. And last, but far from least, Amundson, in *The Silenced Majority,* has drawn upon theorists of democracy as diverse as Madison, Jefferson, Mill, Dewey, and Dahl to warn that the very survival of democracy, however defined, depends upon the political activation of women.

A third characteristic of the bibliography is the value of the material, whether intended or not, as a means of viewing political institutions and processes. The various studies of women in Congress provide some useful discussions about the operations and power relationships of that body. A comparison of the activities, attitudes, and perceptions of men and women at national party nominating conventions sheds light upon what are often regarded as the peculiarities of these gatherings. Descriptions of the functions and roles of women in state, local, and precinct-level politics yield a considerable amount of detailed information about the infinite variety of political organizations and practices, formal and informal, which exist throughout the United States (Horbal, "Women in the DFL"; Segal, "Women in Political Parties"; Wells and Smeal, "Women's Attitudes Toward Women in Politics").

Which brings us back to where we started. If the study of women and politics can teach us something about political life, then, may this be, as it was for Plato, a professionally recognized subject of inquiry for men as well as for women. We may all be the better for it.

BIBLIOGRAPHY

General

MARY BEARD, *Women as a Force in History.* New York: Macmillan, 1946.

SIMONE DE BEAUVOIR, *The Second Sex.* New York: Knopf, 1953.

JUDITH HOLE and ELLEN LEVINE, *Rebirth of Feminism.* New York: Quadrangle, 1971.

KATE MILLET, *Sexual Politics.* Garden City, N.Y.: Doubleday, 1970.

Political Theory

General

HENRY ADAMS, *Mont St. Michel and Chartres.* Boston: Houghton Mifflin, 1905. Especially Chaps. 6, 10, and 11.

ELIZABETH DREW and LESLIE LIPSTON, "The Liberation of Women and Men," unpublished paper prepared for the National Conference of the American Association of Higher Education, Chicago, 1972.

RON CHRISTENSON, "Political Theory of Male Chauvinism: J. J. Rousseau's Paradigm," *Midwest Quart.,* **13,** 291–299 (April 1972).

EVA FIGES, *Patriarchal Attitudes.* New York: Stein and Day, 1970.

PENNY HERRICOURT, *A Woman's Philosophy of Woman; Or Woman Affranchised. An Answer to Michelet, Proudhon, Girardin, Legouve, Comte and other Innovators.* New York: Carleton, 1864.

SUSAN TANENBAUM, "Montesquie and Mme. de Stael: The Woman as a Factor in Political Analysis," *Political Theory* **1,** No. 1, 92–103 (Feb. 1973).

MARY WOLLSTONECRAFT, *A Vindication of the Rights of Women.* New York: Norton, 1967. Originally published in 1792.

Representative Democracy

KIRSTEN AMUNDSON, *The Silenced Majority.* Englewood Cliff, N.J.: Prentice-Hall, 1971.

CARL N. DEGLER, "Revolution Without Ideology: The Changing Place of Women in America," *Daedalus*, **93**, No. 2, 653–670 (Spring 1964).

BETTY FRIEDAN, "Our Revolution is Unique," in Mary Lou Thompson, ed., *Voices of the New Feminism.* Boston: Beacon, 1971.

GERDA LERNER, *The Grimke Sisters from North Carolina: Rebels against Slavery.* Boston: Houghton Mifflin, 1967.

DANIEL LEVINE, *Jane Addams and the Liberal Tradition.* State Historical Society of Wisconsin, 1971.

JOHN STUART MILL and HARRIET TAYLOR MILL, *Essays on Sex Equality,* with an introductory essay by Alice Rossi. Chicago: University of Chicago Press, 1971.

David Potter, "American Women and American Character," in J. Hogue, ed., *American Character and Culture,* DeLand, Fla.: Everett, 1964.

ALICE ROSSI, "Sex Equality: The Beginning of Ideology," in Mary Lou Thompson, ed., *Voices of the New Feminism,* Boston: Beacon, 1971.

ALICE ROSSI, "Equality Between the Sexes: An Immodest Proposal," *Daedalus*, **93**, No. 2, 607–652 (Spring 1964).

Marxism and Socialism

FERDINAND AUGUST BEBEL, *Women and Socialism: Women in the Past, Present and Future.* New York: Socialist Literature, 1910.

CLARA COLON, *Enter Fighting: Today's Woman: A Marxist-Leninist View.* New York: New Outlook, 1970.

ROXANNE DUNBAR, "Female Liberation as a Basis for Liberation," in Mary Lou Thompson, ed., *Voices of the New Feminism.* Boston: Beacon, 1971.

MARX, ENGELS, LENIN, and STALIN, *The Woman Question.* New York: International, 1951.

SHULAMITH FIRESTONE, *The Dialectic of Sex: The Case for a Feminist Revolution.* New York: Morrow, 1971.

JULIETTE MITCHELL, "The Longest Revolution," *New Left Review*, 34–38 (Nov./Dec. 1966).

EVELYN REED, *Problems of Women's Liberation: A Marxist Approach.* New York: Merit, 1969.

Political Anthropology

LUCIAN CARR, "On the Social and Political Position of Women among the Huron-Iroquois Tribes," *Report of the Peabody Museum of American Archeology and Ethnology*, **3**, 207–232 (1880–1887).

FRIEDRICH ENGELS, *The Origins of Family, Private Property and the State.* New York: International, 1942. Originally published in 1842.

JOHN N. B. HEWITT, *Status of Women in Iroquois Polity Before 1784.* Washington: Smithsonian Inst. Annual Report, 1932.

LIONEL TIGER, *Men in Groups.* New York: Random House, 1969.

Comparative Politics

Sub-National

ELLA ANKER, *Women's Suffrage in Norway.* London: National Union of Women's Suffrage Societies, 1913.

KATHLEEN ARCHIBALD, *Sex and the Public Service: A Report to the Public Service Commission of Canada.* Ottawa: Queens Printer, 1971.

WILLIAM J. BLOUGH, "Political Attitudes of Mexican Women," *Jour. of Inter-Amer. Studies and World Affairs,* **14,** 201–224 (May 1972).

BERNADETTE DEVLIN, *The Price of My Soul.* New York: Knopf, 1969.

CLAUDIA DRIEFUS, "St. Joan of the Bogside: An Interview with Bernadette Devlin," *Evergreen Rev.,* **15,** 25–50 (July 1971).

PATRICIA GRIMSHAW, *Women's Suffrage in New Zealand.* Aukland: Aukland University Press, 1972.

ZIPORA KENNER, "Women in the Knesset," *Israel Magazine,* **3,** 74–78 (July/Aug. 1971).

AYSE KUDAT, "Political Views of Peasant Women: A Turkish Case," unpublished paper prepared for the Annual Meeting of the American Political Science Association, Washington, D.C., 1972.

WARD M. MORTON, *Woman Suffrage in Mexico.* Gainesville: University of Florida Press, 1962.

INGUNN NORDEVAL MEANS, "Political Recruitment of Women in Norway," *Western Poli. Quart.,* **25,** 491–521 (Sept. 1972).

INGUNN NORDEVAL MEANS, "Women in Politics: The Norwegian Experience," *Canadian Jour. of Poli. Sci.,* **5,** 365–388 (Sept. 1972).

MARION PHILLIPS, *Women and the Labour Party.* New York: Huebsch, 1918.

CONSTANCE ROVER, *Women's Suffrage and Party Politics in Britain 1866–1941.* London: Routledge Paul, 1967.

MADELEIN SIMMS, "The Abortion Act After Three Years," *Poli. Quart.* (Great Britain), **42,** 269–286 (Sept. 1971).

JACQUELINE VAN VORIS, *Constance de Marklevicz: In the Cause of Ireland.* Amherst: University of Massachusetts Press, 1967.

AUDREY WIPPER, "Equal Rights for Women in Kenya," *Jour. of Modern African Studies,* **9,** 429–442 (Oct. 1971).

Cross-National

JANE CHAPMAN, "Women's Policies and Programs in Western Countries," unpublished paper prepared for the Annual Meeting, American Political Science Association, New Orleans, 1973.

MARGARET COLE, "Woman's Vote: What Has it Attained?" *Poli. Quart.* (Great Britain and the United States), **33,** 74–83 (Jan. 1962).

FLOYD DELL, *Women as World Builders: Studies in Modern Feminism.* Chicago: Forbes, 1913.

MAURICE DUVERGER, *The Political Role of Women.* Paris: UNESCO, 1955.

MARTIN GRUBERG, "Official Commissions of the Status of Women: A World-wide Movement," unpublished paper prepared for the Annual Meeting, American Political Science Association, New Orleans, 1973.

SHIRLEY B. HENDSCH, "Issues and Trends in the Women's Movement in the West," unpublished paper prepared for the Annual Meeting, American Political Science Association, New Orleans, 1973.

JOYCE LADNER, "Tanzanian Women and Nation Building," *Black Scholar,* **3,** 22–29 (Dec. 1971).

ANNIE M. D. LEBEUF, "The Role of Women in the Political Organization of African Societies," in Denise Pauline, ed., *Women of Tropical Africa,* translated by H. M. Wright. Berkeley: University of California Press, 1963.

GRACE MACURDY, *Hellenistic Queens: A Study of Woman Power in Macedonia, Seleucid Syria, and Ptolemic Egypt.* Baltimore: Johns Hopkins Press, 1932.

ANNE MARTIN, "Political Methods of American and British Feminists," *Cur. Hist. Magazine of the N.Y. Times,* **20,** 396–401 (June 1924).

JOSEPHINE MILBURN, "Cross-National Comparison of Women's Legal Status," unpublished paper prepared for the Annual Meeting, American Political Science Association, New Orleans, 1973.

WILLIAM O'NEILL, *The Women's Movement: Feminism in the United States and England.* New York: Barnes and Noble, 1969.

RALPH PATAI, ed., *Women in the Modern World.* New York: Free Press, 1967.

ANN PESCATELLO, ed., *Female and Male in Latin America.* Pittsburgh: University of Pittsburgh Press, 1973.

MARY CORNELIA PORTER and COREY B. VENNING, "Church, State and Society: The Status of Women in Italy and the Republic of Ireland," unpublished paper prepared for the Annual Meeting, American Political Science Association, New Orleans, 1973.

SHEILA ROWBOTHAM, *Women, Resistance and Revolution: A History of Women and Revolution in the Modern World.* New York: Pantheon, 1972.

ROBERT SEDLER, "The Legal Dimension of Women's Liberation: An Overview," *Internat. Law Jour.*, **47**, 419–456 (Spring 1972).

Seminar on the Participation of Women in Public Life. New York: United Nations, 1960.

"Status of Women," *Amer. Jour. of Comparative Law*, **20** (Fall 1972).

SARA STAUFFER WHALEY, "A Cross-National Review of Studies on the Status of Women," unpublished paper prepared for the Annual Meeting, American Political Science Association, New Orleans, 1973.

"Women Around the World," *Annals of the Amer. Acad. of Poli. and Soc. Sci.*, **375** (January 1968).

International Relations

ARISTOPHANES, *Lysistrata.* New York: Caedmon, 1966.

JOHN WESLEY DEKAY, *Women and the New Social State.* Basel: Junger, 1918.

DOROTHY McCONNELL, *Women, War and Fascism.* New York: American League Against Fascism, 1935.

GEORGE LEE, "Rosa Luxemburg and the Impact of Imperialism," *The Economic Journal*, **81**, 847–862 (Dec. 1971).

MAY E. WRIGHT SEWALL, *Women, World War and Permanent Peace.* San Francisco: Newbigin, 1915.

EVELYN SULLEROT, *The Employment of Women and the Problems it Raises in the Member States of the European Community.* Luxembourg: Commission of the European Communities, undated.

American Government and Politics

Suffrage and the First Women's Movement, 1820–1920

JOHN WESLEY DEKAY, *Women and the New Social State.* Basel: Junger, 1918. Adaptability," *The Historian*, **33**, 264–279 (Feb. 1971).

ELEANOR FLEXNER, *Century of Struggle: The Woman's Rights Movement in the United States.* Cambridge: Belknap Press of Harvard University, 1959.

ALAN GRIMES, *The Puritan Ethic and Women's Suffrage.* New York: Oxford University Press, 1967.

JAMES J. KENNEALLY, "Catholicism and Women's Suffrage in Massachusetts," *Catholic Historical Rev.*, **53**, 43–57 (Apr. 1967).

AILEEN S. KRADITOR, *Ideas of the Women's Suffrage Movement, 1890–1920*. New York: Columbia University Press, 1965.

DAVID MORGAN, *Suffragists and Democrats: The Politics of Woman Suffrage in America*. Ann Arbor: University of Michigan Press, 1972.

WILLIAM O'NEILL, *Everyone Was Brave*. Chicago: Quadrangle, 1969.

Elected and Appointed Women

FLORENCE E. ALLEN, "Participation of Women in Government," *Annals of the Amer. Acad. of Poli. and Soc. Sci.*, **251**, 94–103 (May 1947).

NICHOLAS BABCHUCK, "Men and Women in Community Agencies: A Note on Power and Prestige," *Amer. Sociological Rev.*, **25**, 399–403 (June 1960).

FRANK T. COLON, "The Elected Women," *Soc. Studies*, **58**, 256–261 (Nov. 1967).

MARTIN GRUBERG, *Women in American Politics*. Oshkosh, Wisconsin: Academia, 1968.

PEGGY LAMSON, *Few Are Chosen: American Women in Political Life Today*. Boston: Houghton Mifflin, 1968.

CATHARINE PATRICK, "Attitudes about Women Executives in Government Positions," *Jour. of Psych.*, **19**, 3–34 (Feb. 1944).

Women in Public Service. Washington, D.C.: Women's Division, Republican National Committee, 1972. List of women in official capacities in the Republican party; women in Congress, past and current; women presidential appointees; women in the federal service; women in statewide elective and appointive positions.

Political Parties

CHARLES S. BULLOCK and P.L.F. HEYS, "Recruitment of Women for Congress: A Research Note," *Western Poli. Quart.*, **25**, 416–423 (Sept. 1972).

EDWARD COSTANTINI and KENNETH H. CRAIG, "The Social Background Personality and Political Careers of Female Party Leaders," *Jour. of Soc. Issues*, **28**, No. 2, 217–236 (1972).

CLAUDIA DREIFUS, "Women in Politics: An Interview with Edith Green," *Soc. Policy*, 16–22 (Jan./Feb. 1972).

KORYNE HORBAL, "Women in the DFL: Present but Powerless?" unpublished report by the state chairwoman of the Minnesota Democratic Farmer-Labor Party, Minneapolis, Minnesota, undated.

MARGUERITE J. FISHER, "Women in Political Parties," *Annals of the Amer. Acad. of Poli. and Soc. Sci.*, **251**, 87–93 (May 1947).

MARGUERITE J. FISHER and BETTY WHITEHEAD, "Women's Participation in National

Party Nominating Conventions: 1892–1914," *Amer. Poli. Sci. Rev.,* **38,** 895–903 (Oct. 1944).

GERMAINE GREER, "McGovern, The Big Tease," *Harper's,* **245,** 56–60 (Oct. 1972) Women and the 1972 Democratic Convention.

M. KENT JENNINGS and NORMAN THOMAS, "Men and Women in Party Elites: Social Roles and Political Resources," *Midwest Jour. of Poli. Sci.,* **4,** 469–492 (Nov. 1968).

PHYLLIS SEGAL, "Women and Political Parties: The Legal Dimension," *Monograph* (George Washington University Law Center), (January 1971).

RICHARD STILLER, *Queen of the Populists: The Story of Mary Elizabeth Lease.* New York: Crowell, 1970.

Political Participation and Voting Behavior

KIRSTEN AMUNDSON, *The Silenced Majority.* Englewood Cliffs, N.J.: Prentice-Hall, 1971. Chaps. 4 and 7.

EDWARD M. BENNETT and HARRIET M. GOODWIN, "Emotional Aspects of Political Behavior: The Woman Voter," *Genetic Psych. Monographs,* **58** (1958).

ALAN BOOTH, "Sex and Social Participation," *Amer. Sociological Rev.,* **37,** 183–193 (Apr. 1972).

MARJORIE LANSING, "Voting Patterns of American Black Women," unpublished paper prepared for the Annual Meeting, American Political Science Association, New Orleans, 1973.

MORRIS LEVITT, "The Political Role of American Women," *Jour. of Human Relations,* **15,** 23–35 (1st Quart. 1967).

MARIAN SANDERS, *The Lady and the Vote.* Boston: Houghton Mifflin, 1956.

SIDNEY M. SHALETT, "Is There a Woman's Vote?" *Sat. Evening Post,* **233,** 31–37 (Sept. 1960).

ANN SCOTT, *The Southern Lady: From Pedestal to Politics, 1830–1930.* Chicago: University of Chicago Press, 1970.

GLORIA STEINEM, "Women Voters Can't be Trusted," *MS.,* **1,** 47–51 (June 1972).

Political Sociology

Political Socialization

WARREN FARRELL, "The Resocialization of Men's Attitudes Toward Women's Role in Society," unpublished paper prepared for the Annual Meeting, American Political Science Association, Los Angeles, 1970.

FRED GREENSTEIN, "Sex Related Political Differences in Childhood," *Jour. of Politics,* **23,** 353–371 (1961).

ELINA HAAVIO-MANNILA, "Sex Roles in Politics," in Constantina Safilios-Rothschild, ed., *Toward a Sociology of Women*. Lexington, Mass: Xerox, 1972.

LYNNE B. IGLITZIN, "Political Education and Sexual Liberation," *Politics and Soc.*, **2**, No. 2, 241–254 (Winter 1972).

M. KENT JENNINGS and R. G. NIEMI, "The Division of Political Labor between Mothers and Fathers," *Amer. Poli. Sci. Rev.*, **65**, 69–82 (March 1971).

MARIE ROSENBERG, "Pre-electoral Socialization of Women in United States Politics: Case Studies of Congresswomen Edith Green and Julia Butler Hansen," unpublished paper prepared for the Annual Meeting, Western Political Science Association, 1971.

Political Efficacy

EARL KRUSCHKE, "Levels of Optimism as Related to Female Political Behavior," *Soc. Sci.*, **41**, 67–75 (Apr. 1966).

Public Opinion

"Daniel Ellsberg Talks about Women and War," *MS.*, 36–39 (Spring 1972).

HAZEL ERSKINE, "The Polls: Women's Role," *Pub. Opinion Quart.*, **35**, 275–290 (Summer 1971).

Interest Groups, Pressure Groups and Group Theory

PAMELA ALLEN, *Free Space: A Perspective on the Small Group in Women's Liberation*. New York: Times Change, 1970.

BERNARD BERELSON and PAUL F. LAZARSFELD, "Women: A Problem of the P.A.C.," *Pub. Opinion Quart.*, **9**, 79–82 (1945).

DOROTHY DETZER, *Appointment on the Hill*. New York: Holt, 1938. The Women's International League for Peace and Freedom.

JO FREEMAN, "The Origins of the Women's Liberation Movement," in Joan Huber, ed., *Changing Women in a Changing Society*. Chicago: The University of Chicago, 1973.

HELEN HACKER, "Women as a Minority Group," *Soc. Forces*, **30**, 60–69 (Oct. 1951).

INEZ H. IRWIN, *Up the Hill with Banners Flying*. Maine: Traversity, 1964. The Women's Party and the Equal Rights Amendment.

DOROTHY E. JOHNSON, *Organized Women and National Legislation 1920–1941*, unpublished doctoral dissertation, Western Reserve University, 1966.

AILEEN S. KRADITOR, ed., *Up from the Pedestal: Selected Writings from the History of American Feminism*. New York: Quadrangle, 1968.

NOW, *And Justice for All.* Chicago: NOW, 1972. Description of efforts of the National Organization of Women to persuade government agencies to enforce federal laws on sex discrimination.

PETER H. ODEGAARD, *Pressure Politics: The Story of the Anti Saloon League.* New York: Columbia University Press, 1928.

MARY H. ROBERTSON, "Constitutuional Revisions in Illinois. The League of Women Voters Role," *Nat. Civic Rev.,* **60,** 438–443 (Sept. 1971).

AILEEN D. Ross, "Control and Leadership in Women's Groups: An Analysis of Philanthropic Money Raising Activity," *Soc. Forces,* **37,** 124–131 (Dec. 1958).

JUDITH A. TURNER, "Washington Pressures: League of Women Voters Backs Study with Lobbying to Influence Policy," *Nat. Jour.,* **4,** 860–870 (May 20, 1972).

CELLESTINE WARE, *Woman Power: The Movement for Women's Liberation.* New York: Tower, 1970.

"Women's Liberation," *Annals of the Amer. Acad. of Poli. and Soc. Sci.,* **397** (Sept. 1971).

Constitutional Law

"Are Sex-based Classifications Constitutionally Suspect?" *Northwestern U. Law Rev.,* **66,** 481–501 (Sept./Oct. 1971).

JULIUS G. GETMAN, "The Emerging Constitutional Principle of Sexual Equality," in Philip B. Kurland, ed., *The Supreme Court Review, 1972.* Chicago: University of Chicago Press, 1973.

ALPHEUS THOMAS MASON, "The Case of the Overworked Laundress," in John A. Garraty, ed., *Quarrels That Have Shaped the Constitution.* New York: Harper and Row, 1966.

PAULI MURRAY and MARY EASTWOOD, "Jane Crow and the Law: Sex Discrimination and Title VII," *George Washington Law Rev.,* **34,** No. 2, 232–256 (1965). Contains discussion of the uses of the 14th Amendment to combat sex discrimination.

JOSEPH OTERI et al., "Abortion and the Religious Liberty Clauses," *Harvard Civil Rights Civil Liberties Law Rev.,* **7,** No. 3, 559–599 (May 1972).

The Equal Rights Amendment

BARBARA BROWN et al., "A Constitutional Basis for Equal Rights for Women," *Yale Law Jour.,* **80** (April 1970).

"Congress and the Equal Rights Amendment," *Cong. Dig.,* **50,** 1–32 (Jan. 1971).

"Equal Rights for Women: A Symposium on the Proposed Constitutional Amendment," *Harvard Civil Rights Civil Liberties Law Rev.*, **6**, No. 2, 215–289 (Mar. 1971).

Hearings on the Equal Rights Amendment, Subcommittee on Constitutional Amendments of the Committee on the Judiciary, U.S. Senate, on S.J. Res. 61, 2nd Session, 1970.

"The Equal Rights Amendment," *Women's Law Jour.*, **57** (Winter, 1971).

Legal Status of Women: Legislation, Common-Law and the Courts

MARTHA GRIFFITHS, "The Law Must Reflect the New Image of Women," *Hastings Law Jour.*, **23**, 1–14 (Nov. 1971).

MARTHA GRIFFITHS, "Women and Legislation," in Mary Lou Thompson, ed., *Voices of the New Feminism*. Boston: Beacon, 1970.

JOHN D. JOHNSON and CHARLES L. KNAPP, "Sex Discrimination by Law: A Study in Judicial Perspective," *New York University Law Rev.*, **46**, 675–747 (Oct. 1971).

LEO KANOWITZ, *Women and the Law: The Unfinished Revolution*. Albuquerque: University of New Mexico Press, 1969.

ROBERT S. MILLER, JR., "Sex Discrimination and Title VII of the Civil Rights Act of 1964," *Minn. Law Rev.*, **50**, 877–897 (Apr. 1967).

ROBERT D. MORAN, "Reducing Discrimination: The Role of the Equal Pay Act," in Nona and Waehrer Glazer-Malbin and Helen Youngelson, eds., *Women in a Man Made World: Socio-Economic Handbook*. Chicago: Rand McNally, 1972.

PAULI MURRAY, "The Rights of Women," in Norman Porsen, ed., *The Rights of Americans*. (New York: Random House, 1971).

"Symposium—Women and the Law," *Valparaiso Law Rev.* **5**, No. 2 (Summer, 1971).

JONATHAN WILCOX, "The Sex Discrimination Provisions of Title VII: A Maturing Controversy," *Pac. Law Jour.*, **3**, 37–62 (Jan. 1972).

The Federal System

HANS W. BLADE, "Marriage and Divorce in American Conflict Law," *Columbia Law Rev.*, **72**, 329–381 (Feb. 1972).

JOSEPH KENNEDY, "Sex Discrimination: State Protective Labor Laws Since Title VII," *Notre Dame Lawyer*, **42**, 514–549 (Feb. 1972).

The Equal Rights Amendment: How Would It Affect Wisconsin Statutes? Madison, Wis.: The Legislative Reference Bureau, 1971.

BARBARA YAFFE and BYRON YAFFE, "State Protective Legislation: An Anachronism under Title VII?" *Issues in Ind. Soc.*, **2**, No. 1, 54–61 (1971).

The Congress

BELLA ABZUG, *Bella! Ms. Abzug Goes to Washington.* New York: Saturday Review, 1972.

SHIRLEY CHISHOLM, *Unbought and Unbossed.* New York: Houghton Mifflin, 1971.

FRIEDA L. GEHLEN, "Women in Congress: Their Power and Influence in a Man's World," *Trans-action,* **6,** 36–40 (Oct. 1969).

FRANK GRAHAM, *Margaret Chase Smith: Woman of Courage.* New York: Day, 1964.

DAVID LITH, *A Long Way Forward: The Biography of Congresswoman Frances P. Bolton.* New York: Longmans Green, 1957.

ANNABEL PAXTON, *Women in Congress.* Richmond, Va.: Dietz, 1945.

MARRIGENE VAN HELDEN, *Women in Congresses of the United States.* Wash., D.C.: Library of Congress, 1968.

EMMY WERNER, "Women in Congress: 1917–1964," *Western Poli. Quart.,* **19,** 16–30 (Mar. 1966).

The Presidency and the Executive Branch

MARY ANDERSON, *Women at Work.* Minneapolis: University of Minnesota Press, 1951. Study of the Women's Bureau by its first director.

JOSEPH P. LASH, *Eleanor and Franklin.* New York: Norton, 1971. Parts III and IV.

"Majority of Americans Would Vote for a Woman for President," *Gallup Poll 1,* No. 74 (August 1971).

WILLIAM MARTIN, "Equal Employment Opportunities and Government Contracting: Three Theories for Obtaining Judicial Review of Executive Order 11246 Determinations," *Wis. Law Rev.,* **197,** No. 1, 133–152 (1972).

PAUL SEABURY, "HEW and the Universities," *Commentary,* **53,** 38–44 (Feb. 1972).

DAVID SENDLER, ed., "Helen Gurly Brown Predicts: What it Will Be Like When We Elect a Woman President," *Today's Health,* **49,** 26–31 (Dec. 25, 1971).

GENE SMITH, *When the Cheering Stopped.* New York: Morrow, 1964. Part III, Mrs. Woodrow Wilson.

Sex Discrimination and Contract Compliance. Washington, D.C.: American Council on Education, 1972.

Public Administration

HELEN MARKOFF, "The Federal Woman's Program," *Pub. Admin. Rev.,* **32,** 144–151 (Mar. 1972).

ANN SCOTT, "Feminism vs. the Feds," *Issues in Ind. Soc.,* **2,** No. 132, 32–46 (1971).

U.S. Civil Service Commission, *A Study of Employment of Women in the Federal Government.* Washington, D.C.: GPO, 1968.

"Women in Government: Interview with Six in Top Jobs," *U.S. News and World Report*, 62–69 (Jan. 1972).

Issues and Public Policy

Domestic

A Matter of Simple Justice: The President's Task Force on Women's Rights and Responsibilities (Washington, D.C.: GPO, 1970).

JANE ADDAMS, in *A Centennial Reader*, Emily Cooper Johnson, ed., *A Centennial Reader.* New York: Macmillan, 1971.

JESSIE BARNARD, *Women and the Public Interest: An Essay on Policy and Protest.* Chicago: Aldine, 1971.

CAROLYN BIRD, *Born Female: The High Cost of Keeping Women Down.* New York: McKay, 1968.

LUCINDA CISLER, "Abortion: A Major Battle is Over—But the War is Not," *Feminist Studies*, **1**, No. 2, 121–131 (Fall 1972).

Citizens Advisory Council on the Status of Women, *American Women.* Washington, D.C.: Department of Labor, 1968.

JOE H. DANZIGER, "Mandatory Maternity Leaves of Absence: An Equal Protection Analysis," *Temple University Quart.*, **45**, 240–258 (Winter 1972).

THOMAS C. DIENES, *Law, Politics and Birth Control.* Urbana: University of Illinois Press, 1972.

EMILY T. DOUGLAS, *Pioneer of the Future: Margaret Sanger.* New York: Holt, 1970.

ROBERT DRINNON, *Rebel in Paradise: A Biography of Emma Goldman.* Boston: Beacon, 1971.

KATE ELLIS, "The Politics of Day Care," in Roberta Salper, ed., *Female Liberation.* New York: Knopf, 1972.

ALICE FLEMING, *Ida Tarbell: First of the Muckrakers.* New York: Crowell, 1972.

MARJORIE H. FRIEDBURG and CAROL MILLSTROM, "Communal Child Care: Isolation or Constellation," *N.Y.U. Educational Quart.*, **3**, 6–11 (Spring 1972).

CAROL GLASSMAN, "Women and the Welfare System," in Robin Morgan, ed., *Sisterhood is Powerful.* New York: Vintage, 1970.

JUDITH HOLE and ELLEN LEVINE, *Rebirth of Feminism.* New York: Quadrangle, 1971. Chaps. 7 and 8.

DAVID KENNEDY, *Birth Control in America.* New Haven: Yale University Press, 1971.

HELEN MATTHEWS LEWIS, *The Woman's Movement and the Negro Movement: Parallel Struggle for Rights.* Charlottesville: University of Virginia Press, 1949.

MARGARET MEAD and FRANCES B. KAPLAN, eds., *American Women: Report of the President's Commission on the Status of Women and Other Publications of the Commission.* New York: Scribner's, 1965.

LEE RAINWATER and WILLIAM L. YANCEY, eds., *The Moynihan Report and the Politics of Controversy.* Cambridge, Mass.: MIT Press, 1967. Black matriarchy.

PAMELA ROBY, "Politics and Prostitution: A Case Study of the Revision, Enforcement and Administration of the New York Penal Laws on Prostitution," *Criminology,* **9,** 425–447 (Fall 1972).

MARGARET K. ROSENHEIM, "Shapiro v. Thompson: The Beggars are Coming to Town," in Philip B. Kurland, ed., *The Supreme Court Review 1969.* Chicago: University of Chicago Press, 1969. Rights of welfare recipients.

FLORENCE RUDERMAN, *Child Care and Working Mothers: A Study of Arrangements Made for Daytime Care of Children.* New York: Child Welfare League of America, 1968.

ROGER WERTHEIMER, "Understanding the Abortion Argument," *Phil. and Pub. Affairs,* **1,** 67–95 (Fall 1971).

Foreign

JANE ADDAMS, *Peace and Bread in Time of War.* New York: Macmillan, 1922. Women's International League for Peace and Freedom.

MIDGE DECTOR, "The Peace Ladies," in June Sochen, ed., *The New Feminism in Twentieth Century America.* (Lexington, Mass: Heath, 1971).

JOSEPH P. LASH, *Eleanor: The Years Alone.* New York: Norton, 1972.

CAROLYN PARDON, "The Foreign Service Wife and Diplomacy in the 70's," *For. Ser. Jour.,* **48,** 34–35 (Sept. 1971).

State and Local Government and Politics

PATRICIA G. BACH, *Women in Public Life: A Preliminary Report.* Washington, D.C.: ERIC, Clearing House on Higher Education, 1971.

MARY BEARD, *Woman's Work in Municipalities.* New York: Appleton, 1915. Reprinted in *Women State Legislators, Report from a Conference,* Eagleton Center for the American Women and Politics, Rutgers University, New Brunswick, N.J., May 1973.

BETH GILLAN, "No Taxation without Ms. Representation," *Today, The Philadelphia Inquirer Magazine* (June 18, 1972) reprinted by Eagleton Center for the American Women and Politics, Rutgers University, New Brunswick, N.J.

PATRICIA HUCKLE, *Employment of Women in Local Government,* unpublished (1972). Available from author at Center for Urban Affairs, University of Southern California, Los Angeles.

JOAN A. ROTHSCHILD, "On Building a Female Constituency: The Case of Massachusetts," unpublished paper prepared for the Annual Meeting of the American Political Science Association, Washington, D.C., 1972.

IDA F. S. SCHMIDT, "Women State Legislators: Impressions from a Conference," prepared for National Conference of State Legislative Leaders 1972 Yearbook, Eagleton Center for the American Women and Politics, Rutgers University, New Brunswick, N.J.

BERNICE T. VAN DER VRIES, "Women in Government," *State Gov.,* **21,** 127–128 + (June 1948).

EMMY WERNER, "Women in State Legislatures," *Western Poli. Quart.,* **21,** 40–50 (Mar. 1968).

Women's Research Center of Boston, *Who Rules Massachusetts Women?* Cambridge, Mass.: Women's Research Center of Boston, 1971.

NOTES

1. Plato, *The Republic,* Book V, Sec. 455. B. Jowett, trans. New York: Modern Library, 1955.

2. Mary Beard, *Woman as a Force in History.* New York: Macmillan, 1946, p. 71.

3. For an effort to define a political system, see David Easton, *The Political System.* New York: Knopf, 1960.

4. For a discussion and comparison of the women's rights and women's liberation movements, see Judith Hole and Ellen Levine, *Rebirth of Feminism.* New York: Quadrangle, 1971, Part I.

5. Angus Campbell et al., *The Voter Decides.* Evanston: Row Peterson, 1954; also, *The American Voter.* New York: Wiley, 1960.

6. Fred Greenstein, *Children and Politics.* New Haven: Yale University Press, 1965. David Easton and Jack Dennis, *Children in the Political System.* New York: McGraw-Hill, 1969.

7. Harry Eckstein and David E. Apter, ed., *Comparative Politics.* New York: Free Press, 1964, Parts III–VI.

Index